THE SEVEN DEADLY SINS

nakaba suzuki presents

31

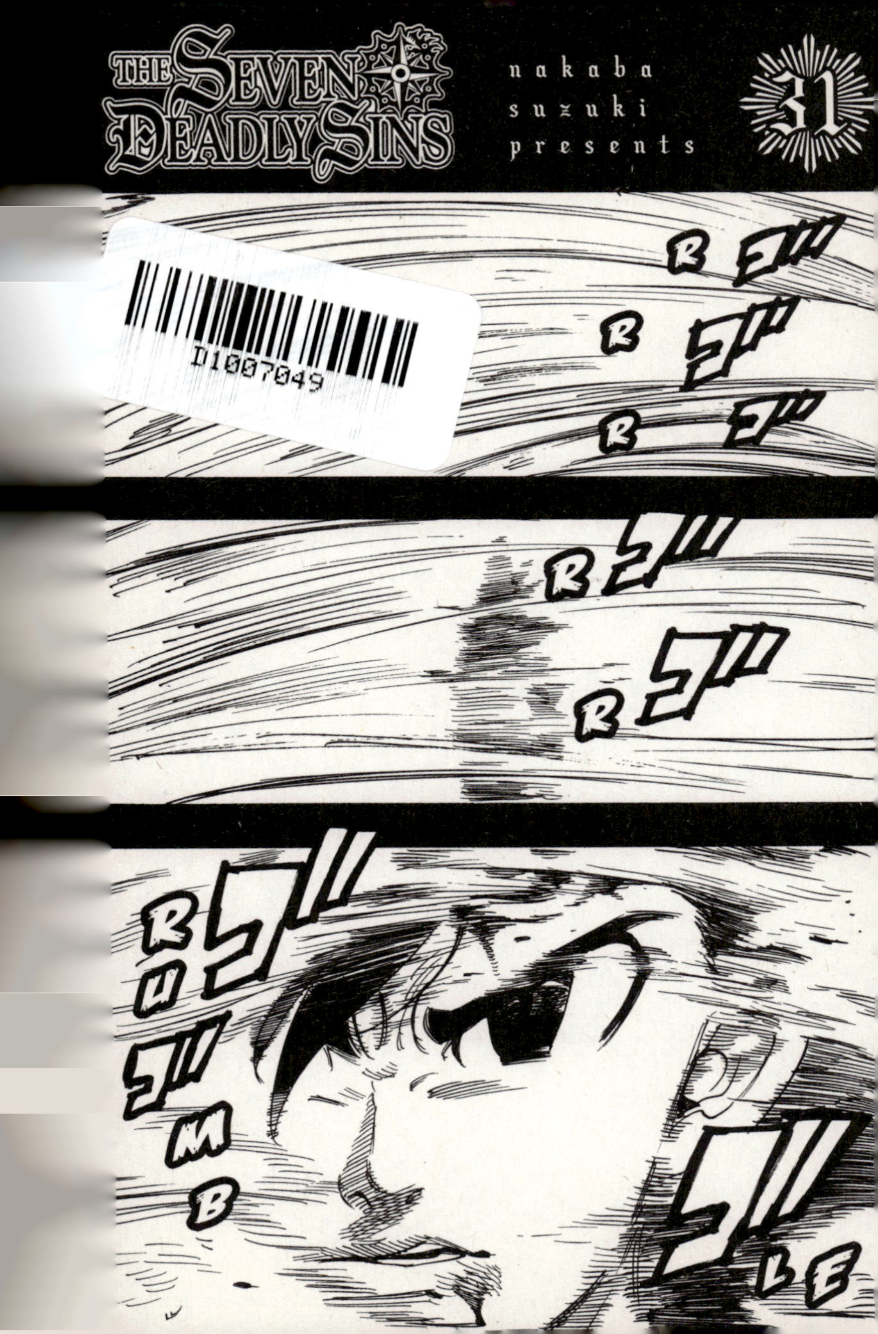
R
R
R
R
R
RUMBLE

CONTENTS

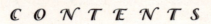

BOAR HAT

The Seven Deadly Sins

Chapter 250 - Her Resolve

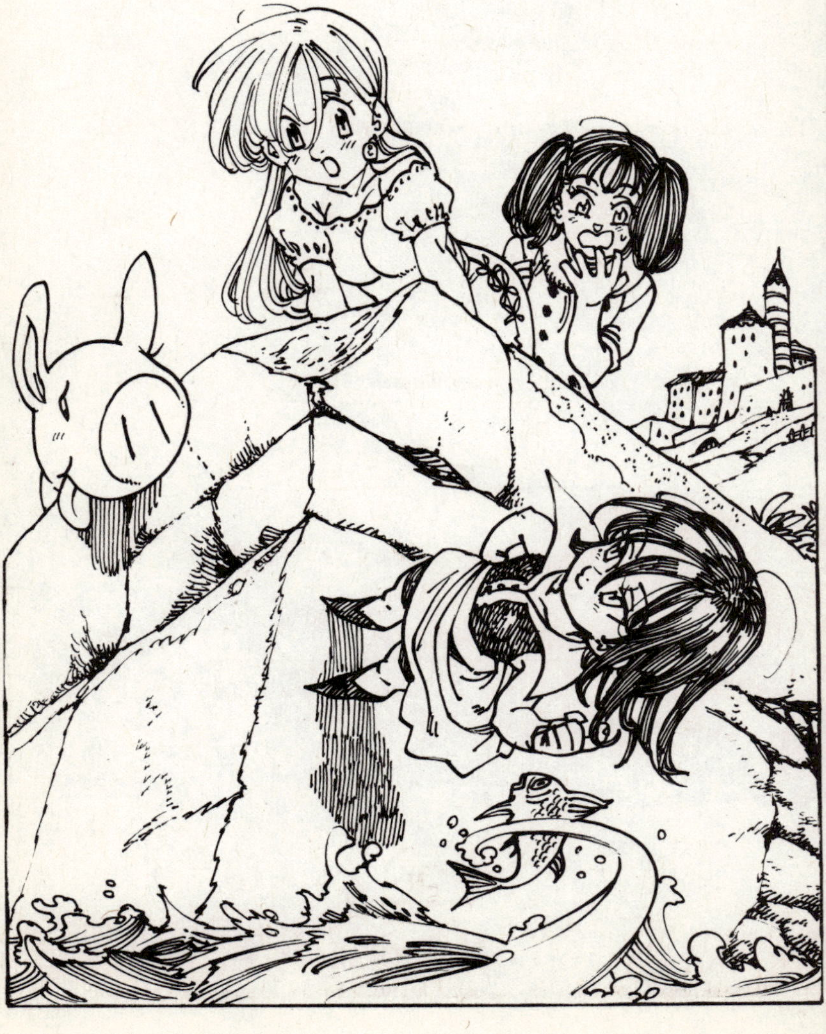

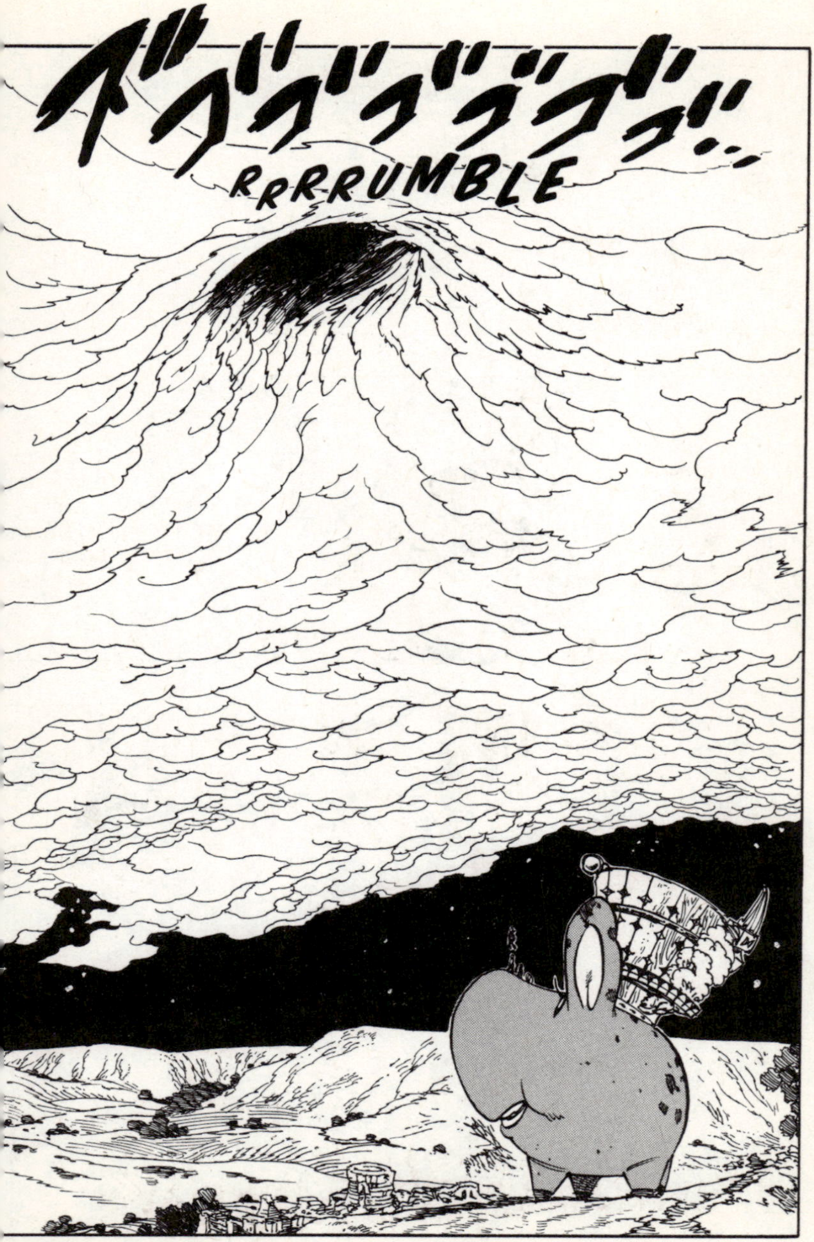
RRRRUMBLE

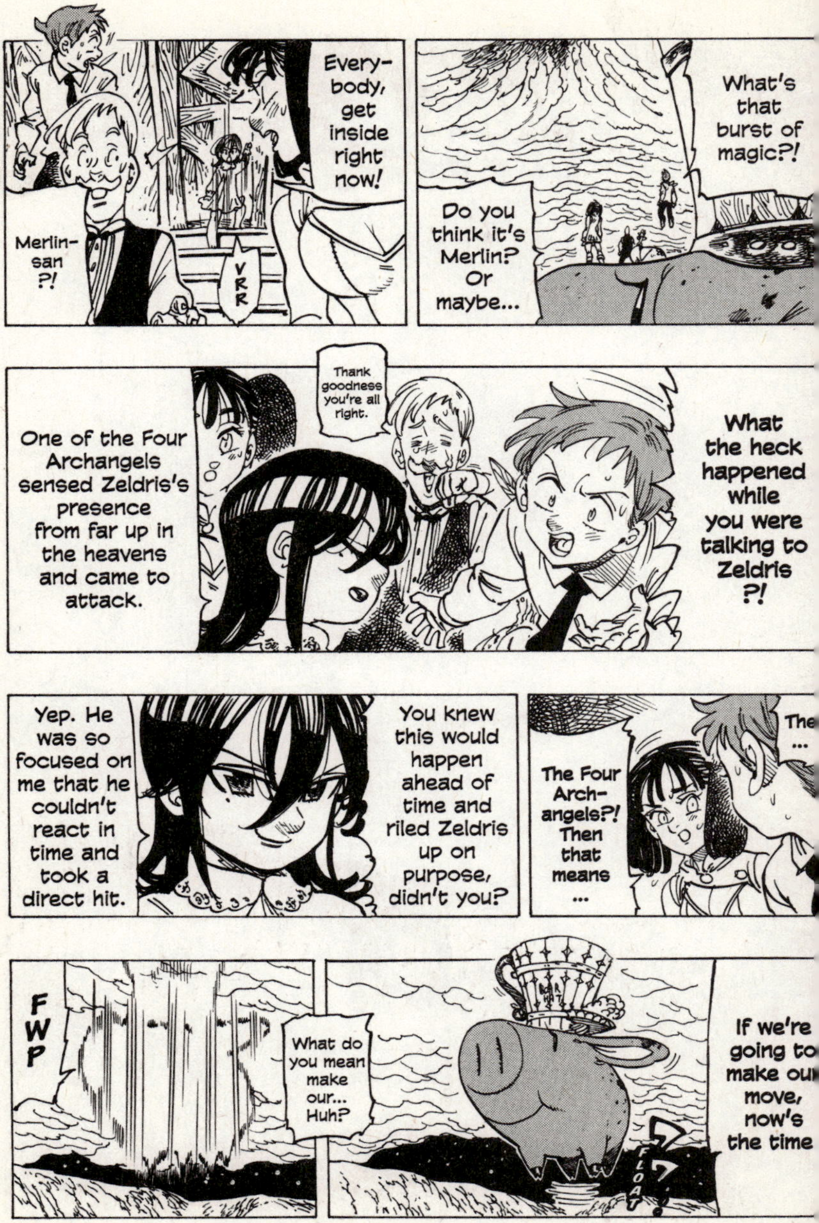
What's that burst of magic?!
Do you think it's Merlin? Or maybe...
Everybody, get inside right now!
VRR
Merlin-san?!
What the heck happened while you were talking to Zeldris?!
Thank goodness you're all right.
One of the Four Archangels sensed Zeldris's presence from far up in the heavens and came to attack.
The...
The Four Arch-angels?! Then that means...
You knew this would happen ahead of time and riled Zeldris up on purpose, didn't you?
Yep. He was so focused on me that he couldn't react in time and took a direct hit.
If we're going to make ou move, now's the time
FLOAT
What do you mean make our... Huh?
FWP

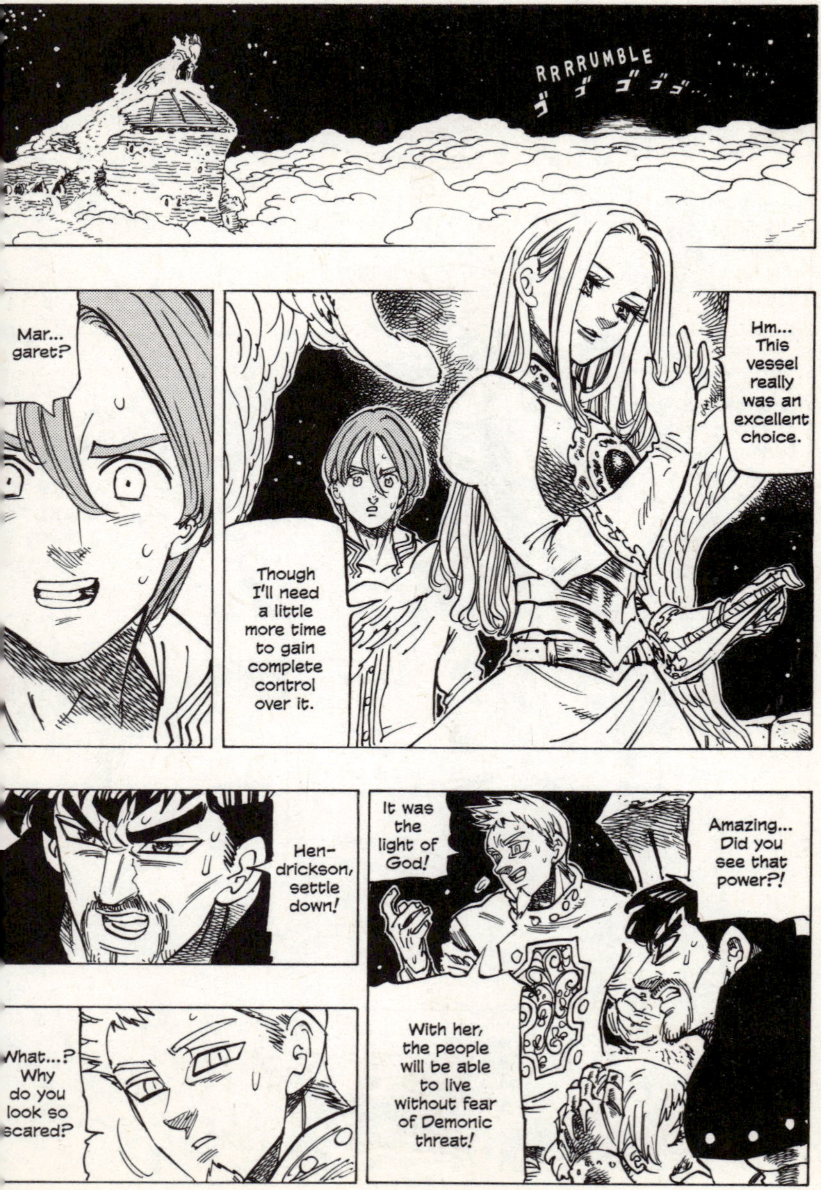
RRRRUMBLE
ゴゴゴゴゴ...
Hm... This vessel really was an excellent choice.
Though I'll need a little more time to gain complete control over it.
Mar... garet?
Amazing... Did you see that power?!
It was the light of God!
With her, the people will be able to live without fear of Demonic threat!
Hen-drickson, settle down!
What...? Why do you look so scared?

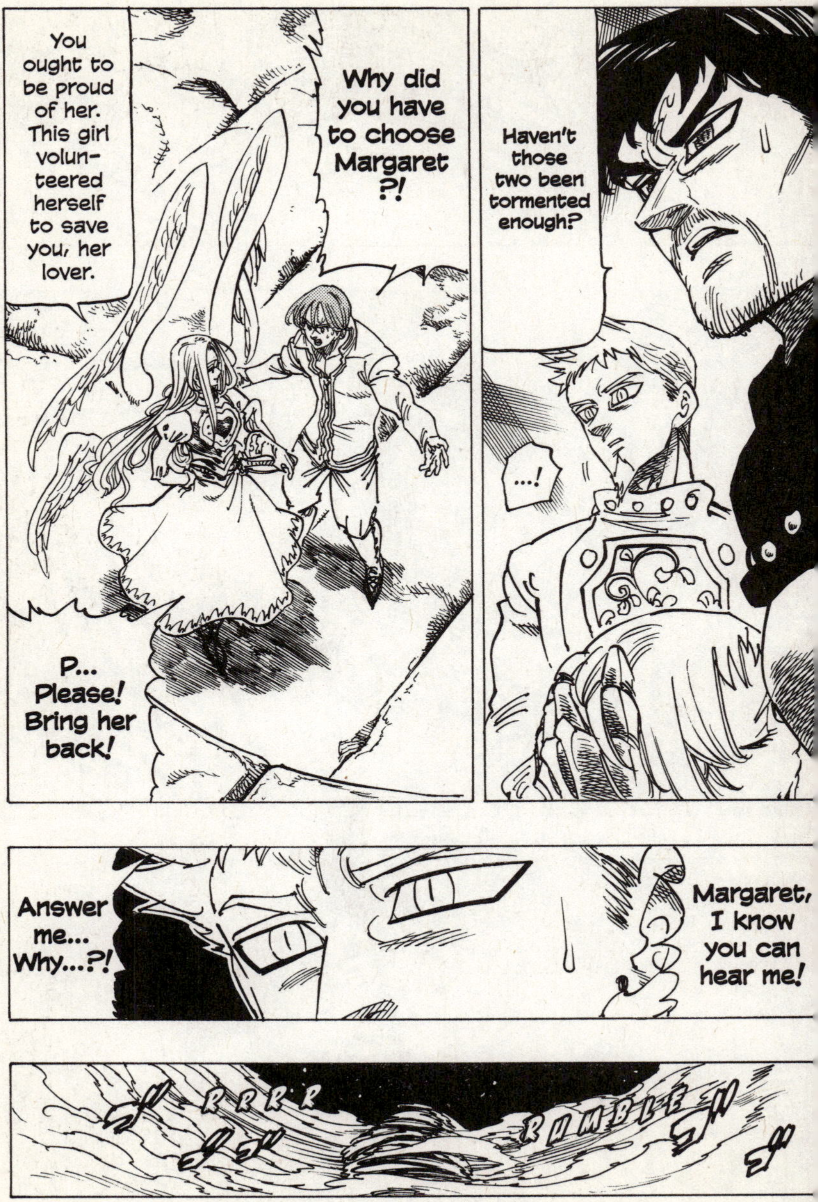
Haven't those two been tormented enough?
...!
Why did you have to choose Margaret?!
You ought to be proud of her. This girl volunteered herself to save you, her lover.
P... Please! Bring her back!
Margaret, I know you can hear me!
Answer me... Why...?!
RUMBLE
RRRR

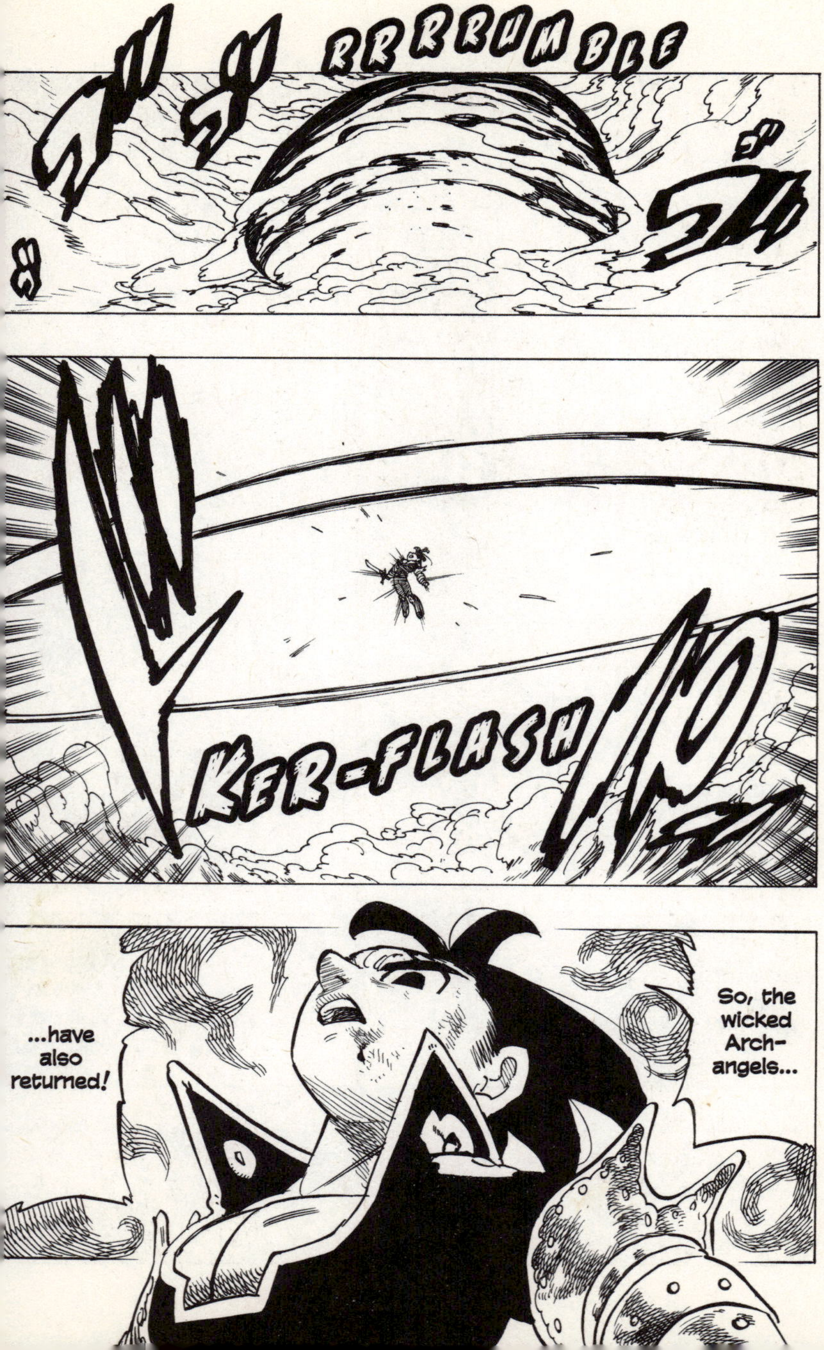
RRRRUMBLE
KER-FLASH
So, the wicked Arch-angels...
...have also returned!

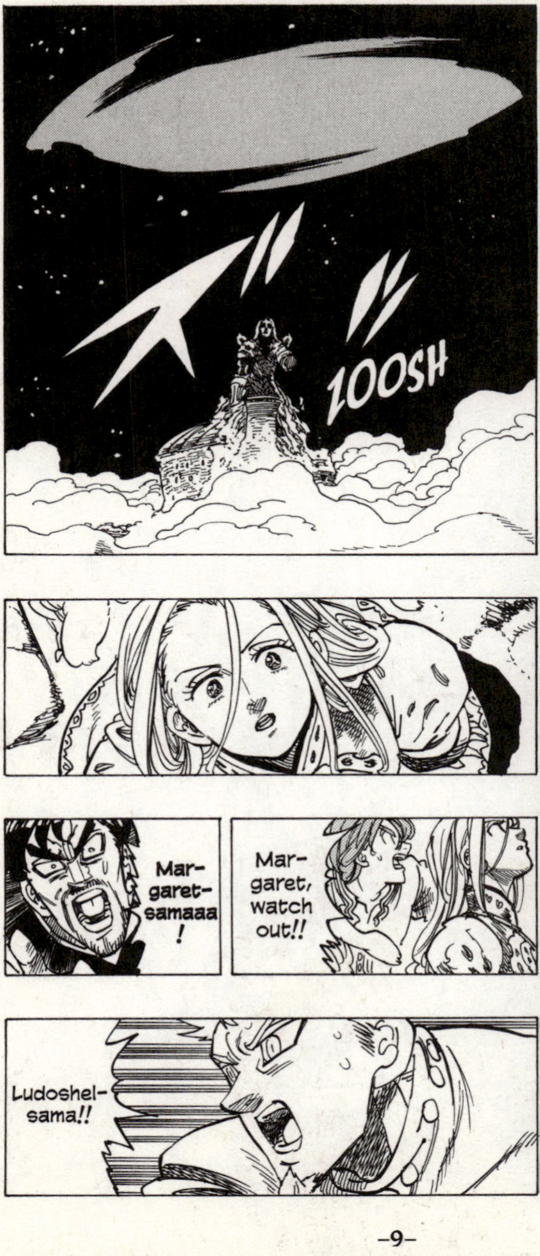
ZOOSH
Margaret, watch out!!
Margaret-samaaa!
Ludoshel-sama!!

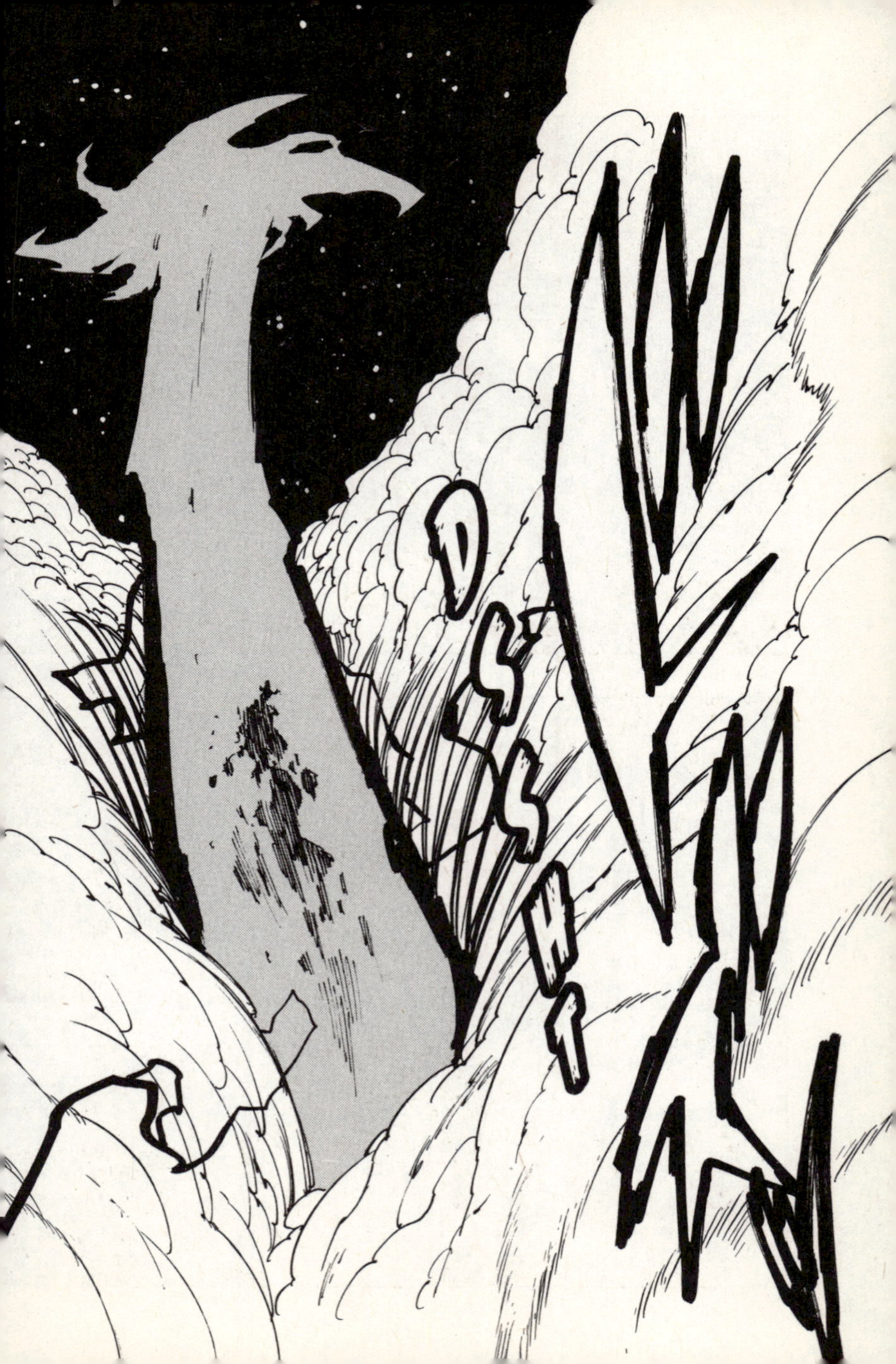
DSSHT

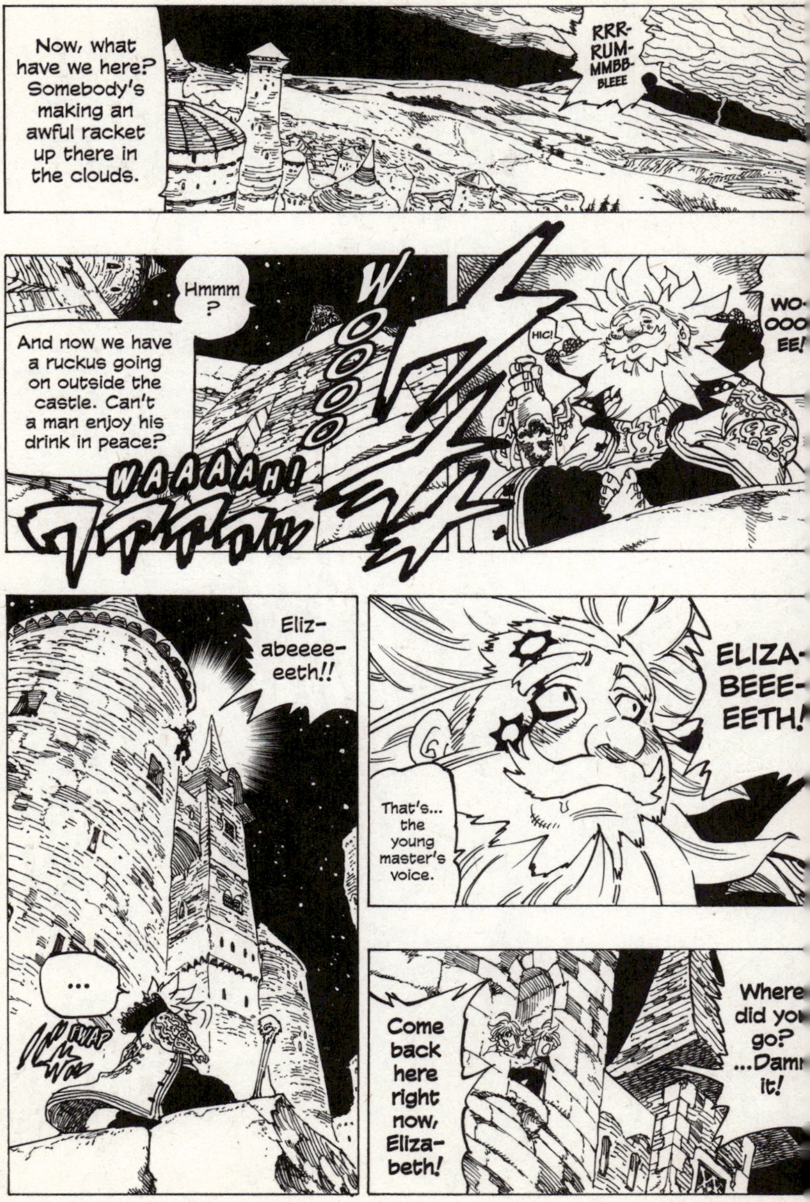
RRR-RUM-MMBB-BLEEE
Now, what have we here? Somebody's making an awful racket up there in the clouds.
WO-OOO EE!
HIC!
Hmmm?
And now we have a ruckus going on outside the castle. Can't a man enjoy his drink in peace?
WOOOOOO
WAAAAAH!
ELIZA-BEEEE-EETH!
That's... the young master's voice.
Where did yo go? ...Dam it!
Come back here right now, Eliza-beth!
Eliz-abeeee-eeth!!
...
FWAP

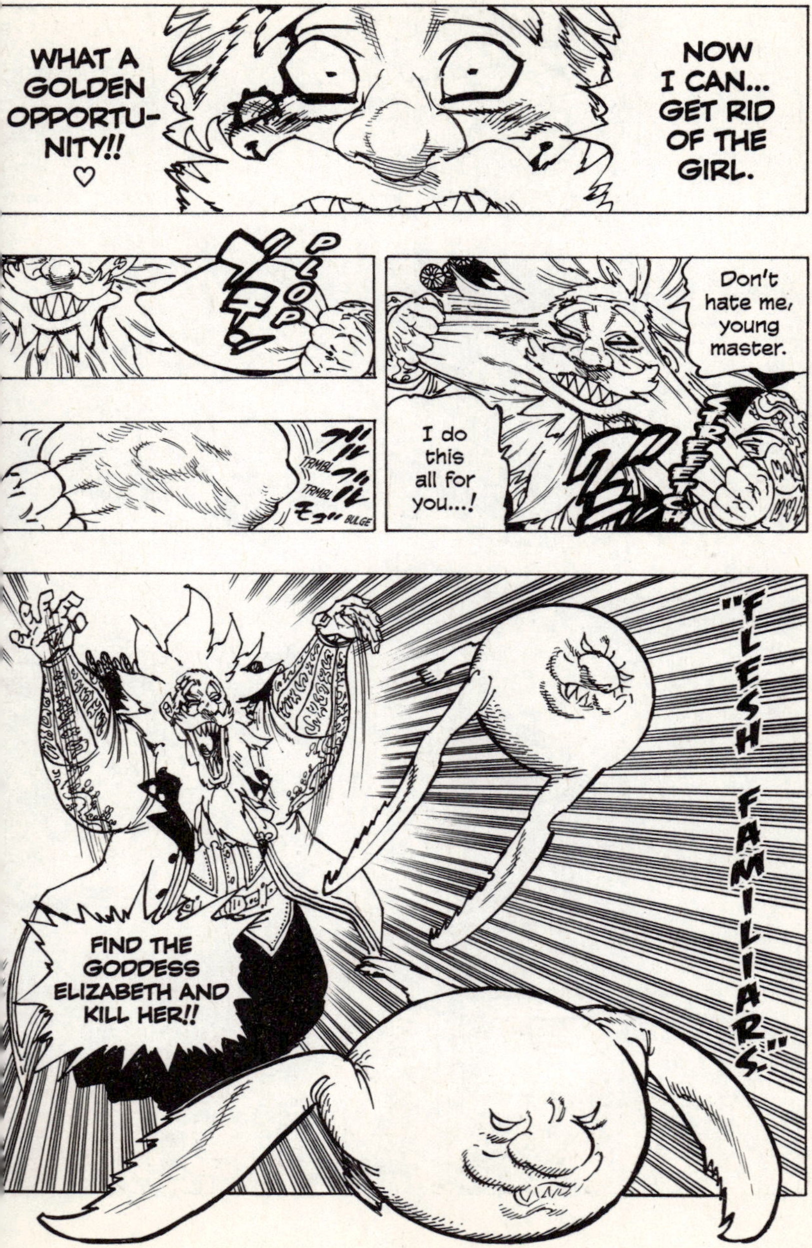

NOW I CAN... GET RID OF THE GIRL.
WHAT A GOLDEN OPPORTU-NITY!! ♡
Don't hate me, young master.
STREEETCH
I do this all for you...!
PLOP
TRMBL TRMBL
BULGE
"FLESH FAMILIARS."
FIND THE GODDESS ELIZABETH AND KILL HER!!

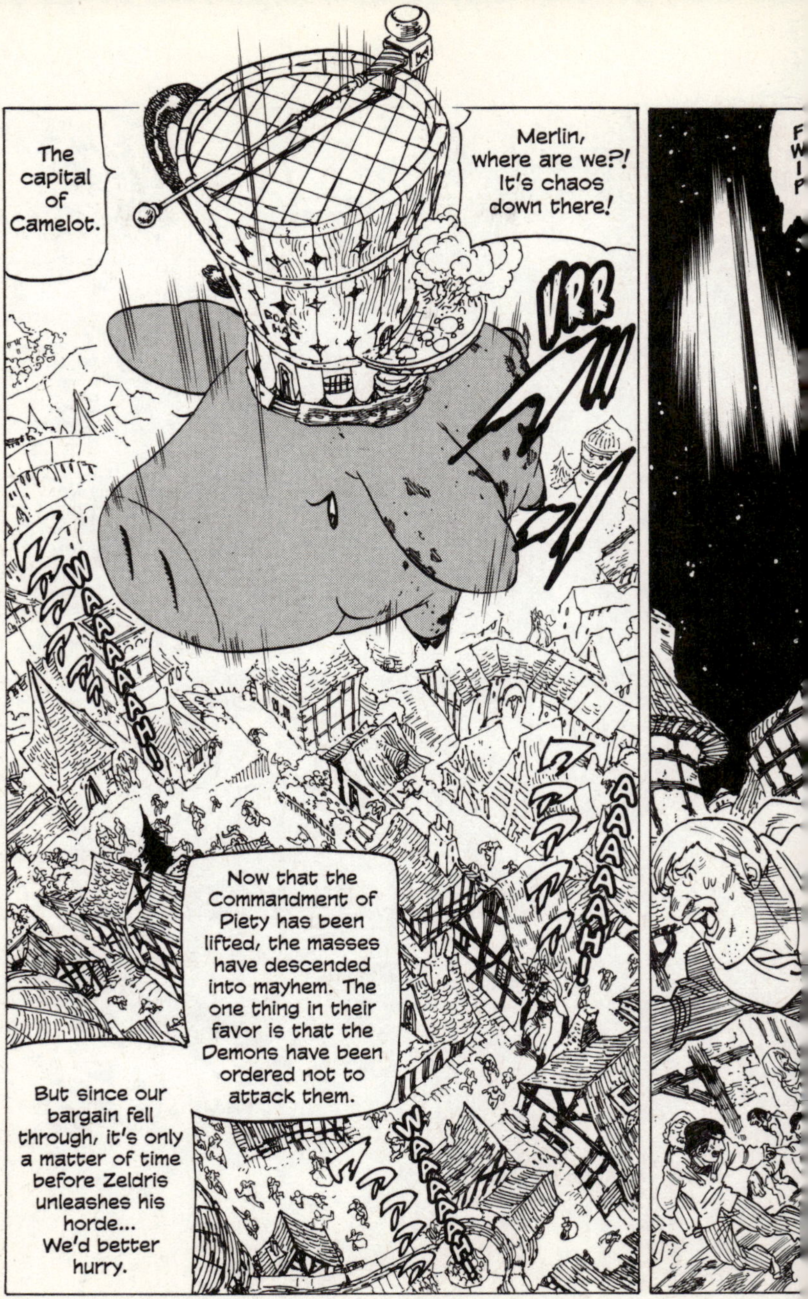
FWIP
Merlin, where are we?! It's chaos down there!
The capital of Camelot.
VRR
WAAAAAAH!
AAAAAAAH!
Now that the Commandment of Piety has been lifted, the masses have descended into mayhem. The one thing in their favor is that the Demons have been ordered not to attack them.
But since our bargain fell through, it's only a matter of time before Zeldris unleashes his horde... We'd better hurry.
WAAAAAAH!

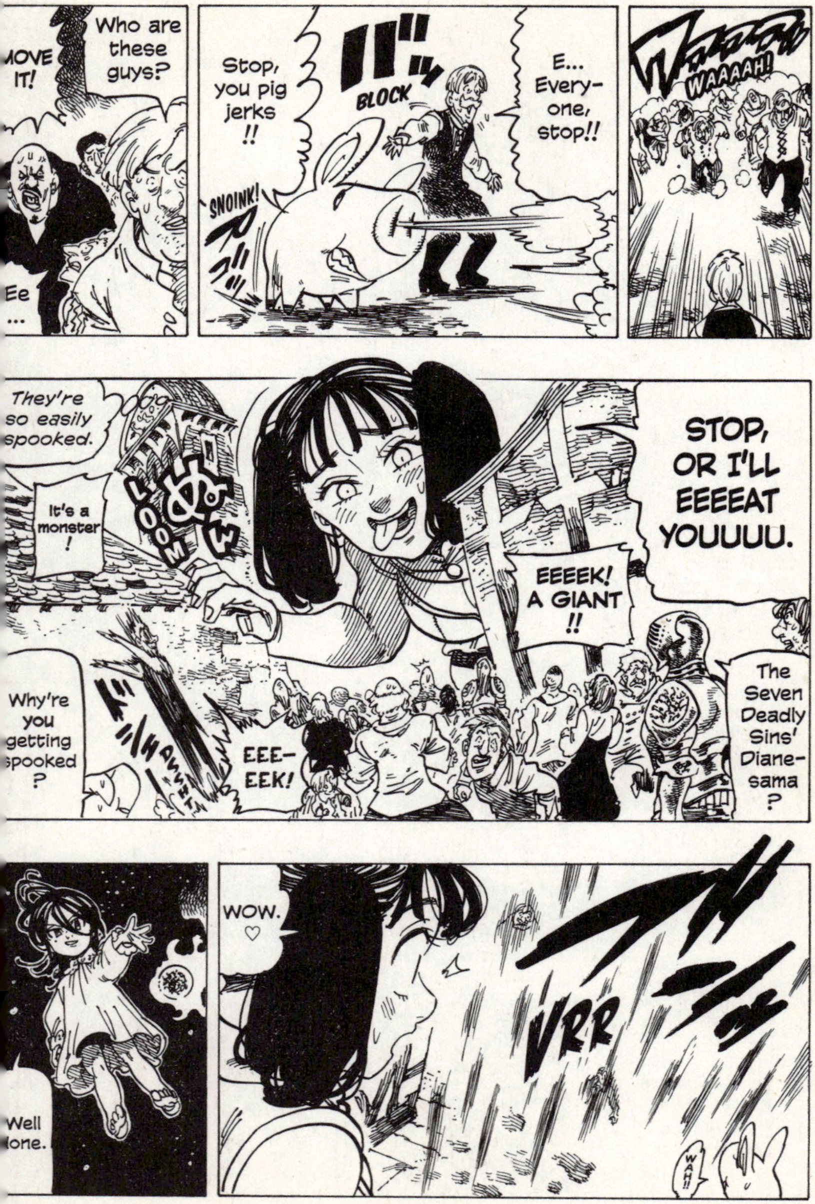
WAAAAH!
E... Every-one, stop!!
BLOCK
Stop, you pig jerks!!
SNOINK!
Who are these guys?
MOVE IT!
Ee...
STOP, OR I'LL EEEEAT YOUUUU.
They're so easily spooked.
LOOM
It's a monster!
EEEEK! A GIANT!!
The Seven Deadly Sins' Diane-sama?
EEE-EEK!
Why're you getting spooked?
WOW. ♡
VRR
WAH!!
Well done.

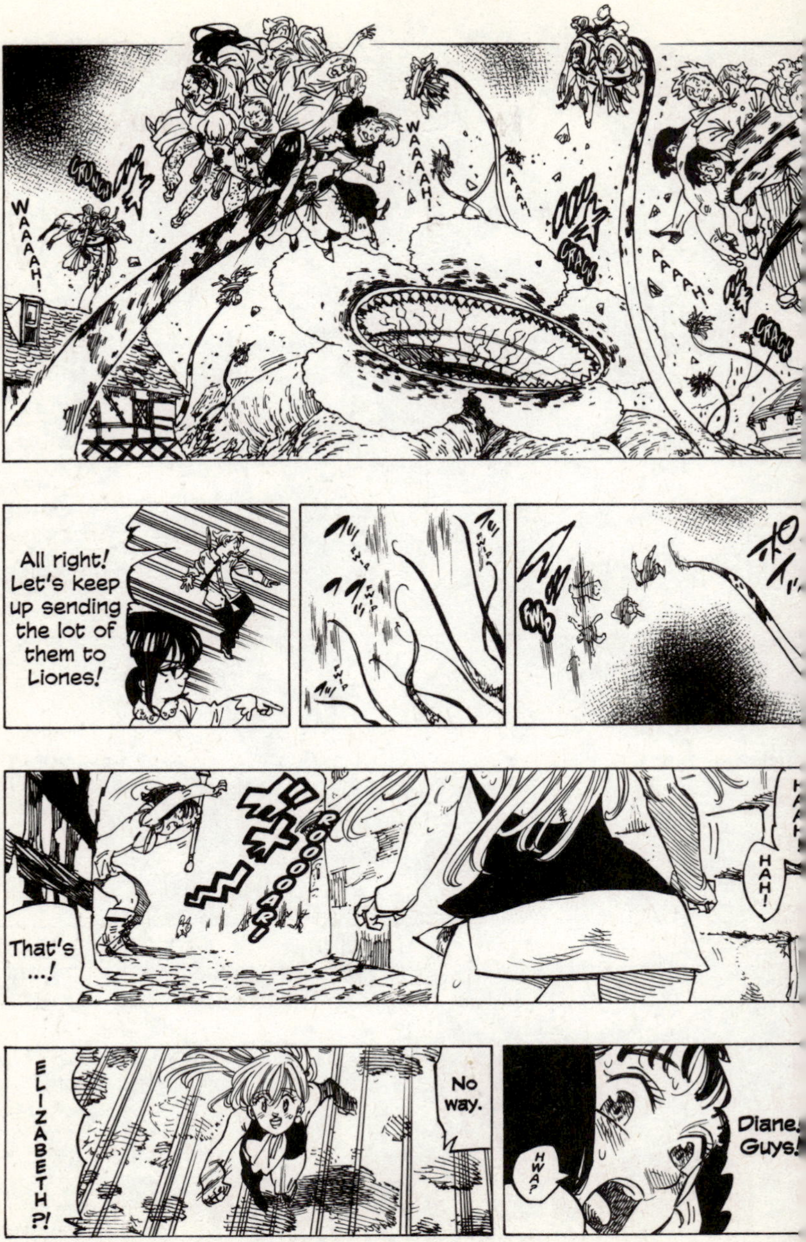
AAAAAH!
CRACK
CRACK
AAAAH!
WAAAAH!
CRUNCH
WAAAAH!
FWIP
FWIP
FWIP
FWIP
All right! Let's keep up sending the lot of them to Liones!
HAAH!
HAH!
ROOOOAR!
That's ...!
Diane. Guys!
HWA?
No way.
ELIZABETH?!

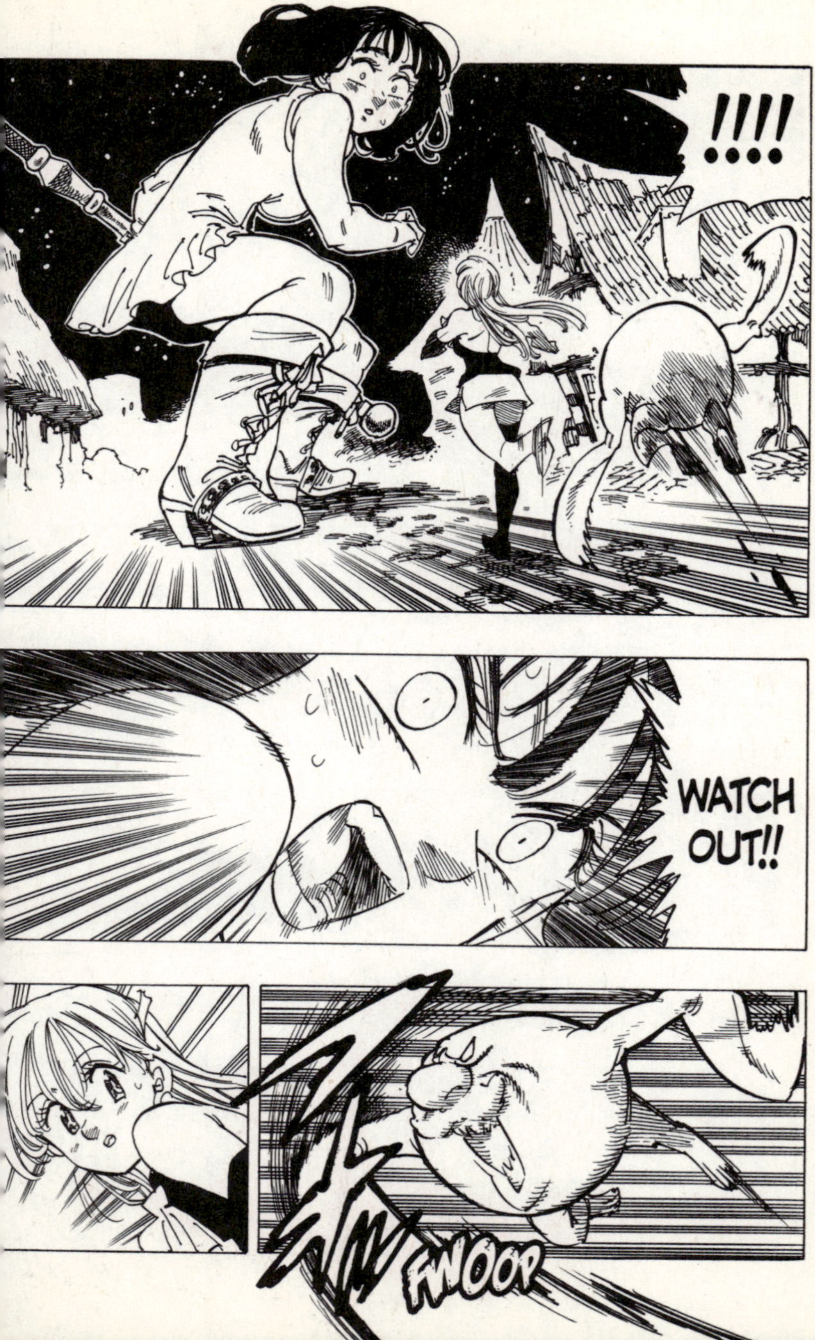
!!!!
WATCH OUT!!
FWOOP

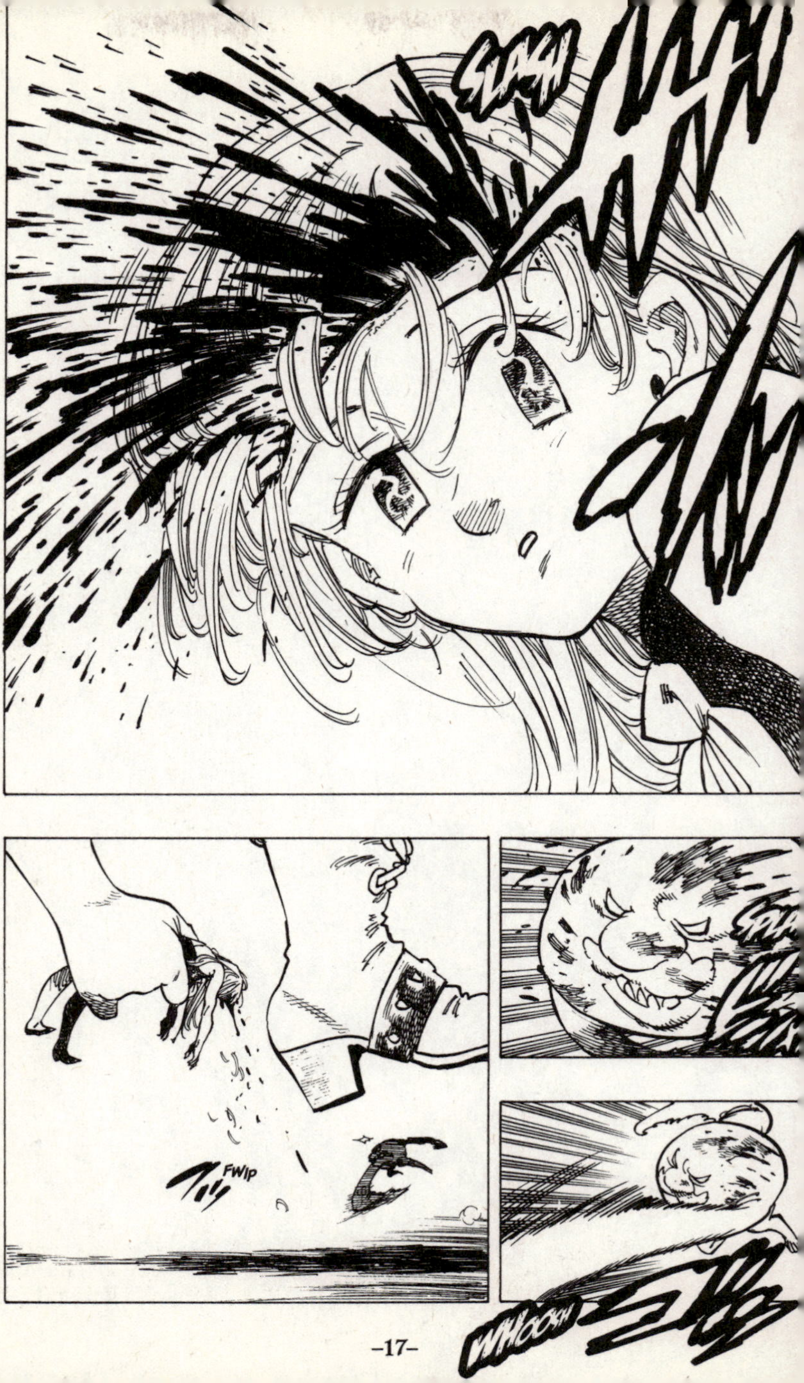
SLASH
WHOOSH
FWIP

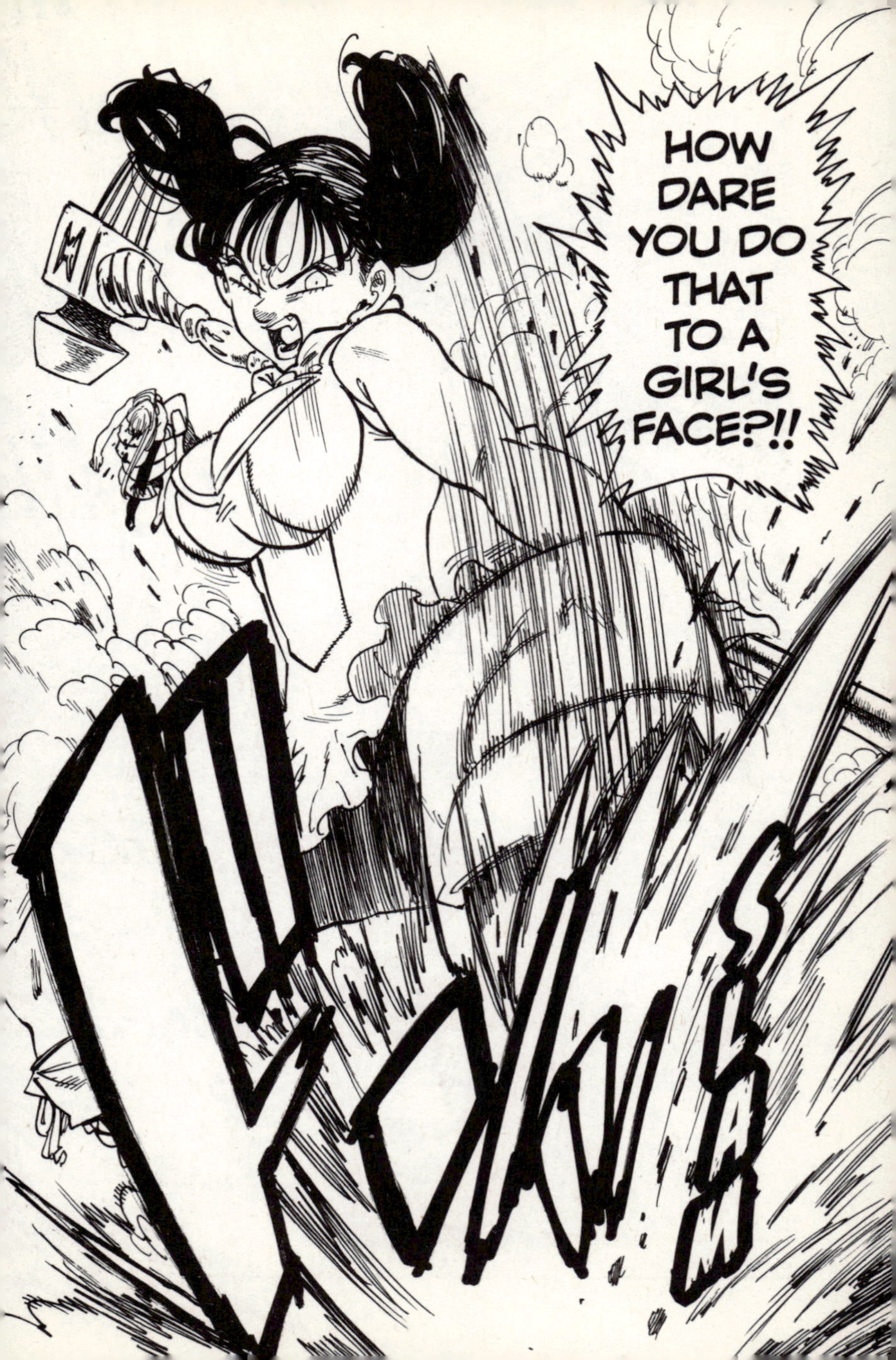
HOW DARE YOU DO THAT TO A GIRL'S FACE?!!

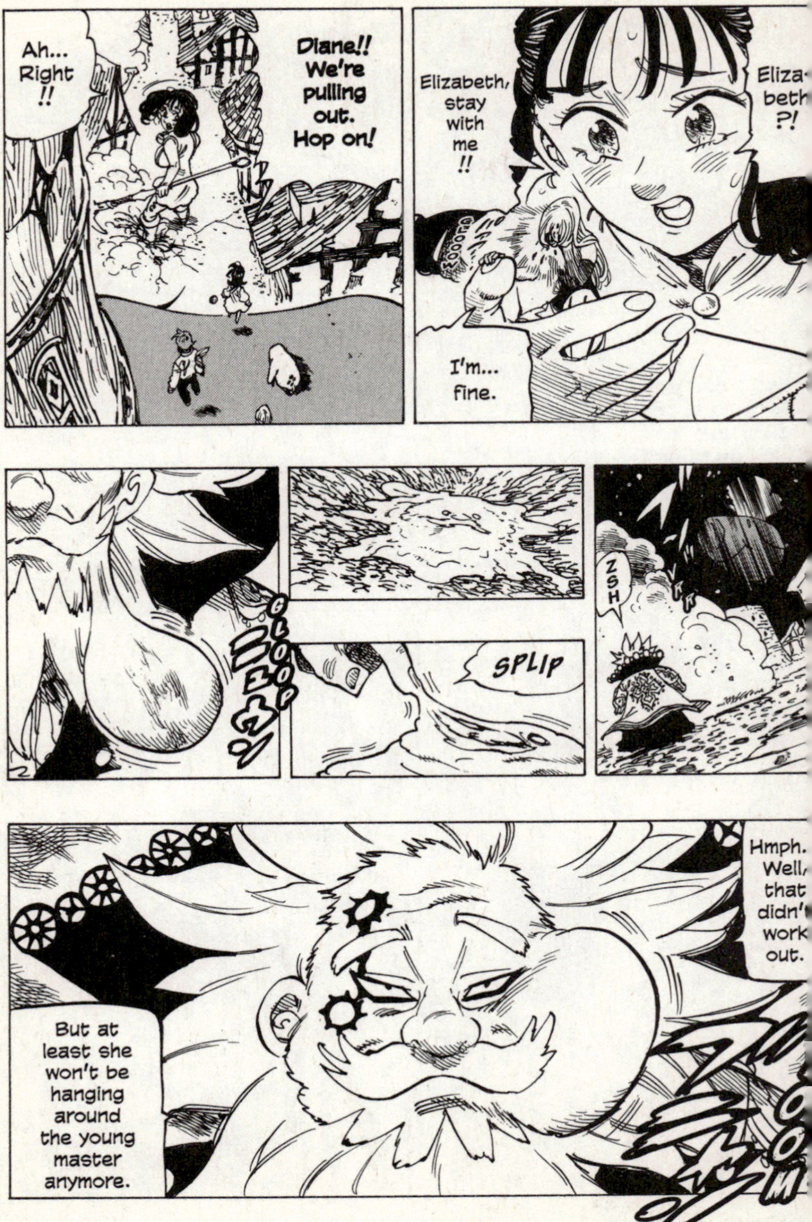
Elizabeth ?!
Elizabeth, stay with me !!
GLOOOW
I'm... fine.
Diane!! We're pulling out. Hop on!
Ah... Right !!
ZSH
SPLIP
GLOOP
Hmph. Well, that didn't work out.
But at least she won't be hanging around the young master anymore.

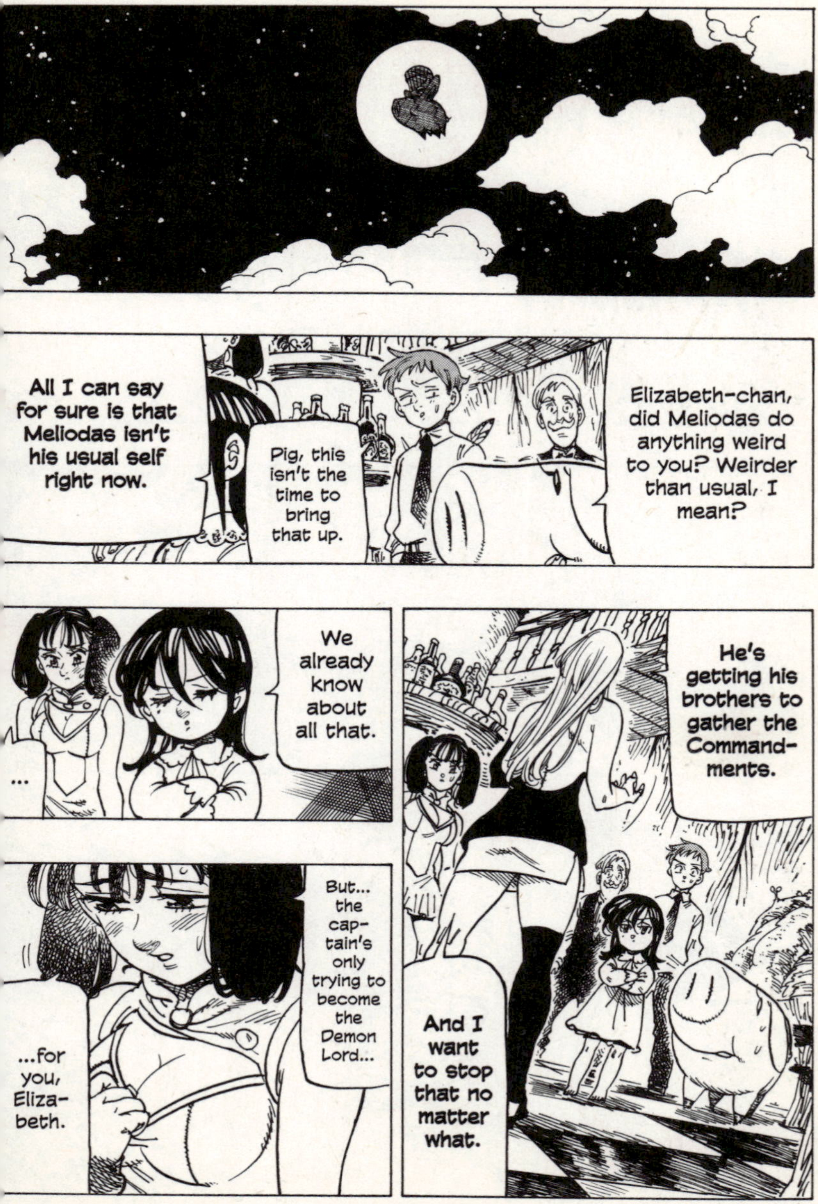

Elizabeth-chan, did Meliodas do anything weird to you? Weirder than usual, I mean?
Pig, this isn't the time to bring that up.
All I can say for sure is that Meliodas isn't his usual self right now.
He's getting his brothers to gather the Command-ments.
And I want to stop that no matter what.
We already know about all that.
...
But... the cap-tain's only trying to become the Demon Lord...
...for you, Eliza-beth.

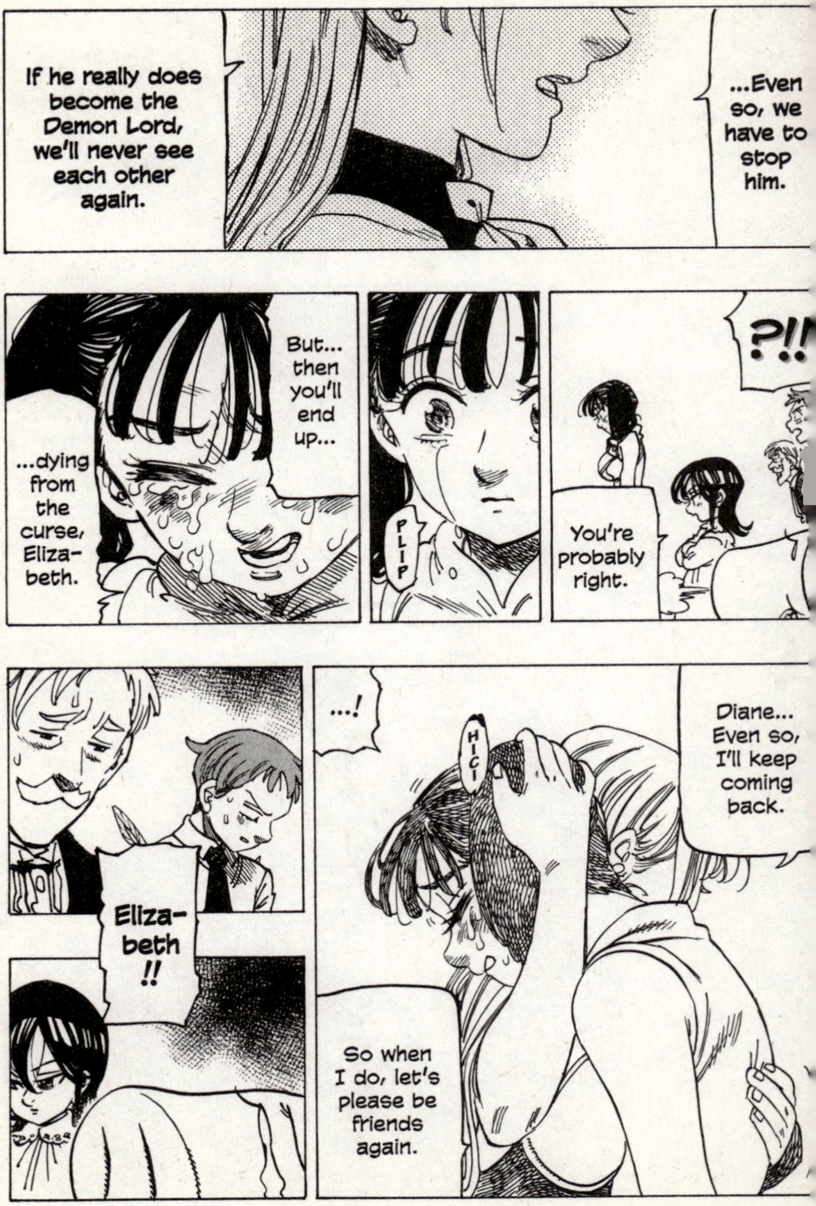
...Even so, we have to stop him.
If he really does become the Demon Lord, we'll never see each other again.
?!!
You're probably right.
PLIP
But... then you'll end up...
...dying from the curse, Elizabeth.
Diane... Even so, I'll keep coming back.
HIC
...!
So when I do, let's please be friends again.
Eliza-beth!!

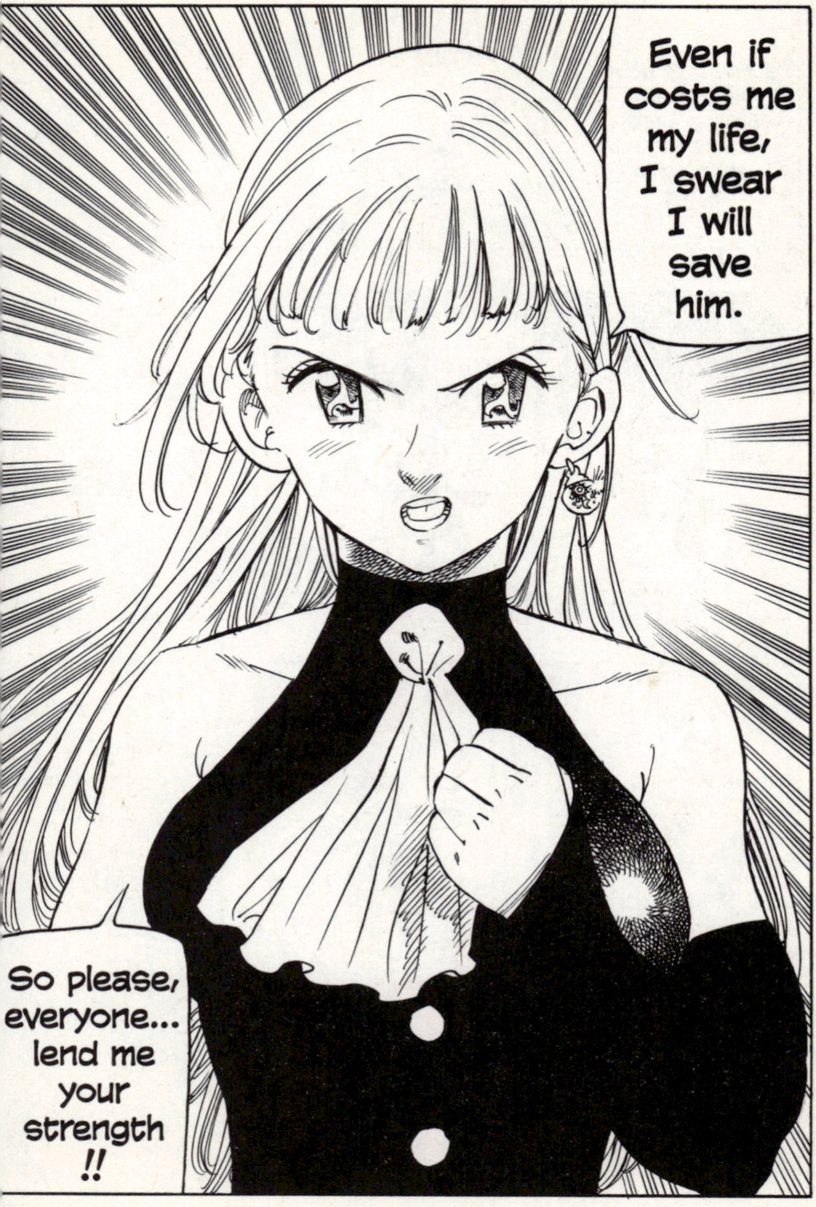
Even if costs me my life, I swear I will save him.
So please, everyone... lend me your strength!!

Chapter 251 - The Holy War Accord

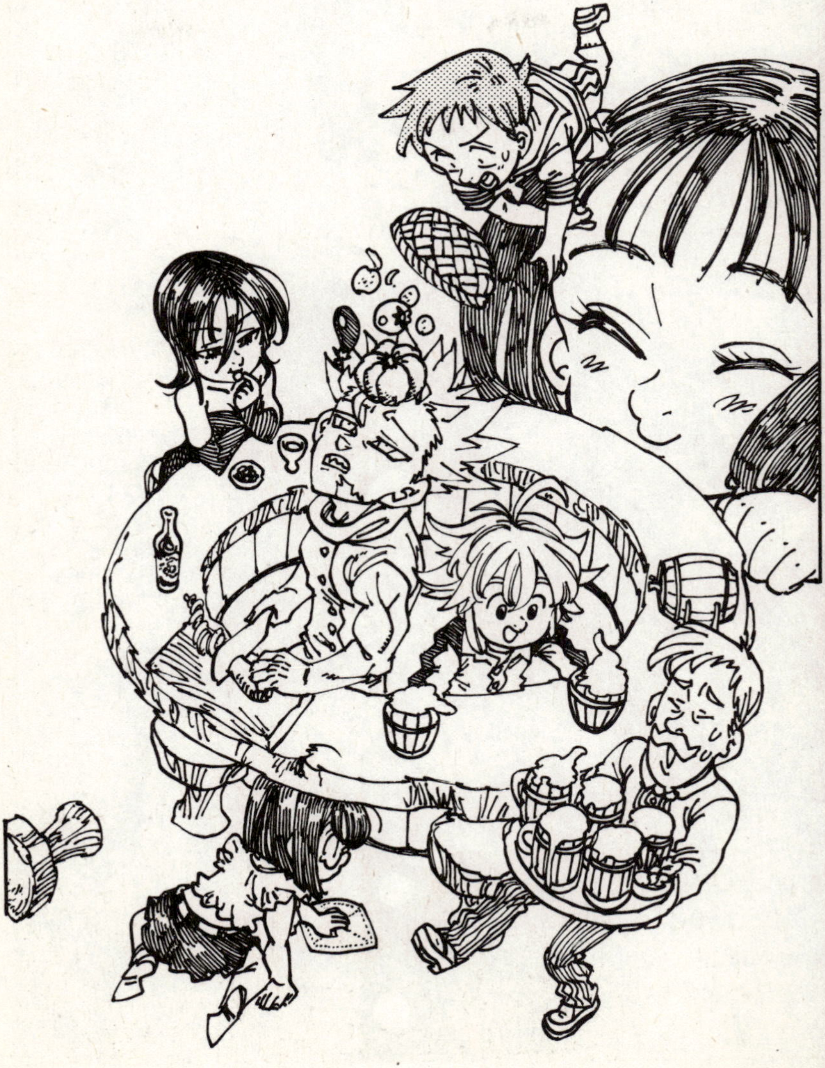

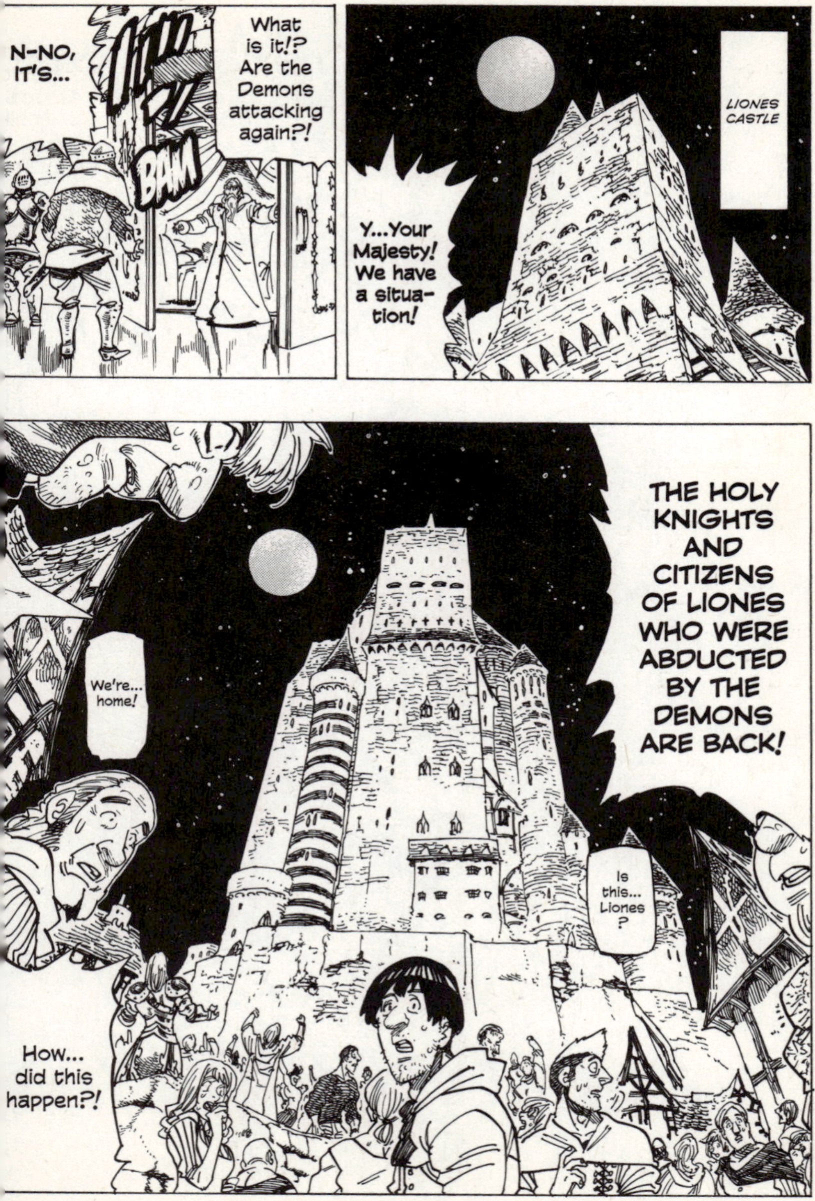
LIONES CASTLE
Y...Your Majesty! We have a situation!
What is it!? Are the Demons attacking again?!
BAM
N-NO, IT'S...
THE HOLY KNIGHTS AND CITIZENS OF LIONES WHO WERE ABDUCTED BY THE DEMONS ARE BACK!
Is this... Liones?
We're... home!
How... did this happen?!

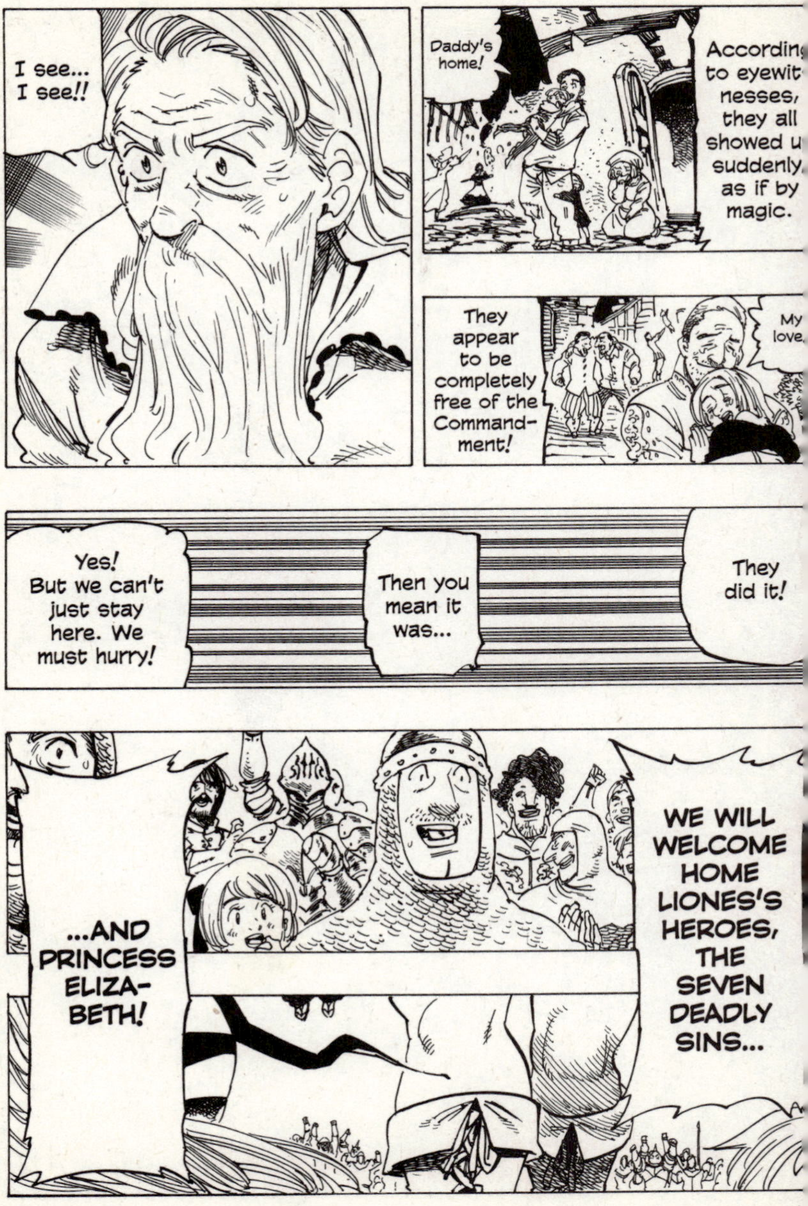
According to eyewit-nesses, they all showed u suddenly, as if by magic.
Daddy's home!
My love.
They appear to be completely free of the Command-ment!
I see... I see!!
They did it!
Then you mean it was...
Yes! But we can't just stay here. We must hurry!
WE WILL WELCOME HOME LIONES'S HEROES, THE SEVEN DEADLY SINS...
...AND PRINCESS ELIZA-BETH!

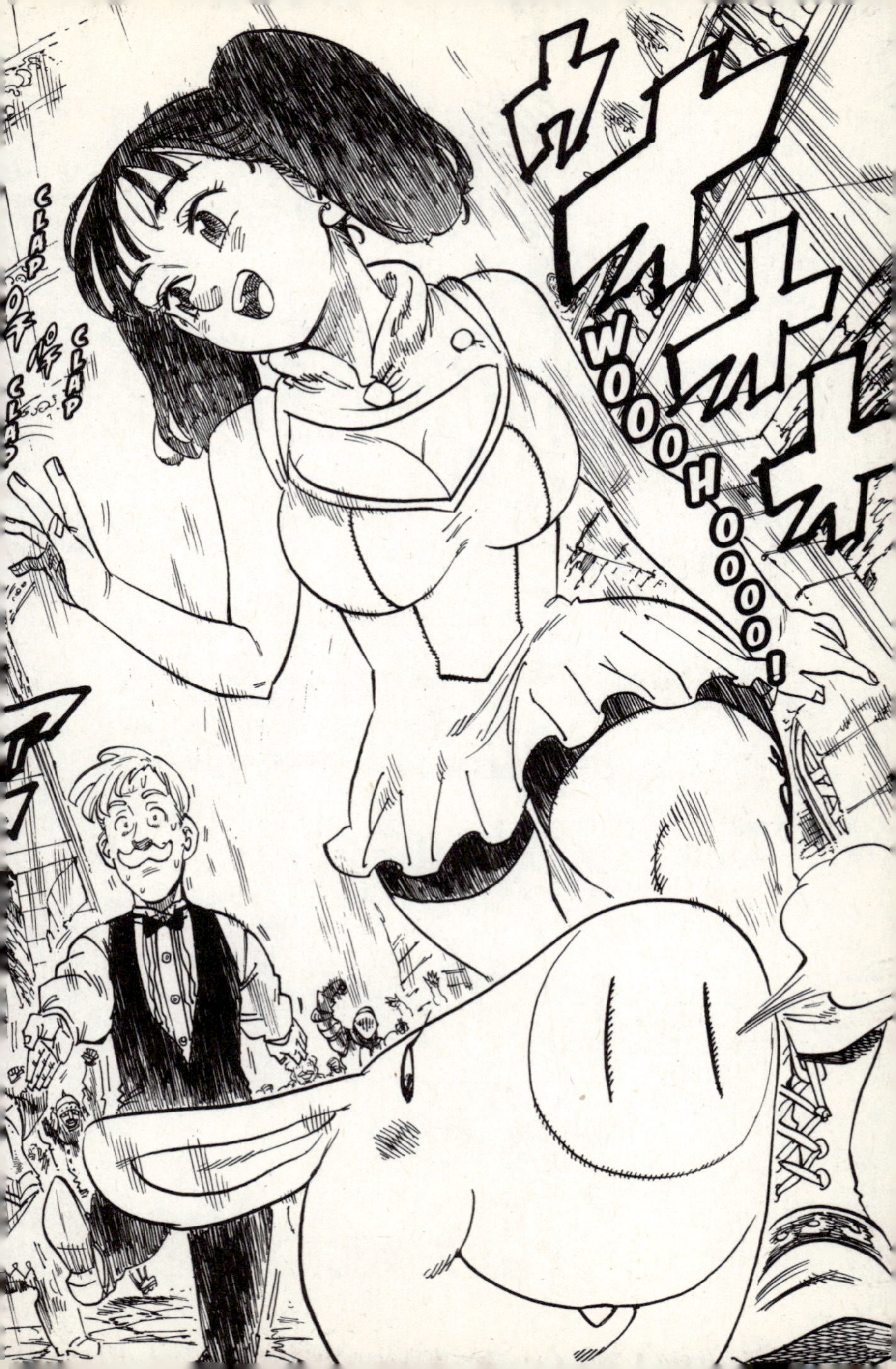
WOOOOHOOOOO!
CLAP CLAP CLAP

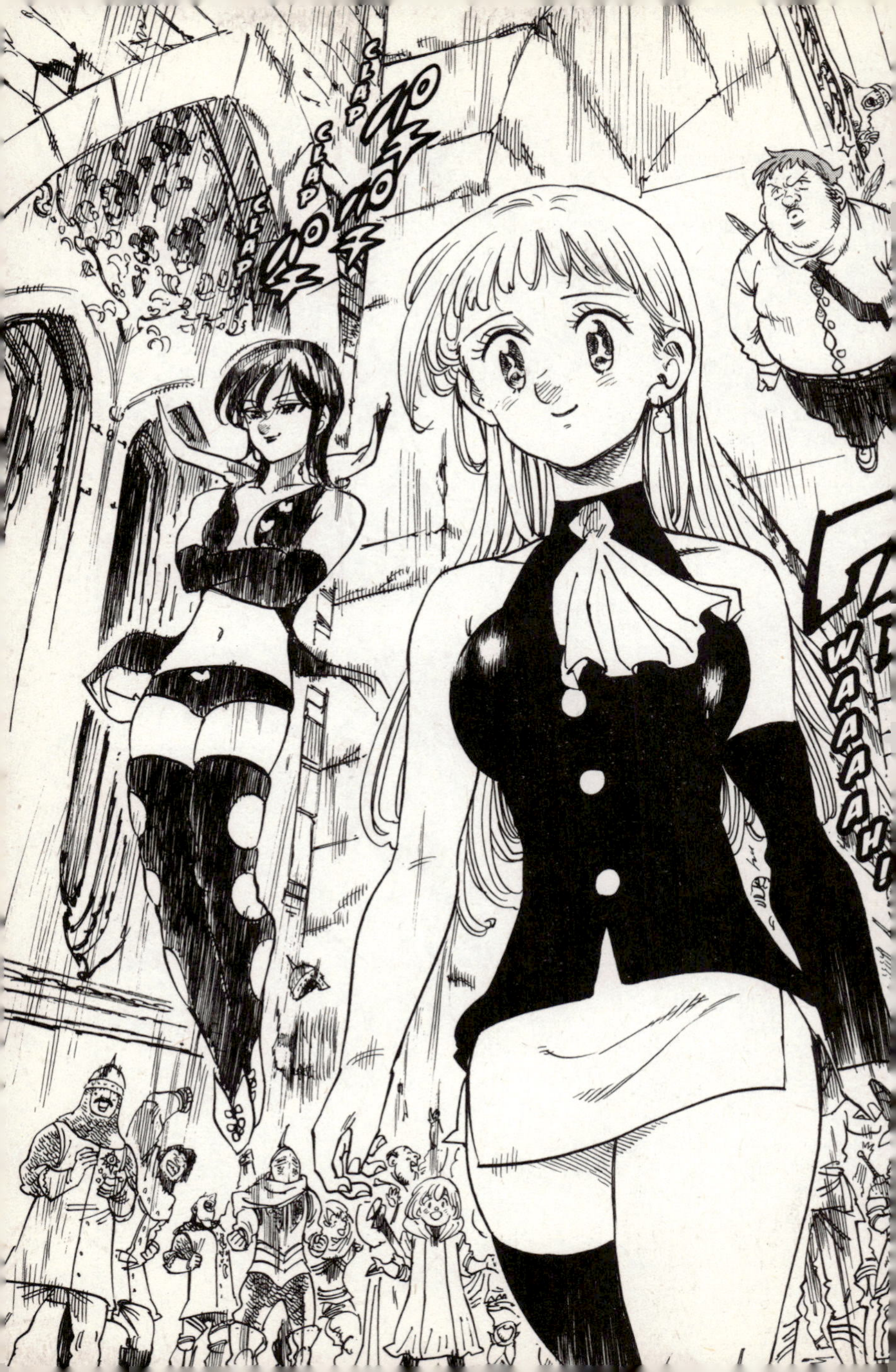
WAAAAAH!
CLAP CLAP CLAP

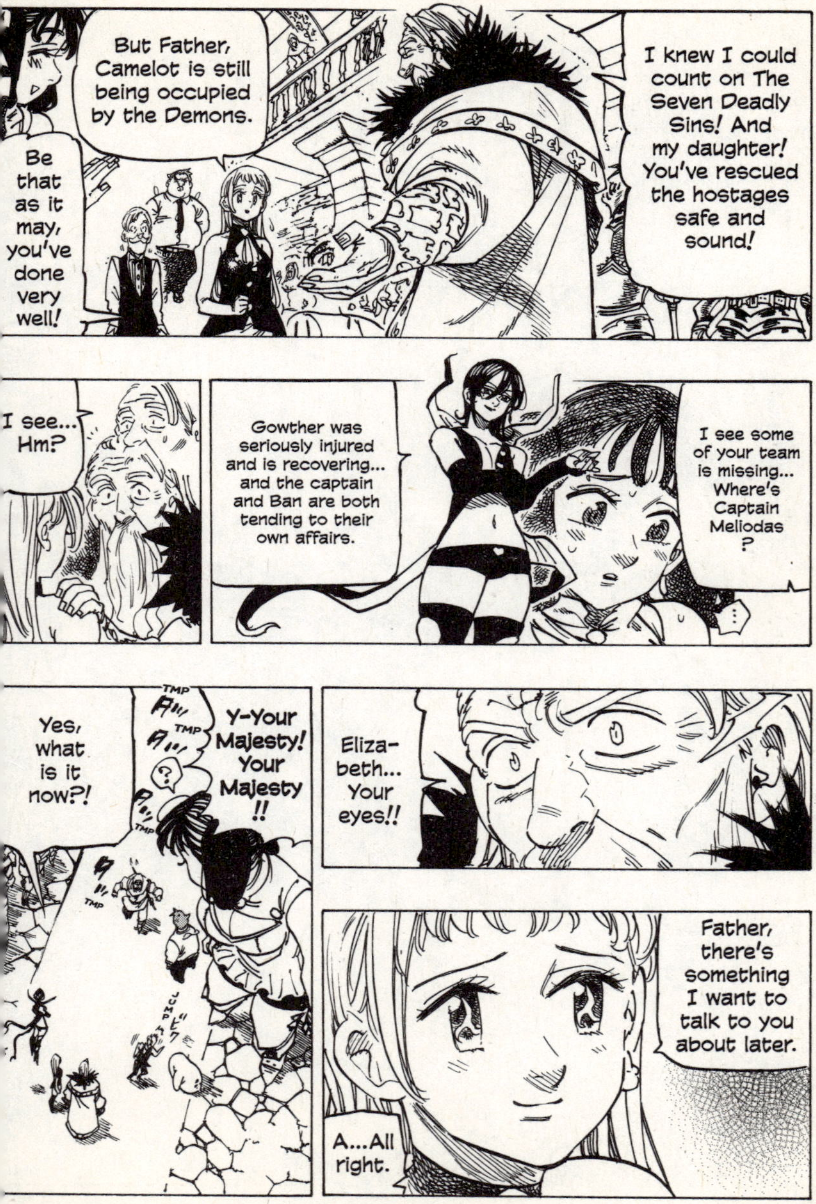
I knew I could count on The Seven Deadly Sins! And my daughter! You've rescued the hostages safe and sound!
But Father, Camelot is still being occupied by the Demons.
Be that as it may, you've done very well!
I see some of your team is missing... Where's Captain Meliodas?
...
Gowther was seriously injured and is recovering... and the captain and Ban are both tending to their own affairs.
I see... Hm?
Eliza-beth... Your eyes!!
Father, there's something I want to talk to you about later.
A...All right.
TMP
TMP
Y-Your Majesty! Your Majesty!!
?
TMP
Yes, what is it now?!
TMP
JUMP

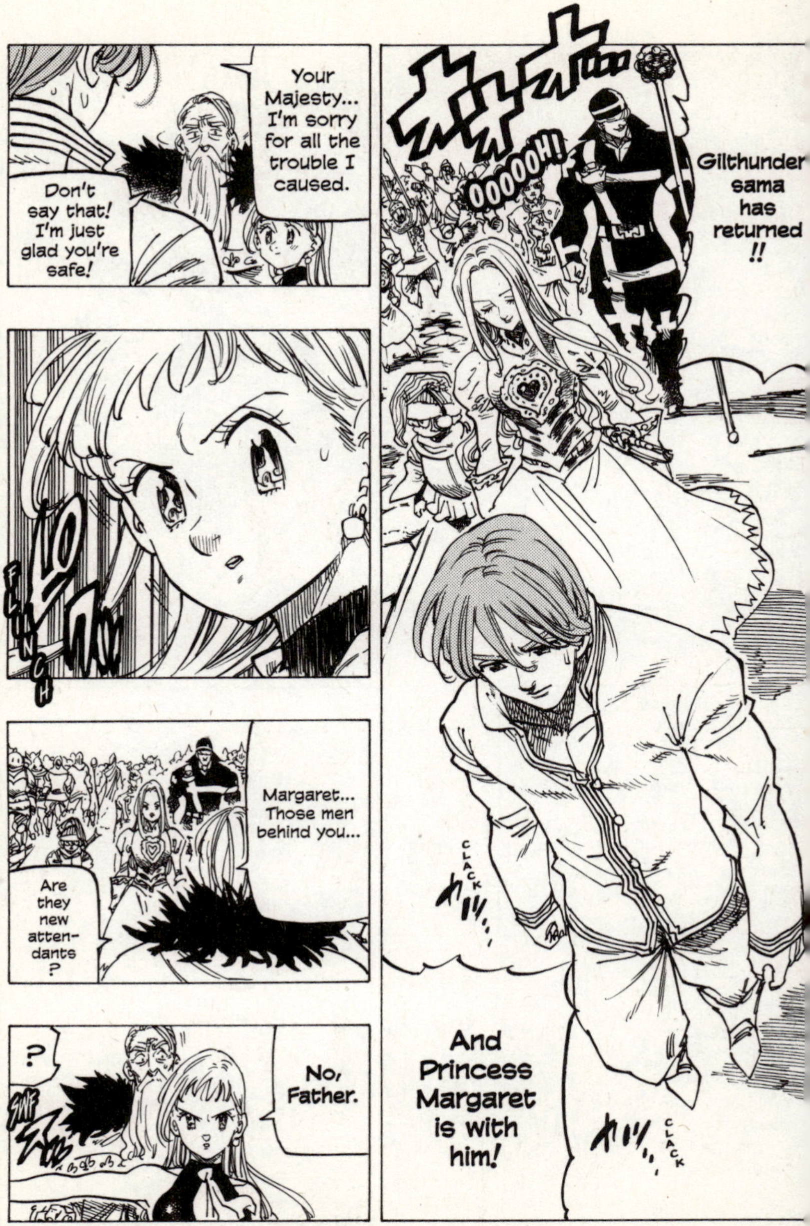
OOOOOOH!!
Gilthunder sama has returned !!
And Princess Margaret is with him!
CLACK
CLACK
Your Majesty... I'm sorry for all the trouble I caused.
Don't say that! I'm just glad you're safe!
FLINCH
Margaret... Those men behind you...
Are they new attendants ?
?
No, Father.

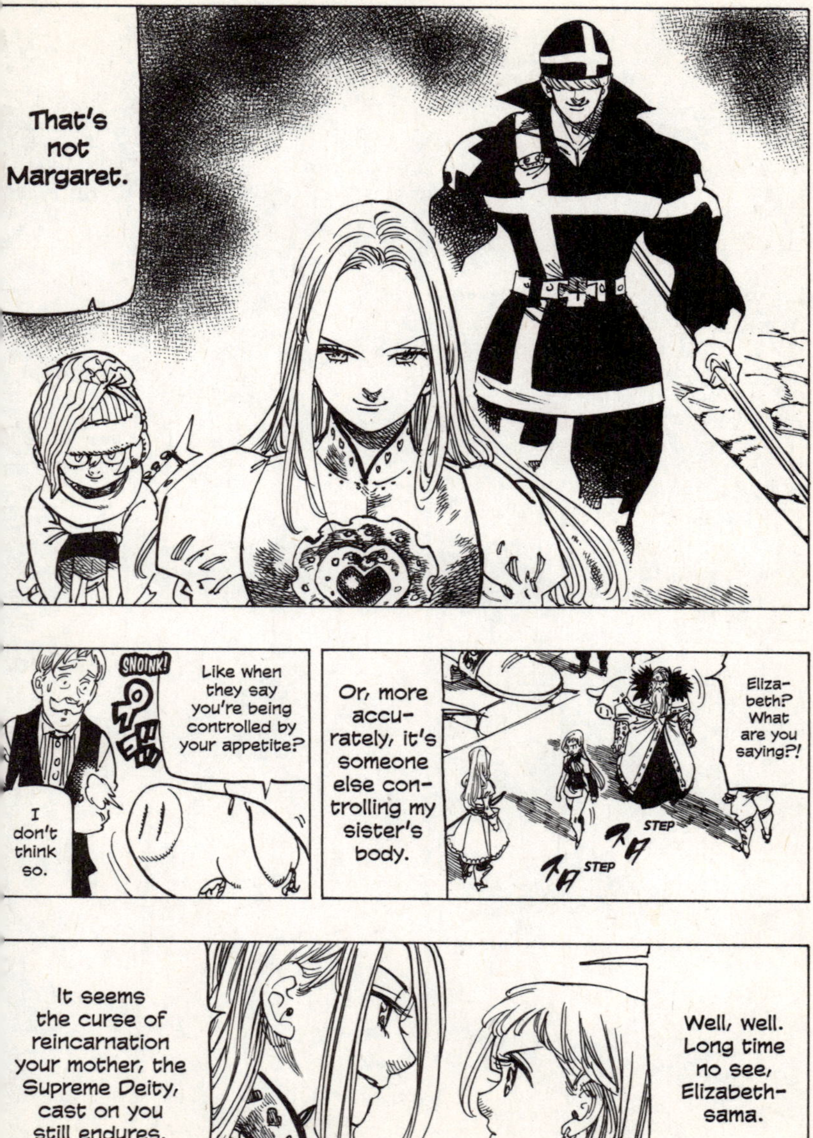
That's not Margaret.
Eliza-beth? What are you saying?!
STEP
STEP
Or, more accu-rately, it's someone else con-trolling my sister's body.
Like when they say you're being controlled by your appetite?
SNOINK!
I don't think so.
Well, well. Long time no see, Elizabeth-sama.
It seems the curse of reincarnation your mother, the Supreme Deity, cast on you still endures.

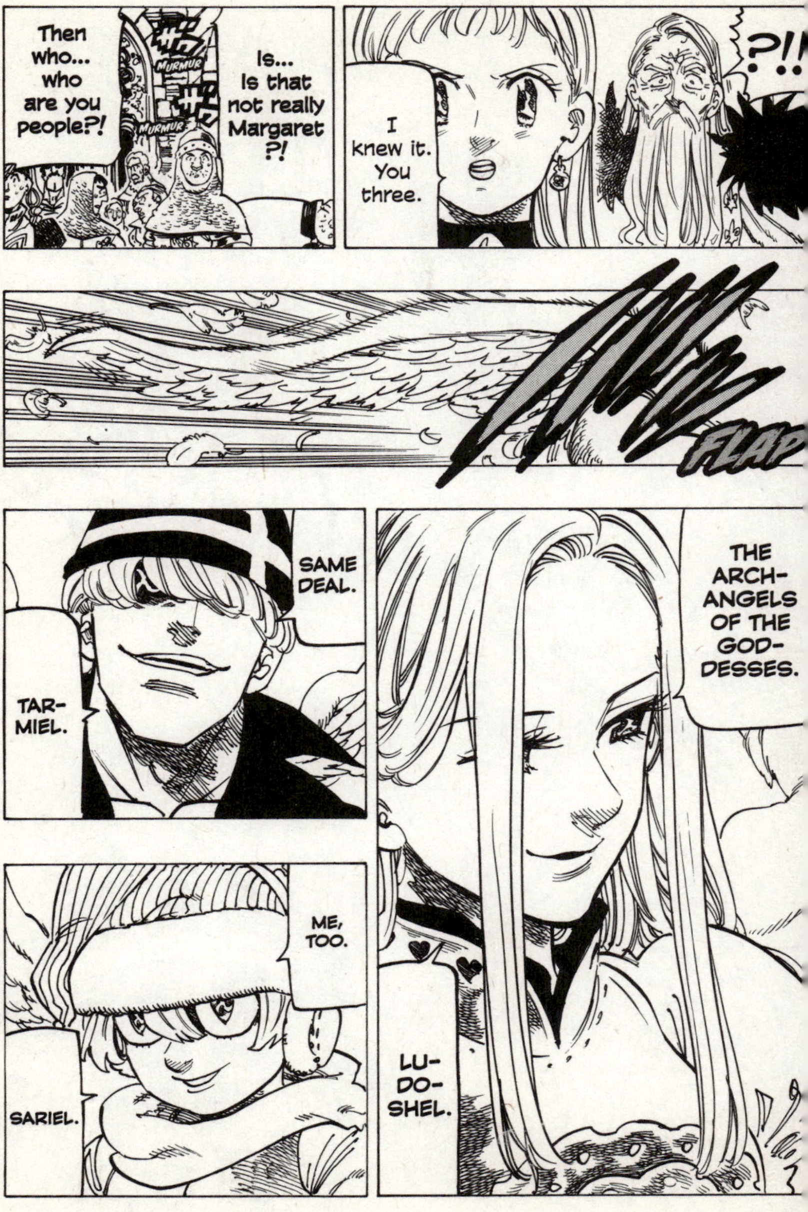
?!!
I knew it. You three.
Is... Is that not really Margaret?!
MURMUR
MURMUR
Then who... who are you people?!
FLAP
THE ARCH-ANGELS OF THE GOD-DESSES.
LU-DO-SHEL.
SAME DEAL.
TAR-MIEL.
ME, TOO.
SARIEL.

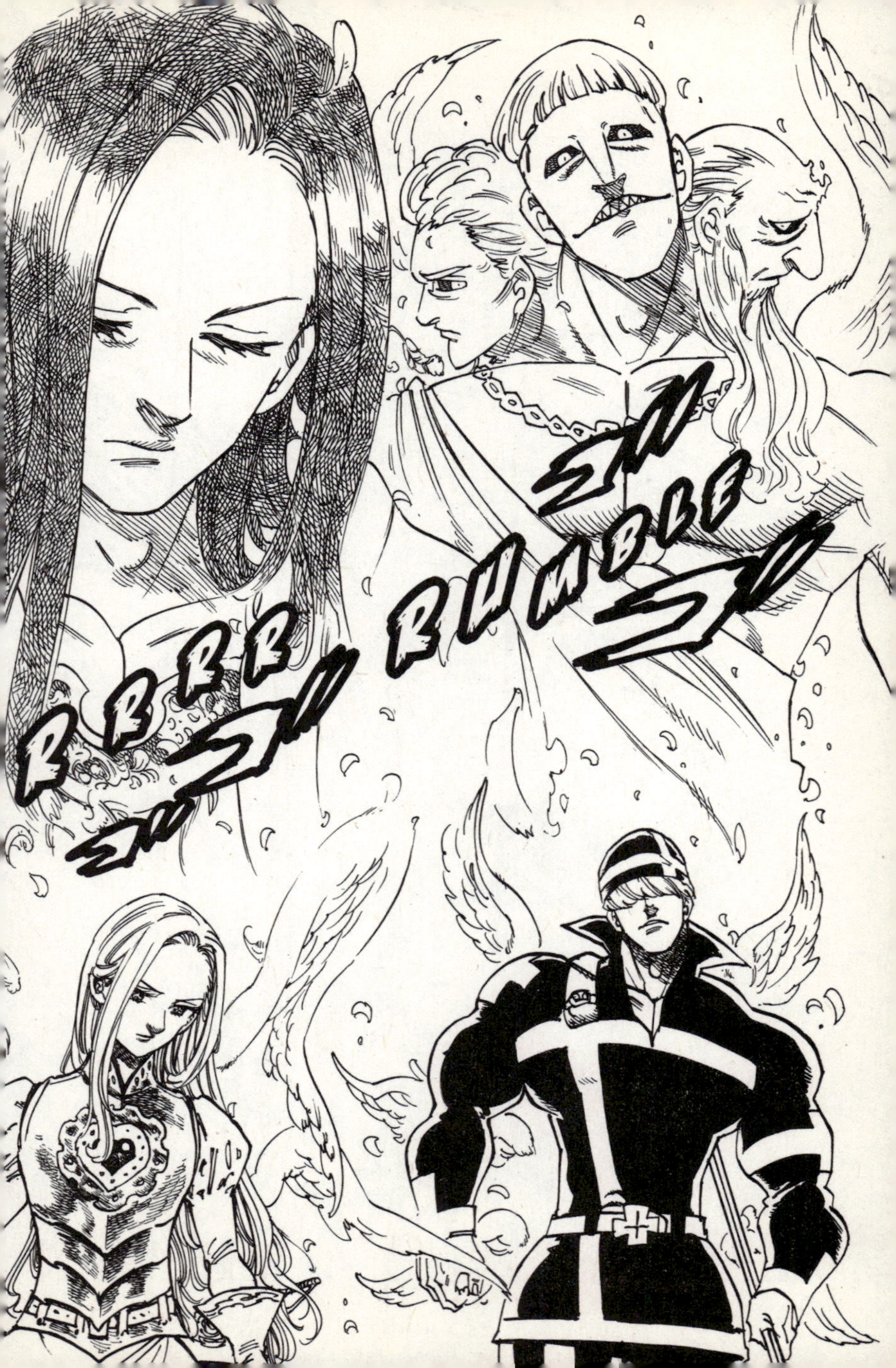
RRRR RUMBLE

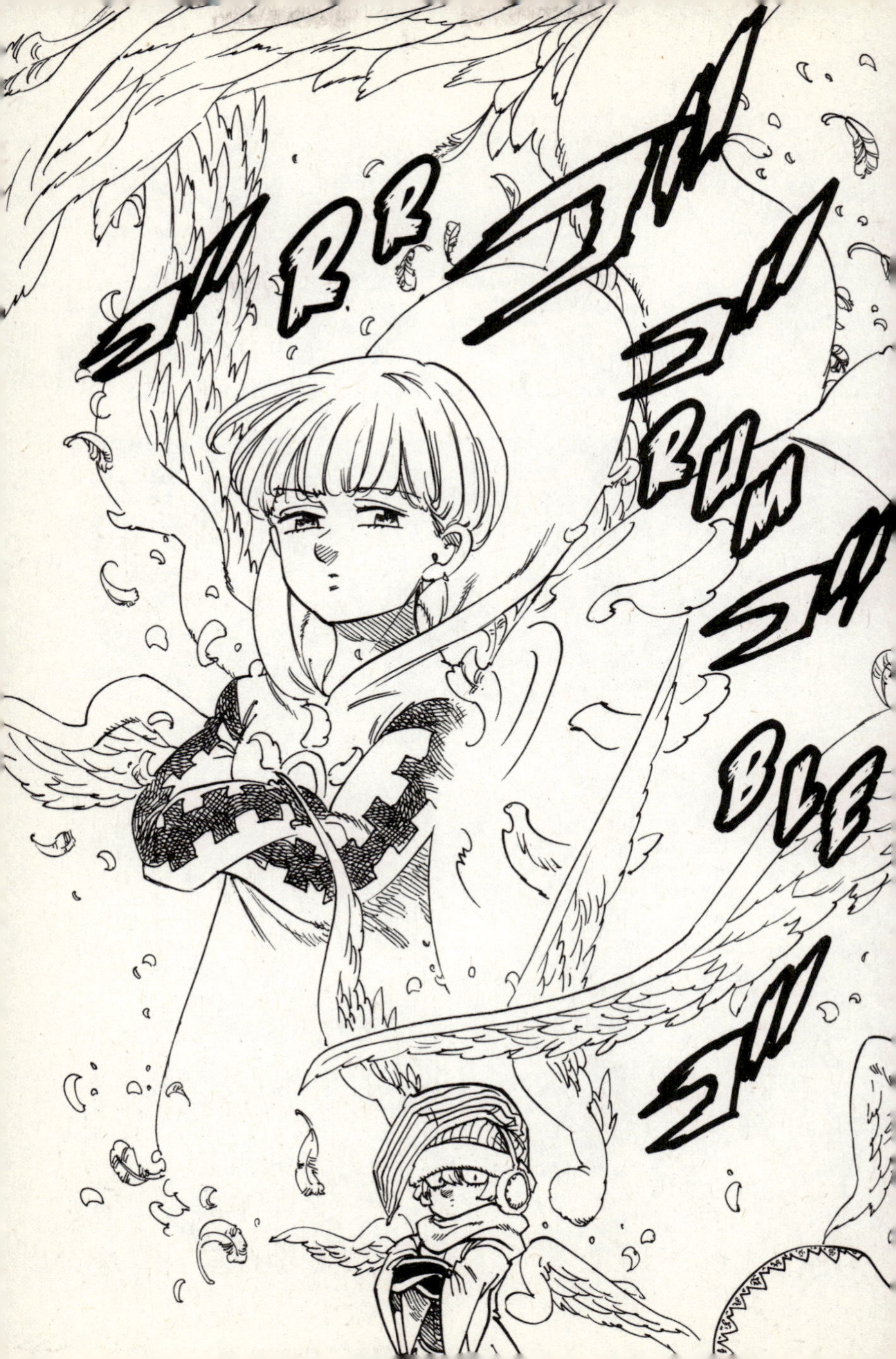

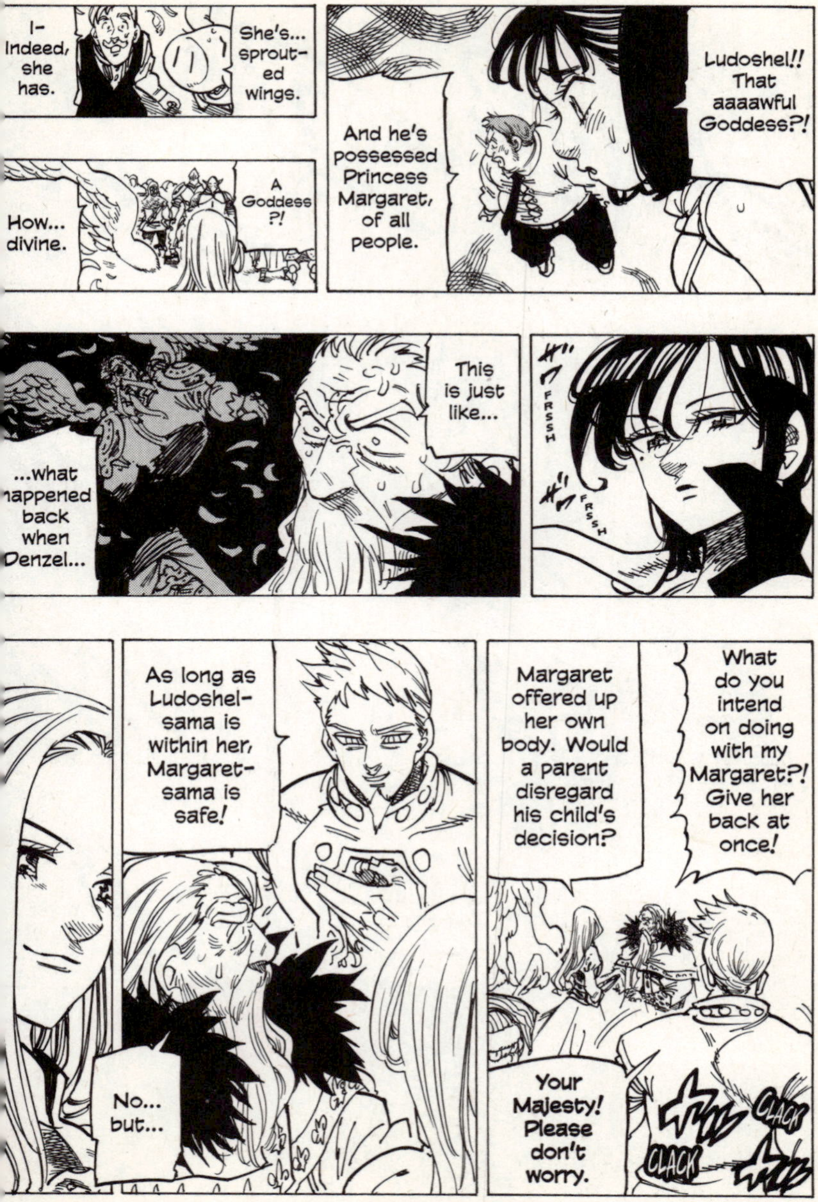
Ludoshel!! That aaaawful Goddess?!
And he's possessed Princess Margaret, of all people.
She's... sprouted wings.
I- Indeed, she has.
A Goddess?!
How... divine.
FRSSH
FRSSH
This is just like...
...what happened back when Denzel...
What do you intend on doing with my Margaret?! Give her back at once!
Margaret offered up her own body. Would a parent disregard his child's decision?
Your Majesty! Please don't worry.
CLACK
CLACK
As long as Ludoshel-sama is within her, Margaret-sama is safe!
No... but...

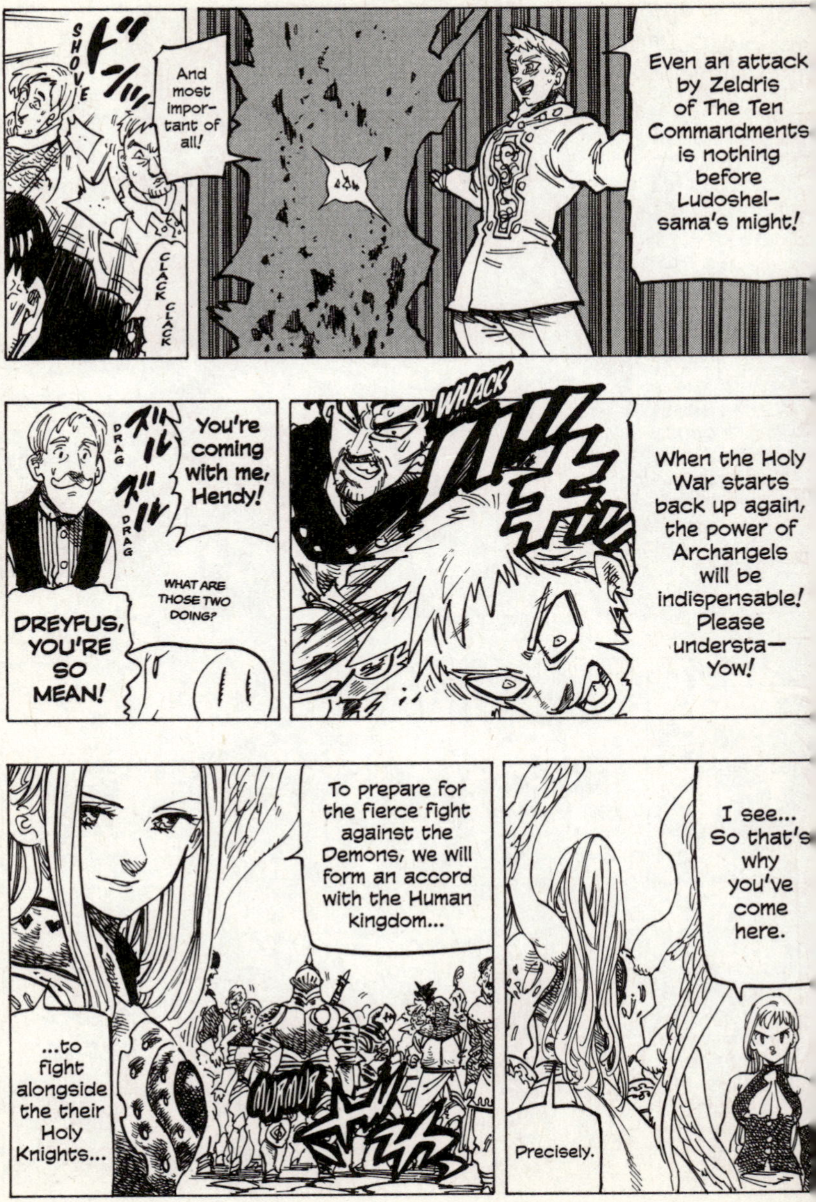
Even an attack by Zeldris of The Ten Commandments is nothing before Ludoshel-sama's might!
And most important of all!
SHOVE
CLACK CLACK
When the Holy War starts back up again, the power of Archangels will be indispensable! Please understa— Yow!
WHACK
DRAG
DRAG
You're coming with me, Hendy!
WHAT ARE THOSE TWO DOING?
DREYFUS, YOU'RE SO MEAN!
I see... So that's why you've come here.
Precisely.
To prepare for the fierce fight against the Demons, we will form an accord with the Human kingdom...
...to fight alongside the their Holy Knights...
MURMUR

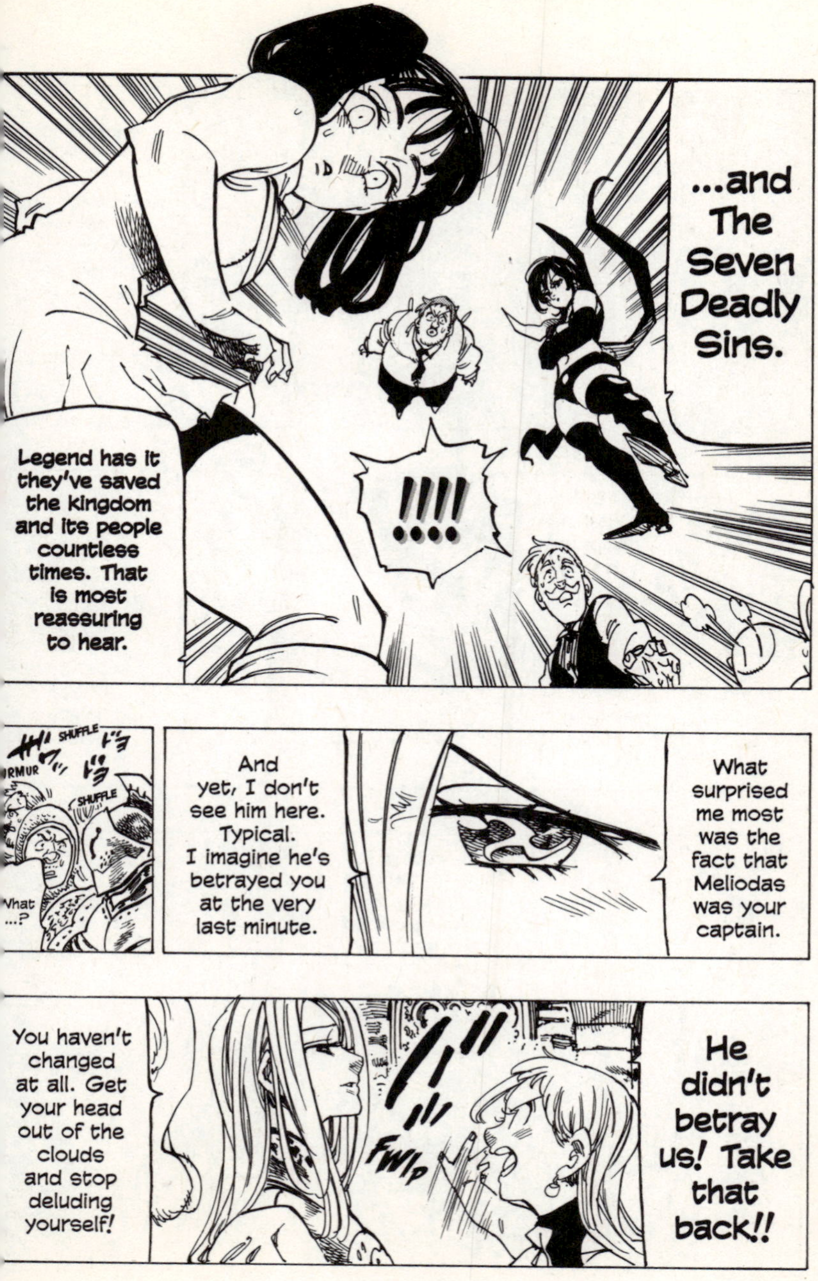

...and The Seven Deadly Sins.
!!!!
Legend has it they've saved the kingdom and its people countless times. That is most reassuring to hear.
What surprised me most was the fact that Meliodas was your captain.
And yet, I don't see him here. Typical. I imagine he's betrayed you at the very last minute.
SHUFFLE
SHUFFLE
What ...?
He didn't betray us! Take that back!!
FWIP
You haven't changed at all. Get your head out of the clouds and stop deluding yourself!

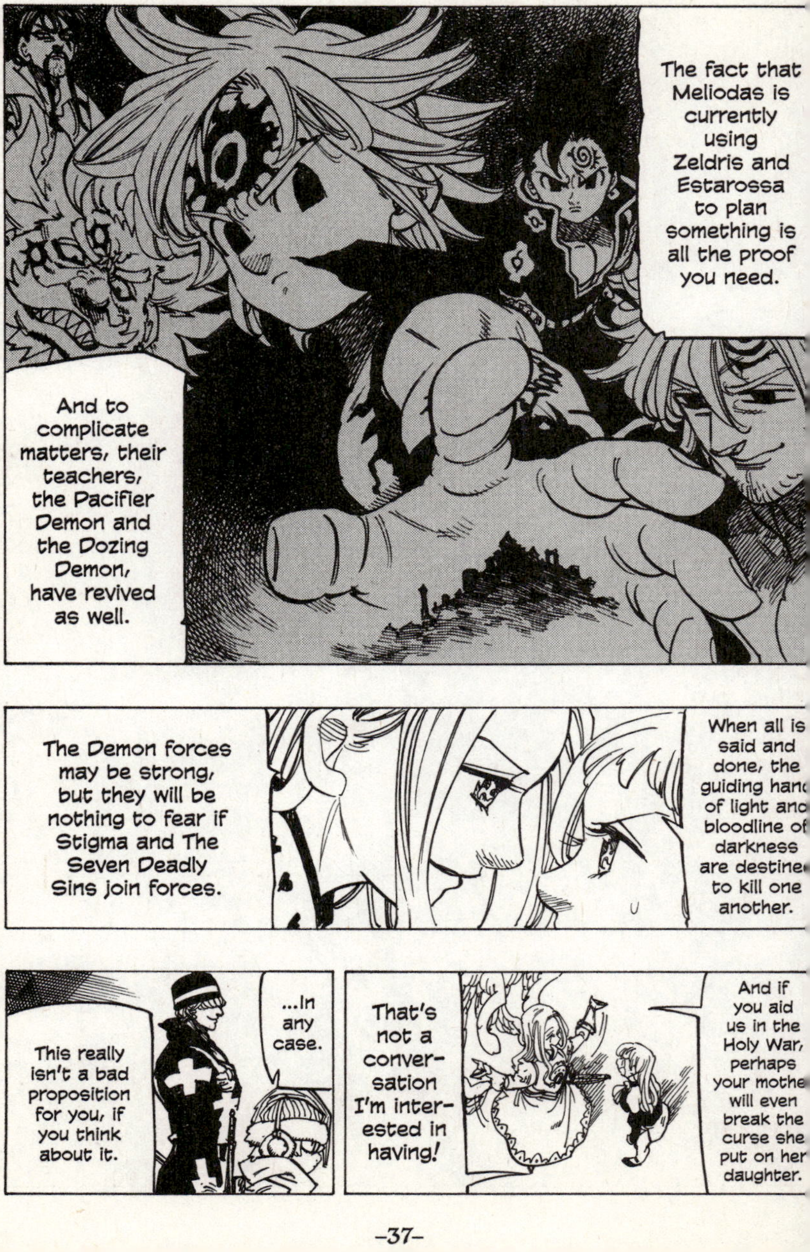
The fact that Meliodas is currently using Zeldris and Estarossa to plan something is all the proof you need.
And to complicate matters, their teachers, the Pacifier Demon and the Dozing Demon, have revived as well.
When all is said and done, the guiding han of light an bloodline of darkness are destine to kill one another.
The Demon forces may be strong, but they will be nothing to fear if Stigma and The Seven Deadly Sins join forces.
And if you aid us in the Holy War, perhaps your mothe will even break the curse she put on her daughter.
That's not a conversation I'm interested in having!
...In any case.
This really isn't a bad proposition for you, if you think about it.

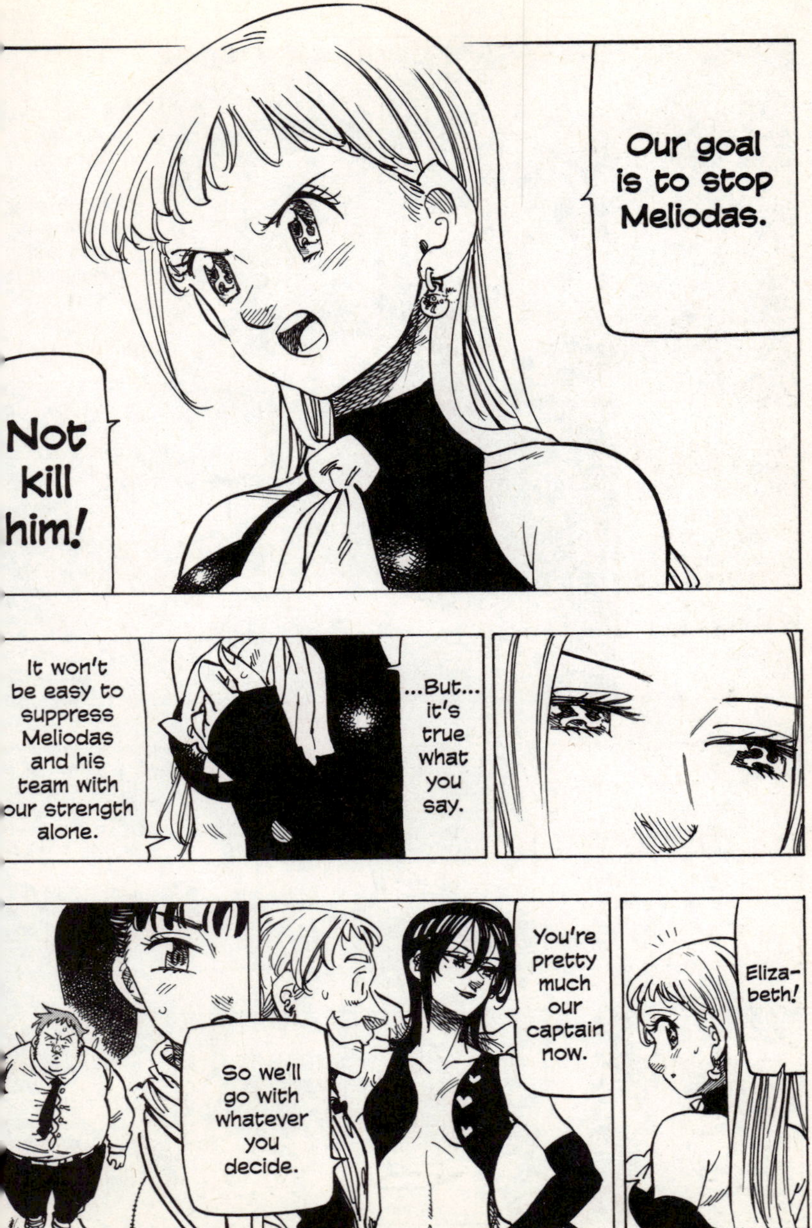
Our goal is to stop Meliodas.
Not kill him!
...But... it's true what you say.
It won't be easy to suppress Meliodas and his team with our strength alone.
Eliza-beth!
You're pretty much our captain now.
So we'll go with whatever you decide.

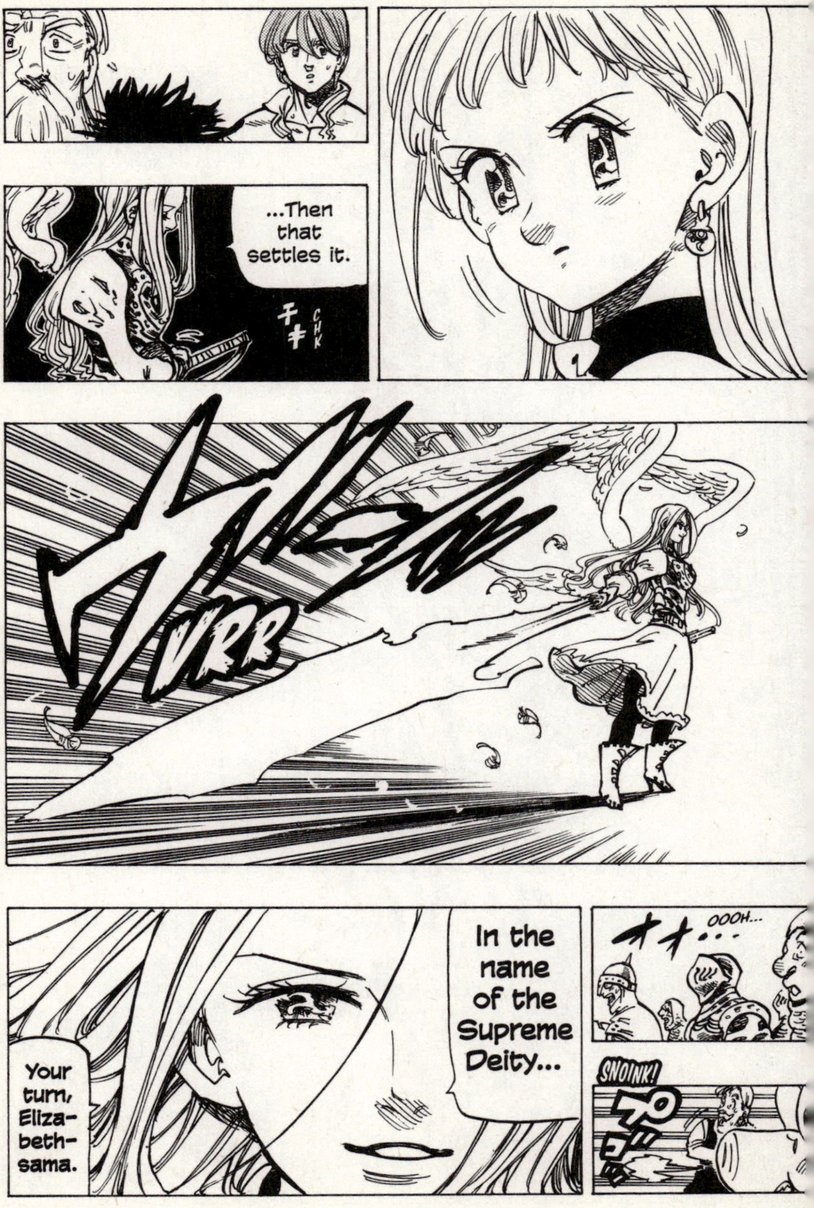
...Then that settles it.
CHK
VRR
OOOH...
SNOINK!
In the name of the Supreme Deity...
Your turn, Eliza-beth-sama.

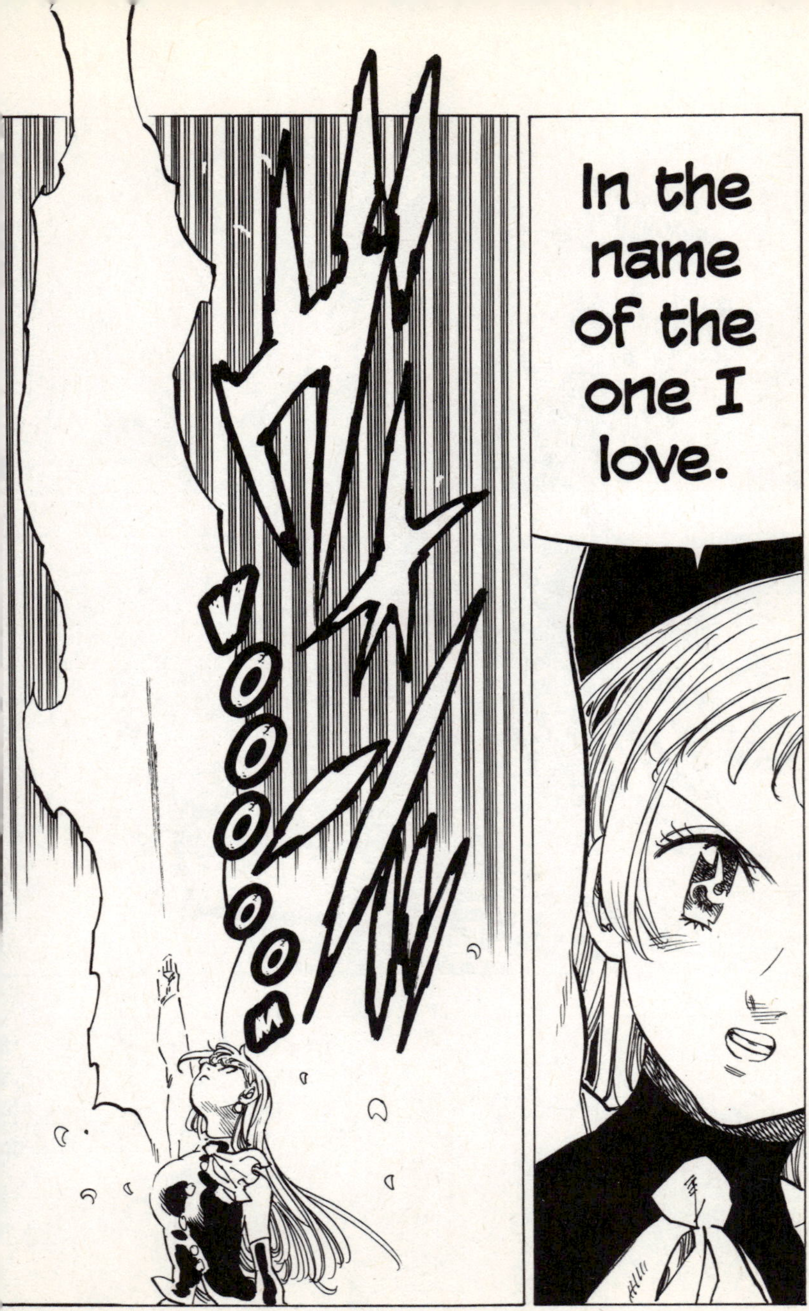
In the name of the one I love.
VOOOOOM

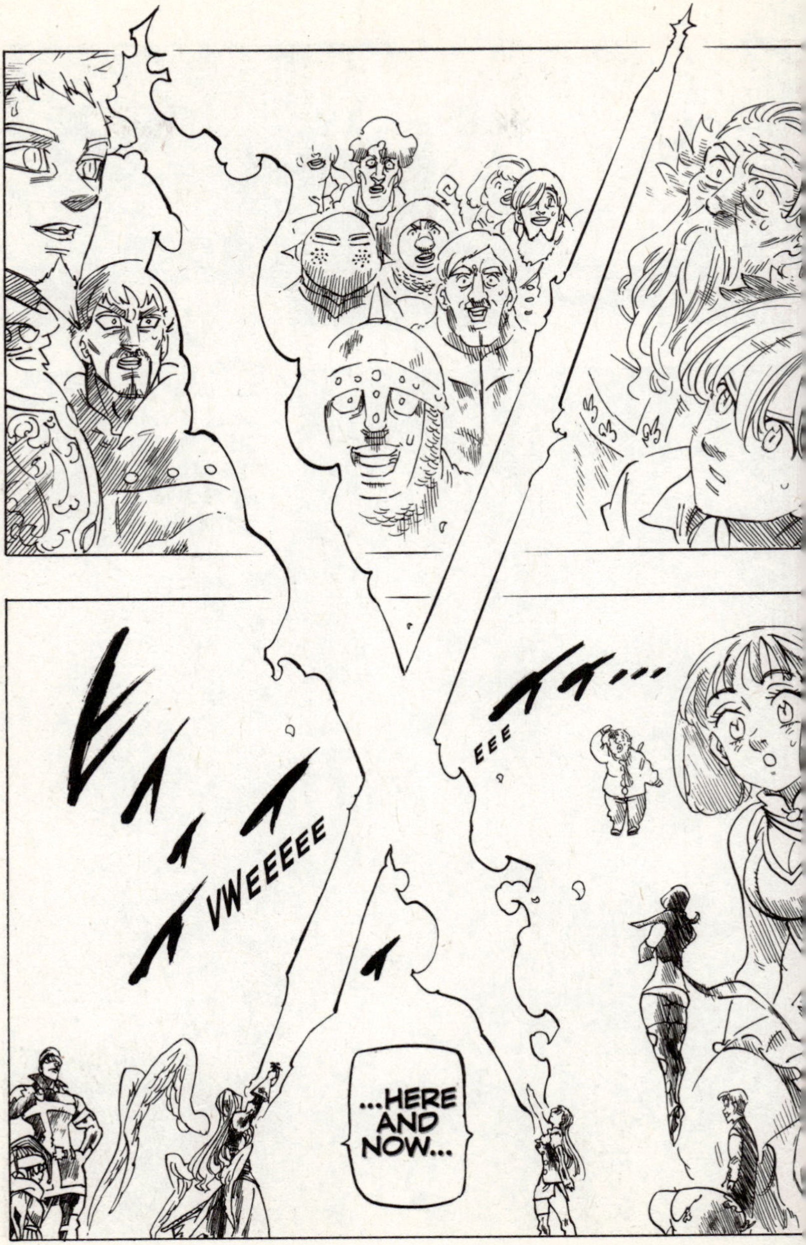
EEE
VWEEEEEE
...HERE AND NOW...

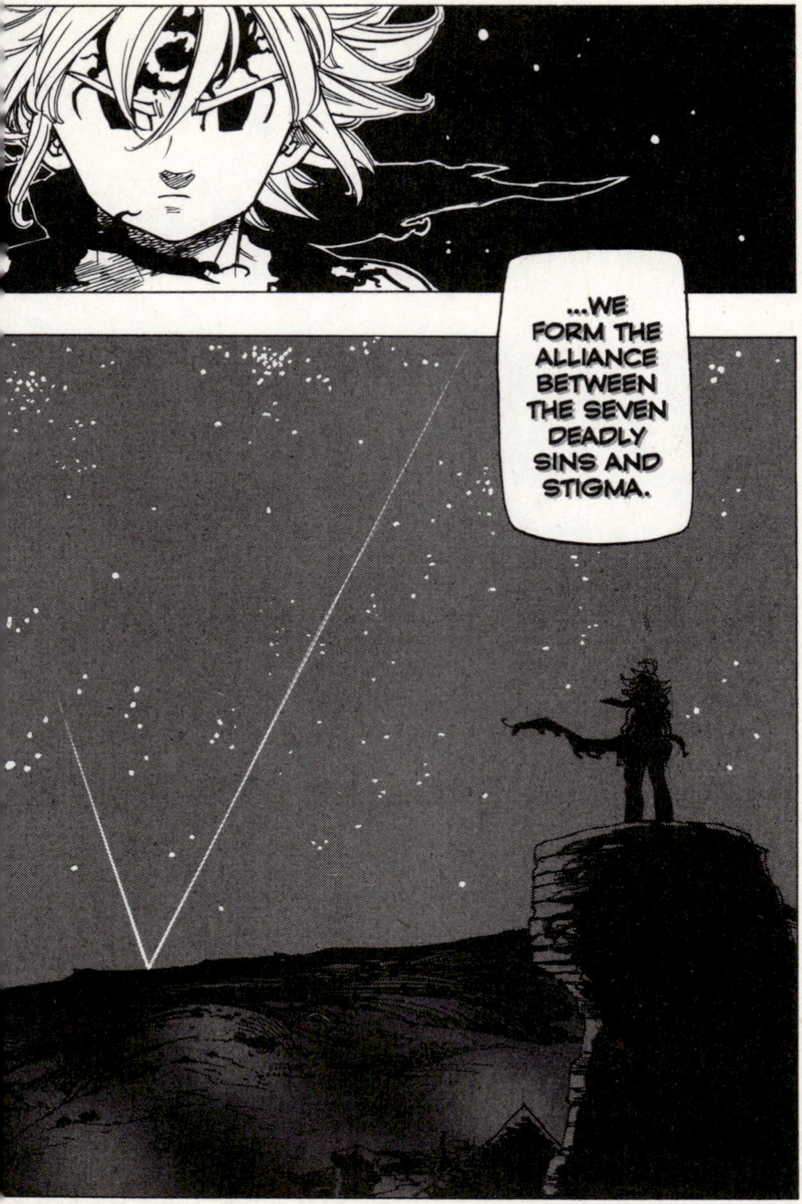
...WE FORM THE ALLIANCE BETWEEN THE SEVEN DEADLY SINS AND STIGMA.

Chapter 252 - An Old Grudge

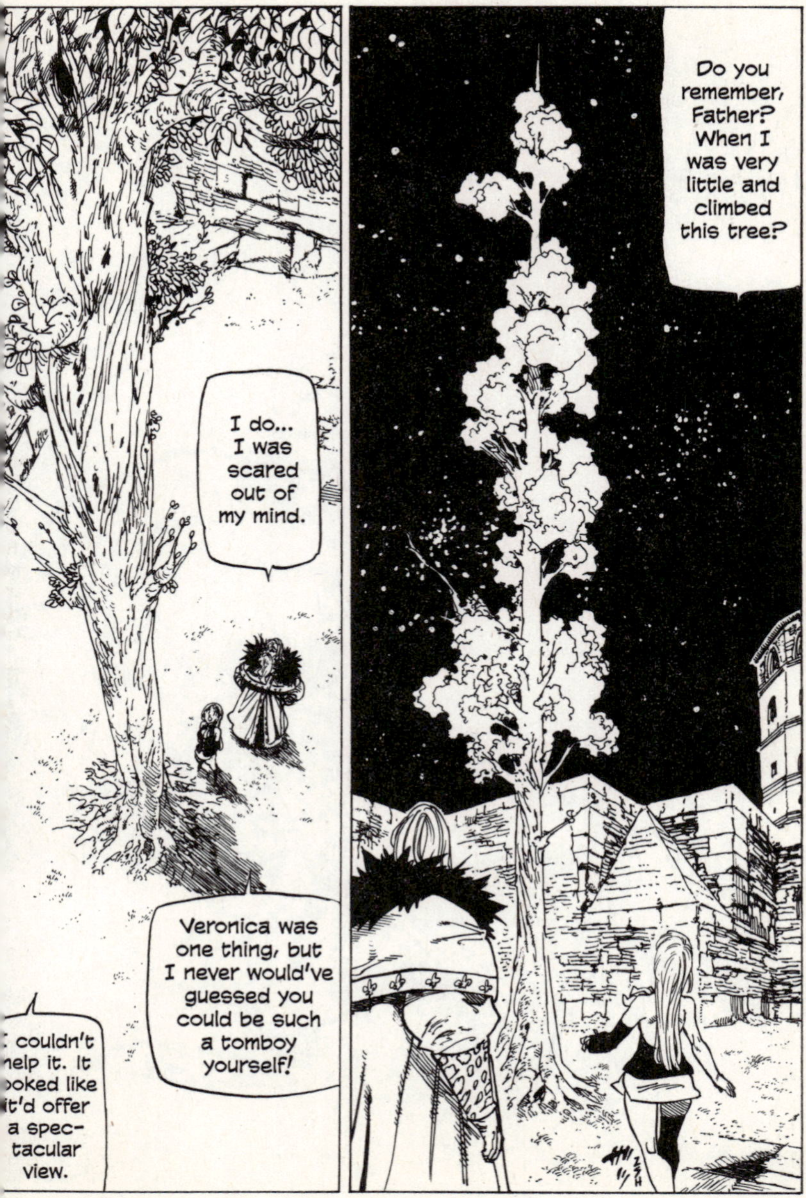
Do you remember, Father? When I was very little and climbed this tree?
I do... I was scared out of my mind.
Veronica was one thing, but I never would've guessed you could be such a tomboy yourself!
couldn't elp it. It ooked like it'd offer a spectacular view.

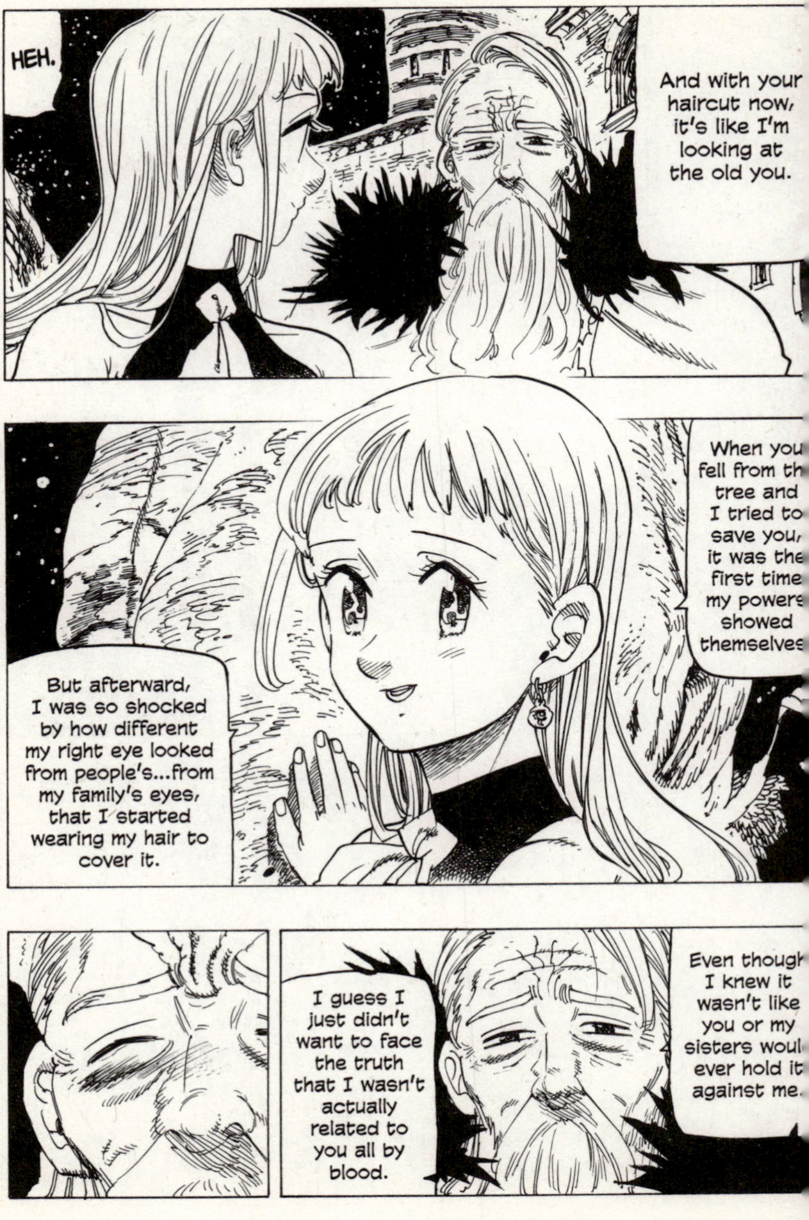
And with your haircut now, it's like I'm looking at the old you.
HEH.
When you fell from th tree and I tried to save you, it was the first time my powers showed themselves
But afterward, I was so shocked by how different my right eye looked from people's...from my family's eyes, that I started wearing my hair to cover it.
Even though I knew it wasn't like you or my sisters woul ever hold it against me.
I guess I just didn't want to face the truth that I wasn't actually related to you all by blood.

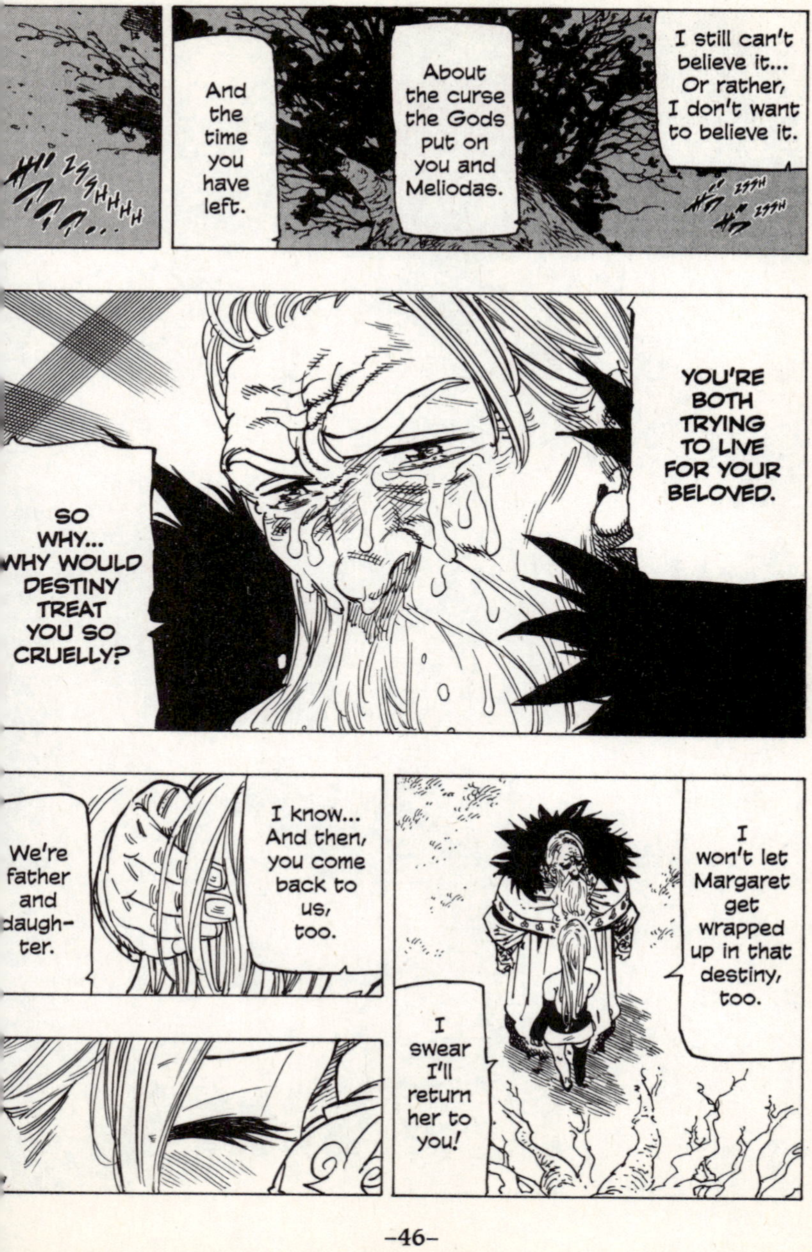
I still can't believe it... Or rather, I don't want to believe it.
ZSSH
ZSSH
About the curse the Gods put on you and Meliodas.
And the time you have left.
YOU'RE BOTH TRYING TO LIVE FOR YOUR BELOVED.
SO WHY... WHY WOULD DESTINY TREAT YOU SO CRUELLY?
I won't let Margaret get wrapped up in that destiny, too.
I swear I'll return her to you!
I know... And then, you come back to us, too.
We're father and daughter.

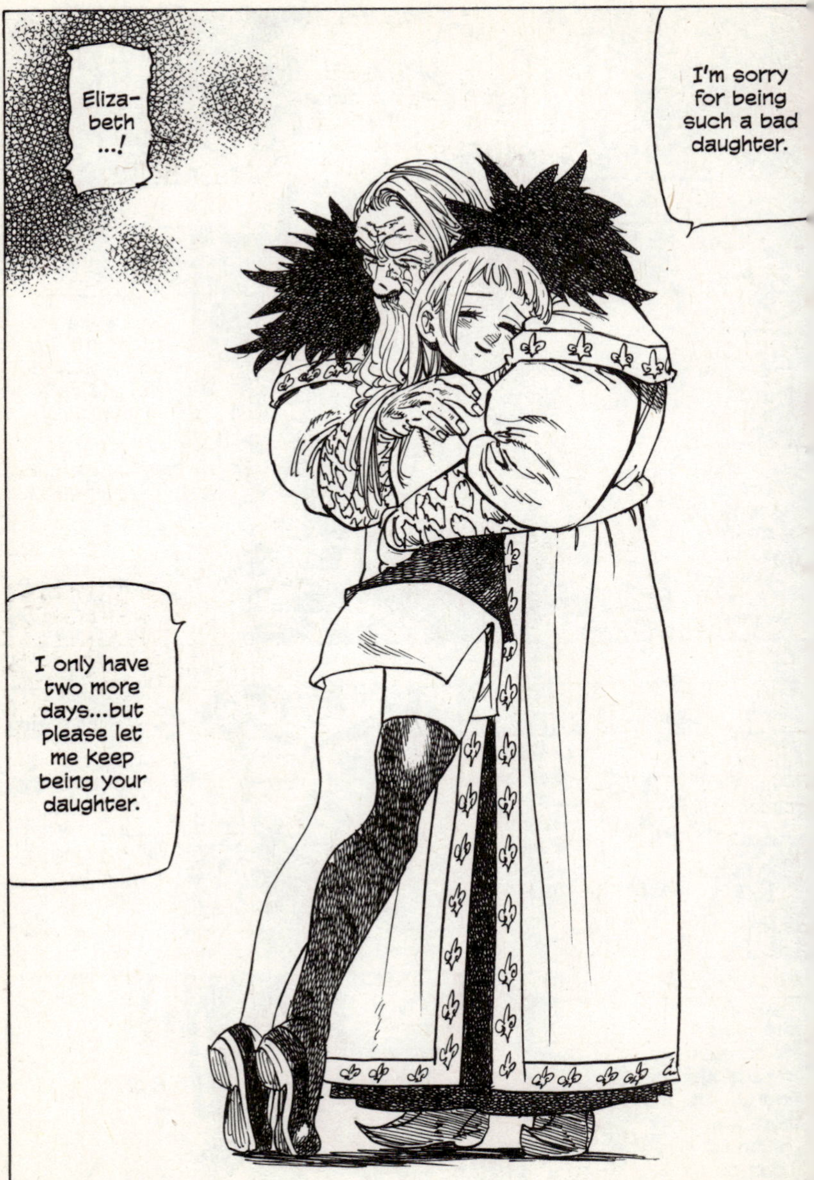
I'm sorry for being such a bad daughter.
Eliza-beth ...!
I only have two more days...but please let me keep being your daughter.

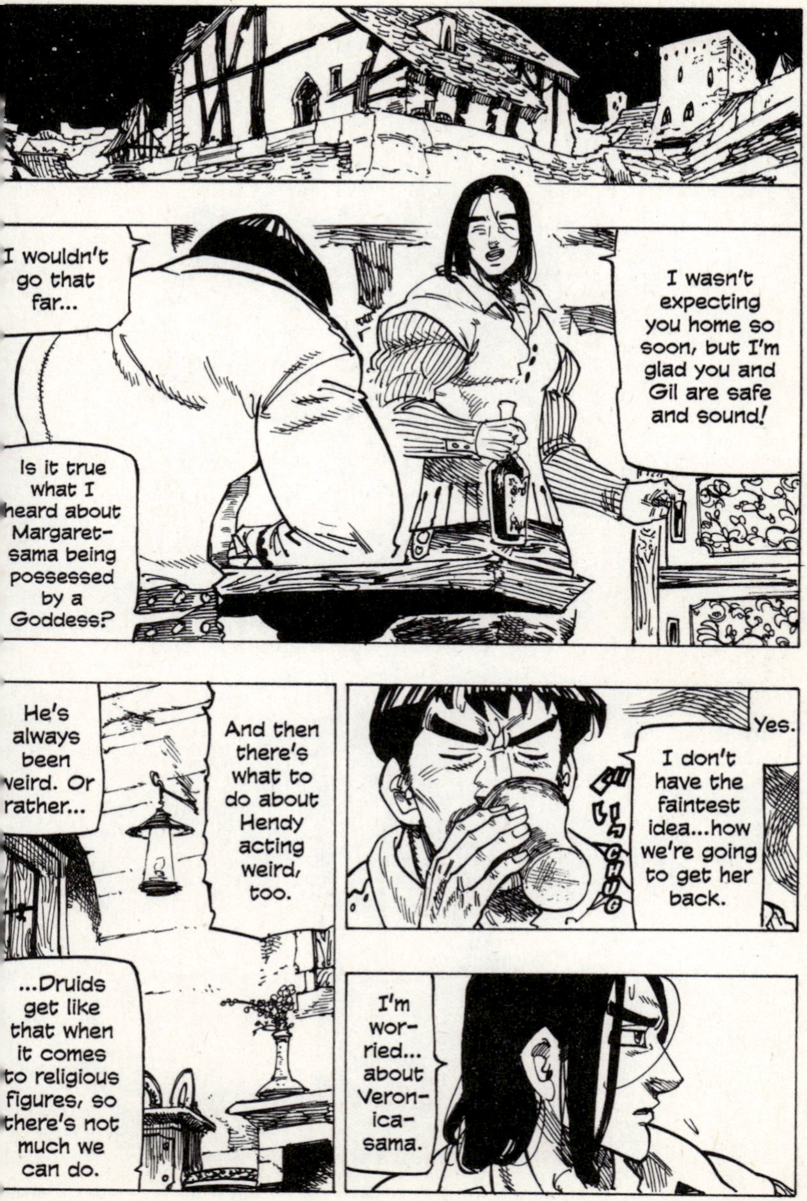
I wasn't expecting you home so soon, but I'm glad you and Gil are safe and sound!
I wouldn't go that far...
Is it true what I heard about Margaret-sama being possessed by a Goddess?
Yes.
I don't have the faintest idea...how we're going to get her back.
CHUG
CHUG
I'm wor-ried... about Veron-ica-sama.
And then there's what to do about Hendy acting weird, too.
He's always been weird. Or rather...
...Druids get like that when it comes to religious figures, so there's not much we can do.

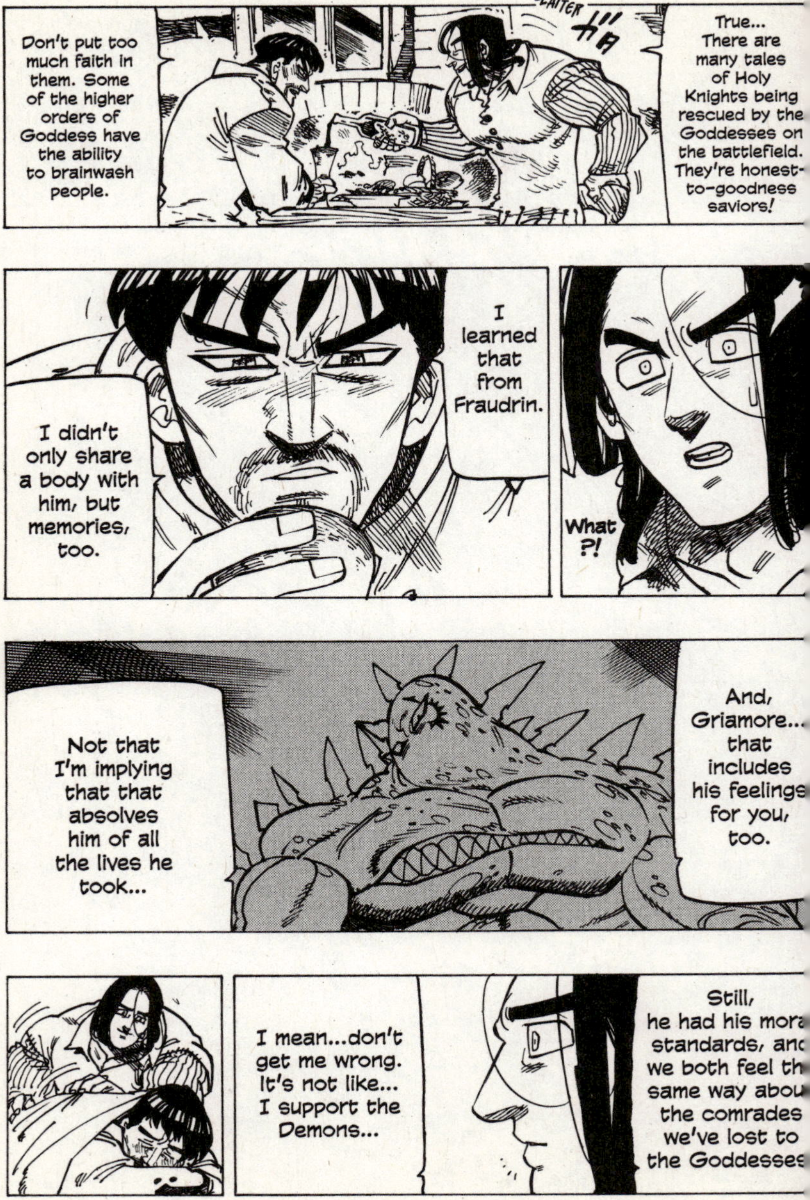
True... There are many tales of Holy Knights being rescued by the Goddesses on the battlefield. They're honest-to-goodness saviors!
CLATTER
ガタ
Don't put too much faith in them. Some of the higher orders of Goddess have the ability to brainwash people.
What?!
I learned that from Fraudrin.
I didn't only share a body with him, but memories, too.
And, Griamore... that includes his feeling for you, too.
Not that I'm implying that that absolves him of all the lives he took...
Still, he had his mora standards, an we both feel th same way abou the comrades we've lost to the Goddesse
I mean...don't get me wrong. It's not like... I support the Demons...

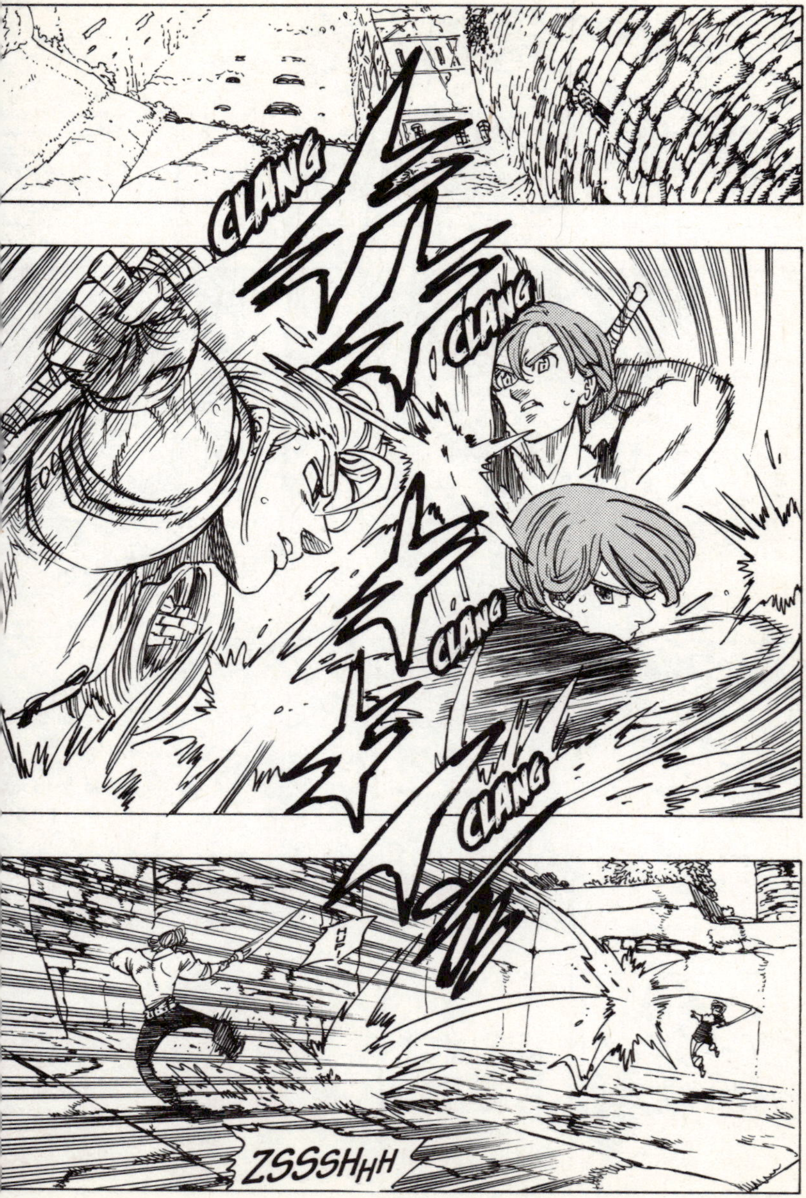
CLANG
CLANG
CLANG
CLANG
HUP!
ZSSSHHH

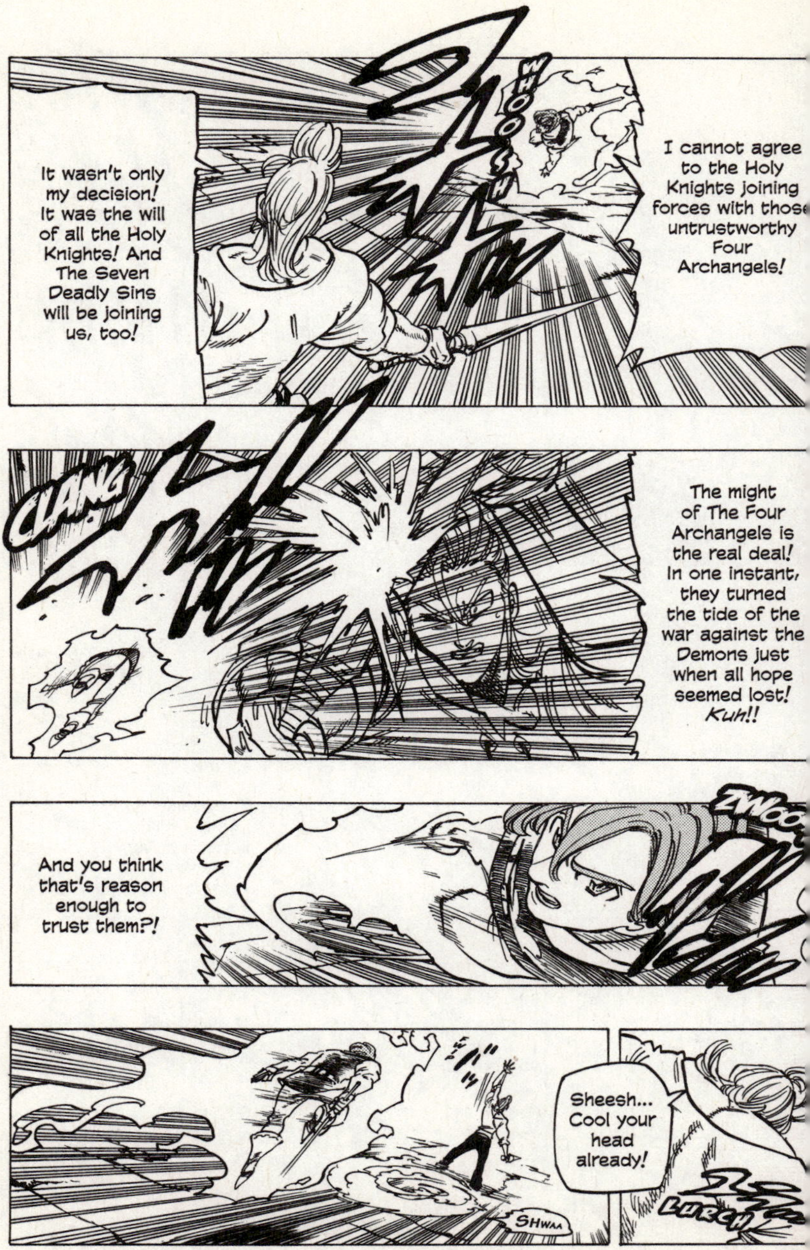
I cannot agree to the Holy Knights joining forces with thos
WHOOSH
It wasn't only my decision! It was the will of all the Holy Knights! And The Seven Deadly Sins will be joining us, too!
The might of The Four Archangels is the real deal! In one instant, they turned the tide of the war against the Demons just when all hope seemed lost! *Kuh!!*
CLANG
ZWOO
And you think that's reason enough to trust them?!
Sheesh... Cool your head already!
LURCH
SHWAA

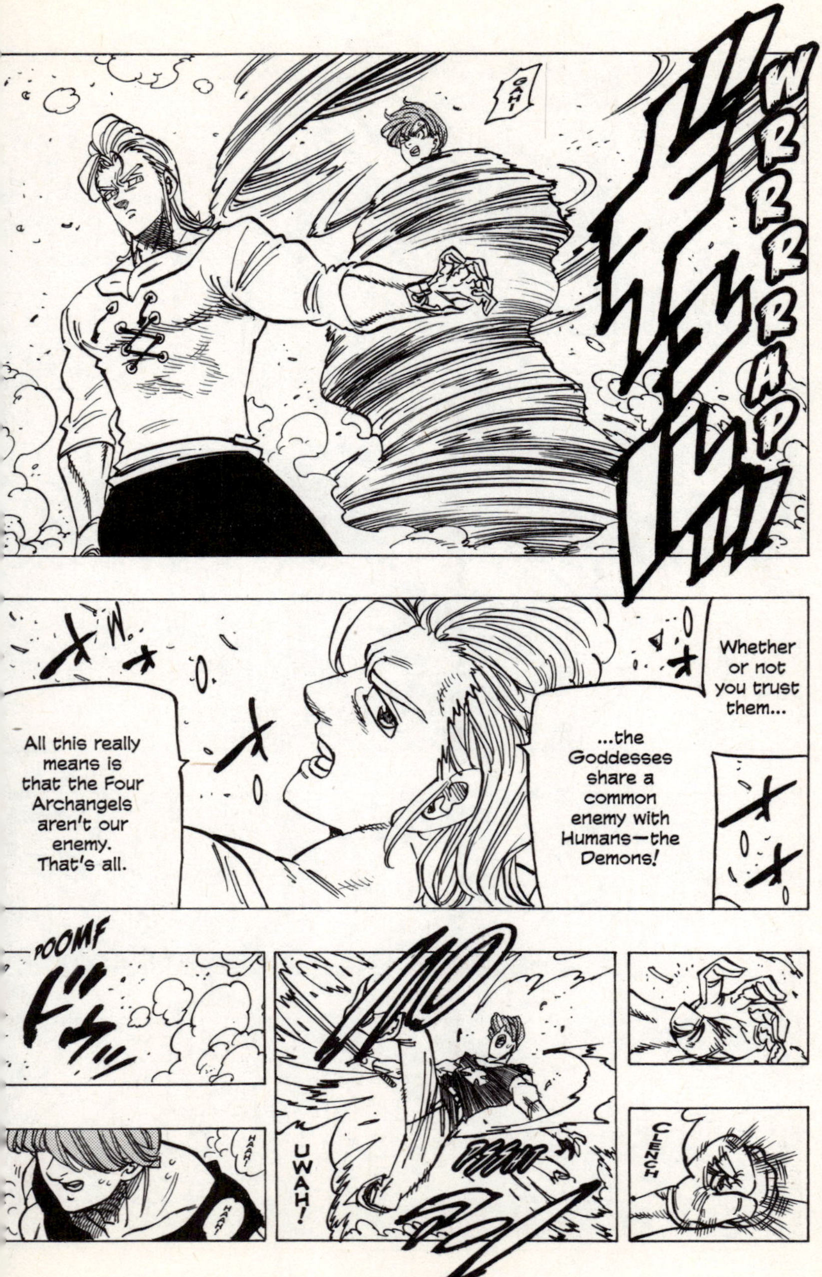
GAH!
WRRRRAP!!
Whether or not you trust them...
...the Goddesses share a common enemy with Humans—the Demons!
All this really means is that the Four Archangels aren't our enemy. That's all.
CLENCH
UWAH!
POOMF
HAAH!
HAAH!

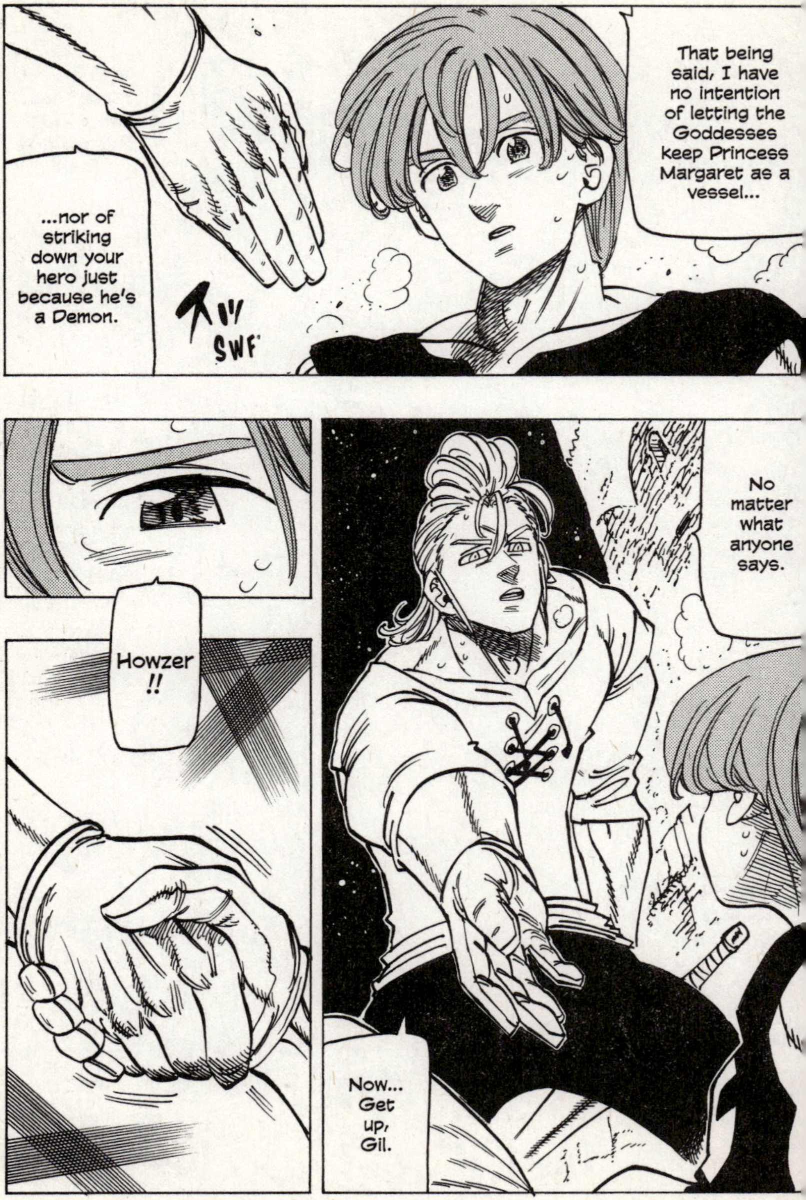
That being said, I have no intention of letting the Goddesses keep Princess Margaret as a vessel...
...nor of striking down your hero just because he's a Demon.
SWF
No matter what anyone says.
Now... Get up, Gil.
Howzer !!

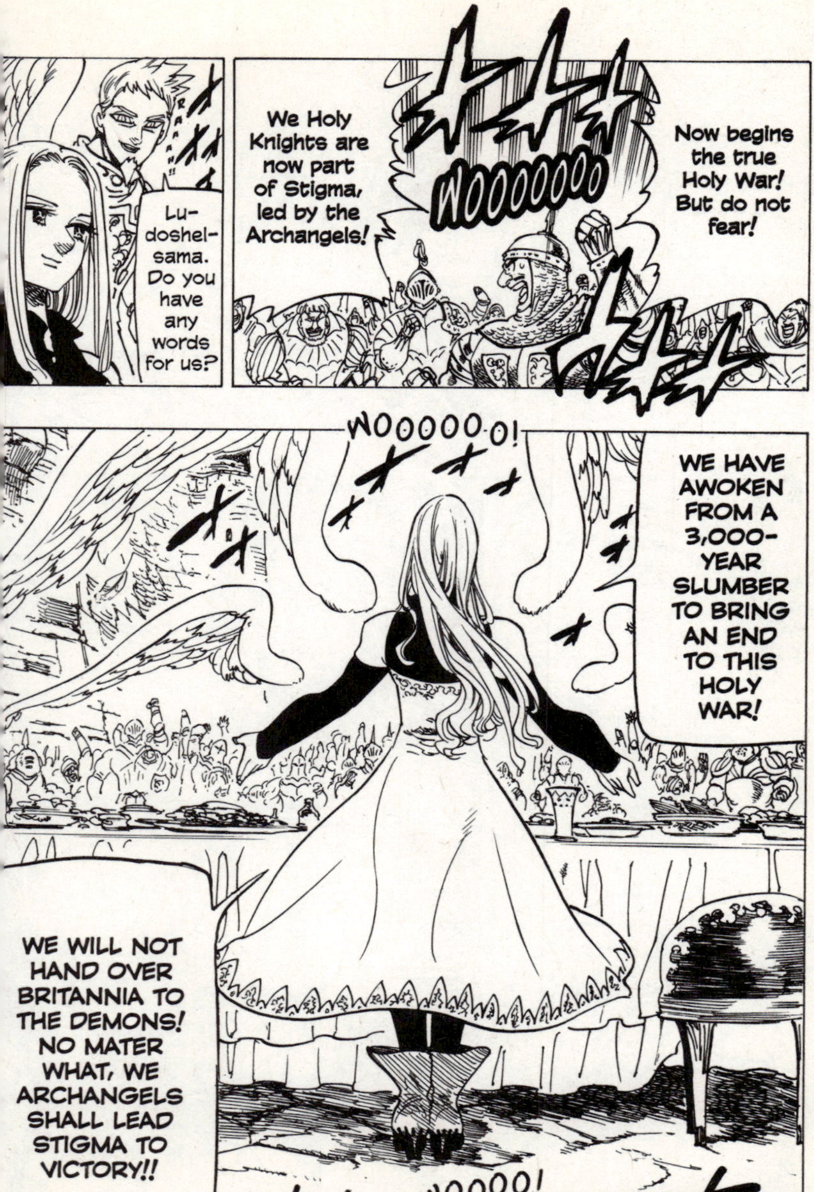
Now begins the true Holy War! But do not fear!
WOOOOOOO
We Holy Knights are now part of Stigma, led by the Archangels!
Ludoshel-sama. Do you have any words for us?
WE HAVE AWOKEN FROM A 3,000-YEAR SLUMBER TO BRING AN END TO THIS HOLY WAR!
WOOOOO-O!
WE WILL NOT HAND OVER BRITANNIA TO THE DEMONS! NO MATER WHAT, WE ARCHANGELS SHALL LEAD STIGMA TO VICTORY!!
WOOOO!

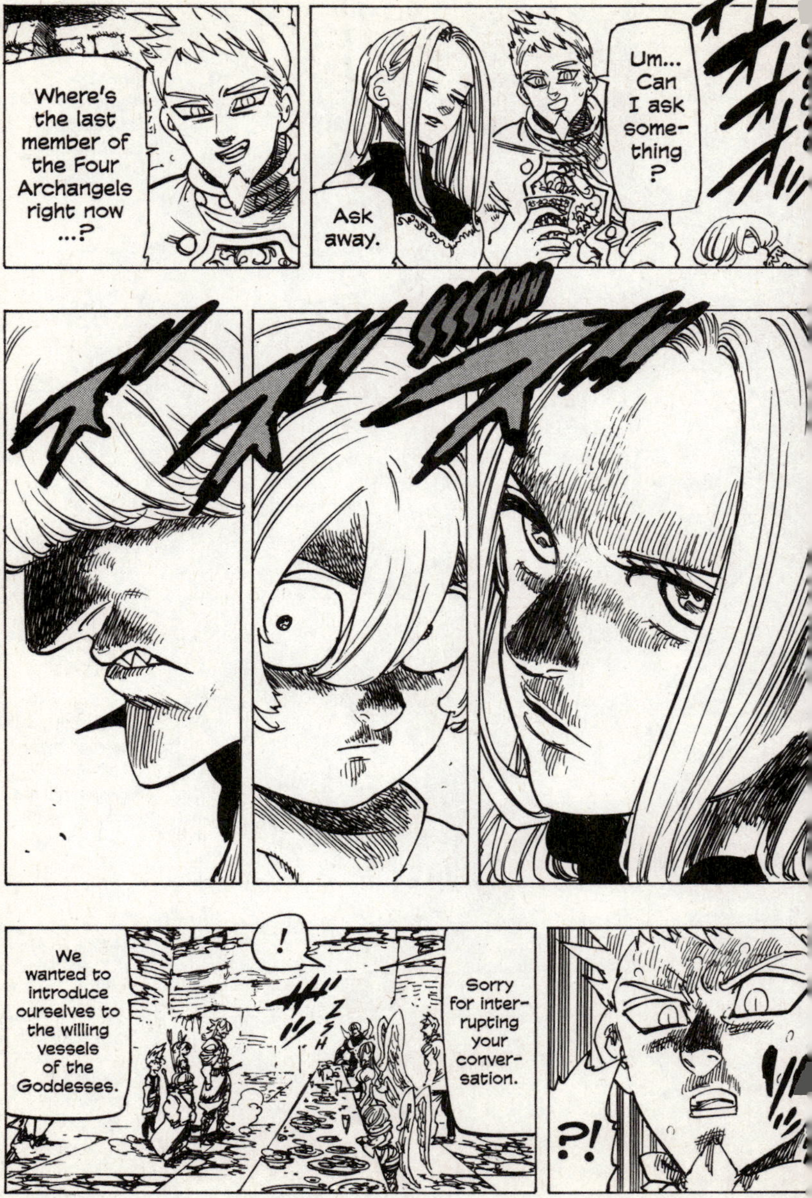
Um... Can I ask some-thing?
Ask away.
Where's the last member of the Four Archangels right now ...?
SSSHHH
?!
Sorry for inter-rupting your conver-sation.
ZSH
!
We wanted to introduce ourselves to the willing vessels of the Goddesses.

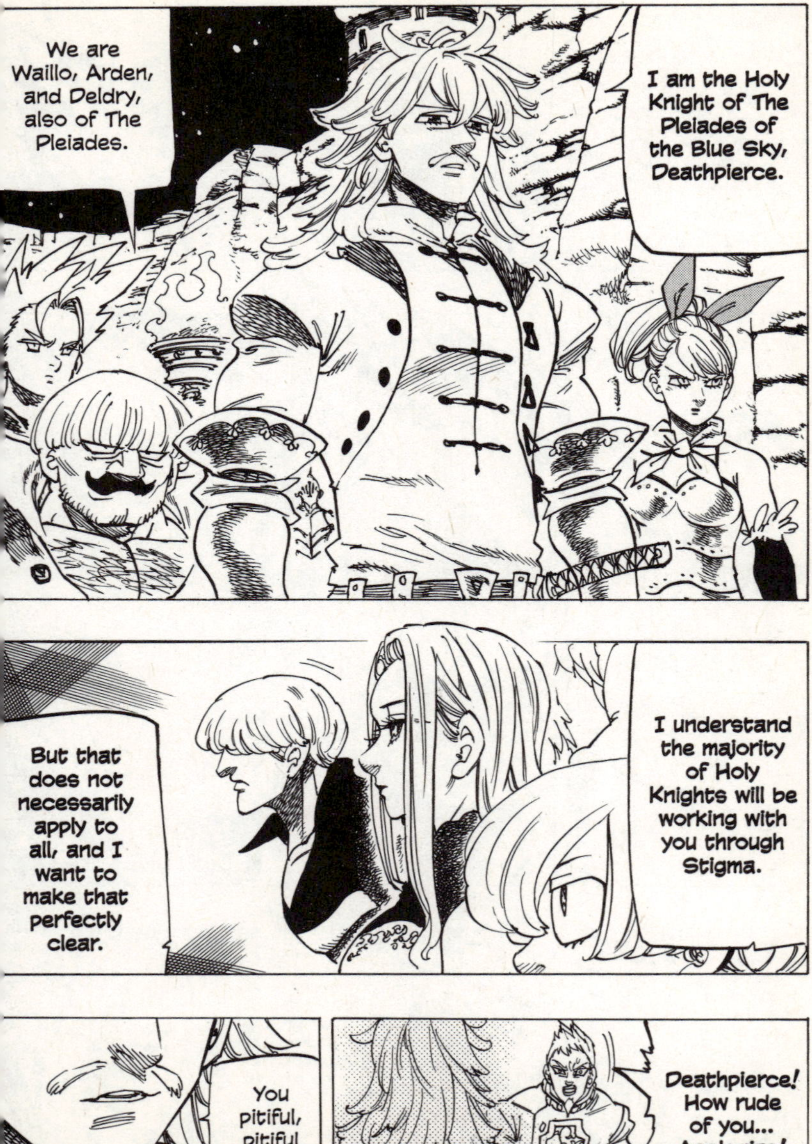
I am the Holy Knight of The Pleiades of the Blue Sky, Deathpierce.
We are Waillo, Arden, and Deldry, also of The Pleiades.
I understand the majority of Holy Knights will be working with you through Stigma.
But that does not necessarily apply to all, and I want to make that perfectly clear.
Deathpierce! How rude of you... Apologize!
You pitiful, pitiful man.

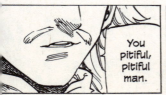

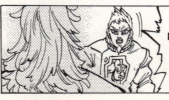

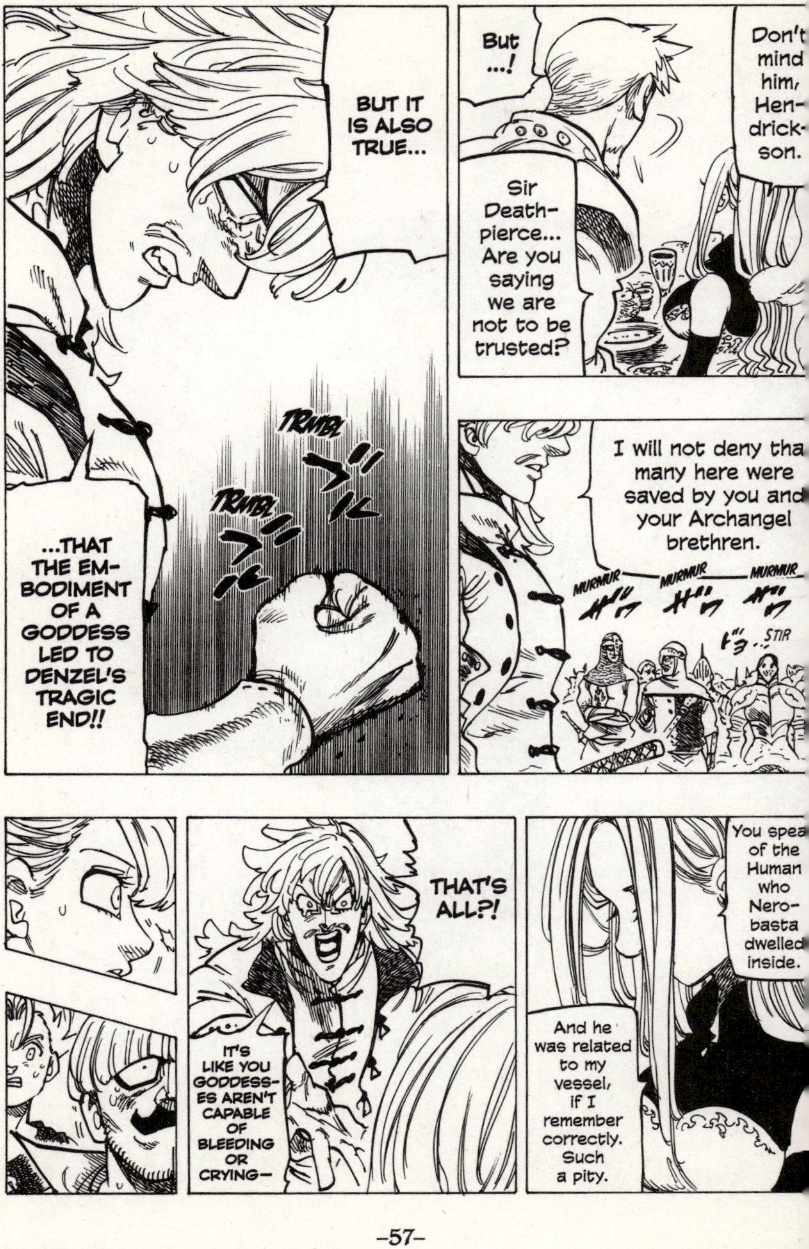
Don't mind him, Hendrickson.
But ...!
Sir Deathpierce... Are you saying we are not to be trusted?
I will not deny tha many here were saved by you and your Archangel brethren.
MURMUR
MURMUR
MURMUR
STIR
BUT IT IS ALSO TRUE...
TRMBL
TRMBL
...THAT THE EMBODIMENT OF A GODDESS LED TO DENZEL'S TRAGIC END!!
You spea of the Human who Nerobasta dwelled inside.
And he was related to my vessel, if I remember correctly. Such a pity.
THAT'S ALL?!
IT'S LIKE YOU GODDESSES AREN'T CAPABLE OF BLEEDING OR CRYING—

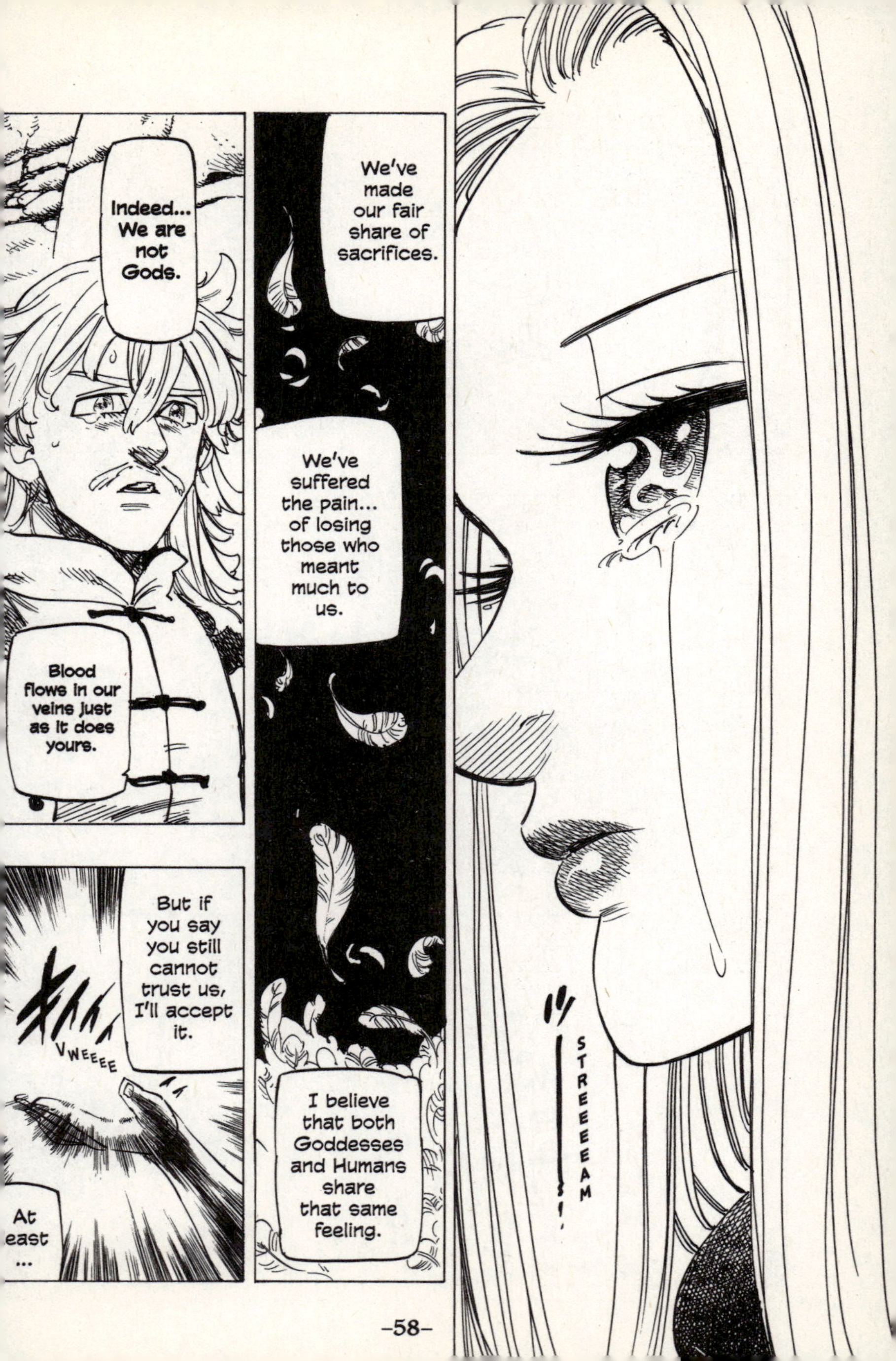
STREEEEAM
We've made our fair share of sacrifices.
We've suffered the pain... of losing those who meant much to us.
I believe that both Goddesses and Humans share that same feeling.
Indeed... We are not Gods.
Blood flows in our veins just as it does yours.
But if you say you still cannot trust us, I'll accept it.
VWEEEEE
At east ...

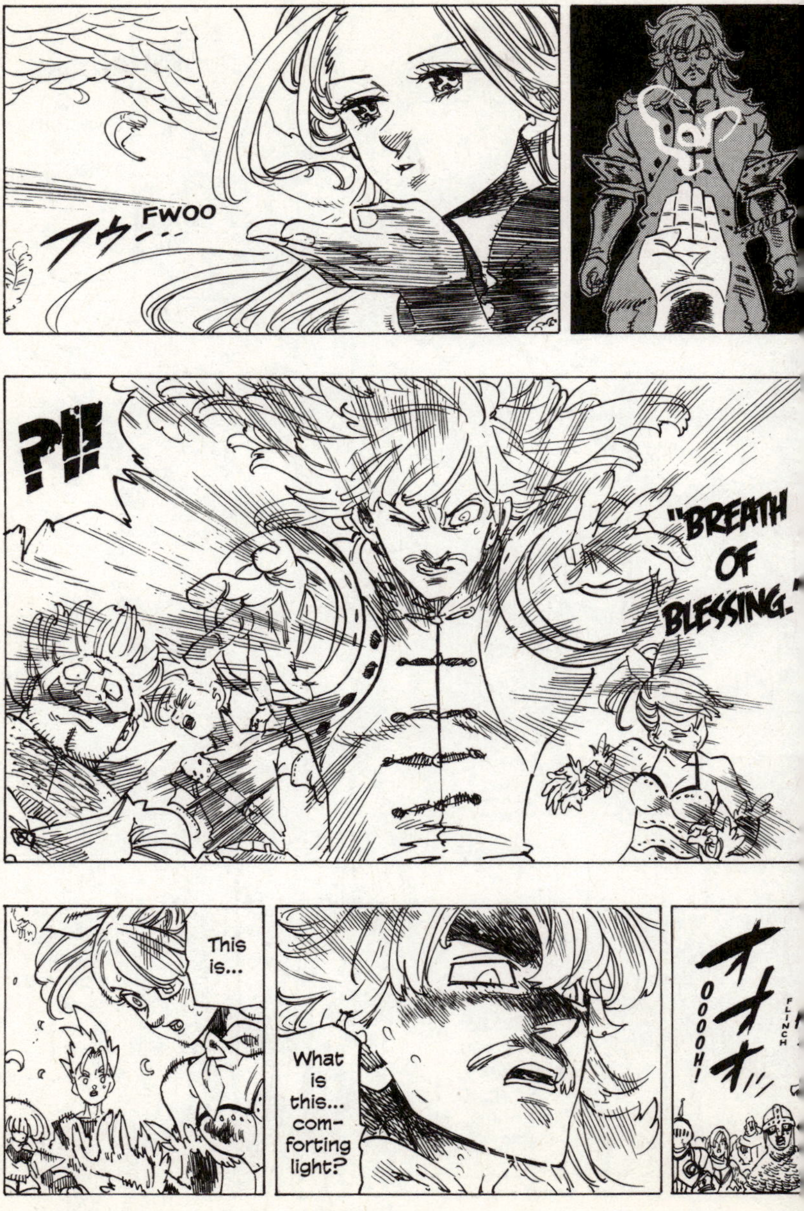
FWOO
"BREATH OF BLESSING."
?!!
OOOOH!
FLINCH
What is this... com-forting light?
This is...

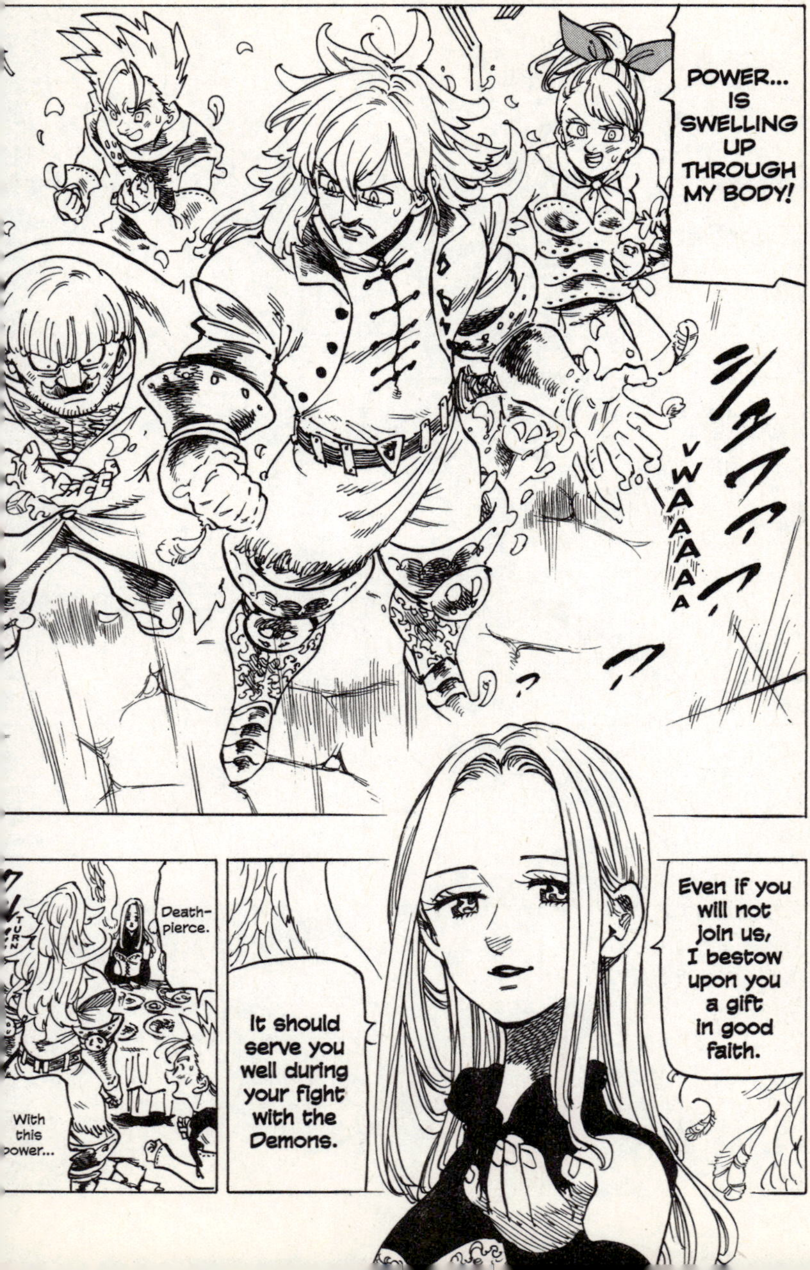
POWER... IS SWELLING UP THROUGH MY BODY!
VWAAAAAA
Even if you will not join us, I bestow upon you a gift in good faith.
It should serve you well during your fight with the Demons.
Death-pierce.
TURN
With this power...

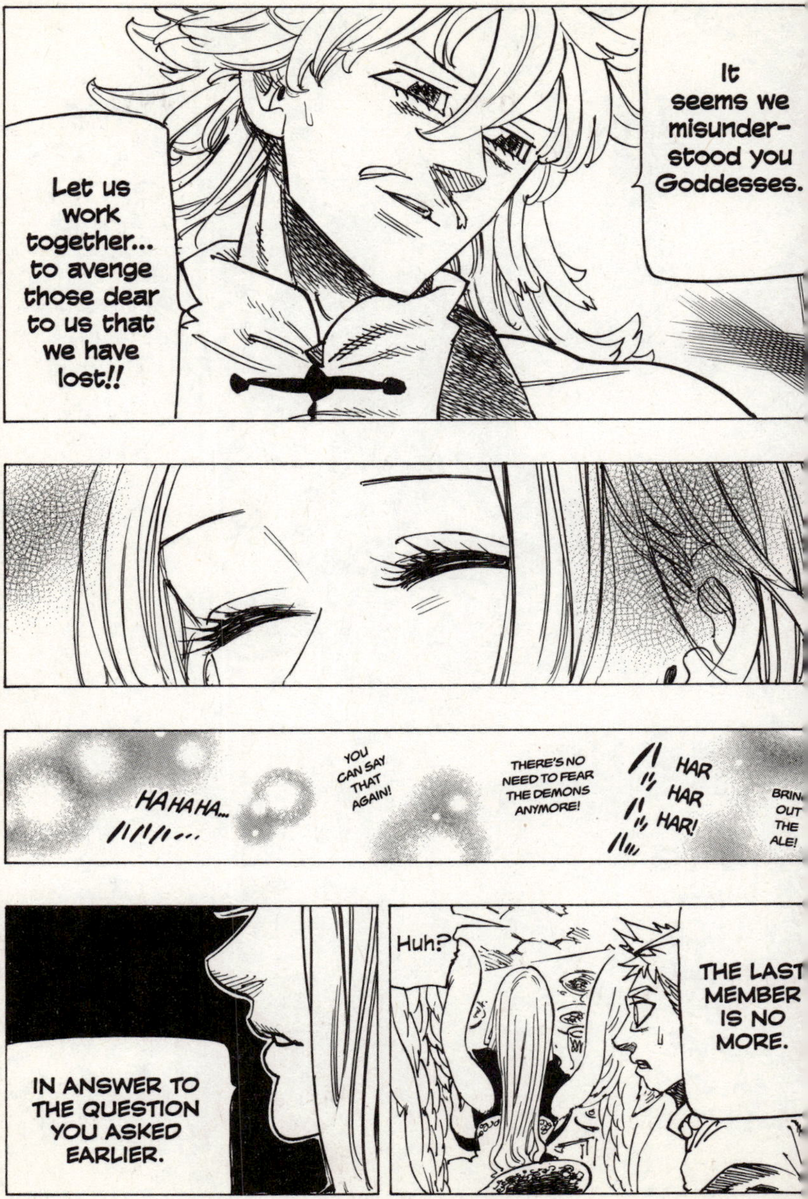
It seems we misunder-stood you Goddesses.
Let us work together... to avenge those dear to us that we have lost!!
BRIN OUT THE ALE!
HAR HAR HAR!
THERE'S NO NEED TO FEAR THE DEMONS ANYMORE!
YOU CAN SAY THAT AGAIN!
HAHAHA...
Huh?
THE LAST MEMBER IS NO MORE.
IN ANSWER TO THE QUESTION YOU ASKED EARLIER.

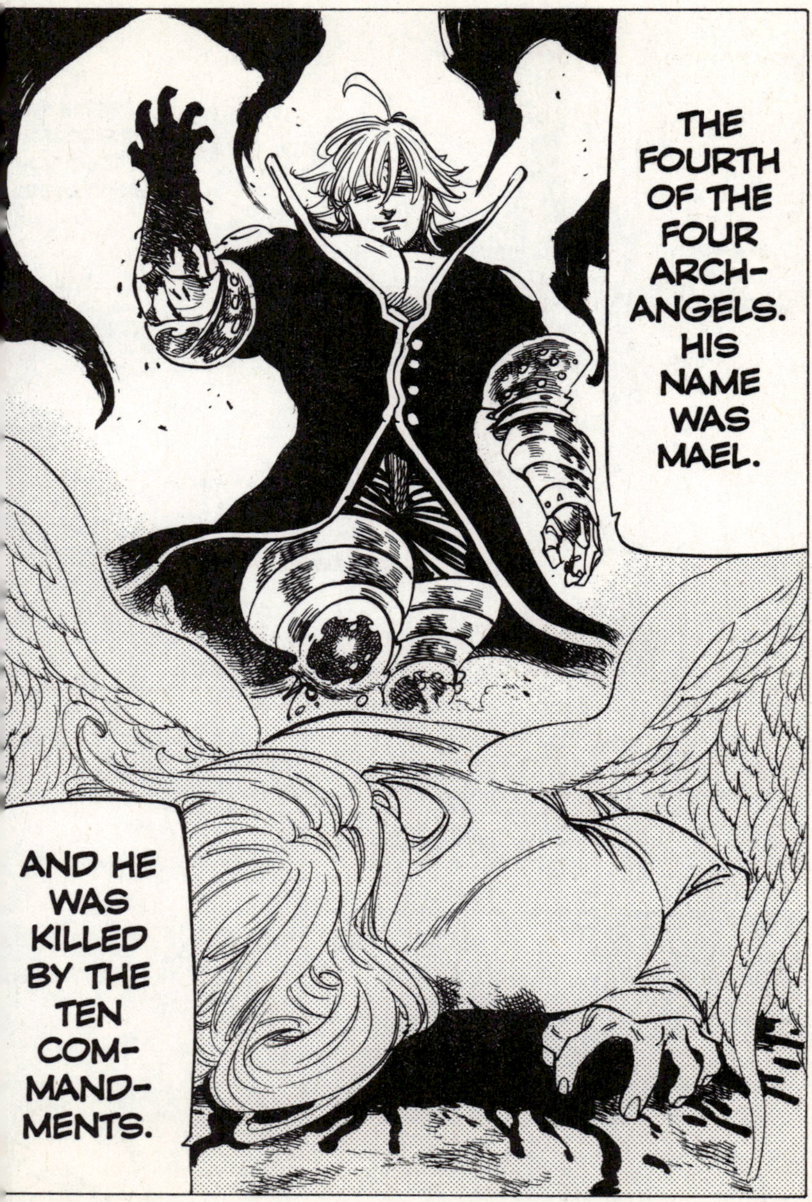
THE FOURTH OF THE FOUR ARCH-ANGELS. HIS NAME WAS MAEL.
AND HE WAS KILLED BY THE TEN COM-MAND-MENTS.

Chapter 253 - Lost Grace

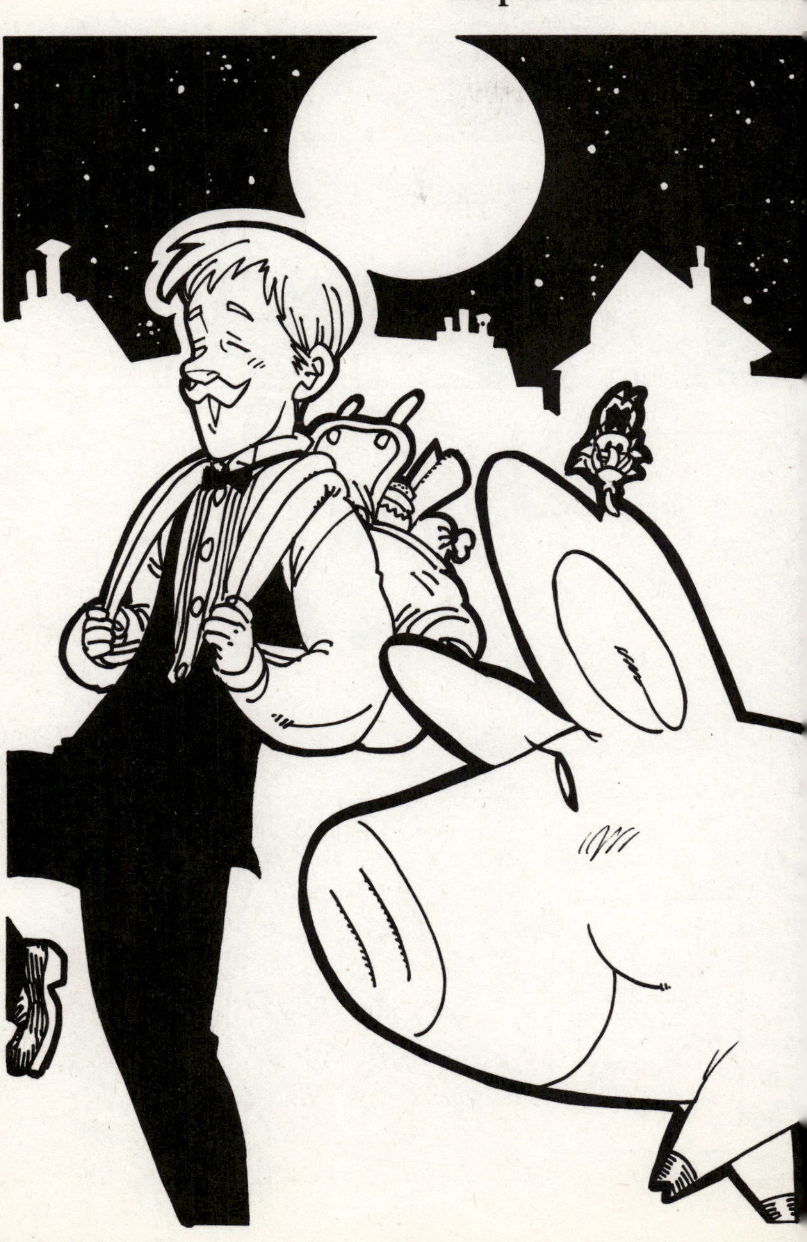

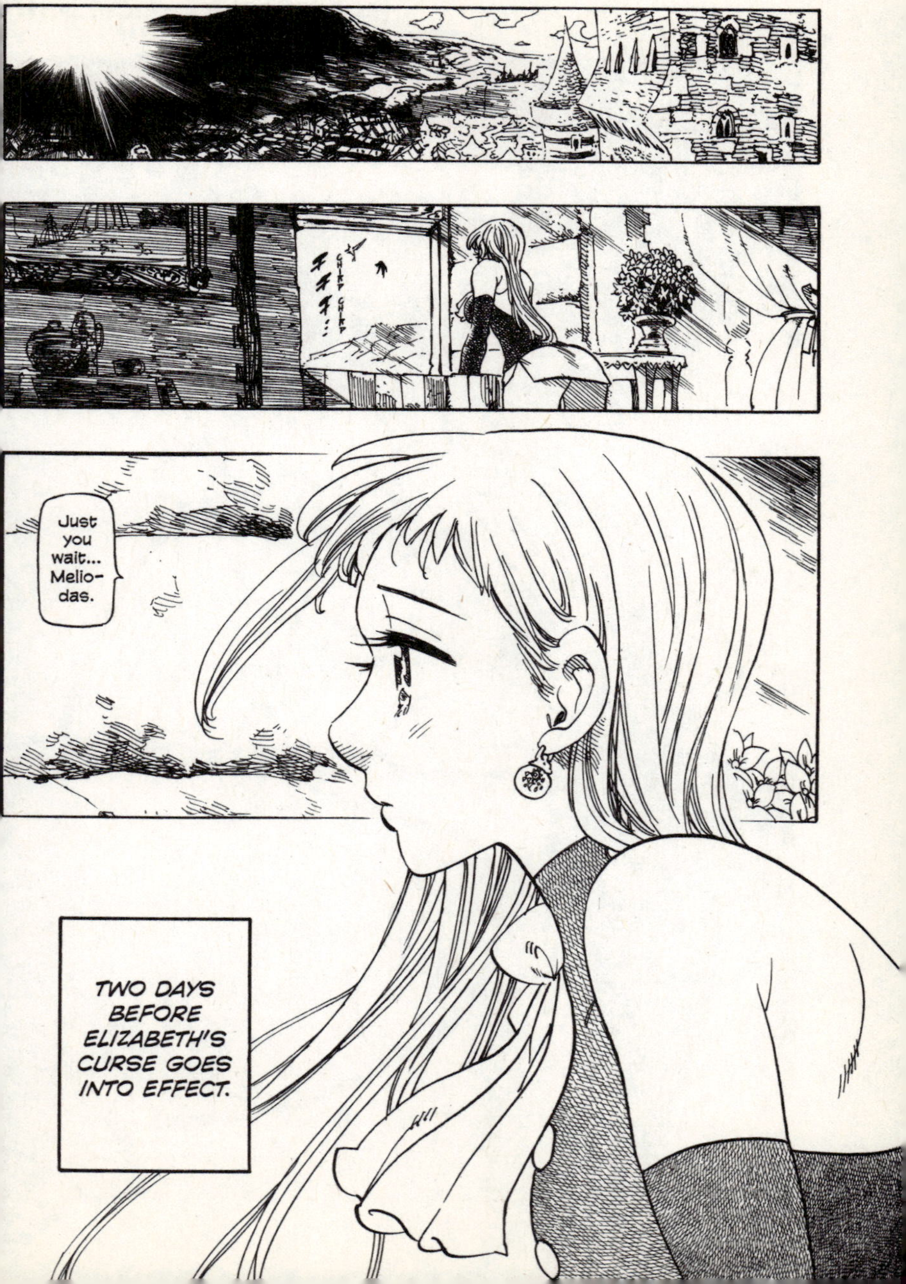
チチチ!!
CHIRP CHIRP
Just you wait... Melio-das.
TWO DAYS BEFORE ELIZABETH'S CURSE GOES INTO EFFECT.

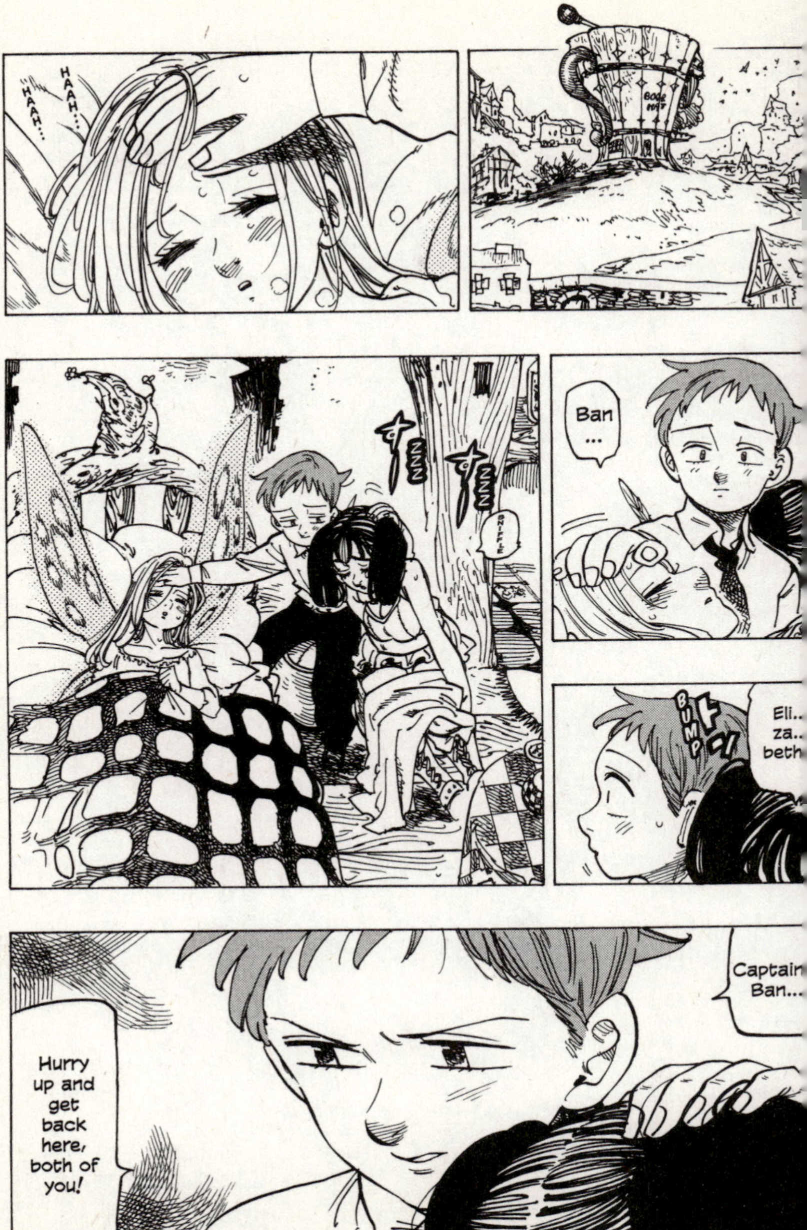
HAAH... HAAH...
Ban ...
BUMP
Eli.. za.. beth
ZZZ
ZZZ
SNIFFLE
Captain Ban...
Hurry up and get back here, both of you!

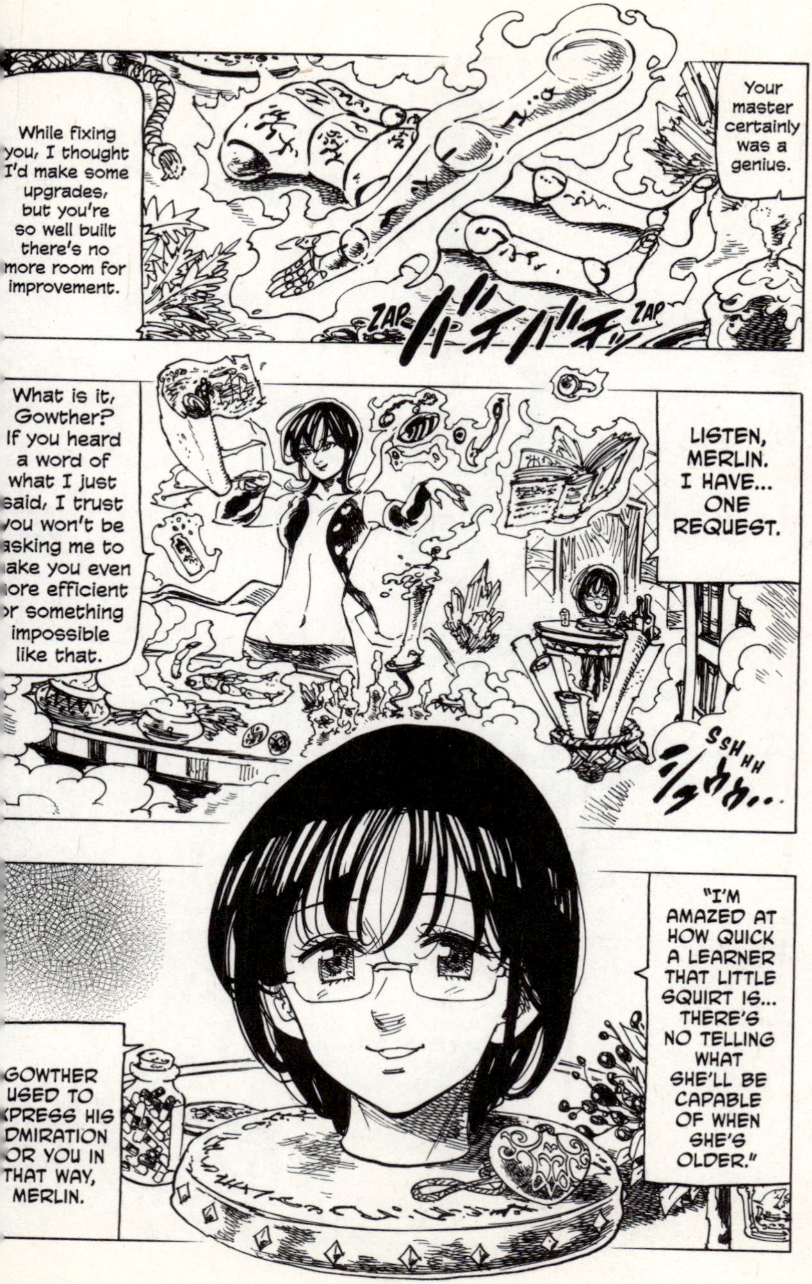

Your master certainly was a genius.
While fixing you, I thought I'd make some upgrades, but you're so well built there's no more room for improvement.
ZAP
ZAP
LISTEN, MERLIN. I HAVE... ONE REQUEST.
What is it, Gowther? If you heard a word of what I just said, I trust ou won't be asking me to ake you even ore efficient r something impossible like that.
SSHHH
"I'M AMAZED AT HOW QUICK A LEARNER THAT LITTLE SQUIRT IS... THERE'S NO TELLING WHAT SHE'LL BE CAPABLE OF WHEN SHE'S OLDER."
GOWTHER USED TO XPRESS HIS DMIRATION OR YOU IN THAT WAY, MERLIN.

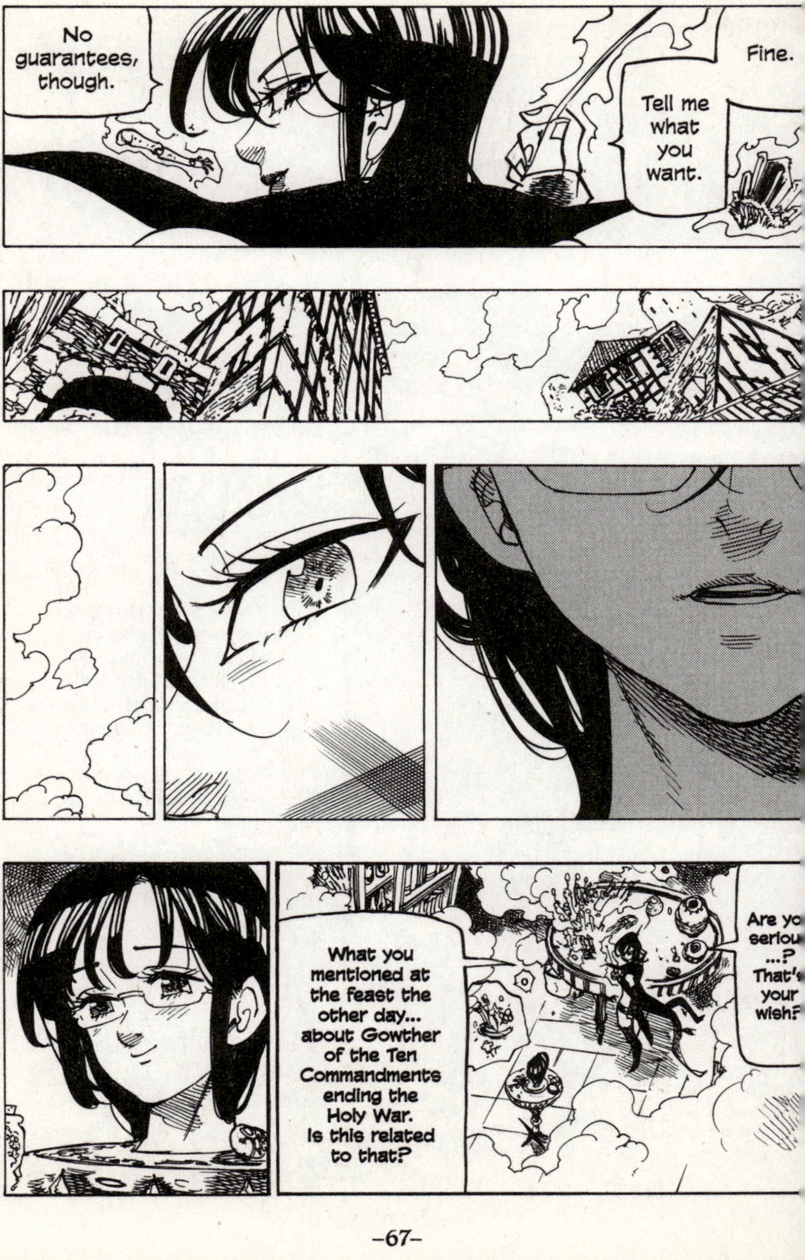
Fine.
Tell me what you want.
No guarantees, though.
Are yo seriou ...? That's your wish?
What you mentioned at the feast the other day... about Gowther of the Ten Commandments ending the Holy War. Is this related to that?

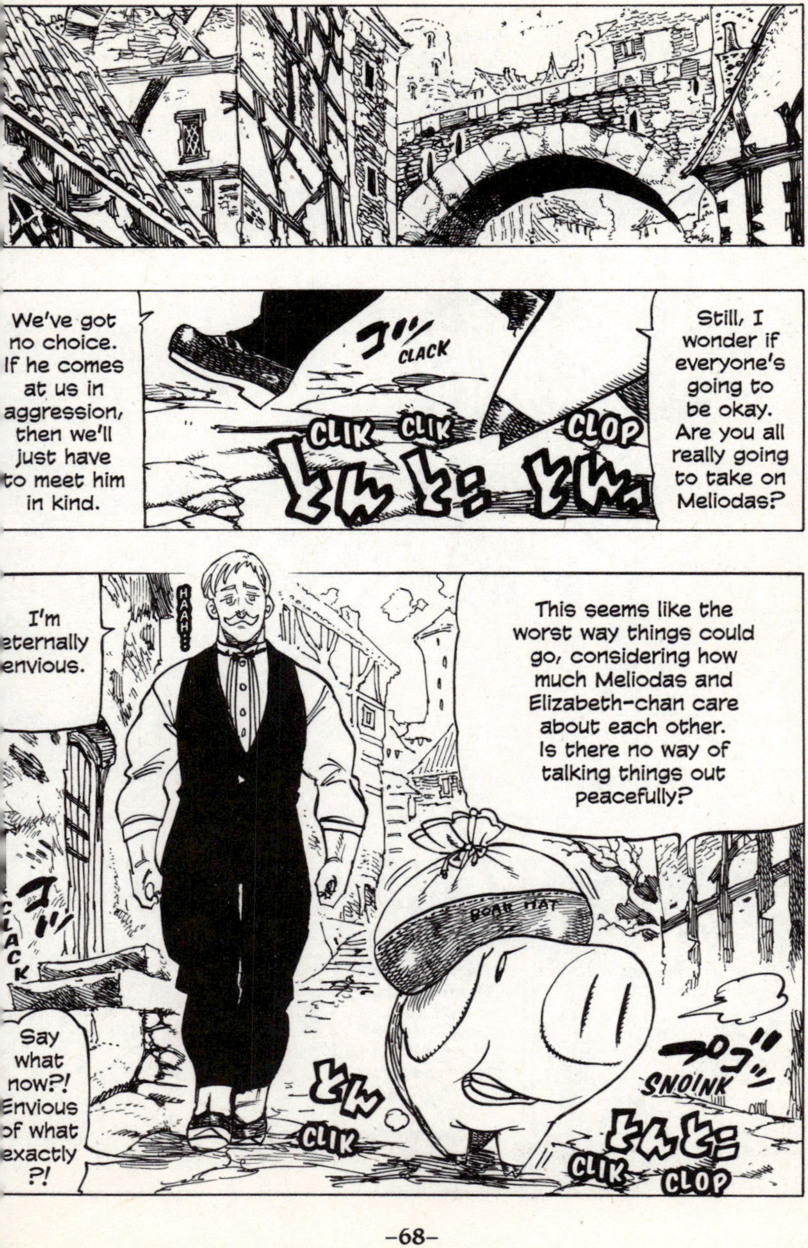
Still, I wonder if everyone's going to be okay. Are you all really going to take on Meliodas?
CLACK
CLOP
CLIK
CLIK
We've got no choice. If he comes at us in aggression, then we'll just have to meet him in kind.
This seems like the worst way things could go, considering how much Meliodas and Elizabeth-chan care about each other. Is there no way of talking things out peacefully?
BOAR HAT
SNOINK
CLOP
CLIK
CLIK
HAAH...
I'm eternally envious.
CLACK
Say what now?! Envious of what exactly ?!

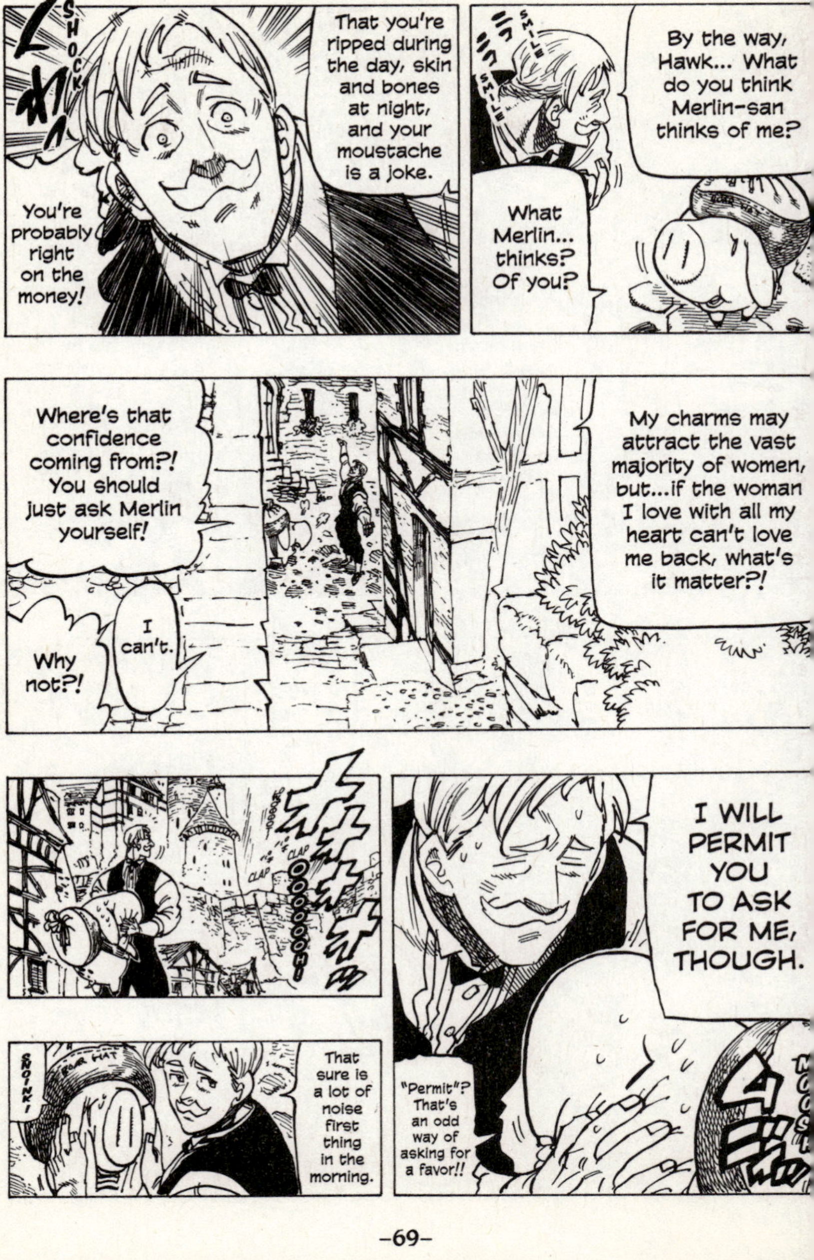
SMILE SMILE
By the way, Hawk... What do you think Merlin-san thinks of me?
What Merlin... thinks? Of you?
SHOCK
That you're ripped during the day, skin and bones at night, and your moustache is a joke.
You're probably right on the money!
My charms may attract the vast majority of women, but...if the woman I love with all my heart can't love me back, what's it matter?!
Where's that confidence coming from?! You should just ask Merlin yourself!
I can't.
Why not?!
I WILL PERMIT YOU TO ASK FOR ME, THOUGH.
MOOSH
"Permit"? That's an odd way of asking for a favor!!
CLAP CLAP
OOOOOOOOOH!
SNOINK!
That sure is a lot of noise first thing in the morning.

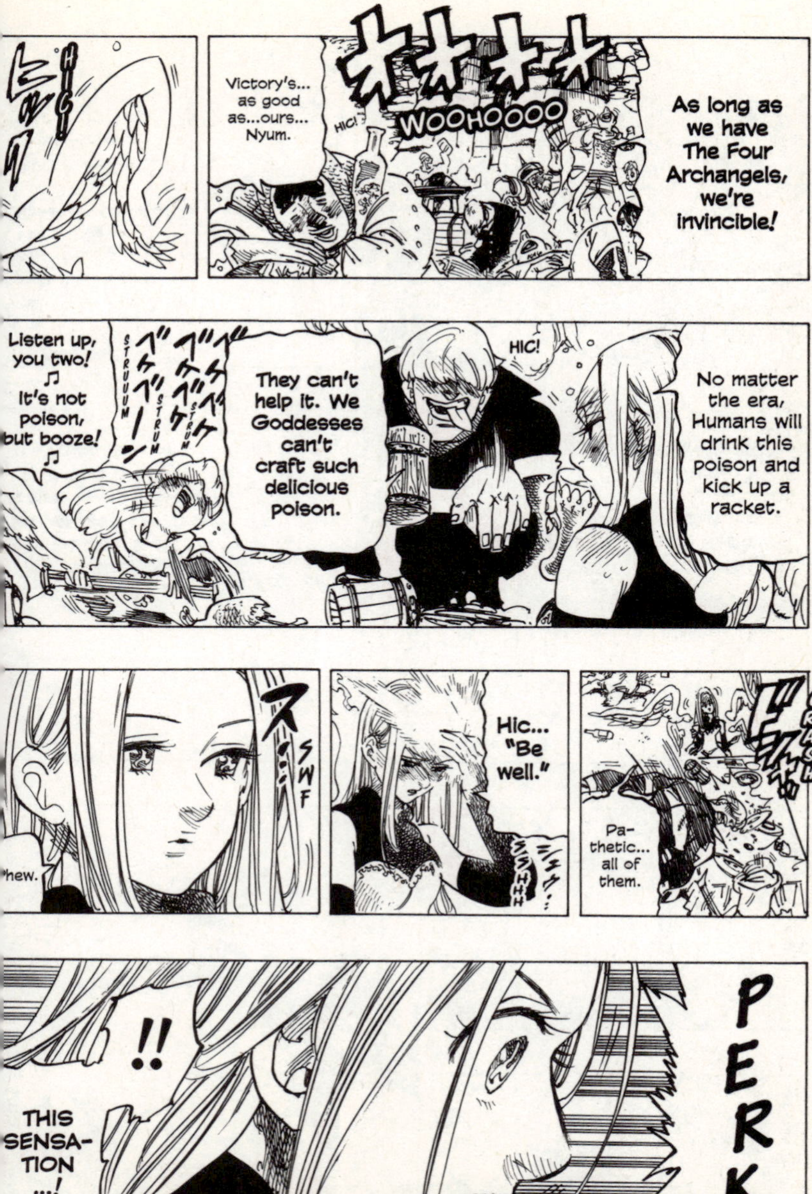
As long as we have The Four Archangels, we're invincible!
WOOHOOOO
HIC!
Victory's... as good as...ours... Nyum.
HIC!
No matter the era, Humans will drink this poison and kick up a racket.
HIC!
They can't help it. We Goddesses can't craft such delicious poison.
STRUM
STRUM
STRUUUM
Listen up, you two! ♫ It's not poison, but booze! ♫
CRASH
Pa-thetic... all of them.
Hic... "Be well."
SHHH
SWF
hew.
PERK
!!
THIS SENSA-TION ...!

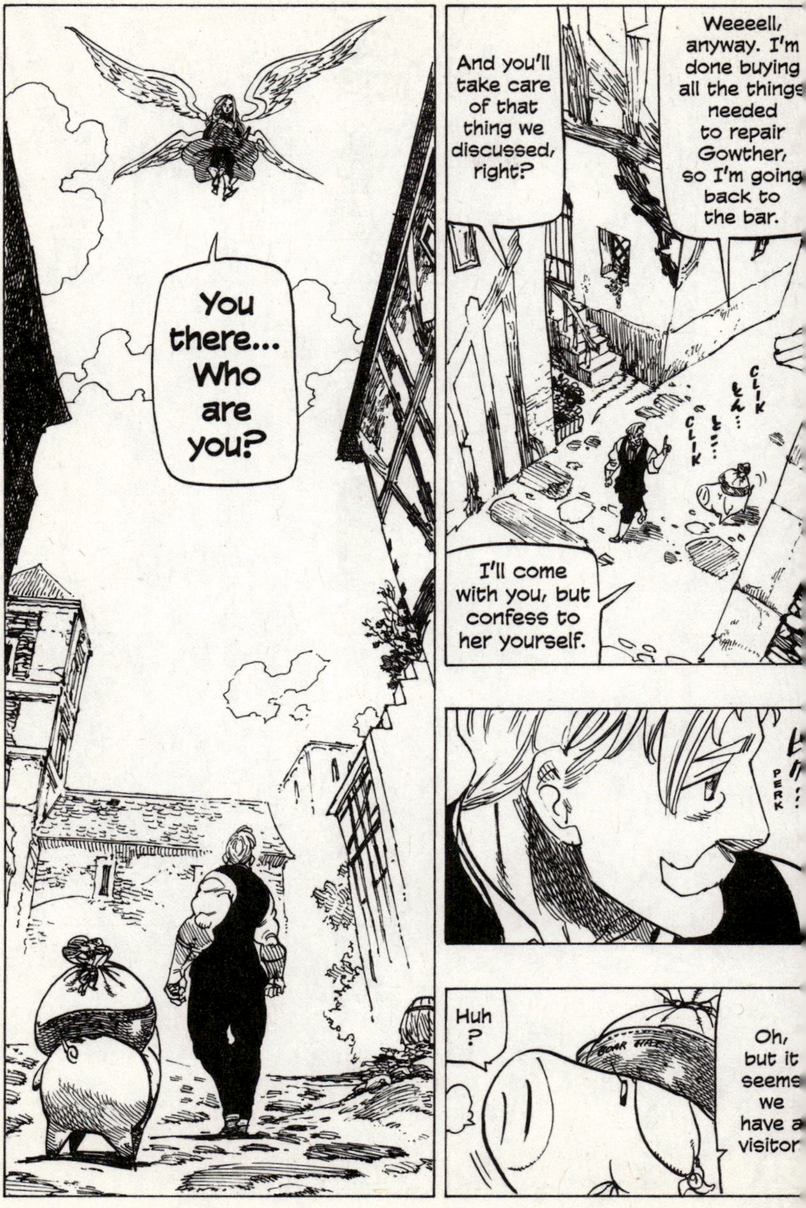
Weeeell, anyway. I'm done buying all the things needed to repair Gowther, so I'm going back to the bar.
And you'll take care of that thing we discussed, right?
CLIK
CLIK
I'll come with you, but confess to her yourself.
PERK
Oh, but it seems we have a visitor
Huh?
You there... Who are you?

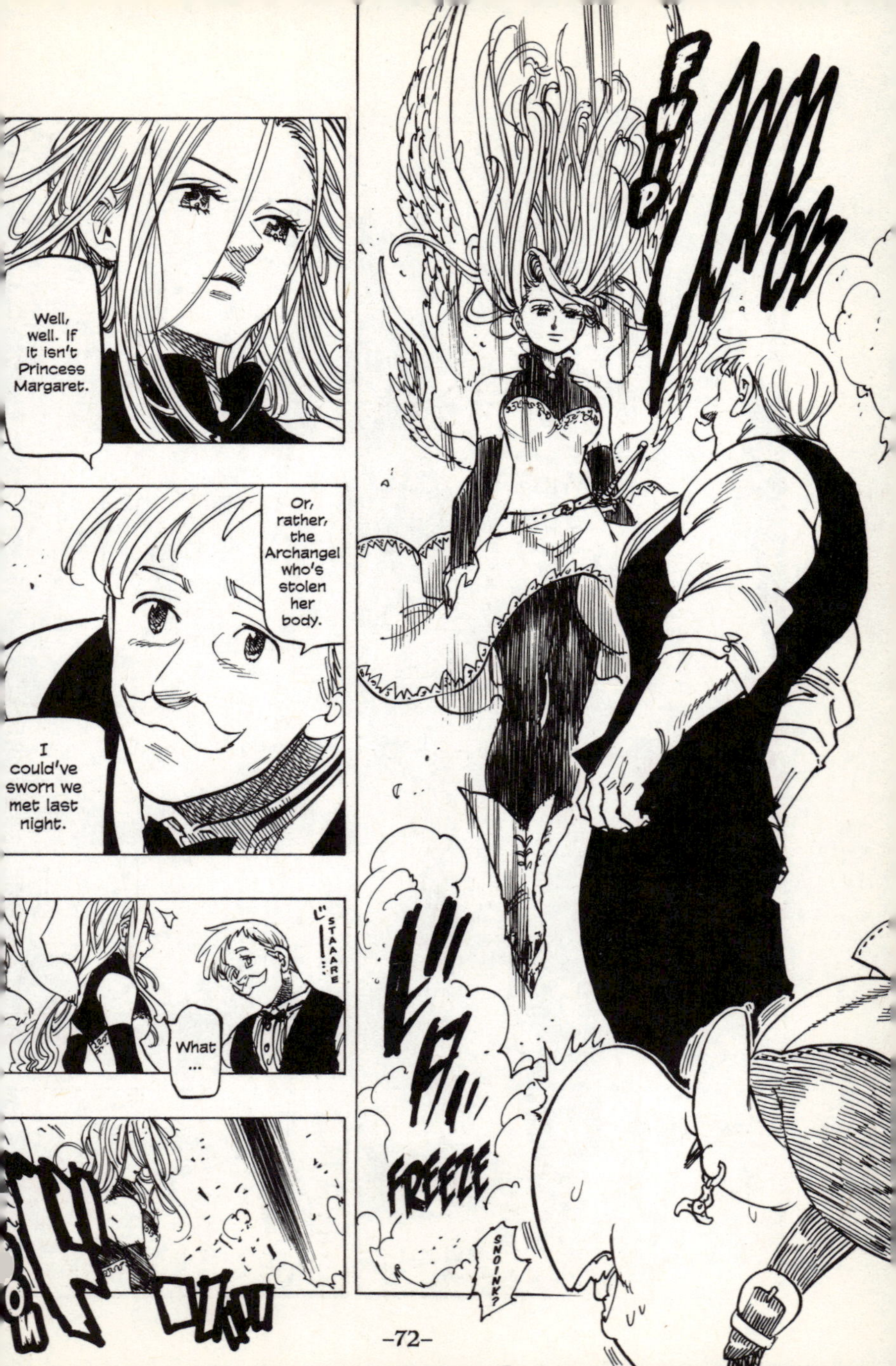
FWIP
FREEZE
SNOINK?
Well, well. If it isn't Princess Margaret.
Or, rather, the Archangel who's stolen her body.
I could've sworn we met last night.
STAAAARE
What...

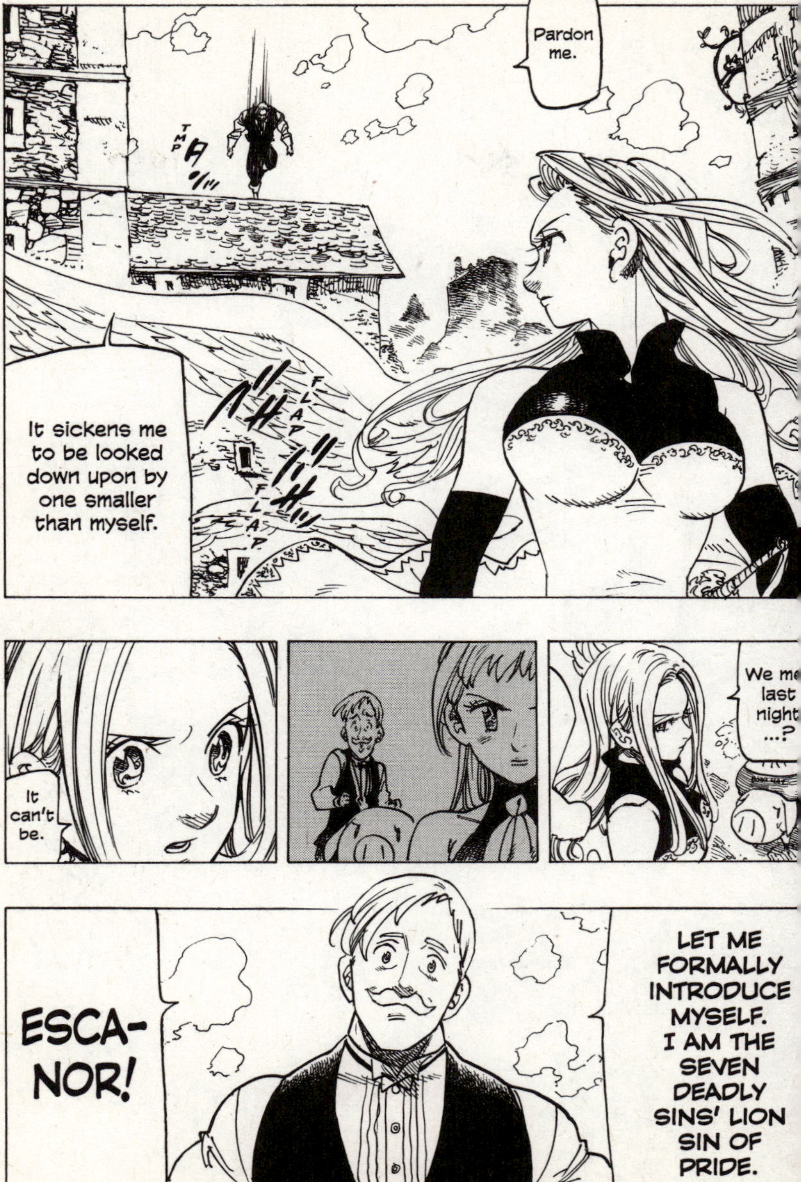
Pardon me.
TMP
FLAP
FLAP
It sickens me to be looked down upon by one smaller than myself.
We me last night ...?
It can't be.
LET ME FORMALLY INTRODUCE MYSELF. I AM THE SEVEN DEADLY SINS' LION SIN OF PRIDE.
ESCA-NOR!

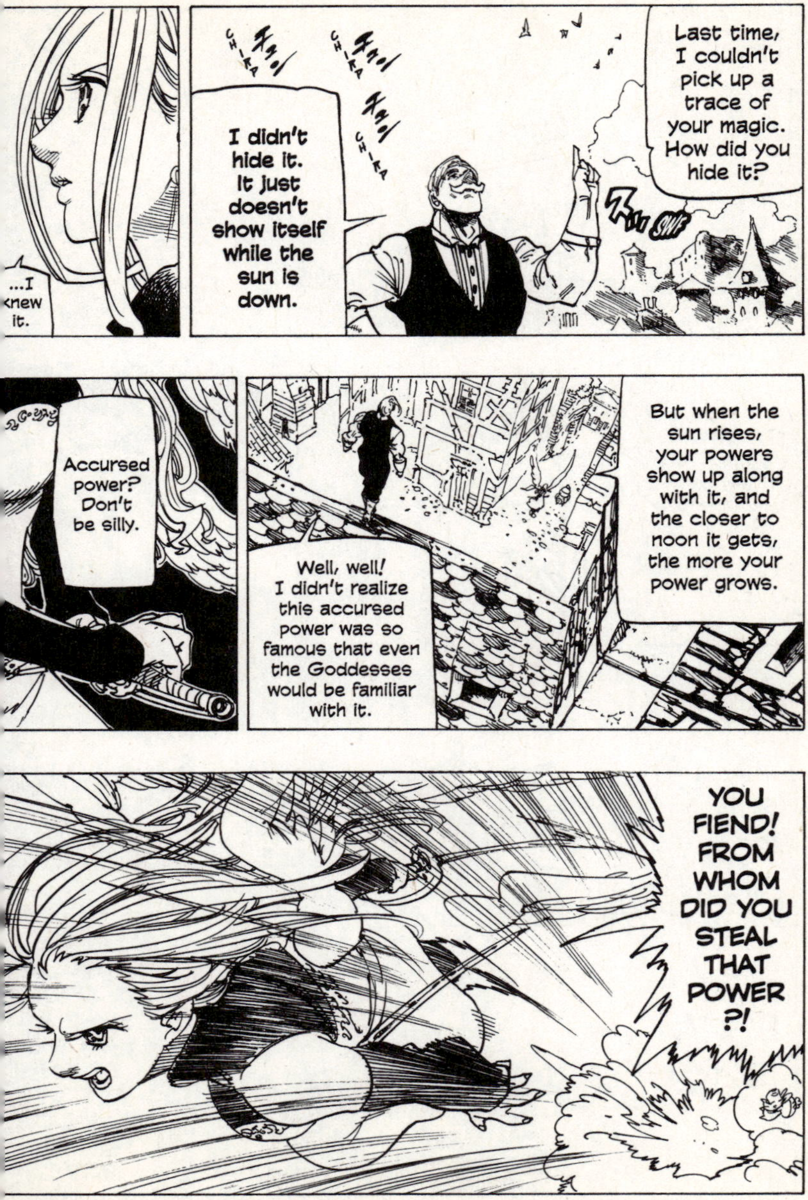
Last time, I couldn't pick up a trace of your magic. How did you hide it?
CHIKA
CHIKA
I didn't hide it. It just doesn't show itself while the sun is down.
CHIKA
SWF
...I knew it.
But when the sun rises, your powers show up along with it, and the closer to noon it gets, the more your power grows.
Well, well! I didn't realize this accursed power was so famous that even the Goddesses would be familiar with it.
Accursed power? Don't be silly.
YOU FIEND! FROM WHOM DID YOU STEAL THAT POWER?!

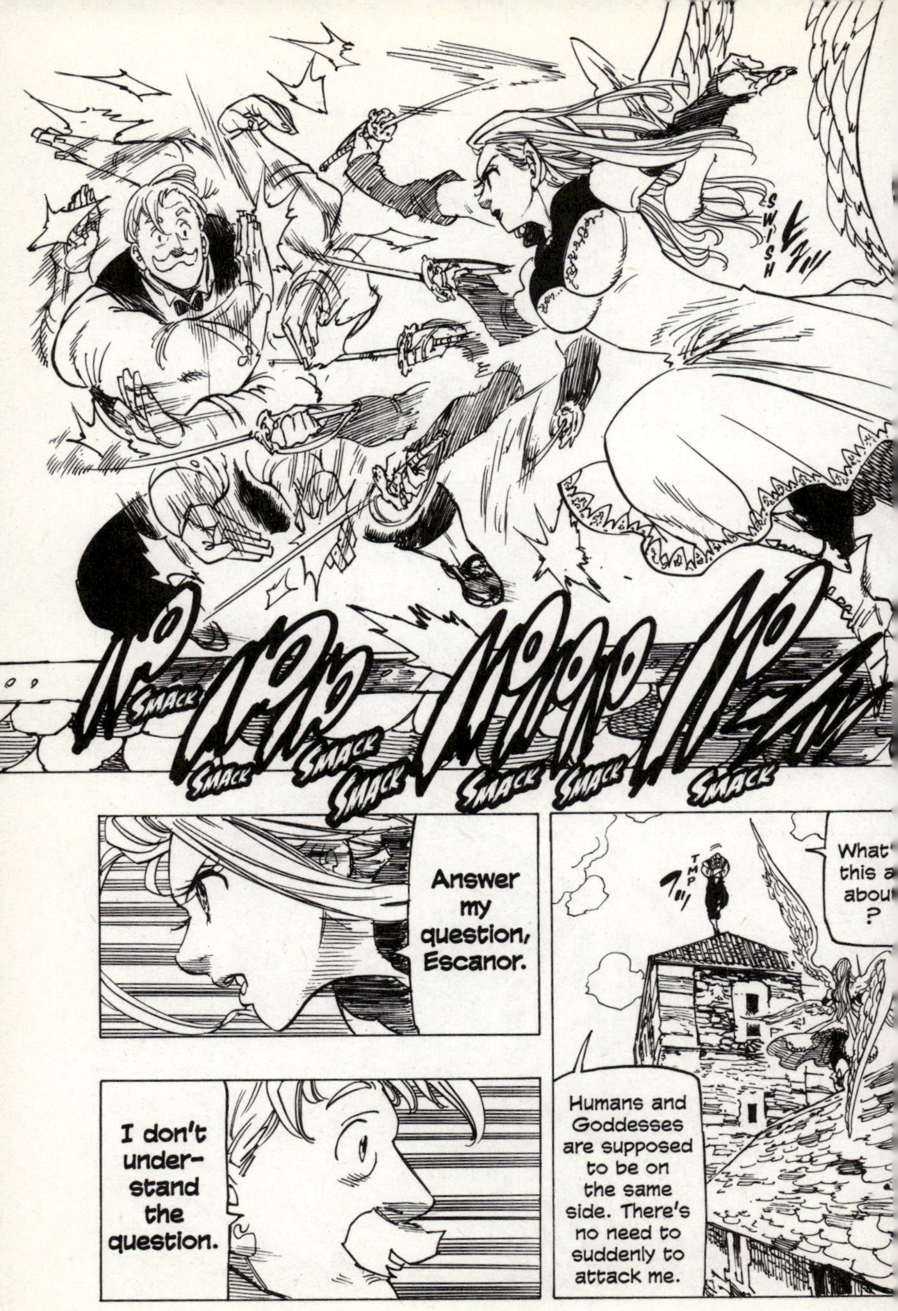
SWISH
SMACK
SMACK
SMACK
SMACK
SMACK
SMACK
SMACK
What' this a abou ?
TMP
Humans and Goddesses are supposed to be on the same side. There's no need to suddenly to attack me.
Answer my question, Escanor.
I don't under-stand the question.

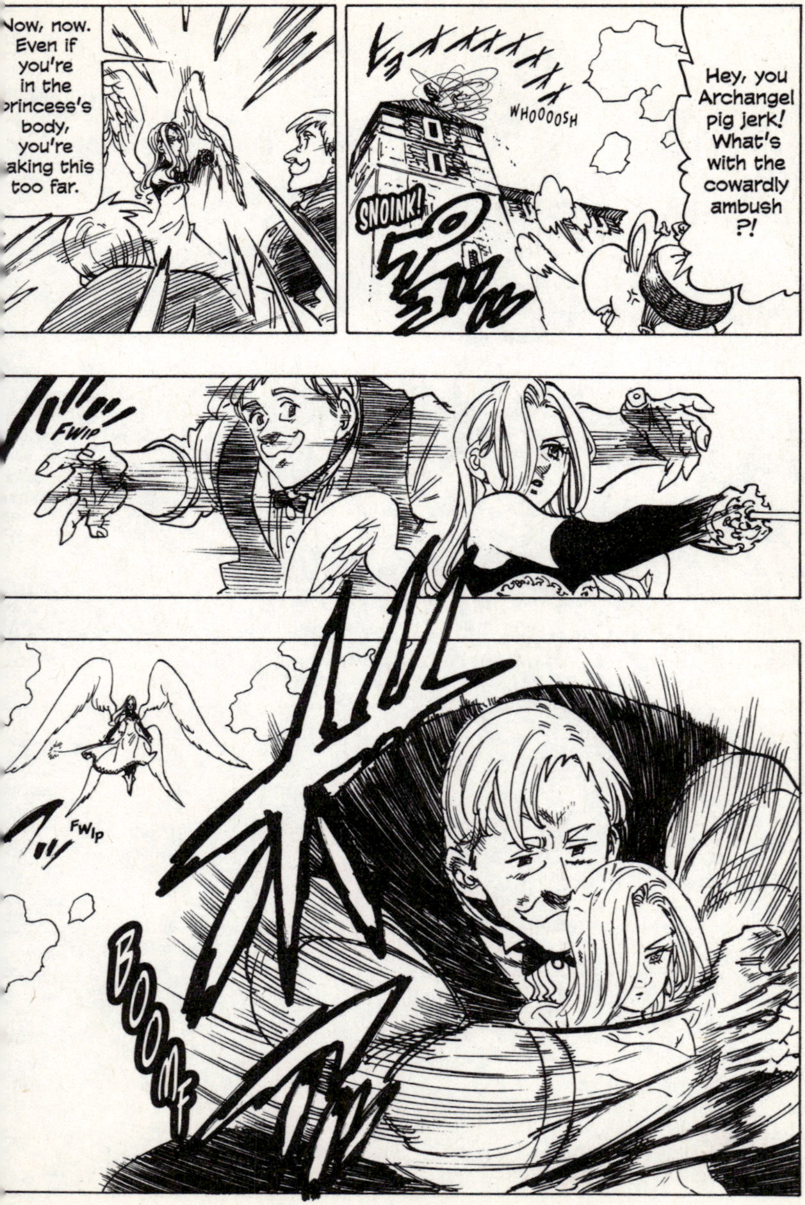
WHOOOOSH
SNOINK!
Hey, you Archangel pig jerk! What's with the cowardly ambush ?!
Now, now. Even if you're in the princess's body, you're aking this too far.
FWIP
FWIP
BOOMF

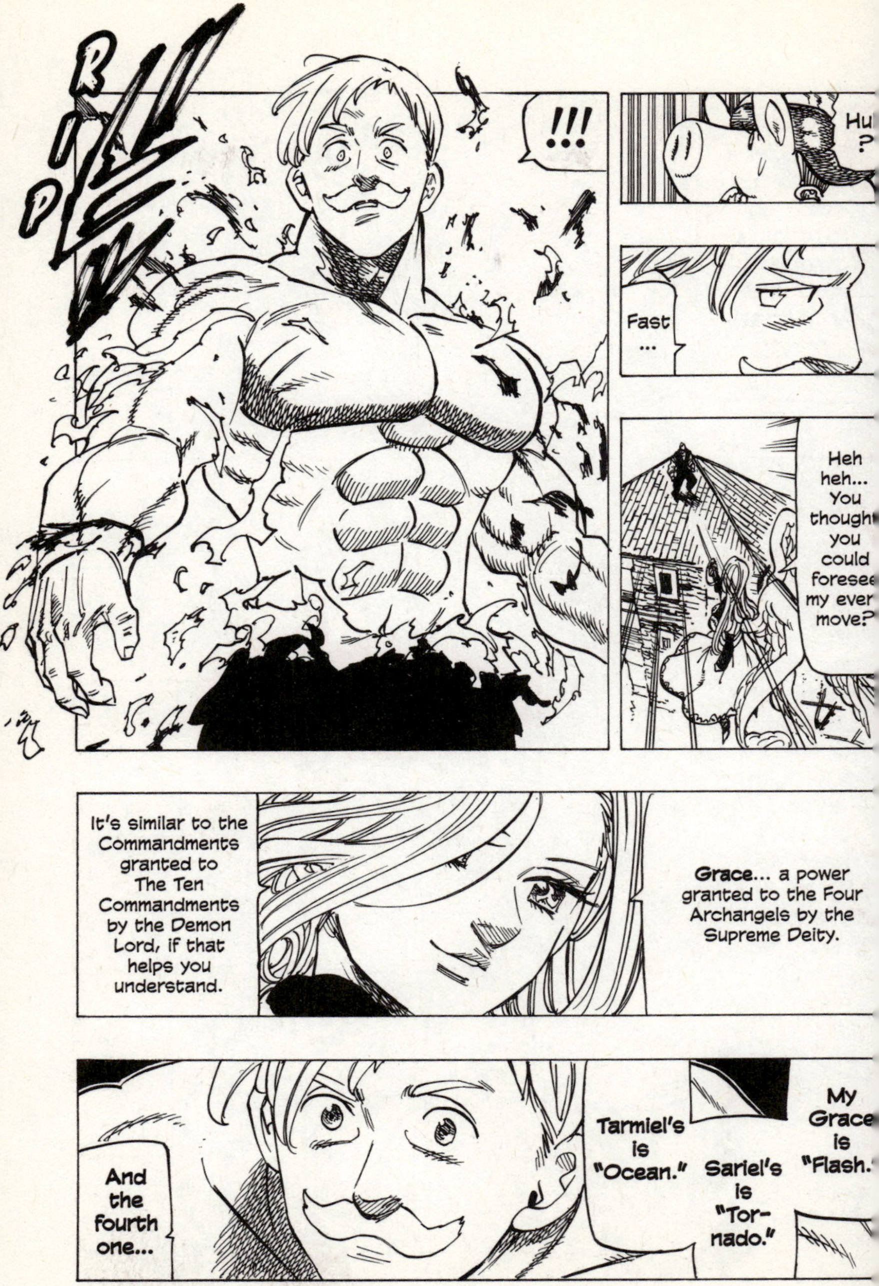

Hu ?
Fast ...
Heh heh... You though you could foresee my ever move?
RIP
!!!
Grace... a power granted to the Four Archangels by the Supreme Deity.
It's similar to the Commandments granted to The Ten Commandments by the Demon Lord, if that helps you understand.
My Grace is "Flash."
Sariel's is "Tor-nado."
Tarmiel's is "Ocean."
And the fourth one...

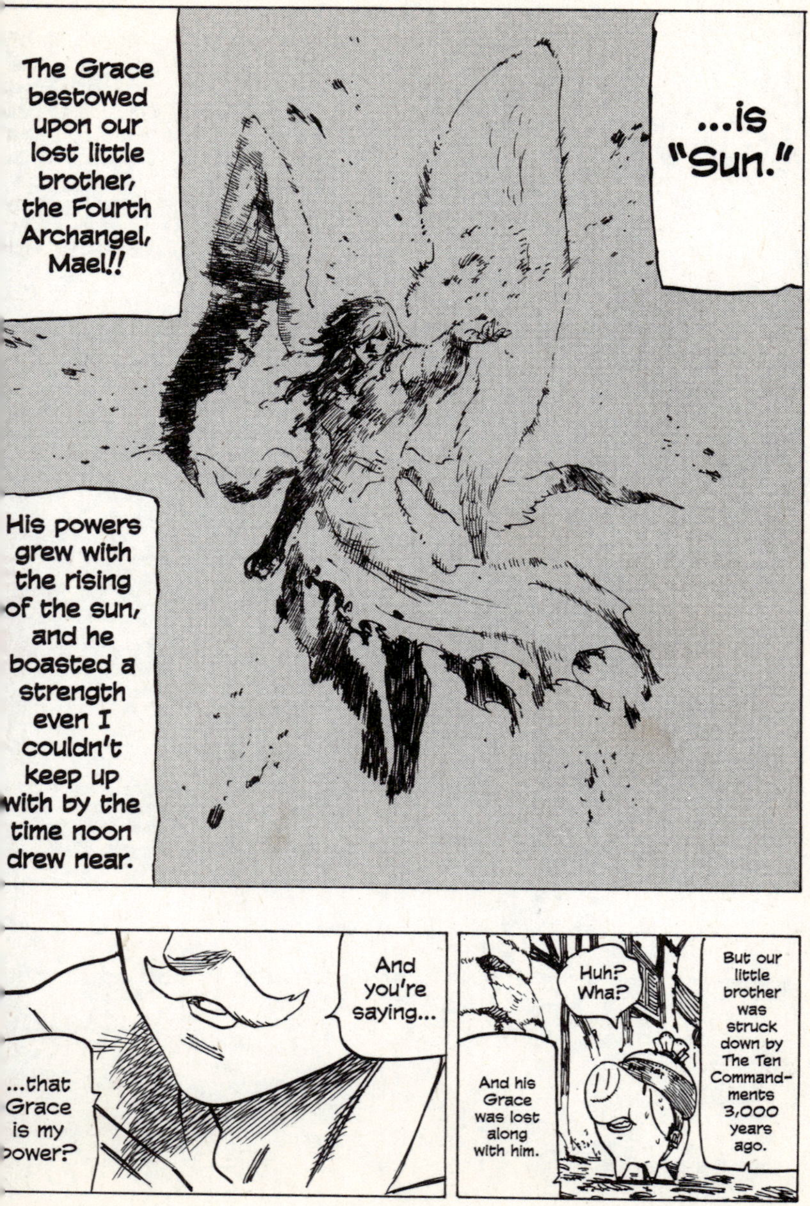
The Grace bestowed upon our lost little brother, the Fourth Archangel, Mael!!
...is "Sun."
His powers grew with the rising of the sun, and he boasted a strength even I couldn't keep up with by the time noon drew near.
But our little brother was struck down by The Ten Commandments 3,000 years ago.
Huh? Wha?
And his Grace was lost along with him.
And you're saying...
...that Grace is my power?

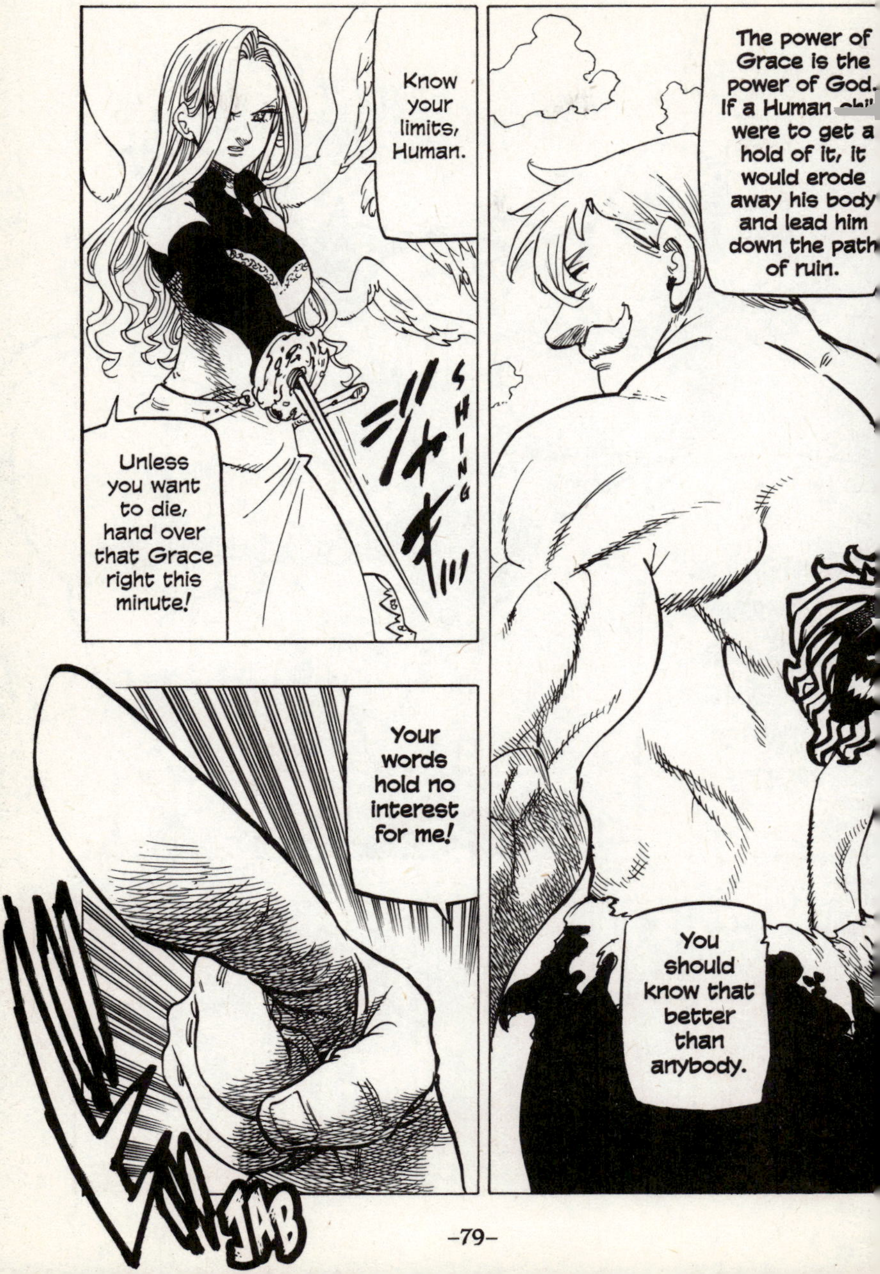

The power of Grace is the power of God. If a Human
were to get a hold of it, it would erode away his body and lead him down the path of ruin.
You should know that better than anybody.
Know your limits, Human.
SHING
Unless you want to die, hand over that Grace right this minute!
Your words hold no interest for me!
JAB

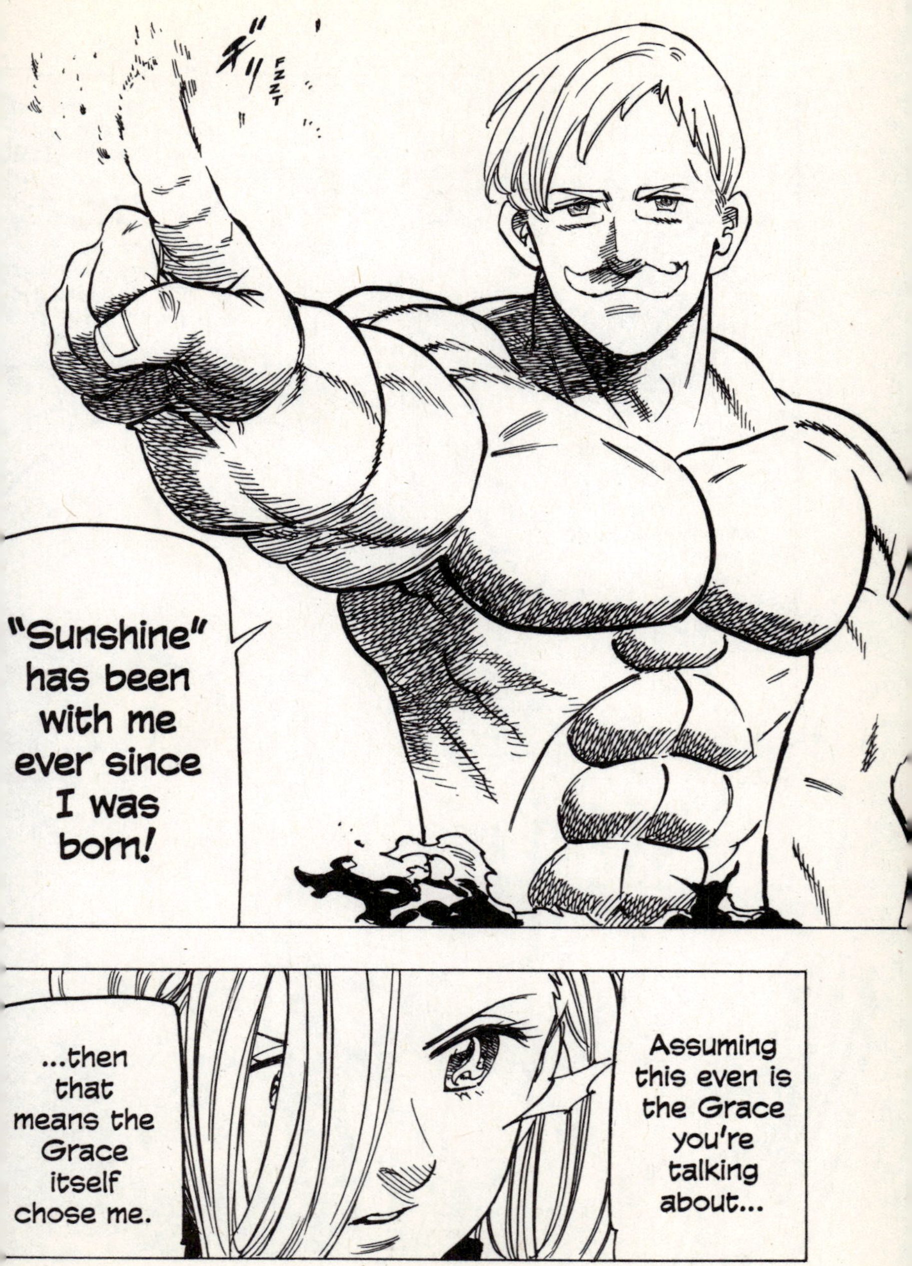
FZZT
"Sunshine" has been with me ever since I was born!
Assuming this even is the Grace you're talking about...
...then that means the Grace itself chose me.

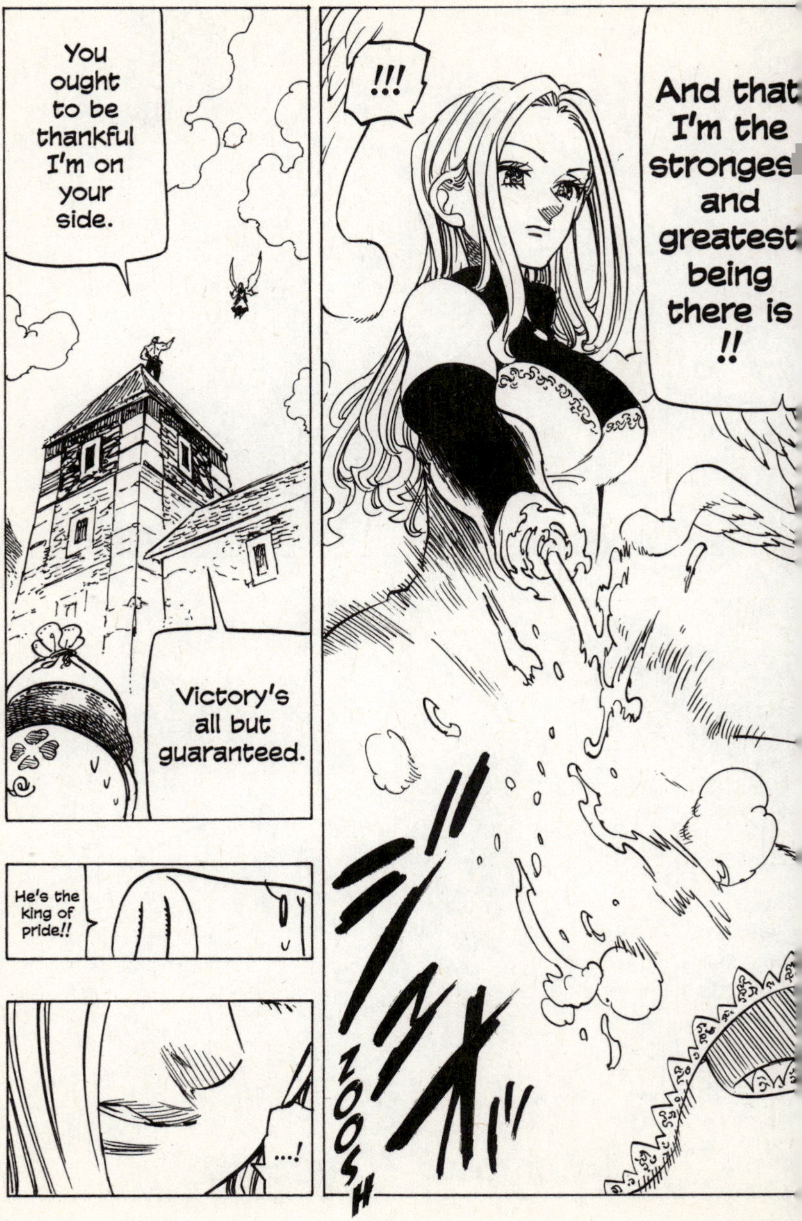
And that I'm the stronges and greatest being there is!!
!!!
ZOOSH
You ought to be thankful I'm on your side.
Victory's all but guaranteed.
He's the king of pride!!
...!

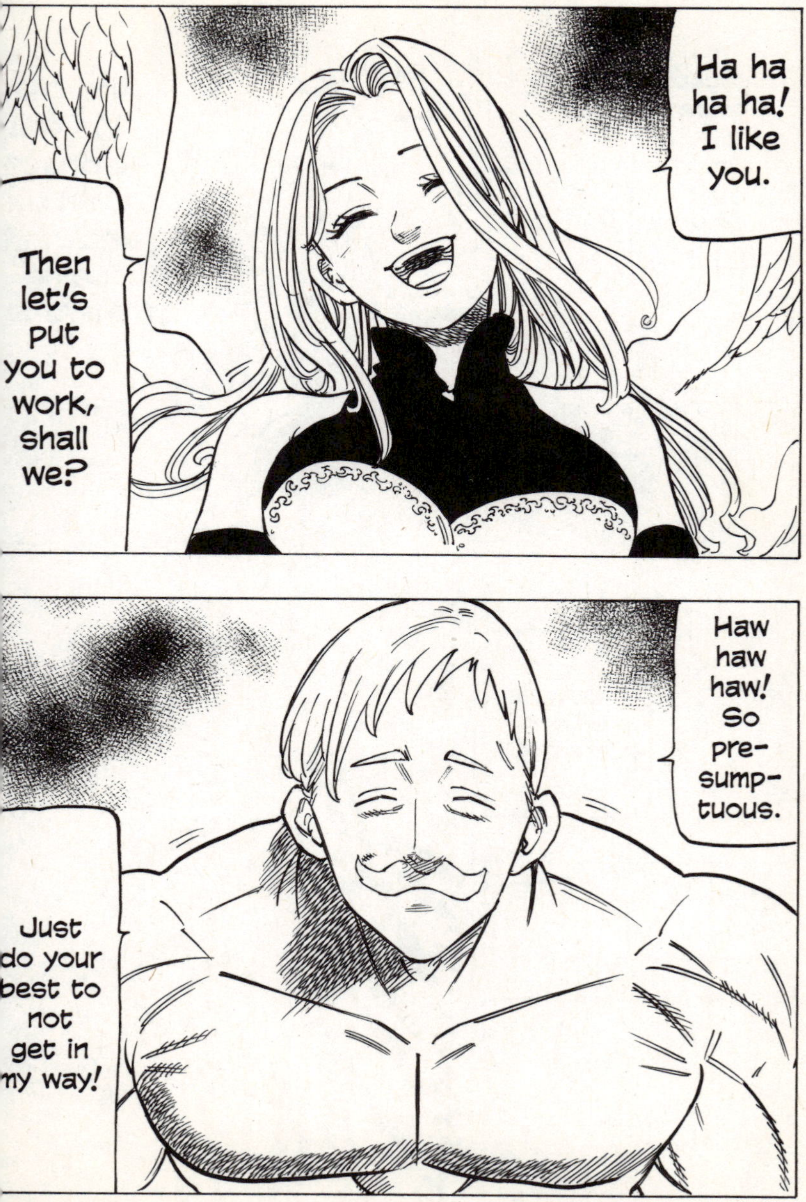
Ha ha ha ha! I like you.
Then let's put you to work, shall we?
Haw haw haw! So pre-sump-tuous.
Just do your best to not get in my way!

Chapter 254 - Camelot in Despair

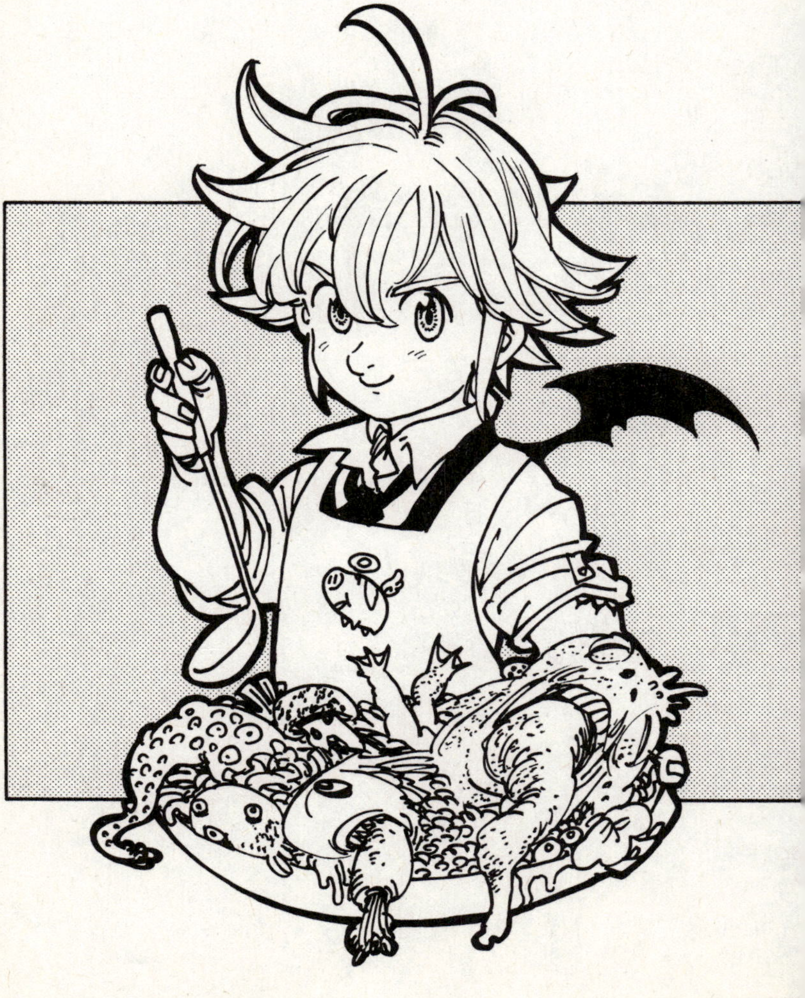

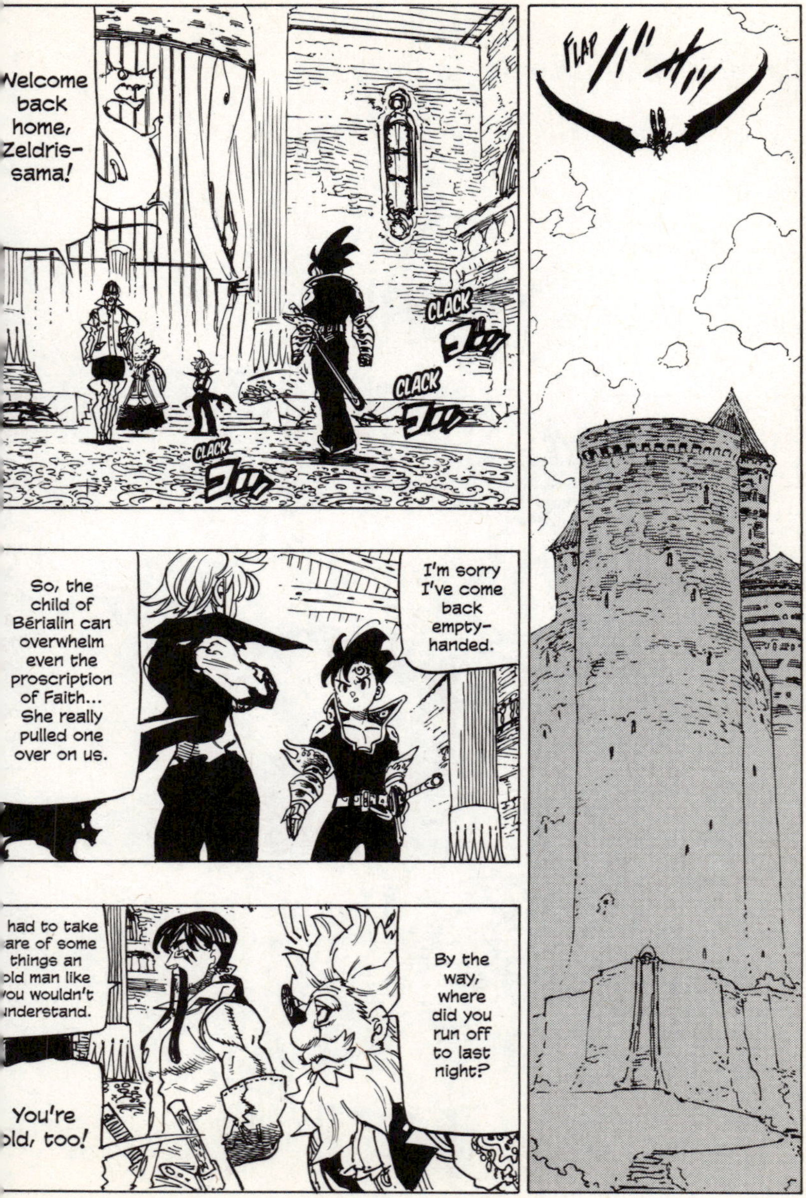
FLAP
Welcome back home, Zeldris-sama!
CLACK
CLACK
CLACK
I'm sorry I've come back empty-handed.
So, the child of Bérialin can overwhelm even the proscription of Faith... She really pulled one over on us.
By the way, where did you run off to last night?
had to take care of some things an old man like you wouldn't understand.
You're old, too!

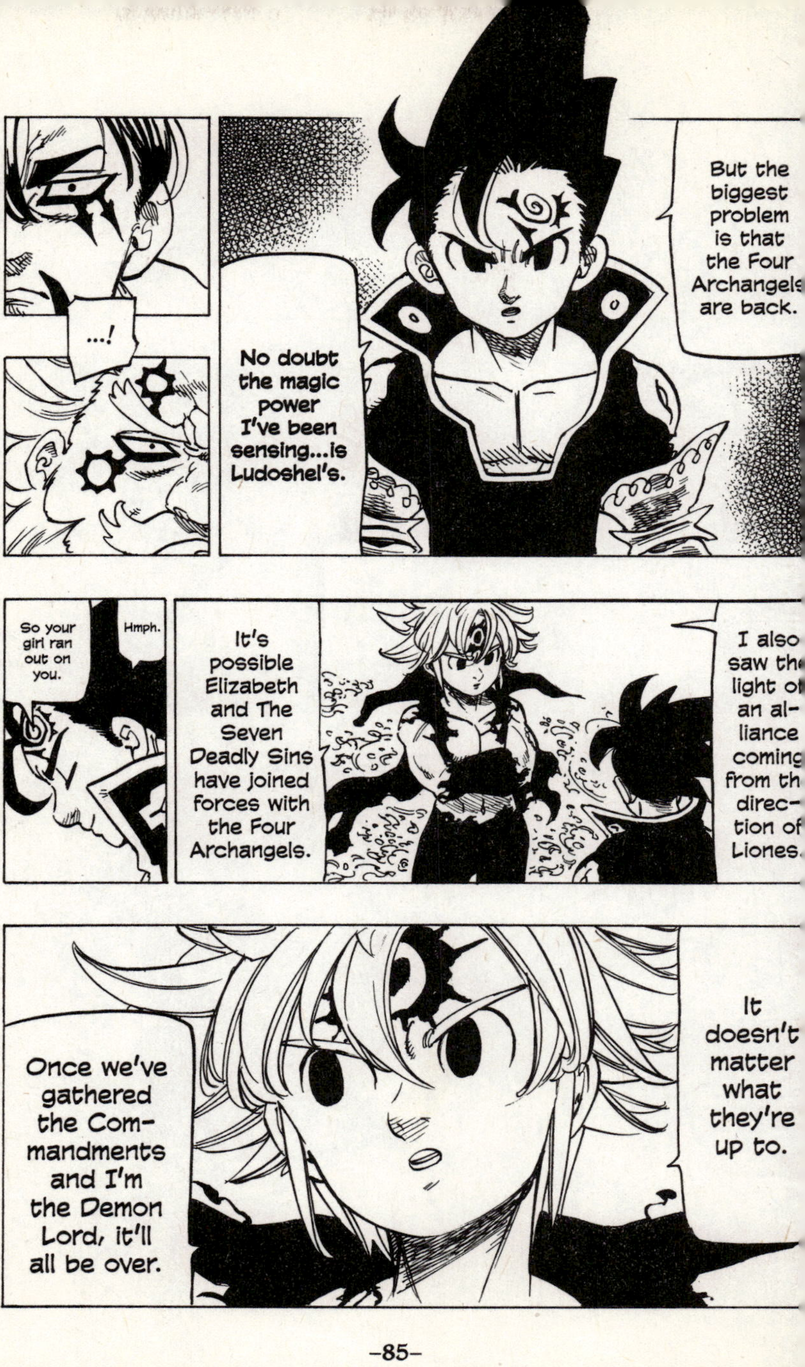
But the biggest problem is that the Four Archangels are back.
No doubt the magic power I've been sensing...is Ludoshel's.
...!
I also saw the light of an alliance coming from the direction of Liones.
It's possible Elizabeth and The Seven Deadly Sins have joined forces with the Four Archangels.
Hmph.
So your girl ran out on you.
It doesn't matter what they're up to.
Once we've gathered the Commandments and I'm the Demon Lord, it'll all be over.

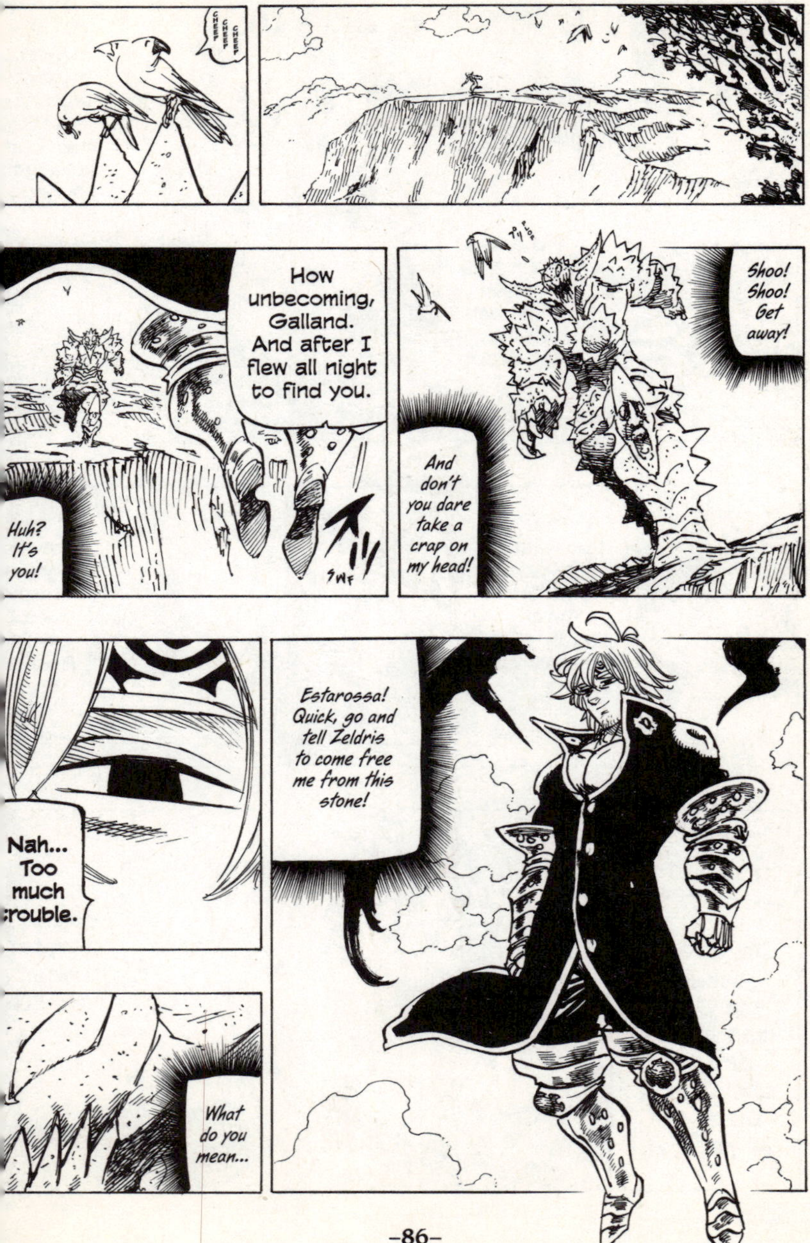
CHEEP CHEEP CHEEP
Shoo! Shoo! Get away!
And don't you dare take a crap on my head!
How unbecoming, Galland. And after I flew all night to find you.
Huh? It's you!
SWF
Estarossa! Quick, go and tell Zeldris to come free me from this stone!
Nah... Too much trouble.
What do you mean...

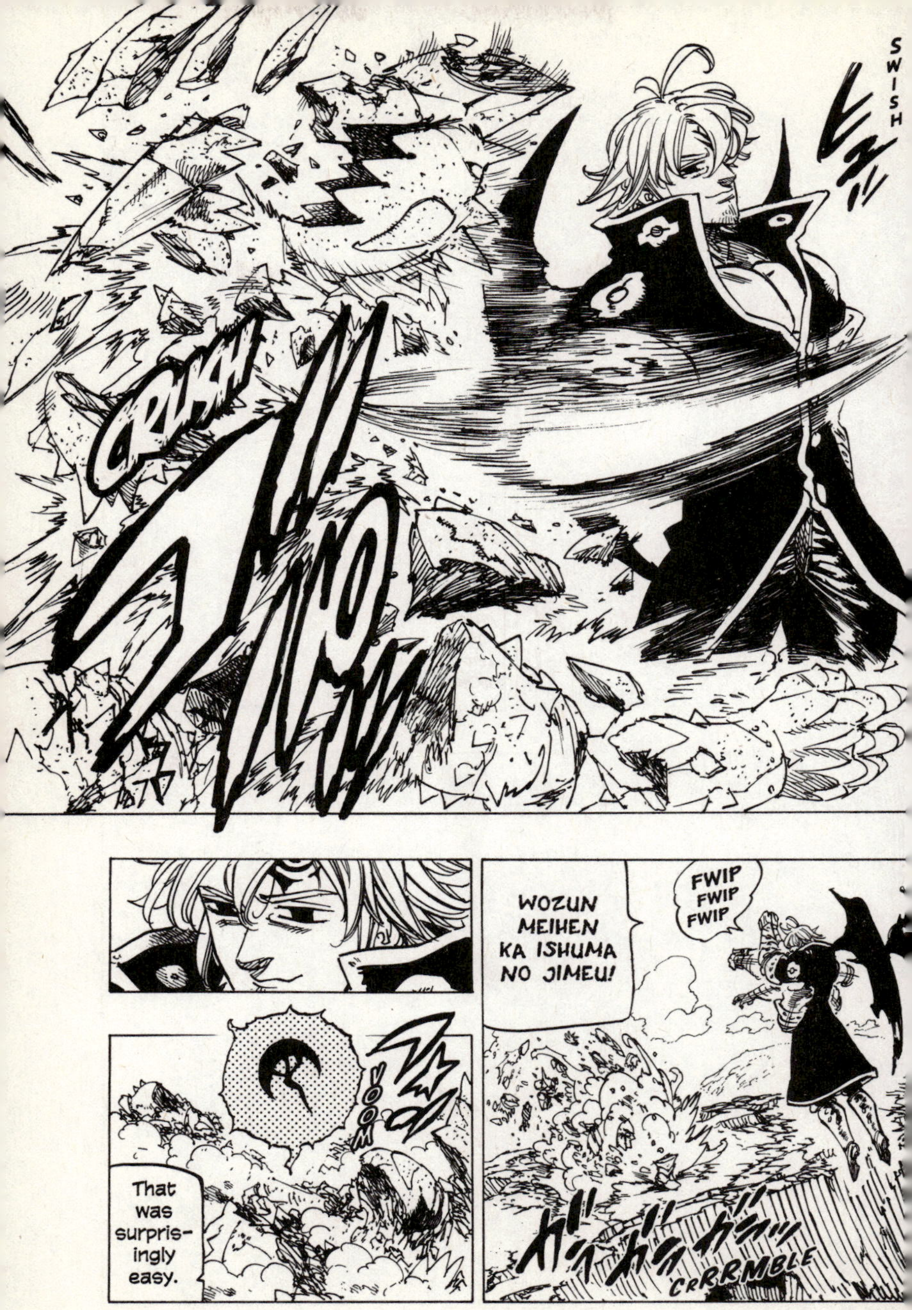
SWISH
CRUSH
FWIP FWIP FWIP
WOZUN MEIHEN KA ISHUMA NO JIMEU!
CRRRMBLE
VOOOM
That was surpris-ingly easy.

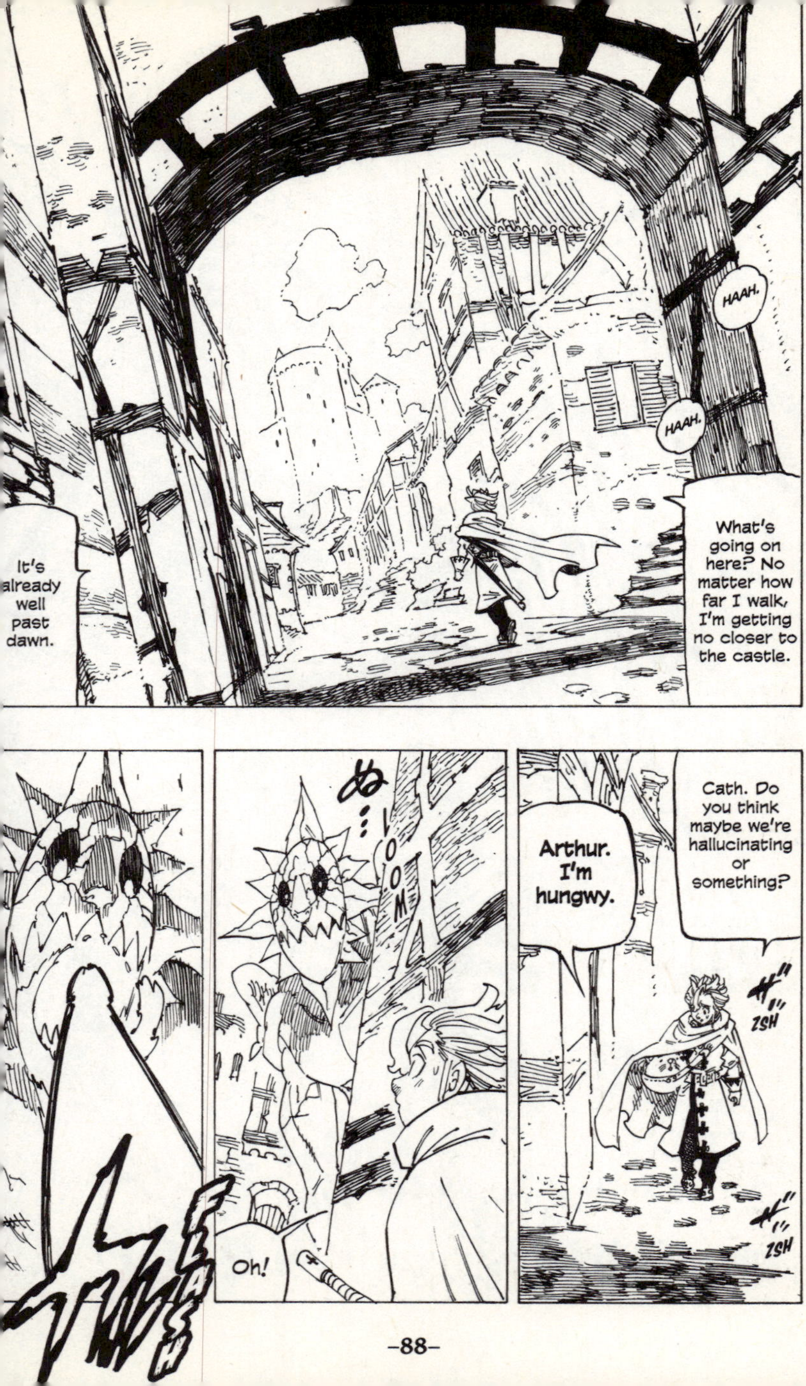
HAAH.
HAAH.
What's going on here? No matter how far I walk, I'm getting no closer to the castle.
It's already well past dawn.
Cath. Do you think maybe we're hallucinating or something?
Arthur. I'm hungwy.
ZSH
ZSH
ぬ…
VOOM
Oh!
FLASH

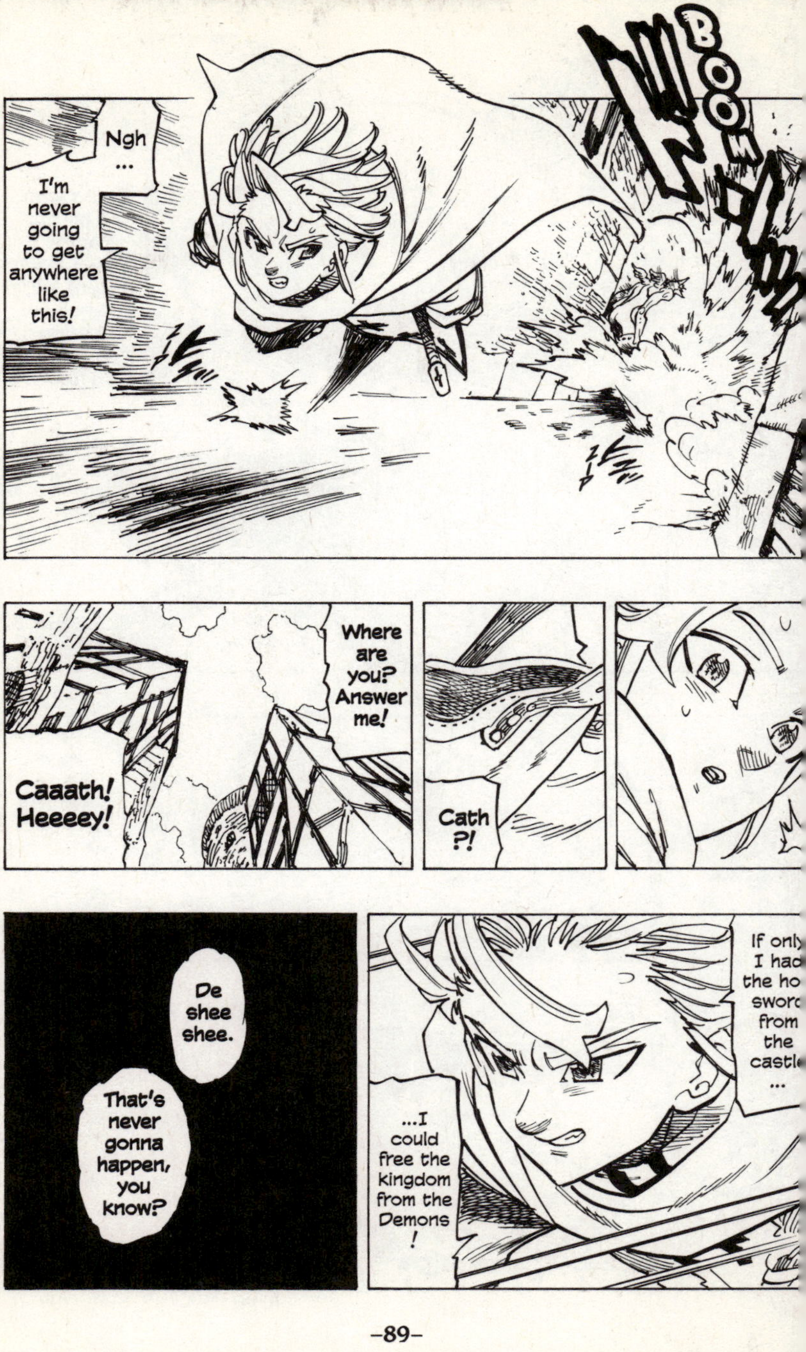
BOOM
Ngh... I'm never going to get anywhere like this!
Cath?!
Where are you? Answer me!
Caaath! Heeeey!
If only I had the ho sword from the castle...
...I could free the kingdom from the Demons!
De shee shee.
That's never gonna happen, you know?

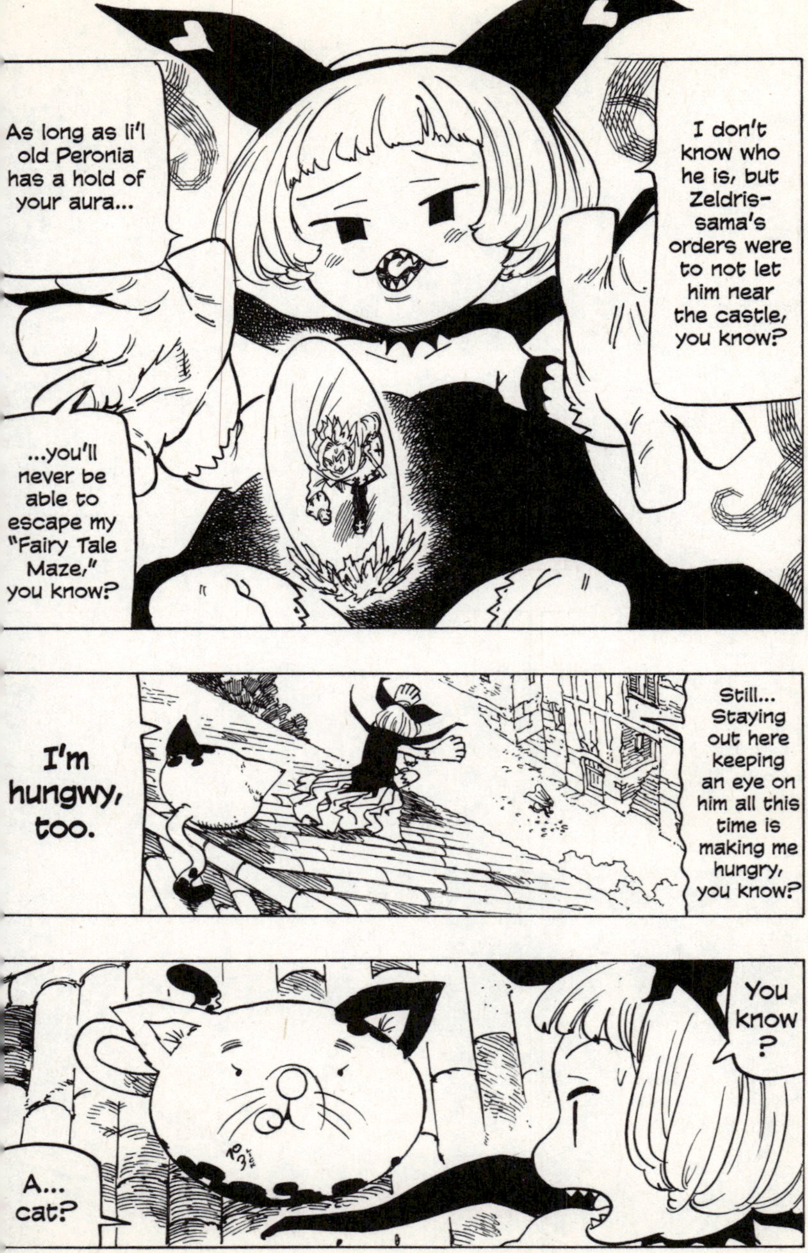
I don't know who he is, but Zeldris-sama's orders were to not let him near the castle, you know?
As long as li'l old Peronia has a hold of your aura...
...you'll never be able to escape my "Fairy Tale Maze," you know?
Still... Staying out here keeping an eye on him all this time is making me hungry, you know?
I'm hungwy, too.
You know?
A... cat?

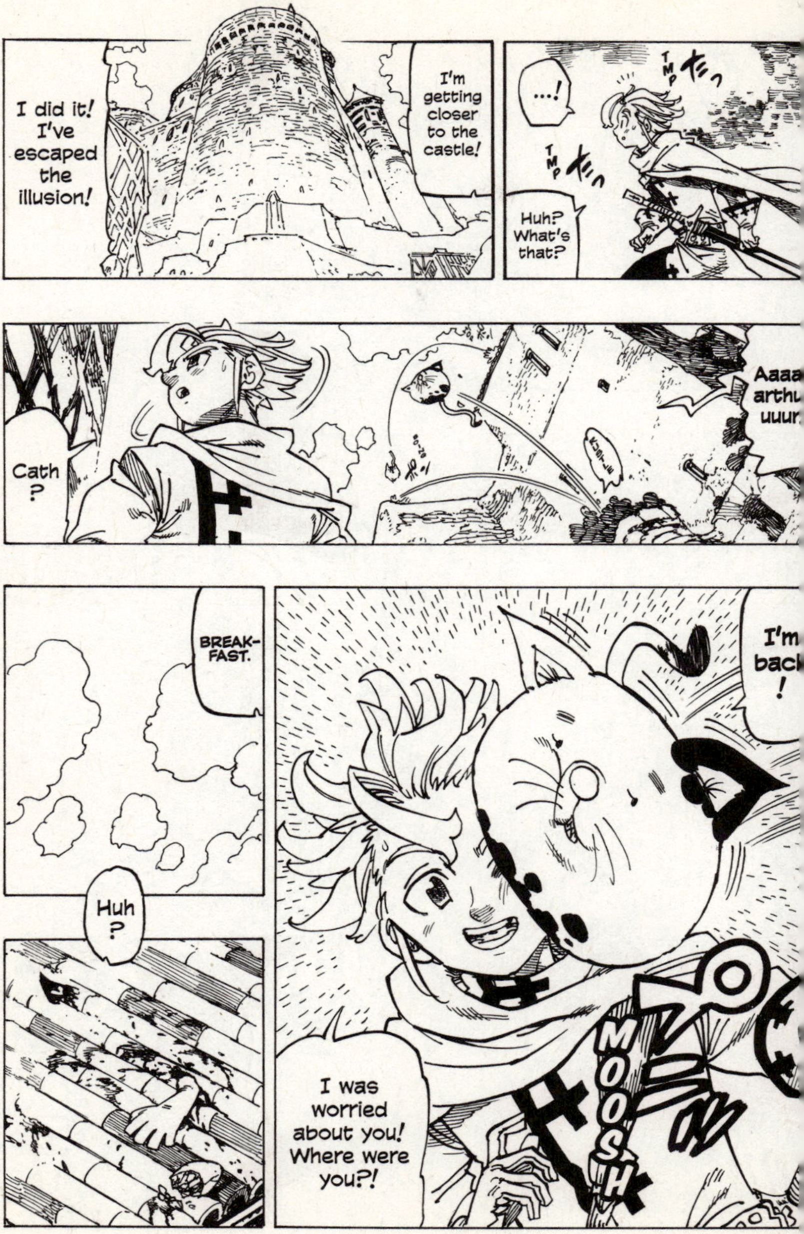
TMP
...!
TMP
Huh? What's that?
I'm getting closer to the castle!
I did it! I've escaped the illusion!
Aaaa arthu uuur.
Cath?
I'm back!
MOOSH
I was worried about you! Where were you?!
BREAK-FAST.
Huh?

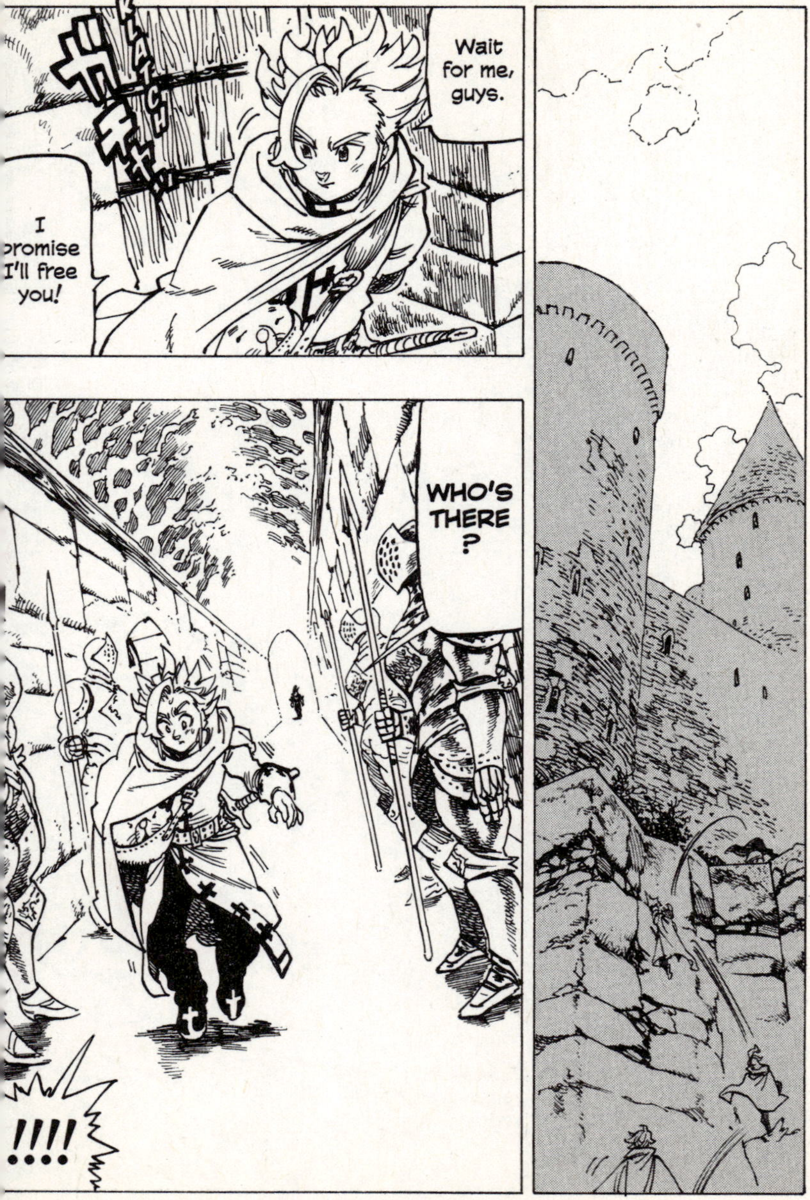
Wait for me, guys.
KLATCH
I promise I'll free you!
WHO'S THERE?
!!!!

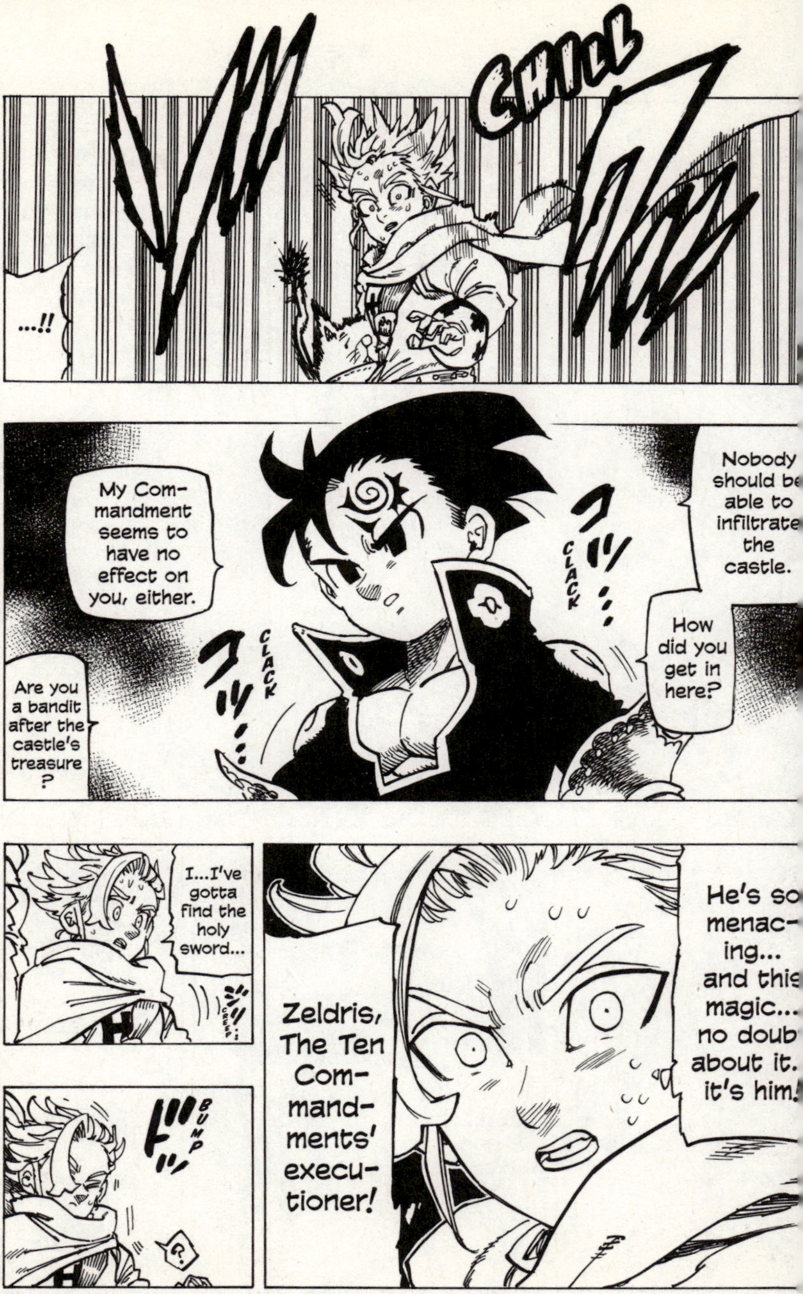

CHILL
...!!
Nobody should be able to infiltrate the castle.
CLACK
How did you get in here?
My Commandment seems to have no effect on you, either.
CLACK
Are you a bandit after the castle's treasure?
He's so menacing... and this magic... no doubt about it. it's him!
Zeldris, The Ten Commandments' executioner!
I...I've gotta find the holy sword...
CREEP
BUMP
?

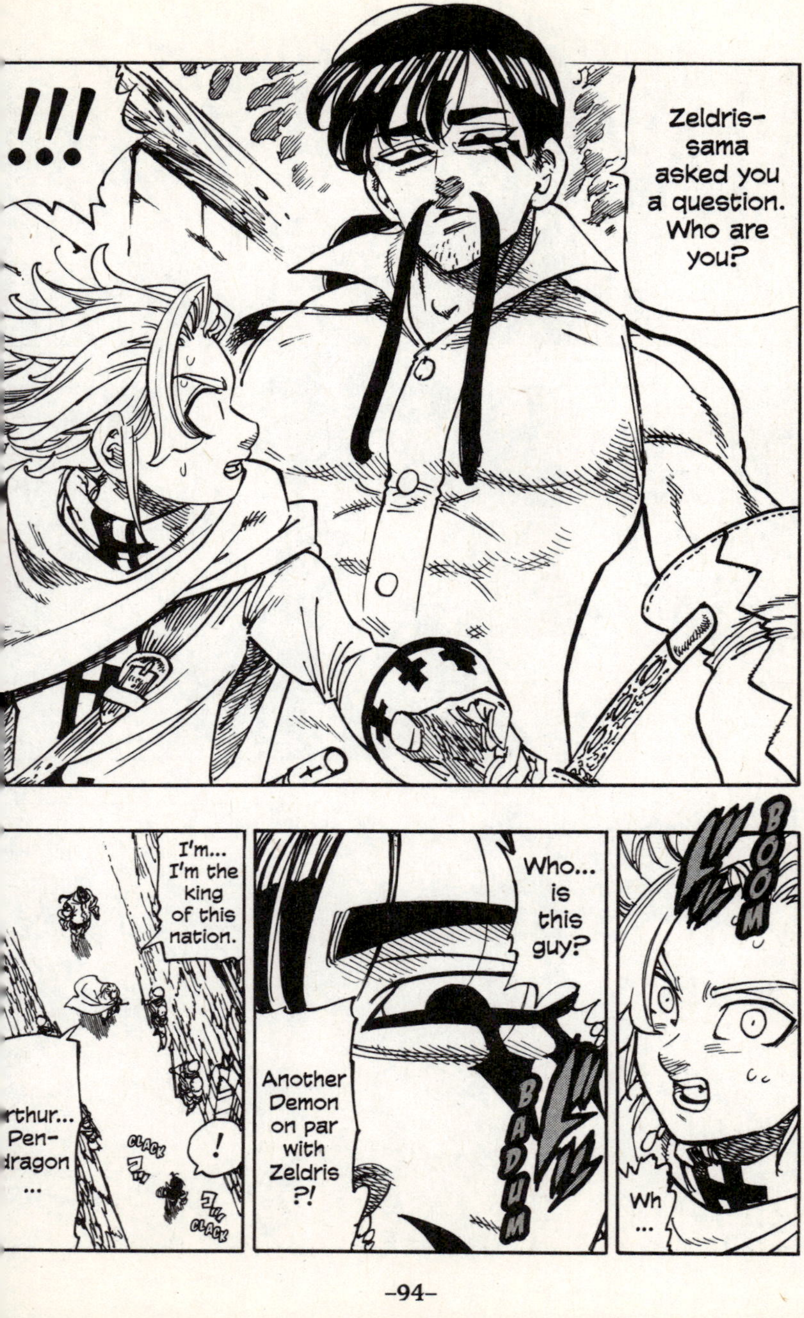
Zeldris-sama asked you a question. Who are you?
!!!
BOOM
Wh ...
Who... is this guy?
BADUM
Another Demon on par with Zeldris ?!
I'm... I'm the king of this nation.
rthur... Pen-dragon ...
!
CLACK
CLACK

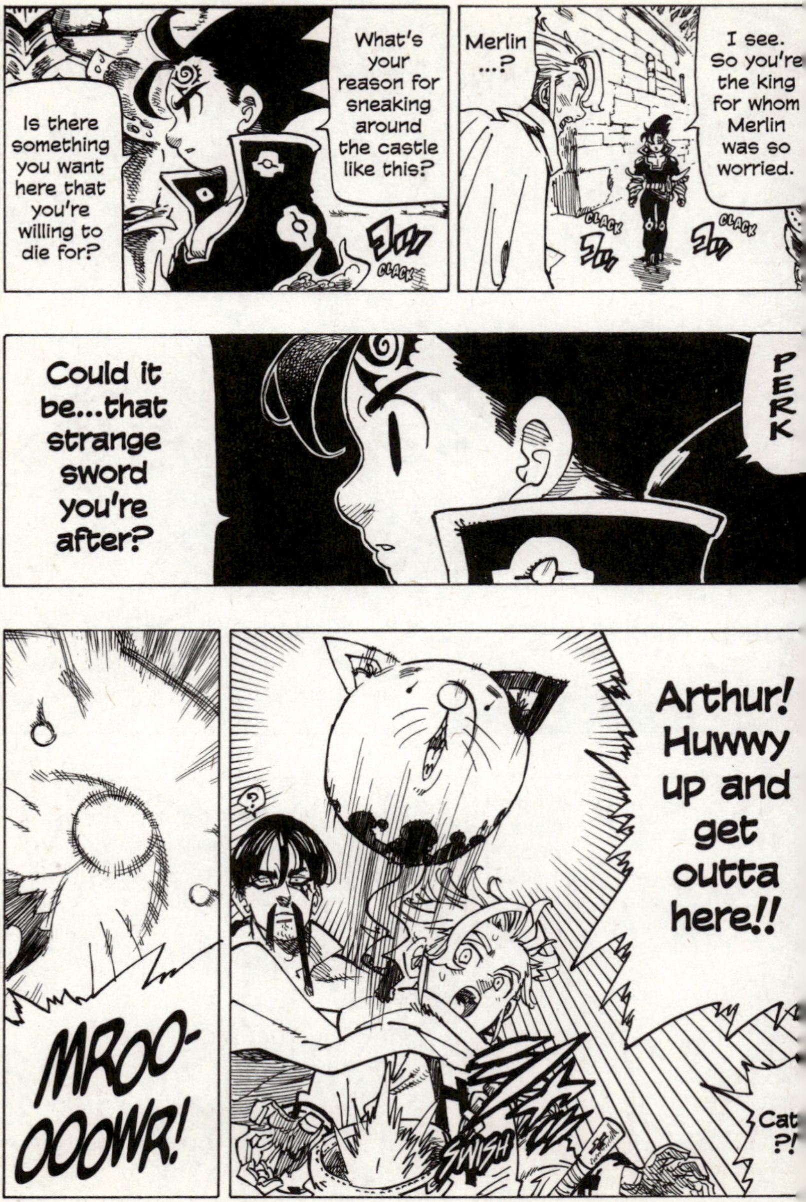
I see. So you're the king for whom Merlin was so worried.
CLACK
CLACK
Merlin ...?
What's your reason for sneaking around the castle like this?
Is there something you want here that you're willing to die for?
CLACK
PERK
Could it be...that strange sword you're after?
Arthur! Huwwy up and get outta here!!
Cat?!
SWISH
MROO-OOOWR!

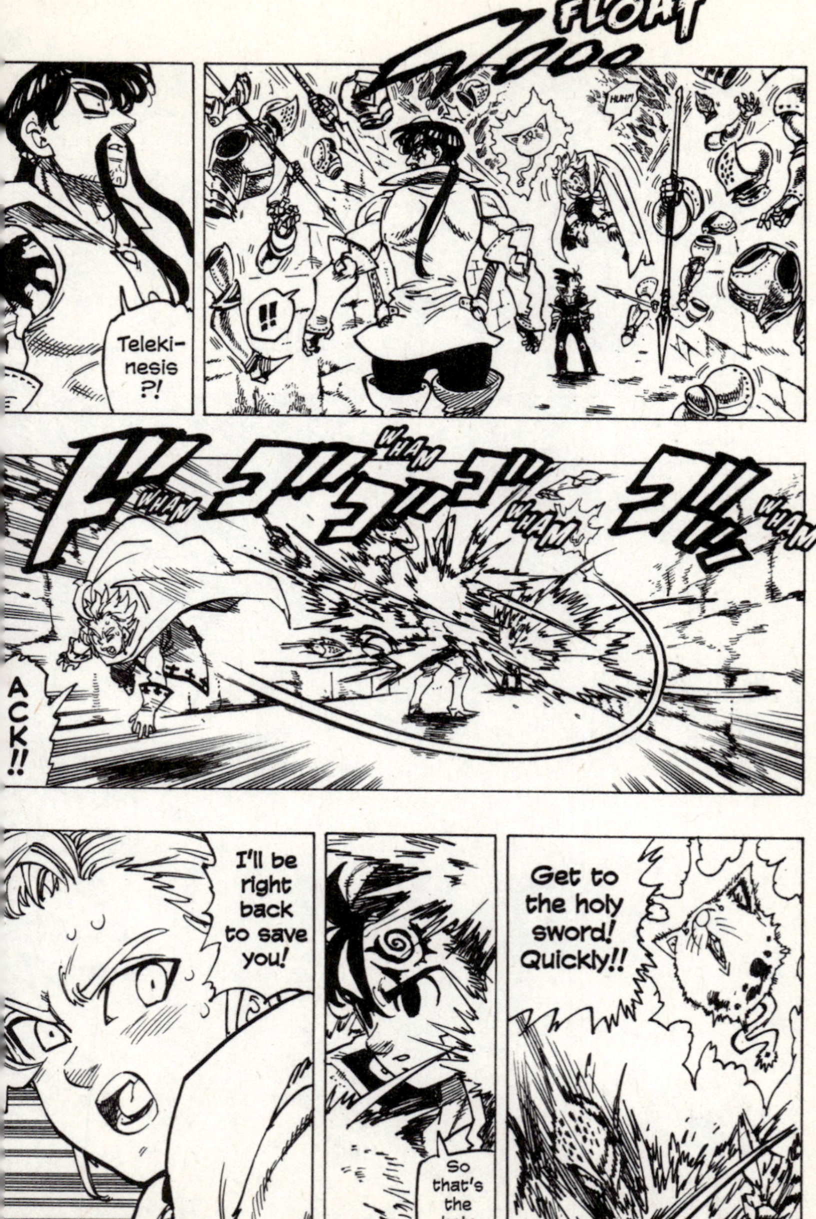
FLOAT
HUH?!
!!
Telekinesis?!
WHAM
WHAM
WHAM
WHAM
ACK!!
Get to the holy sword! Quickly!!
So that's the holy sword?
I'll be right back to save you!

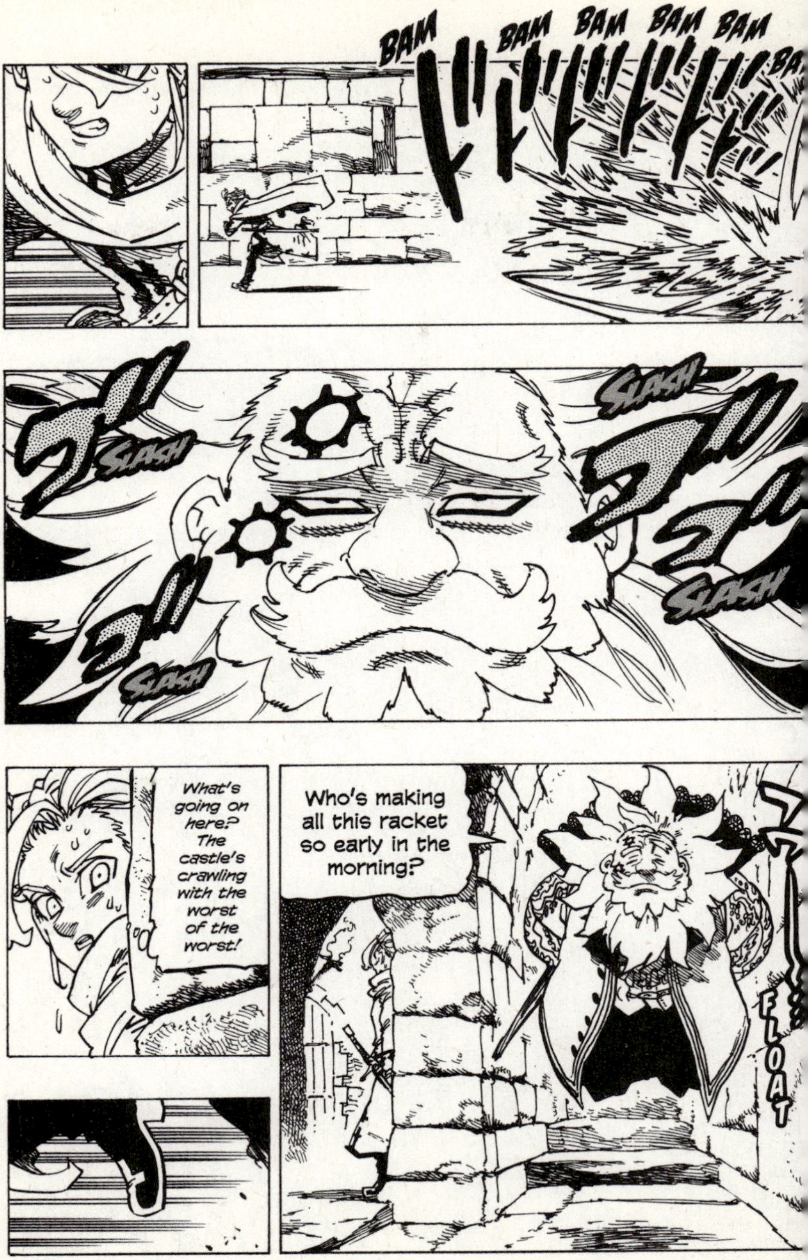
BAM
BAM
BAM
BAM
BAM
SLASH
SLASH
SLASH
SLASH
Who's making all this racket so early in the morning?
FLOAT
What's going on here? The castle's crawling with the worst of the worst!

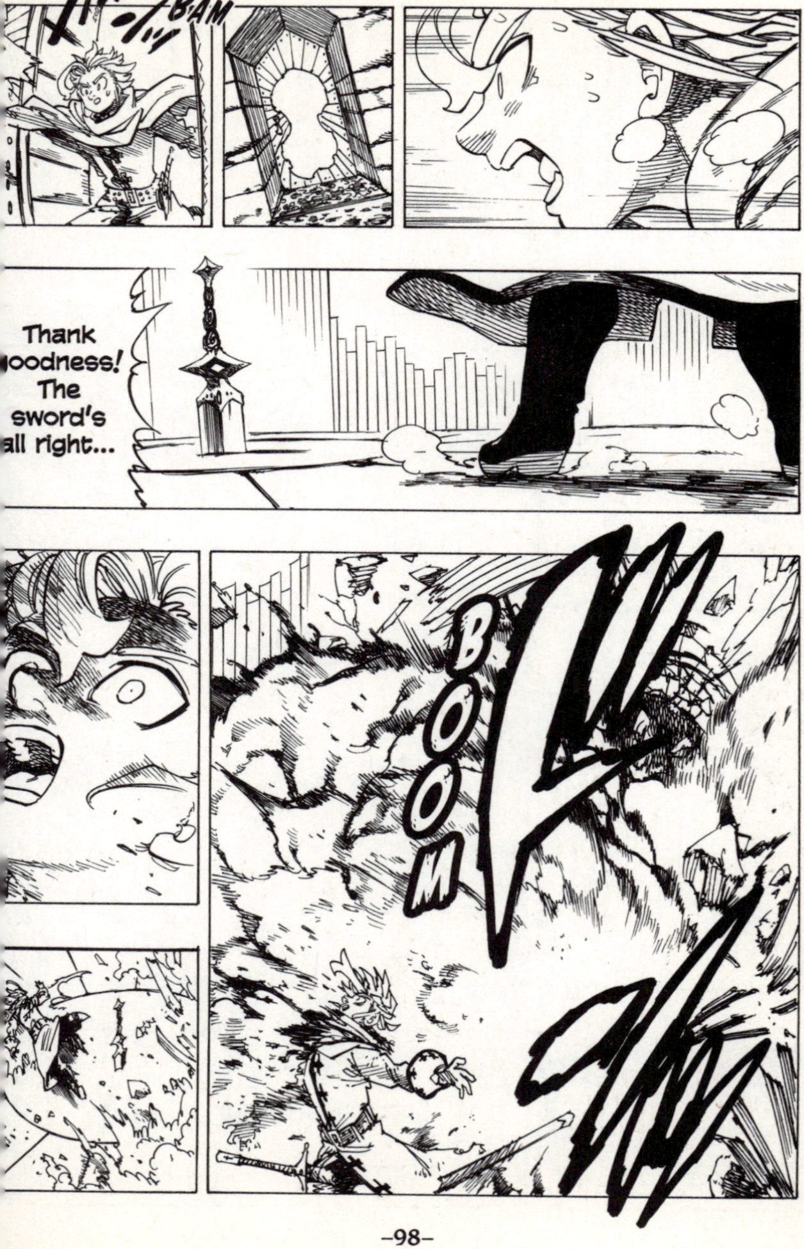
BAM
Thank goodness! The sword's all right...
BOOM

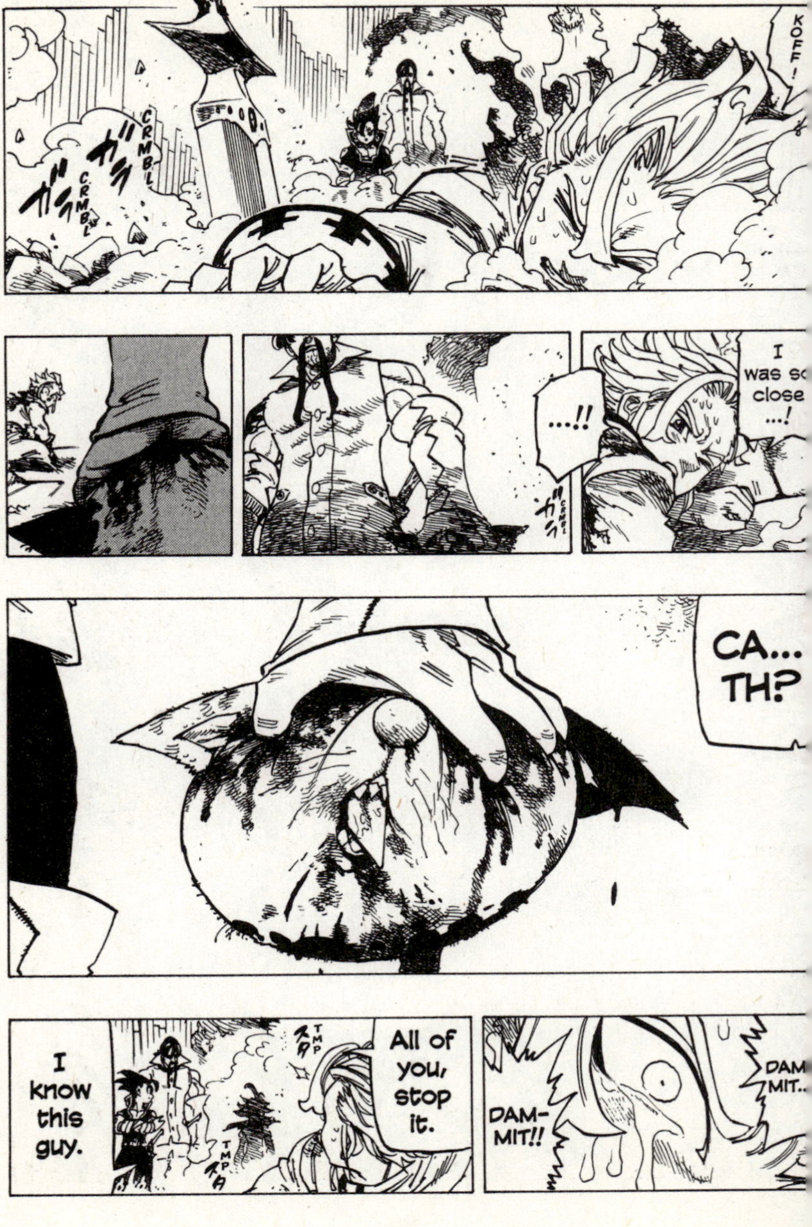
KOFF!
CRMBL
CRMBL
I was so close ...!
...!!
CRMBL
CA... TH?
DAM MIT...
DAM- MIT!!
All of you, stop it.
TMP
I know this guy.
TMP

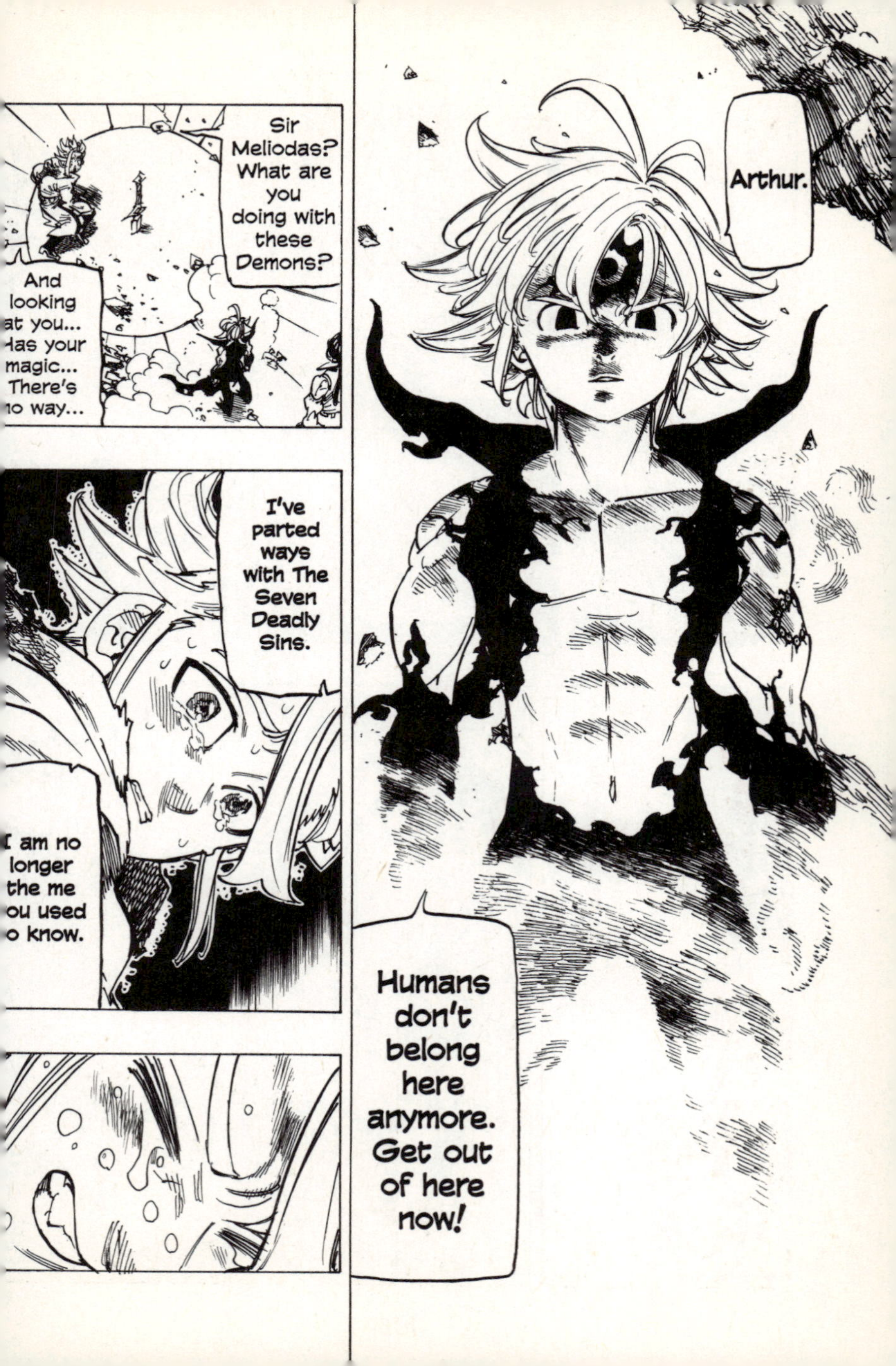
Sir Meliodas? What are you doing with these Demons?
And looking at you... Has your magic... There's no way...
I've parted ways with The Seven Deadly Sins.
I am no longer the me you used to know.
Arthur.
Humans don't belong here anymore. Get out of here now!

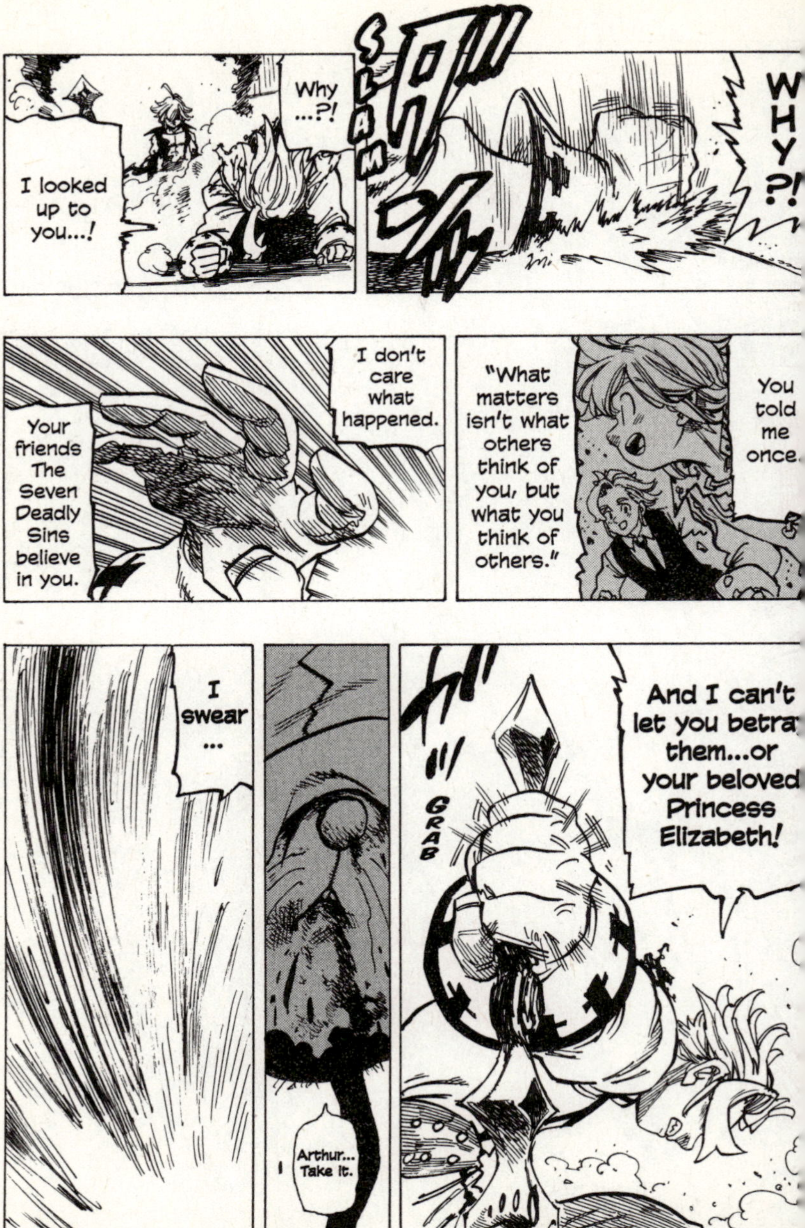
HY?!
SLAM
Why ...?!
I looked up to you...!
You told me once.
"What matters isn't what others think of you, but what you think of others."
I don't care what happened.
Your friends The Seven Deadly Sins believe in you.
And I can't let you betra them...or your beloved Princess Elizabeth!
GRAB
Arthur... Take it.
I swear ...

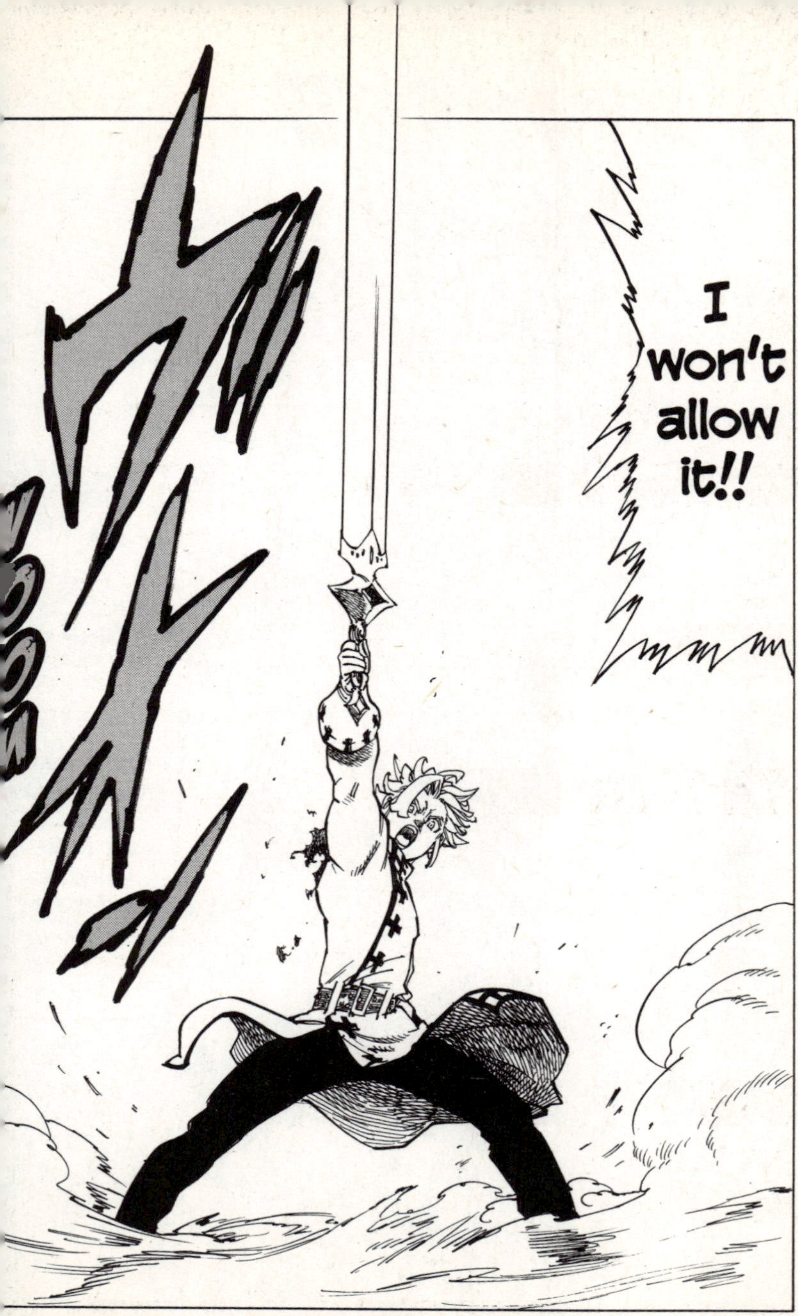
I won't allow it!!

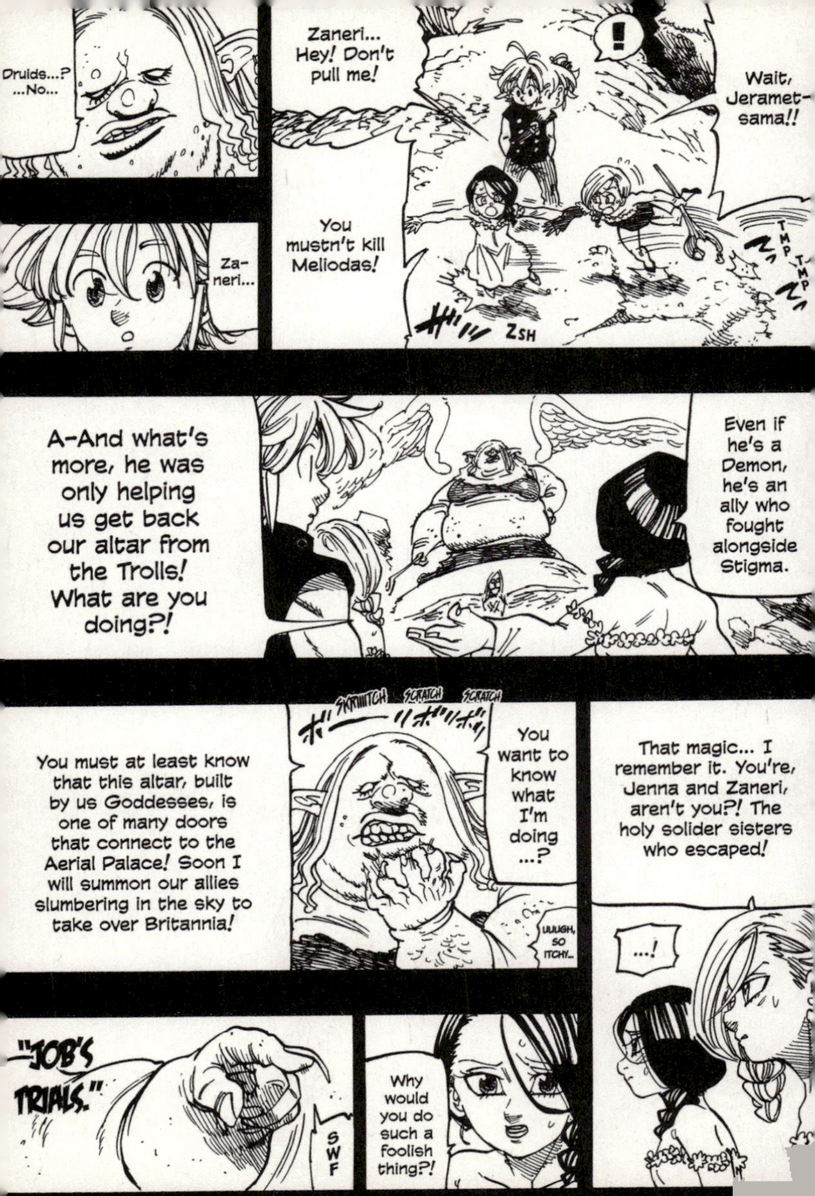
!
Wait, Jeramet-sama!!
Zaneri... Hey! Don't pull me!
You mustn't kill Meliodas!
TMP TMP
ZSH
Druids...? ...No...
Za-neri...
Even if he's a Demon, he's an ally who fought alongside Stigma.
A-And what's more, he was only helping us get back our altar from the Trolls! What are you doing?!
That magic... I remember it. You're, Jenna and Zaneri, aren't you?! The holy solider sisters who escaped!
SKRIIITCH SCRATCH SCRATCH
You want to know what I'm doing...?
UUUGH, SO ITCHY...
You must at least know that this altar, built by us Goddesses, is one of many doors that connect to the Aerial Palace! Soon I will summon our allies slumbering in the sky to take over Britannia!
...!
Why would you do such a foolish thing?!
SWF
"JOB'S TRIALS."

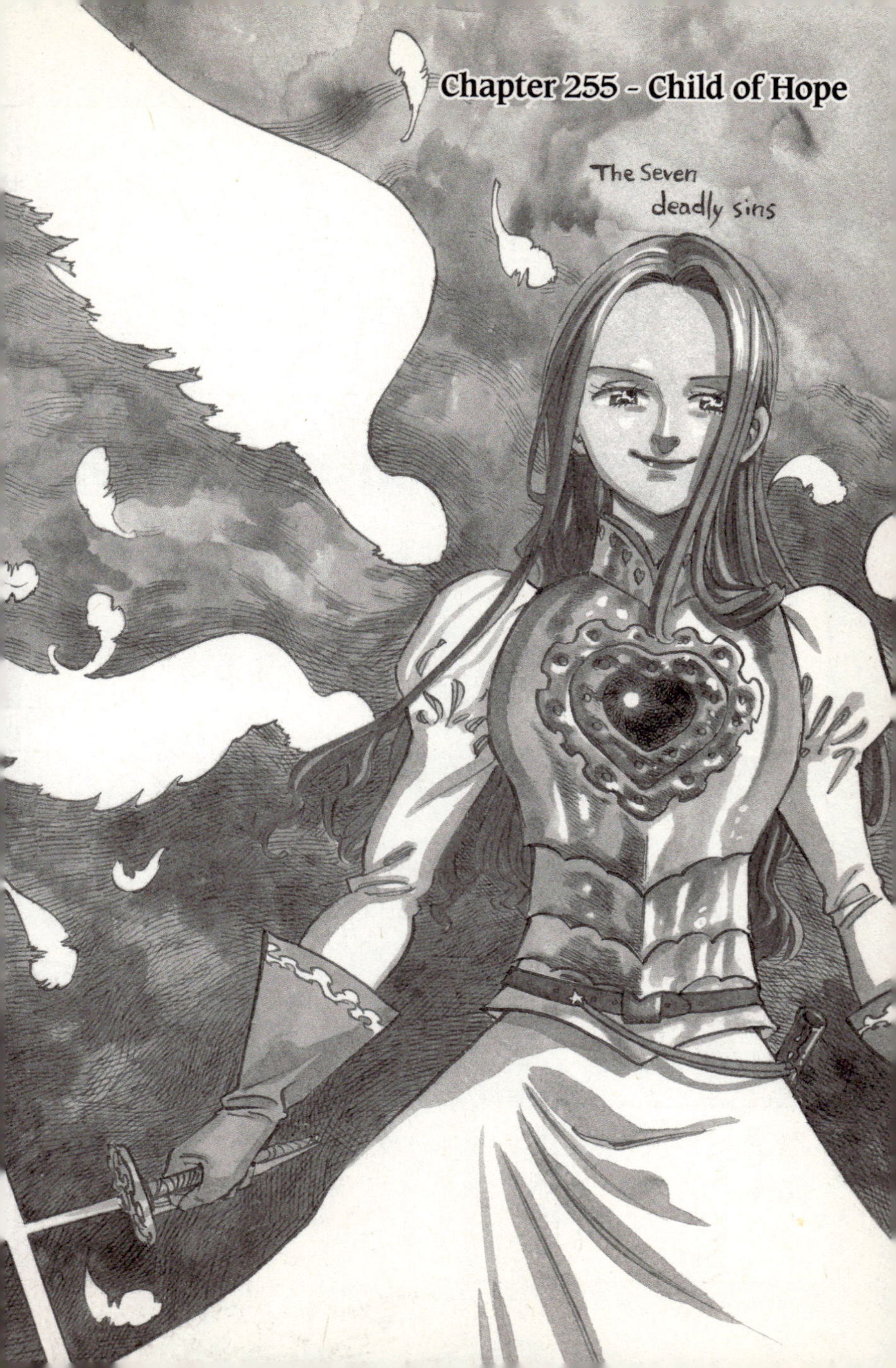

Chapter 255 - Child of Hope
The Seven deadly sins

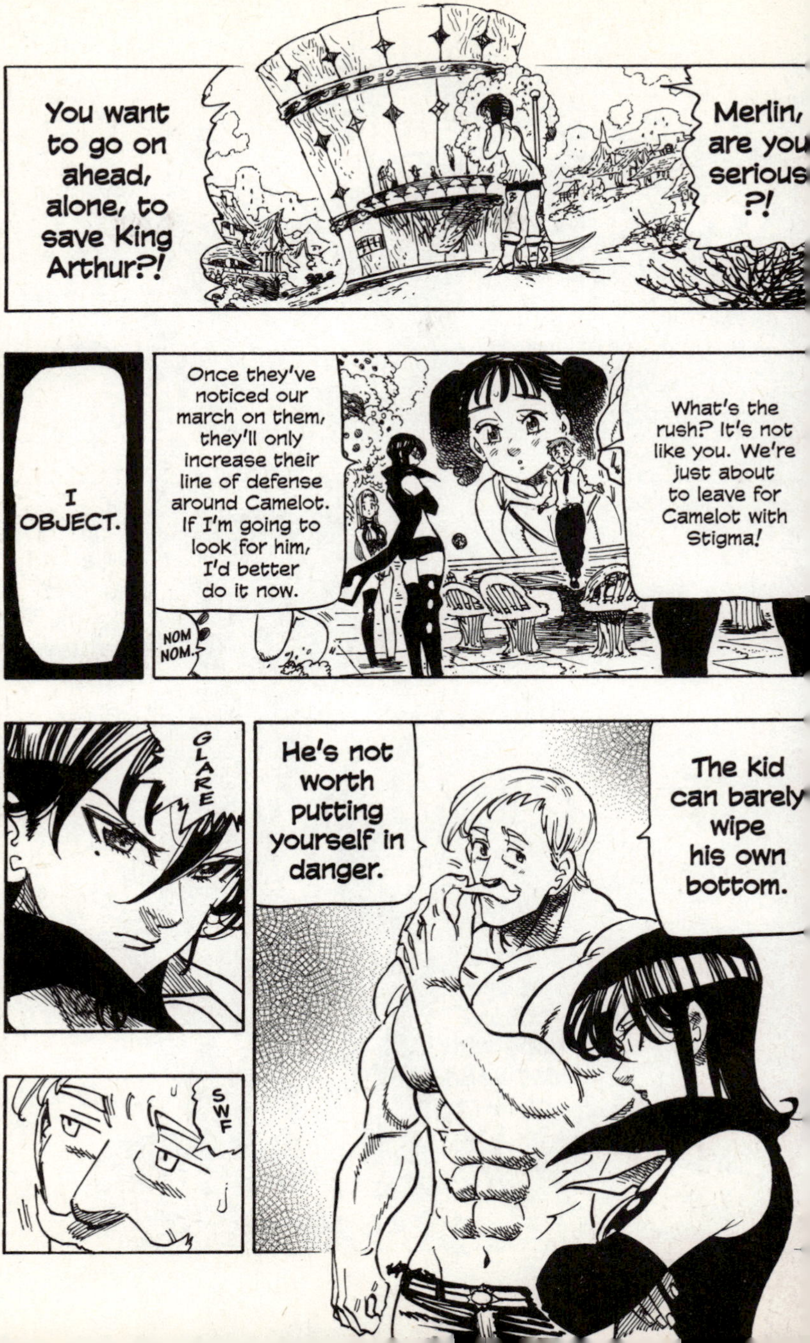
Merlin, are you serious?!
You want to go on ahead, alone, to save King Arthur?!
What's the rush? It's not like you. We're just about to leave for Camelot with Stigma!
Once they've noticed our march on them, they'll only increase their line of defense around Camelot. If I'm going to look for him, I'd better do it now.
NOM NOM.
I OBJECT.
The kid can barely wipe his own bottom.
He's not worth putting yourself in danger.
GLARE
SWF

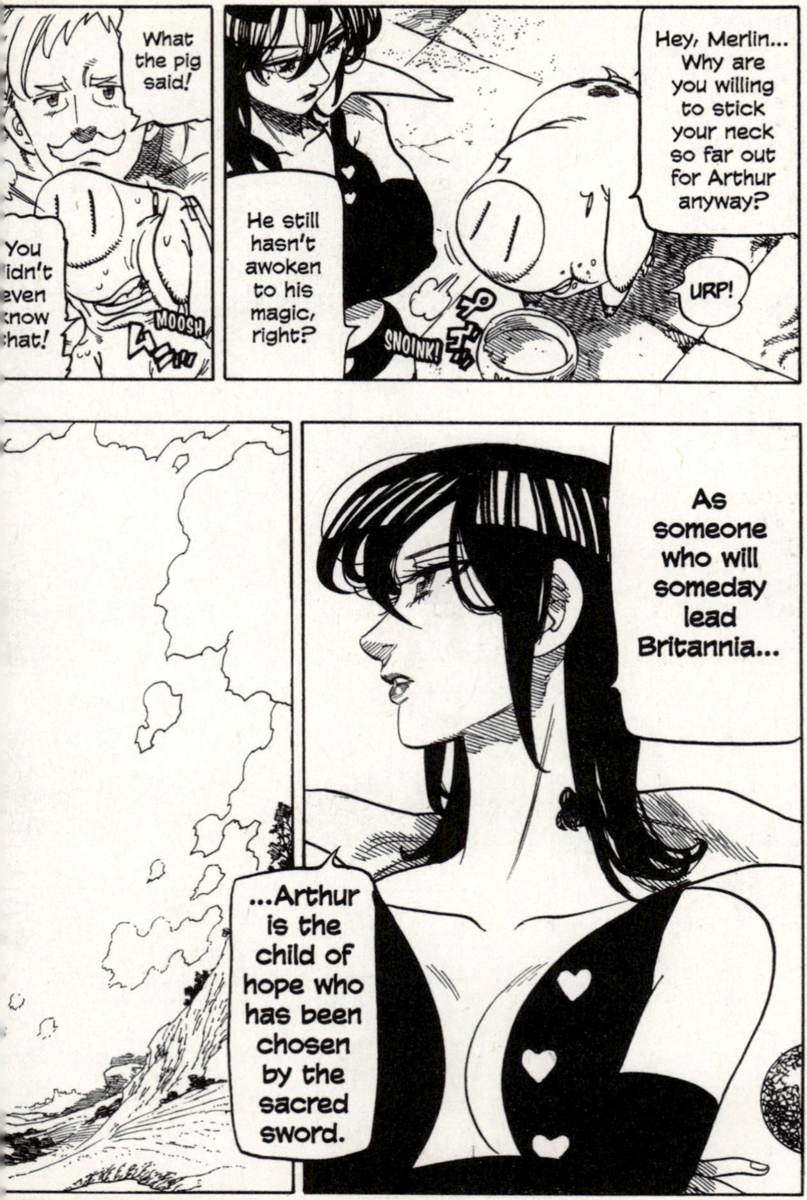

Hey, Merlin... Why are you willing to stick your neck so far out for Arthur anyway?
URP!
He still hasn't awoken to his magic, right?
SNOINK!
What the pig said!
You idn't even now hat!
MOOSH
As someone who will someday lead Britannia...
...Arthur is the child of hope who has been chosen by the sacred sword.

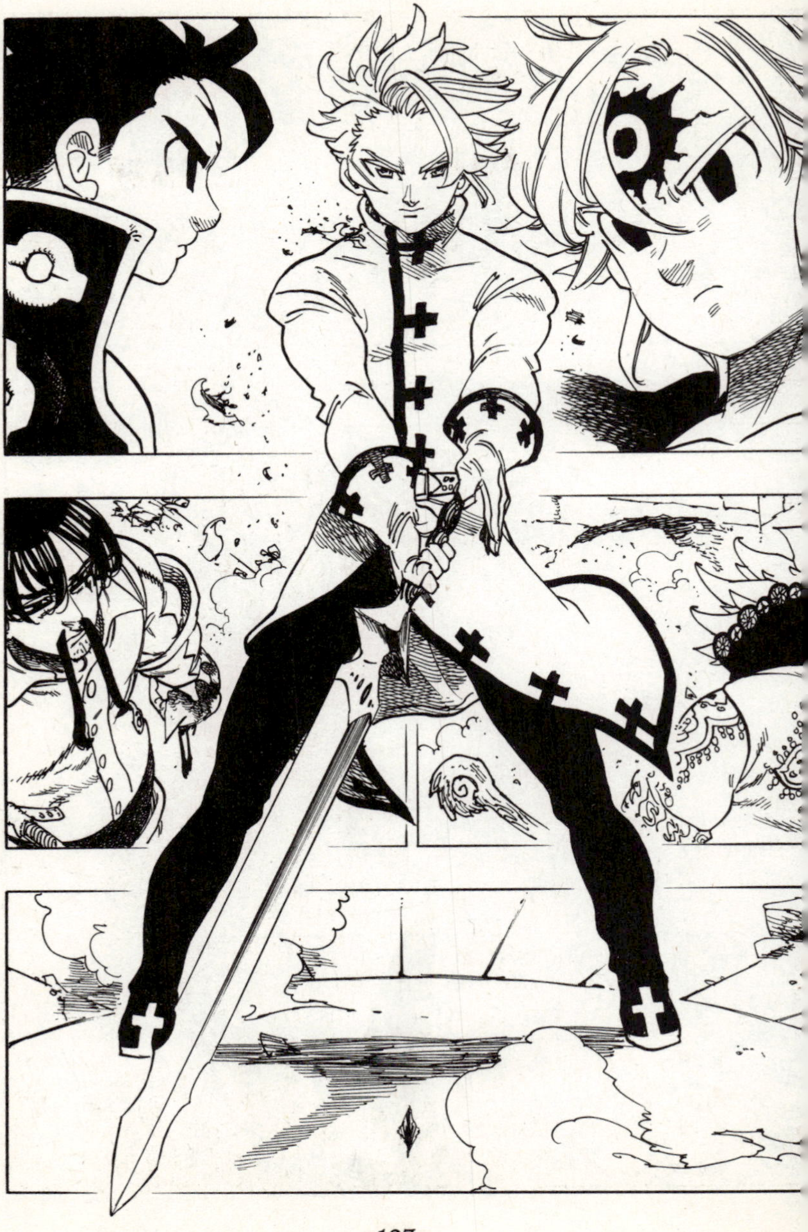

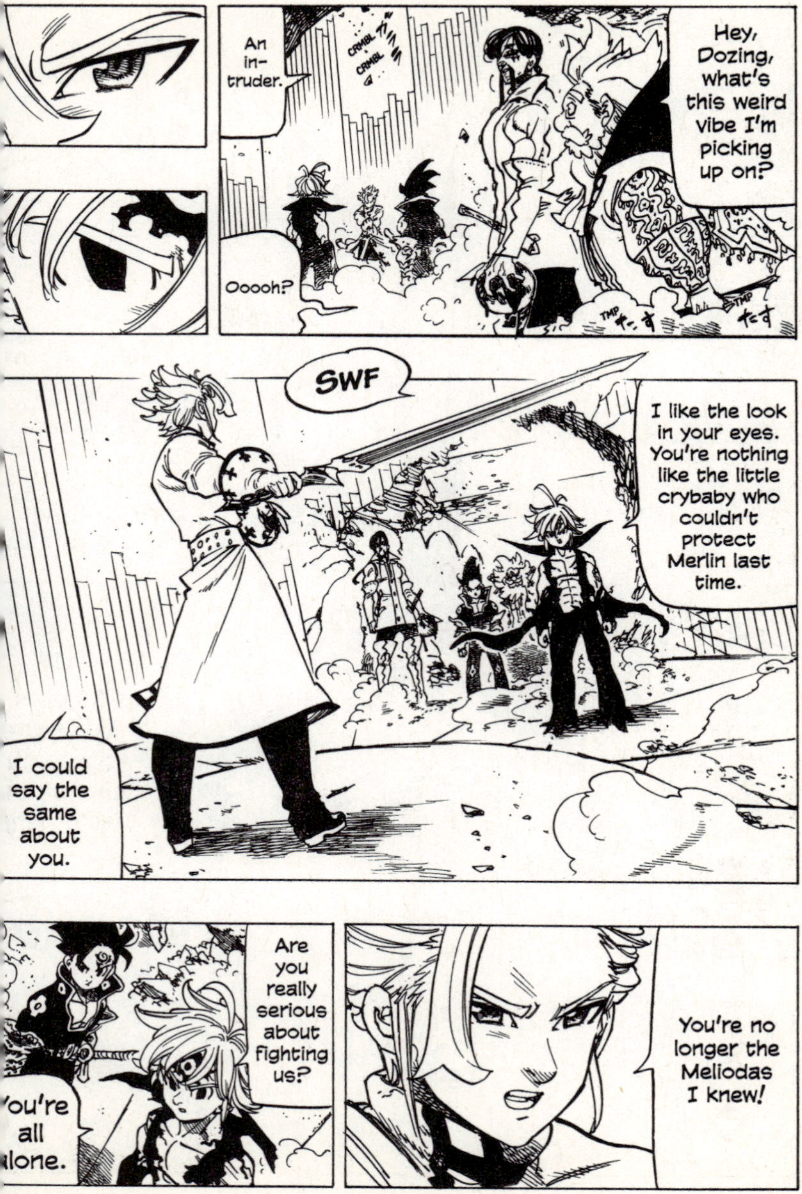
Hey, Dozing, what's this weird vibe I'm picking up on?
TMP
TMP
CRMBL
CRMBL
An in-truder.
Ooooh?
SWF
I like the look in your eyes. You're nothing like the little crybaby who couldn't protect Merlin last time.
I could say the same about you.
You're no longer the Meliodas I knew!
Are you really serious about fighting us?
ou're all lone.

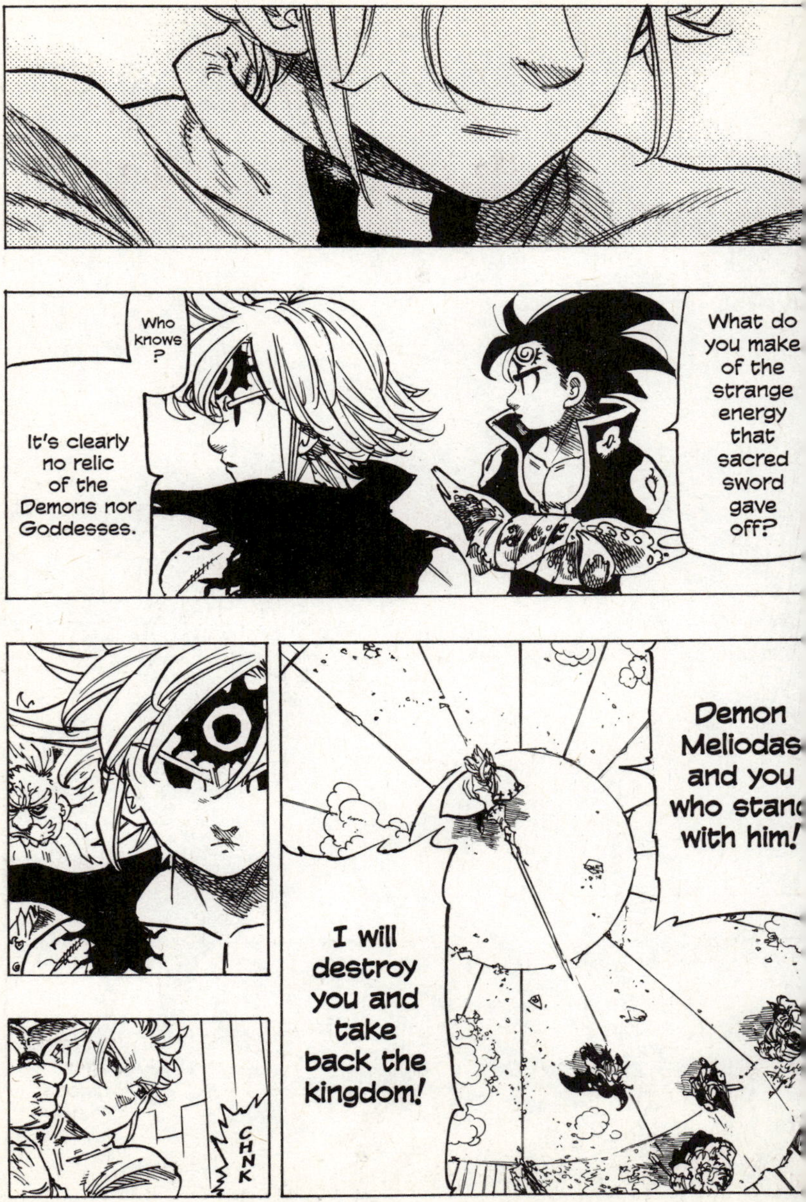
What do you make of the strange energy that sacred sword gave off?
Who knows?
It's clearly no relic of the Demons nor Goddesses.
Demon Meliodas and you who stanc with him!
I will destroy you and take back the kingdom!
CHNK

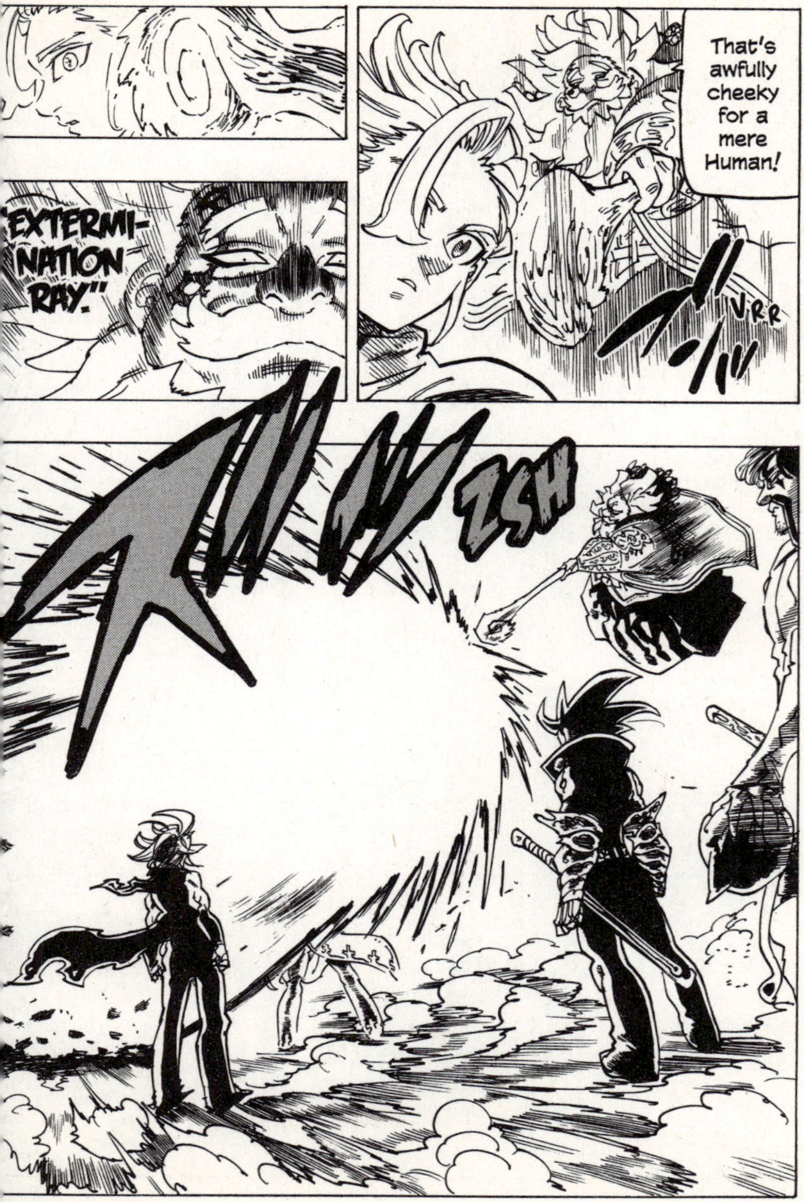
That's awfully cheeky for a mere Human!
VRR
EXTERMI-NATION RAY."
ZSH

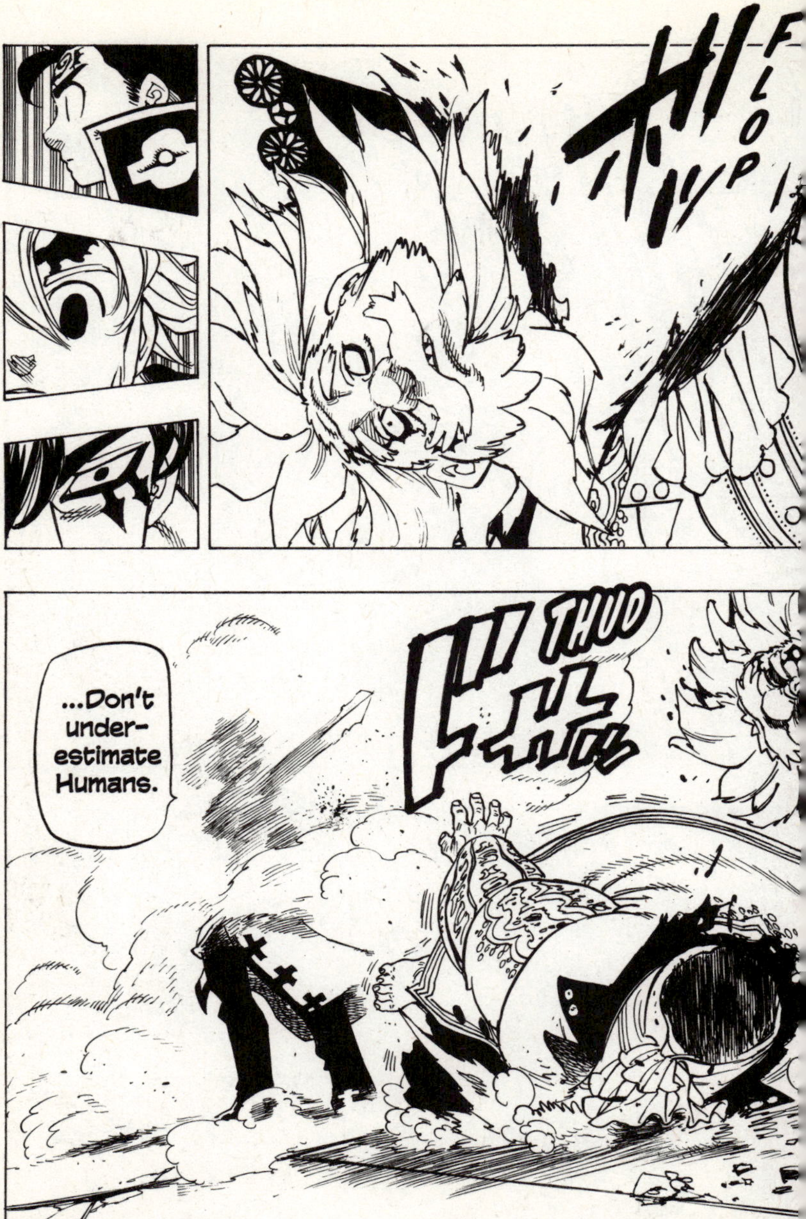
FLOP
THUD
...Don't under-estimate Humans.

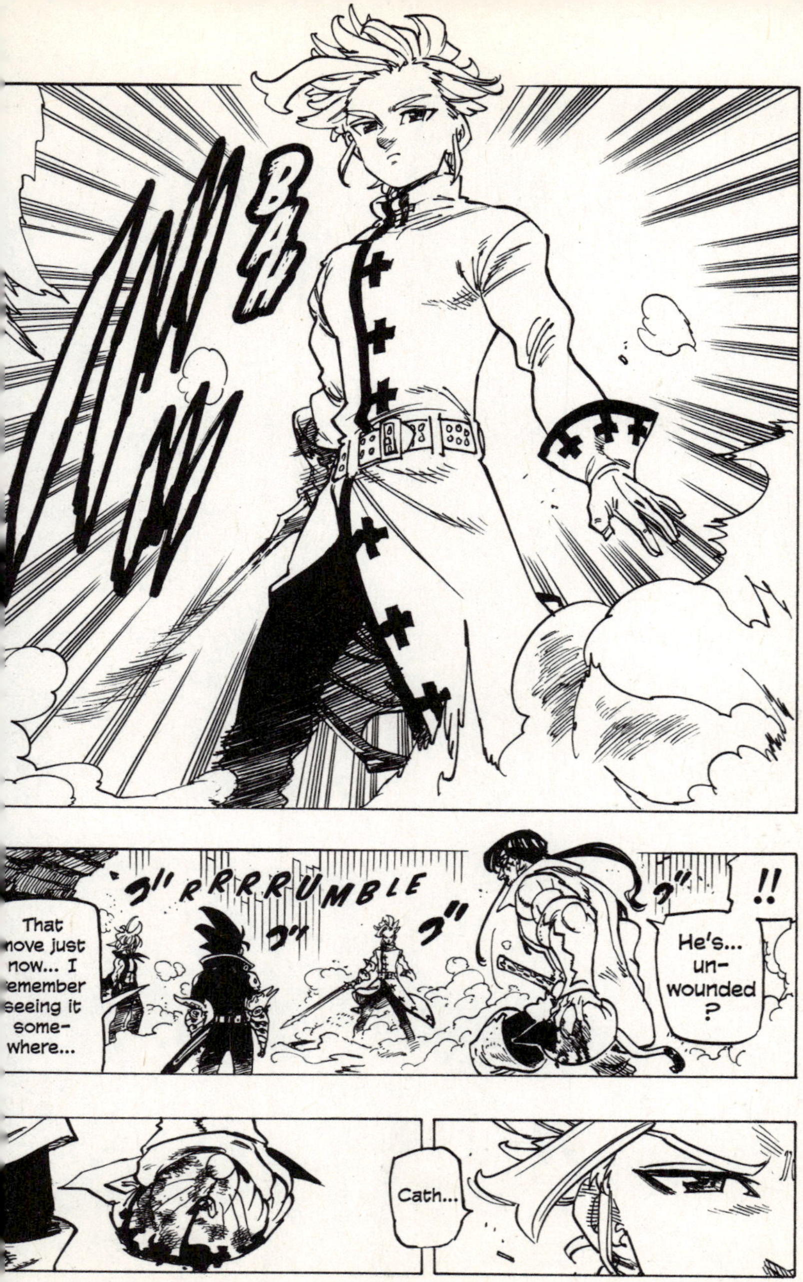
BAAM
!!
He's... un-wounded?
ゴ" ゴ" ゴ"
ゴ" RRRRRUMBLE
That move just now... I remember seeing it some-where...
Cath...

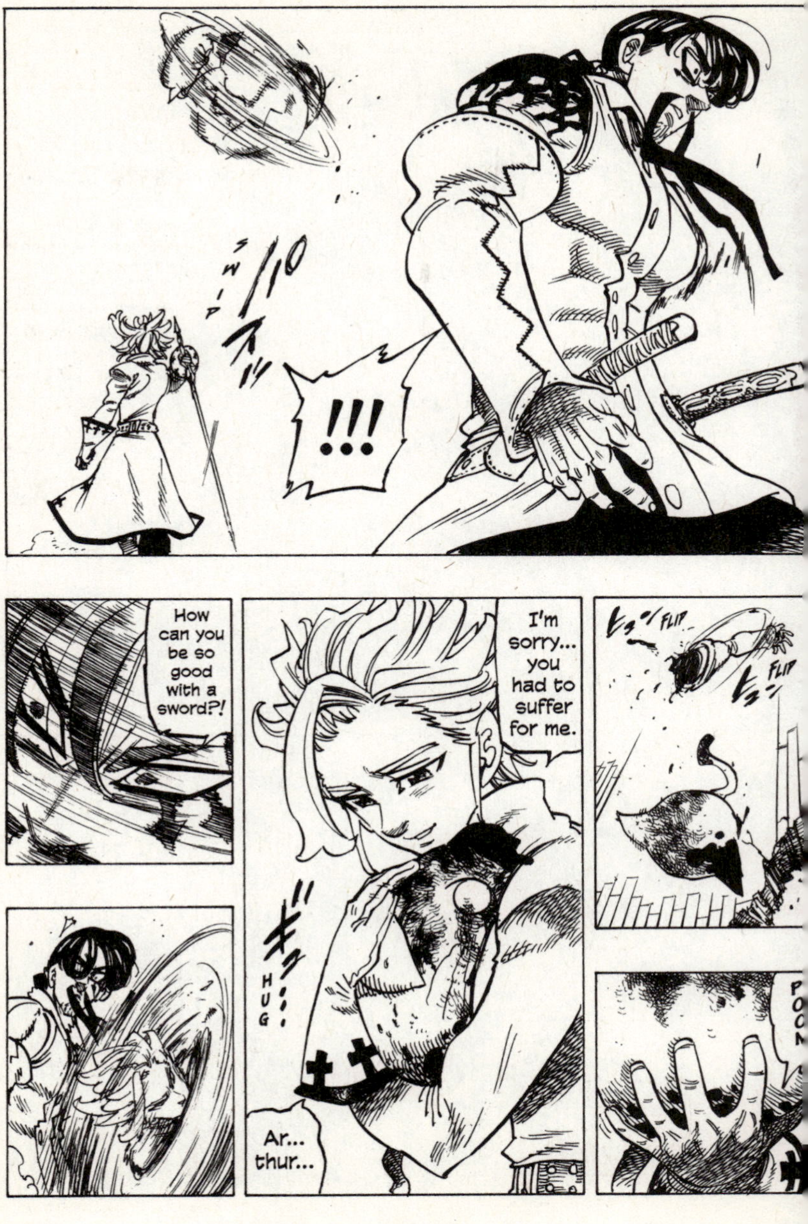
SWIP
!!!
FLIP
FLIP
POO
I'm sorry... you had to suffer for me.
HUG
Ar... thur...
How can you be so good with a sword?!

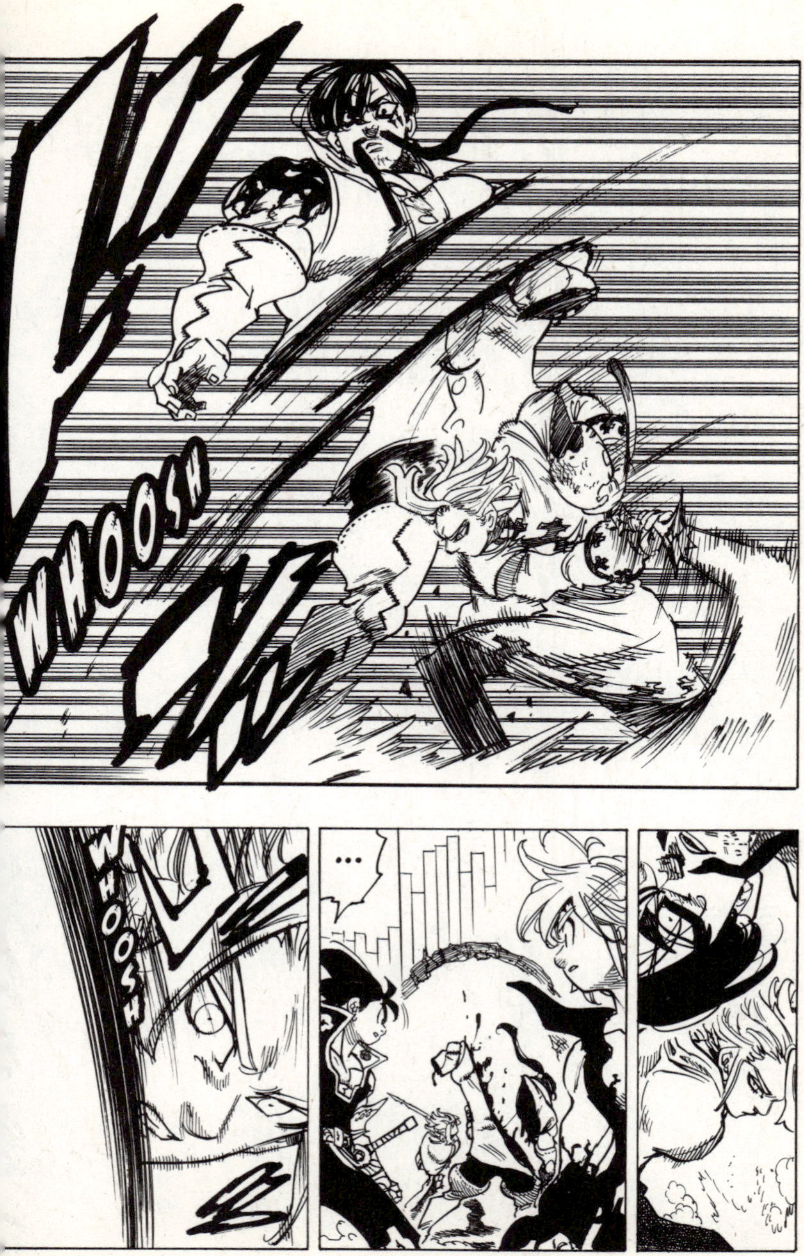
WHOOSH
WHOOSH
...

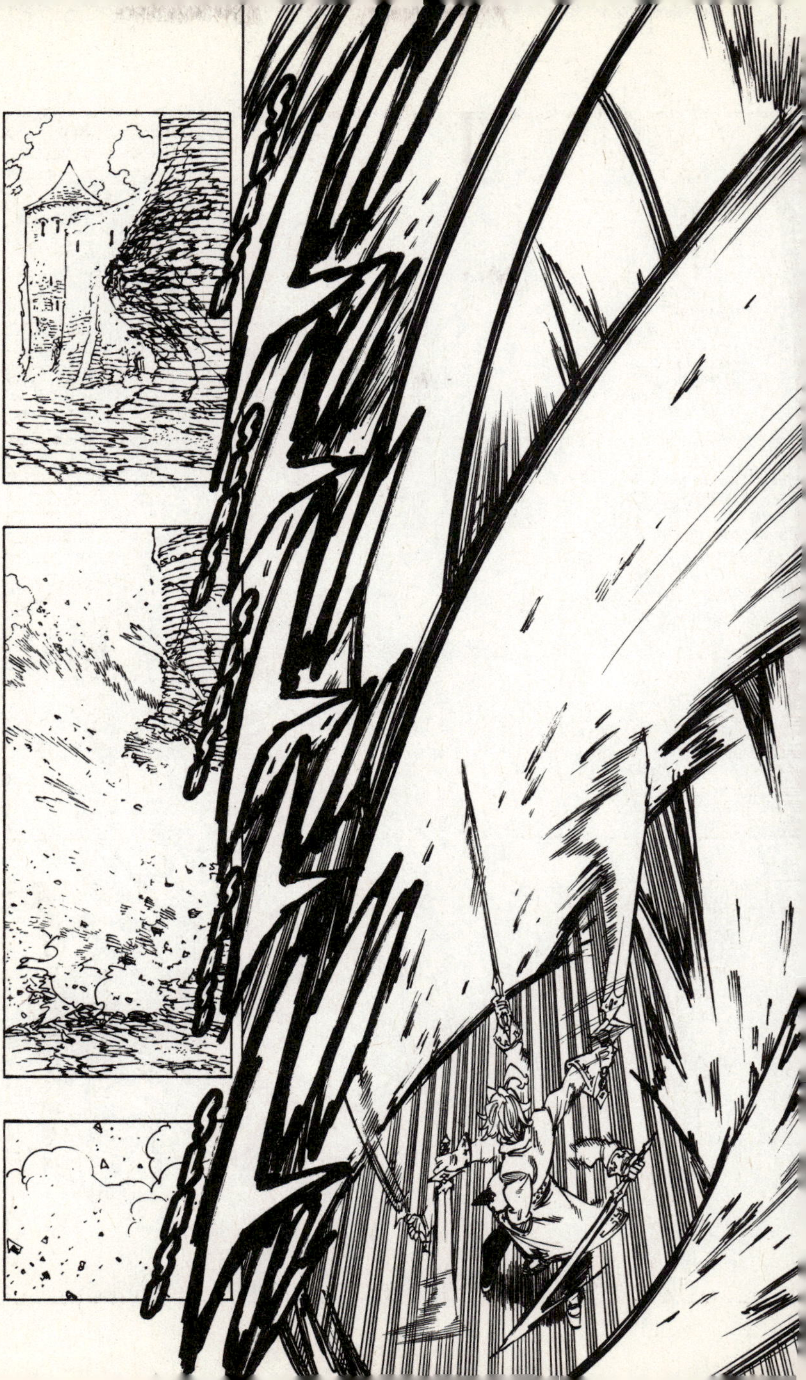

I know. We'll eat together after this.

I'm... hungwy.

CLANG

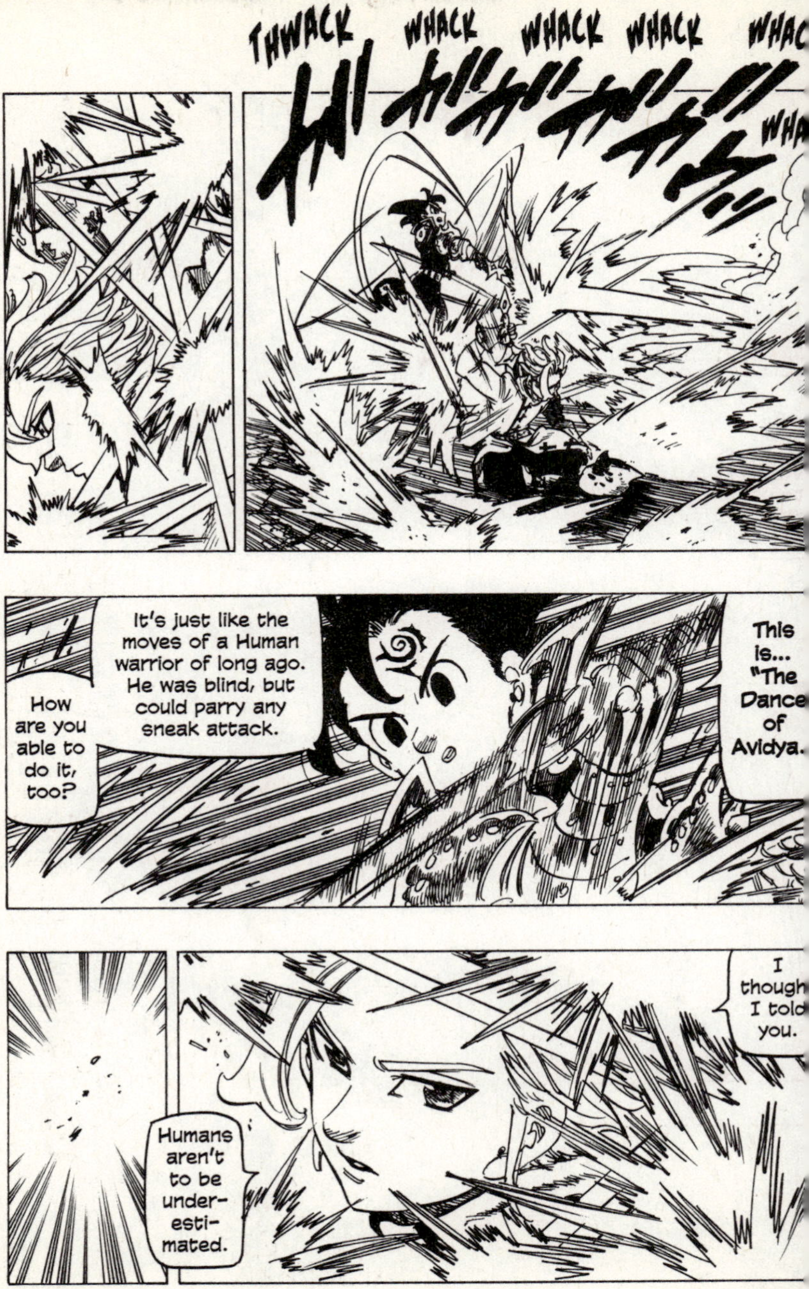

THWACK WHACK WHACK WHACK WHAC
WHA
This is... "The Dance of Avidya.
It's just like the moves of a Human warrior of long ago. He was blind, but could parry any sneak attack.
How are you able to do it, too?
I though I told you.
Humans aren't to be under-esti-mated.

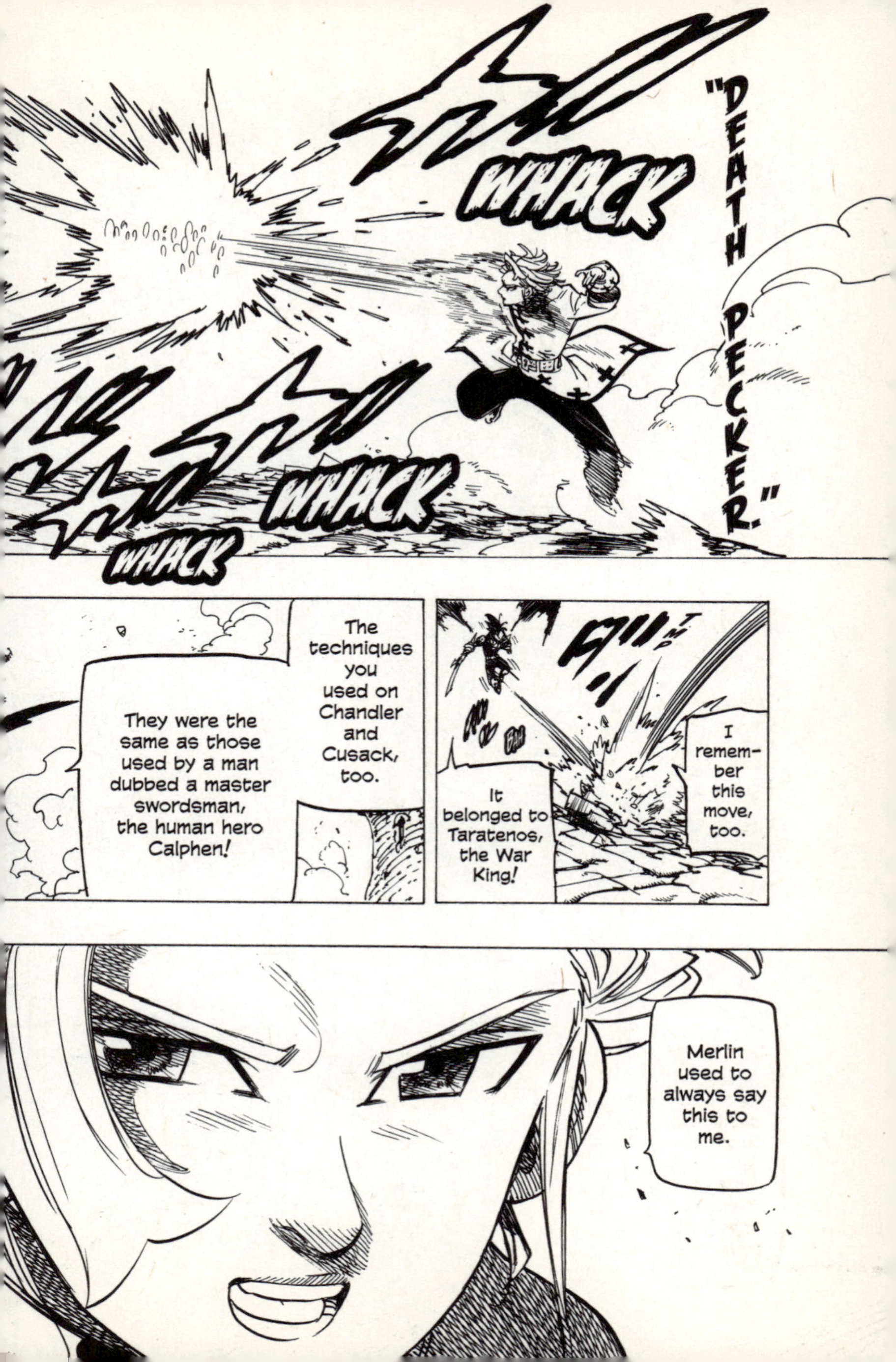
"DEATH PECKER."
WHACK
WHACK
WHACK
I remember this move, too.
It belonged to Taratenos, the War King!
The techniques you used on Chandler and Cusack, too.
They were the same as those used by a man dubbed a master swordsman, the human hero Calphen!
Merlin used to always say this to me.

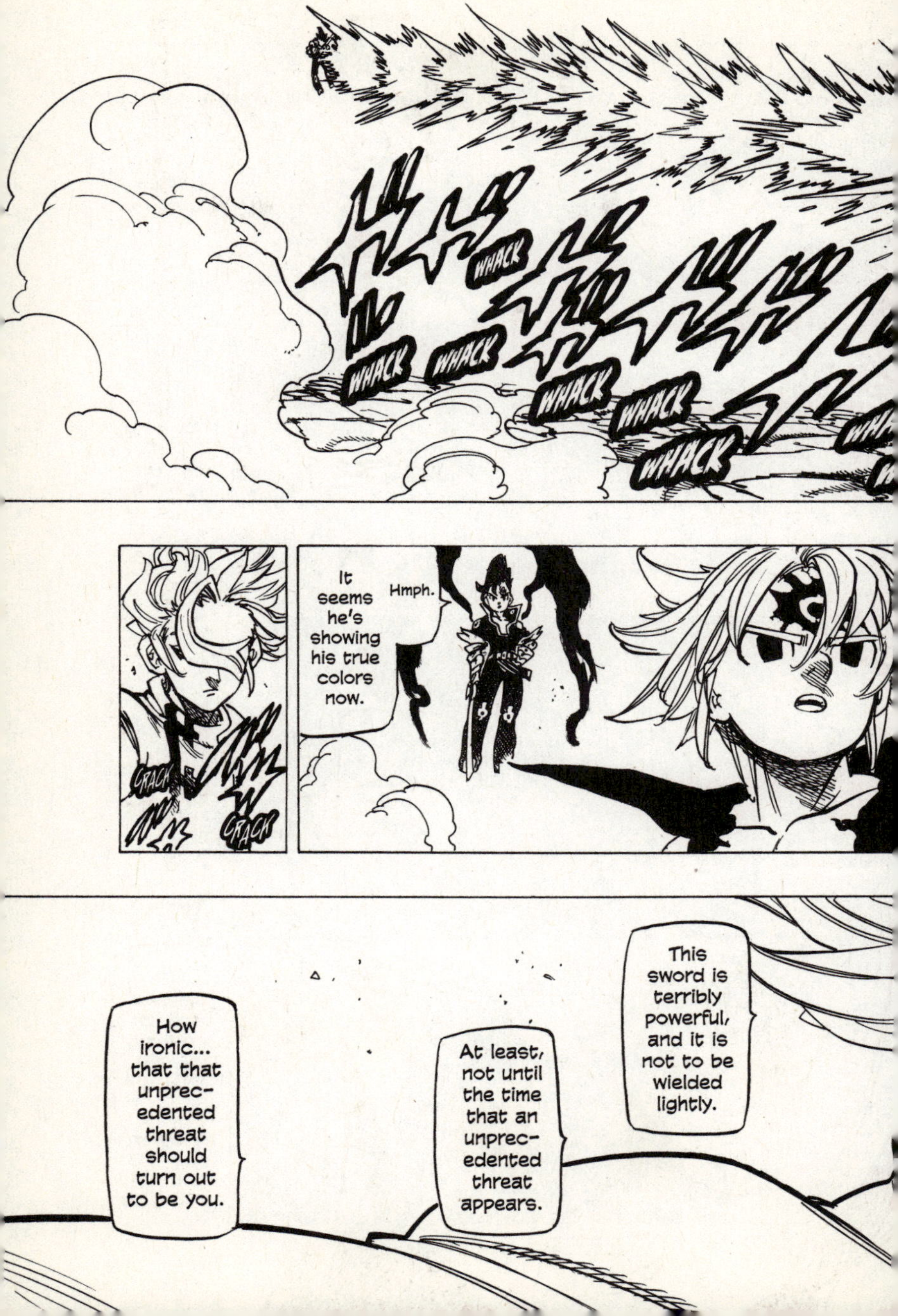
WHACK
WHACK
WHACK
WHACK
WHACK
WHACK
WHACK
Hmph.
It seems he's showing his true colors now.
CRACK
CRACK
This sword is terribly powerful, and it is not to be wielded lightly.
At least, not until the time that an unprecedented threat appears.
How ironic... that that unprecedented threat should turn out to be you.

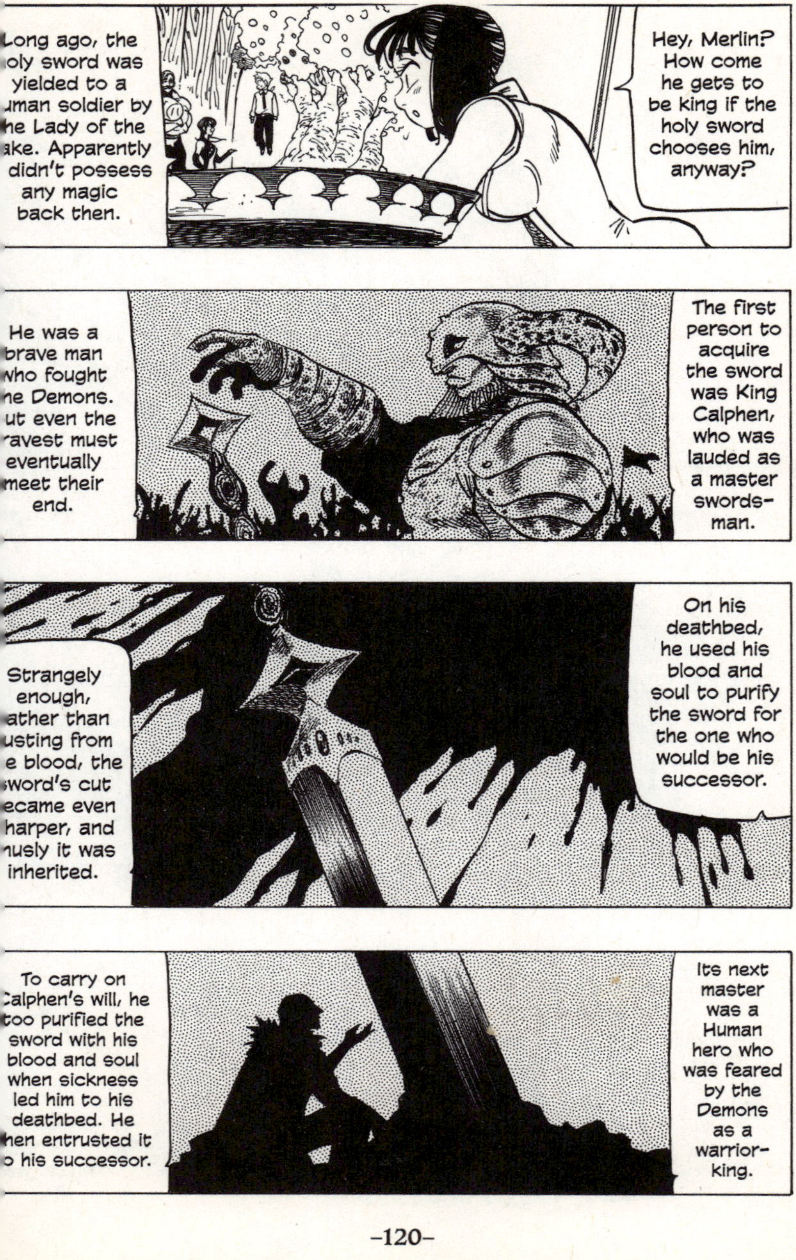
Hey, Merlin? How come he gets to be king if the holy sword chooses him, anyway?
Long ago, the oly sword was yielded to a uman soldier by he Lady of the ake. Apparently didn't possess any magic back then.
The first person to acquire the sword was King Calphen, who was lauded as a master swords-man.
He was a brave man who fought he Demons. ut even the ravest must eventually meet their end.
On his deathbed, he used his blood and soul to purify the sword for the one who would be his successor.
Strangely enough, ather than usting from e blood, the word's cut ecame even harper, and hus it was inherited.
Its next master was a Human hero who was feared by the Demons as a warrior-king.
To carry on Calphen's will, he too purified the sword with his blood and soul when sickness led him to his deathbed. He hen entrusted it o his successor.

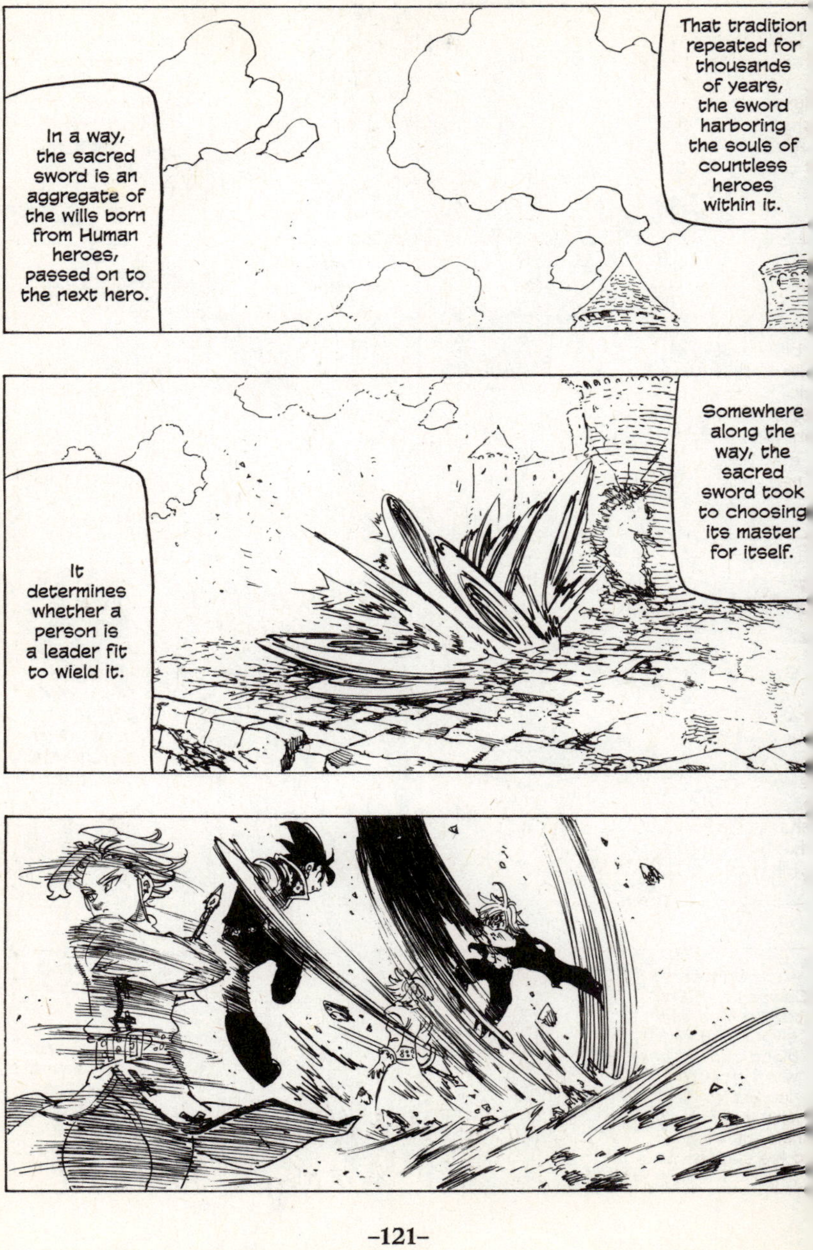
That tradition repeated for thousands of years, the sword harboring the souls of countless heroes within it.
In a way, the sacred sword is an aggregate of the wills born from Human heroes, passed on to the next hero.
Somewhere along the way, the sacred sword took to choosing its master for itself.
It determines whether a person is a leader fit to wield it.

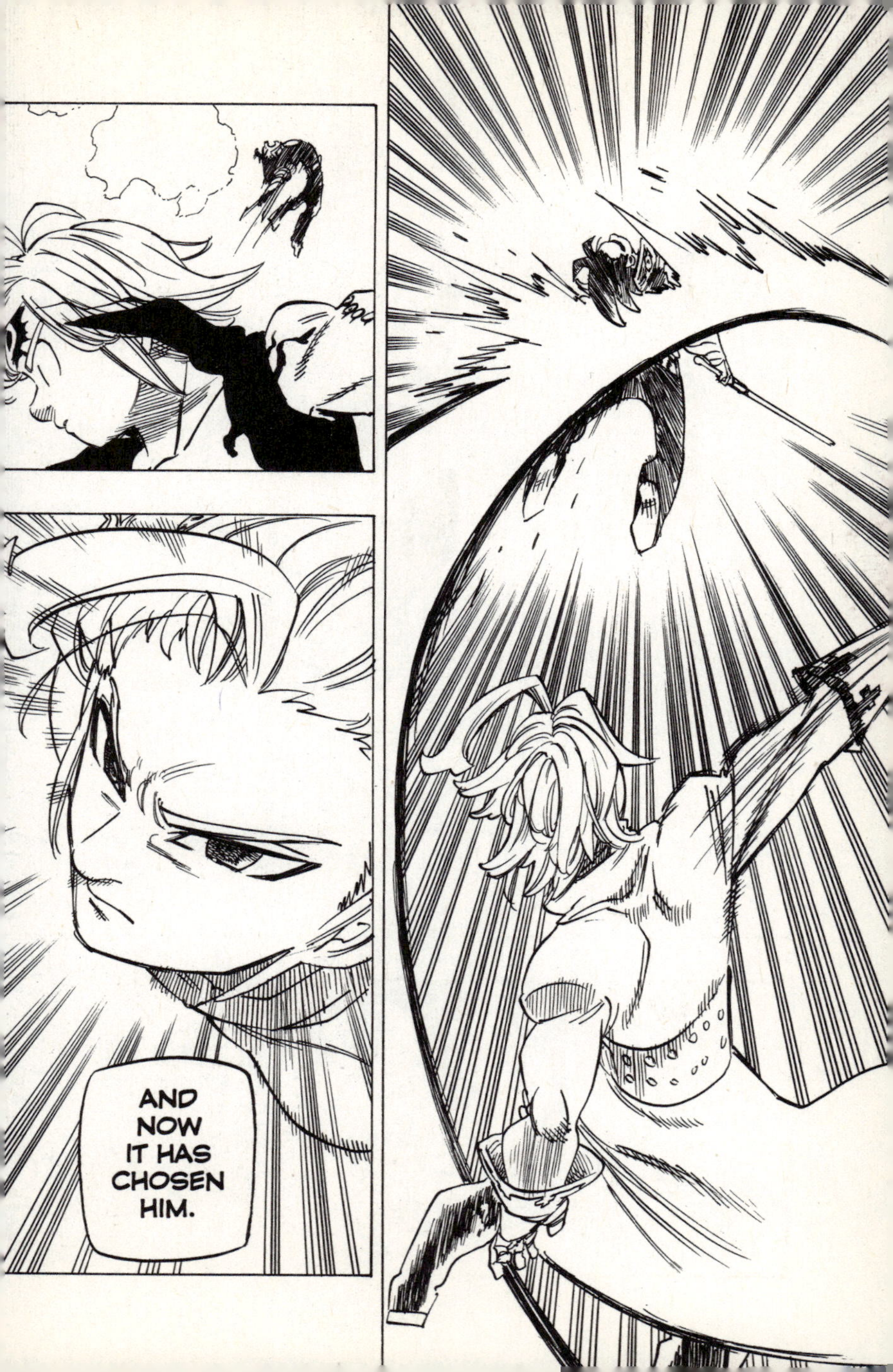
AND NOW IT HAS CHOSEN HIM.

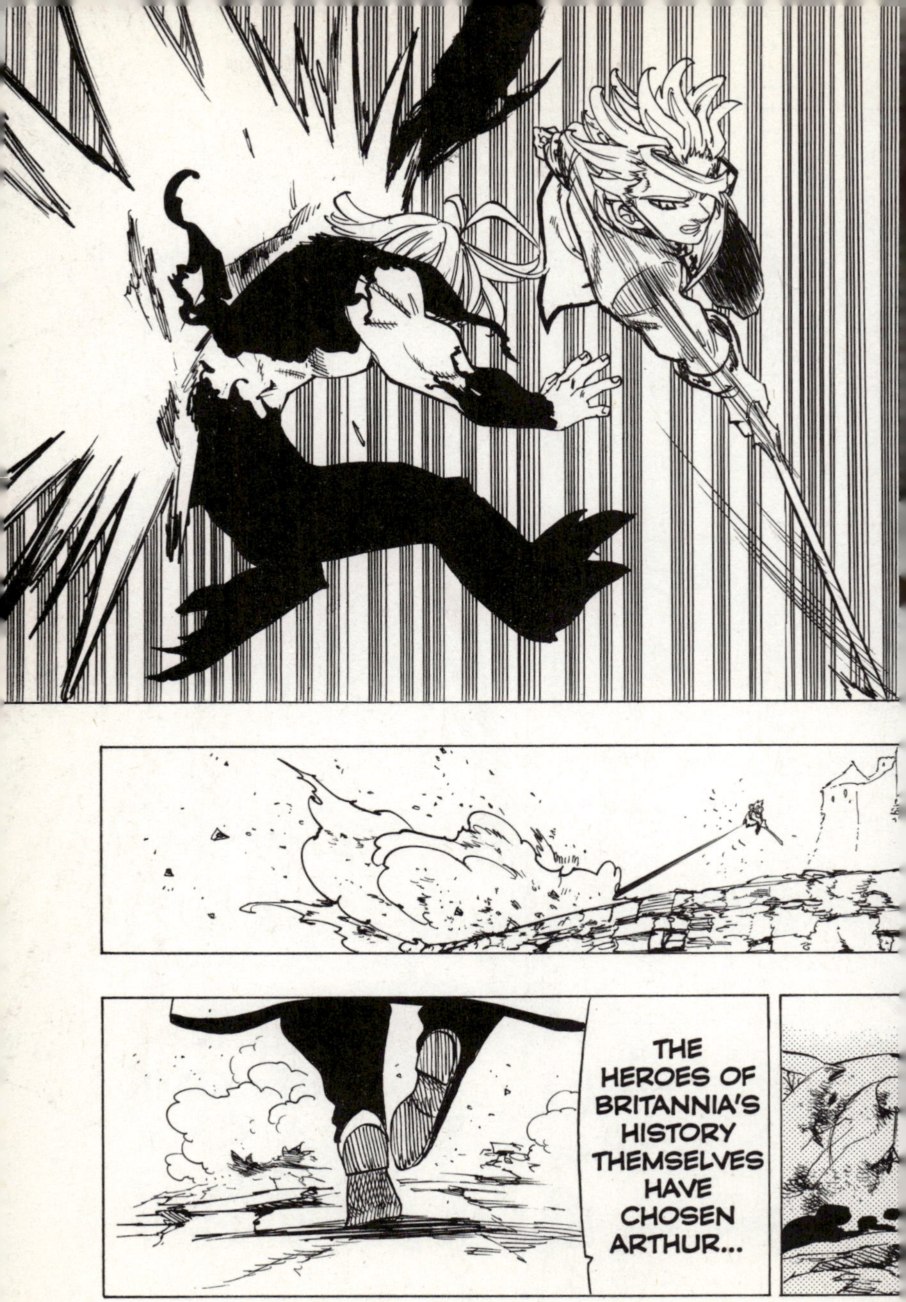
THE HEROES OF BRITANNIA'S HISTORY THEMSELVES HAVE CHOSEN ARTHUR...

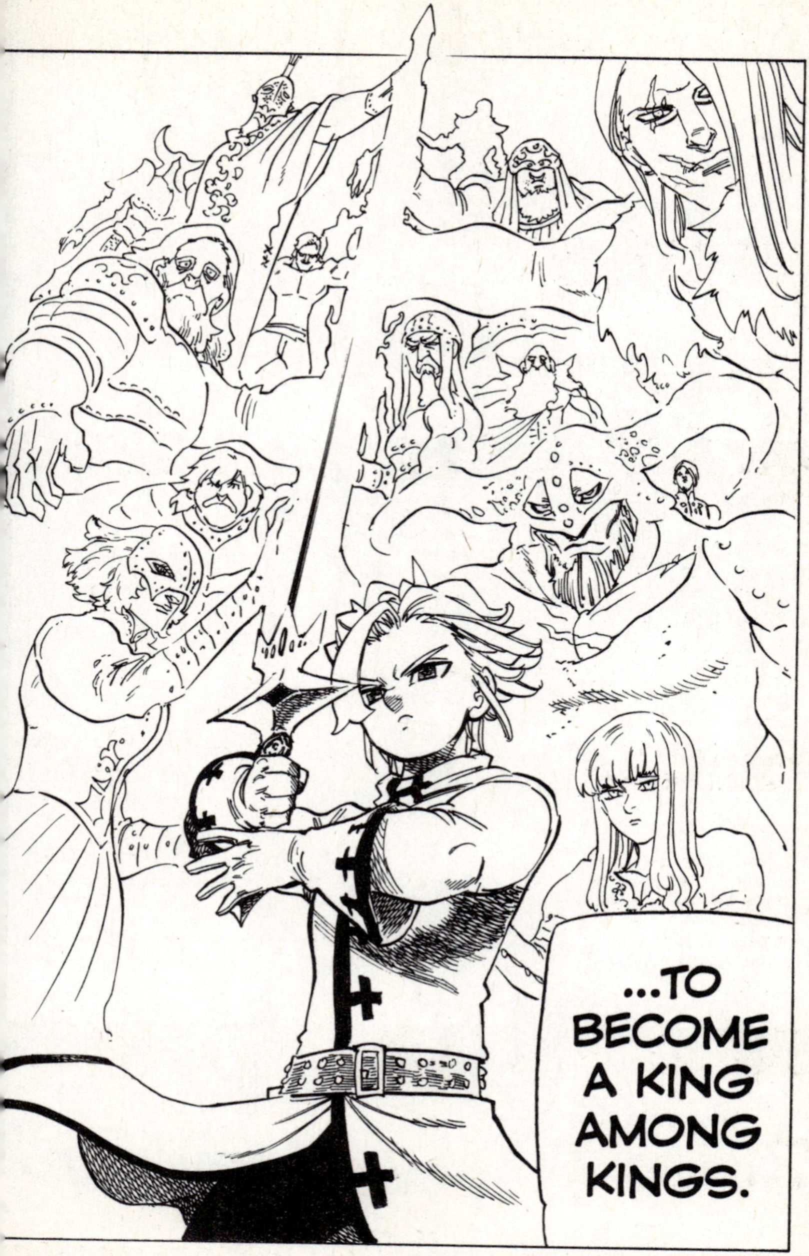
...TO BECOME A KING AMONG KINGS.

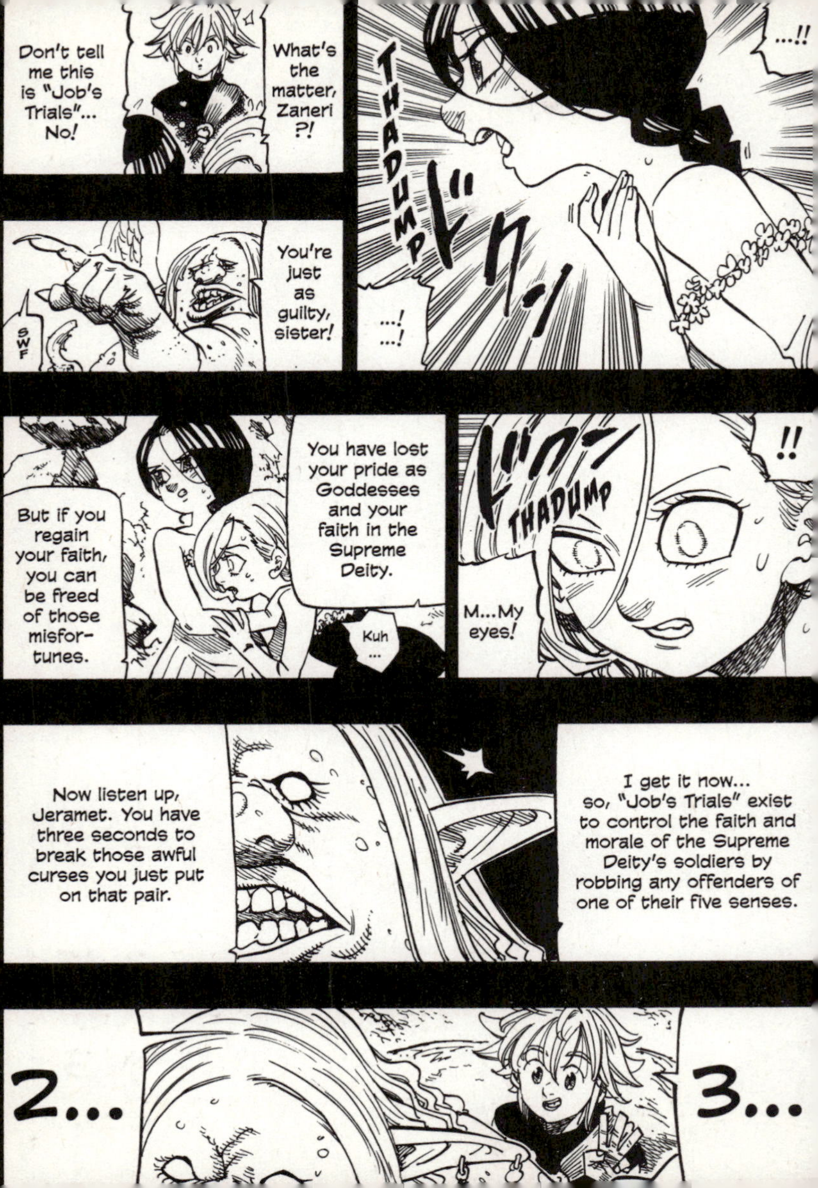
...!!
THADUMP
...!
...!
What's the matter, Zaneri?!
Don't tell me this is "Job's Trials"... No!
You're just as guilty, sister!
SWF
!!
THADUMP
M...My eyes!
You have lost your pride as Goddesses and your faith in the Supreme Deity.
Kuh...
But if you regain your faith, you can be freed of those misfortunes.
I get it now... so, "Job's Trials" exist to control the faith and morale of the Supreme Deity's soldiers by robbing any offenders of one of their five senses.
Now listen up, Jeramet. You have three seconds to break those awful curses you just put on that pair.
3...
2...

Chapter 256 - The Piercing Sacred Sword

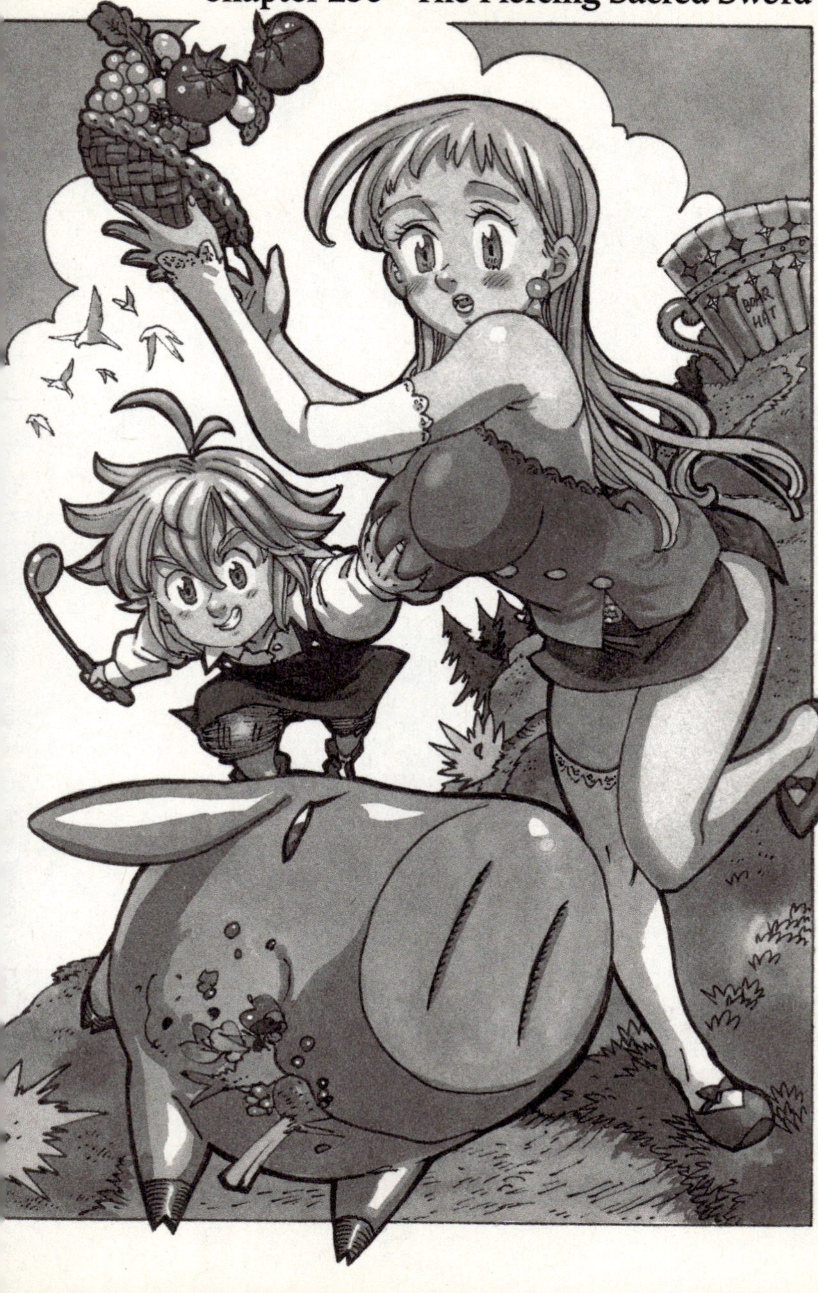

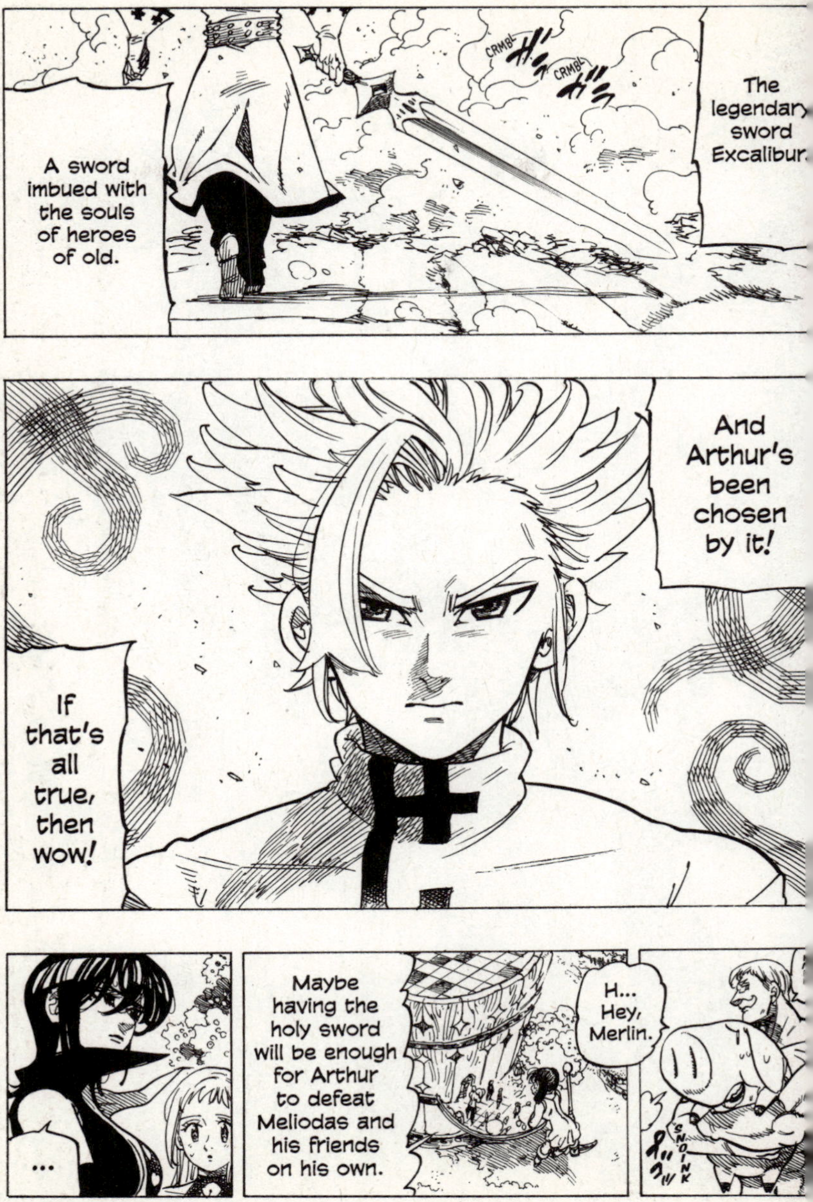
The legendary sword Excalibur.
CRMBL
CRMBL
A sword imbued with the souls of heroes of old.
And Arthur's been chosen by it!
If that's all true, then wow!
H... Hey, Merlin.
SNOINK
Maybe having the holy sword will be enough for Arthur to defeat Meliodas and his friends on his own.
...

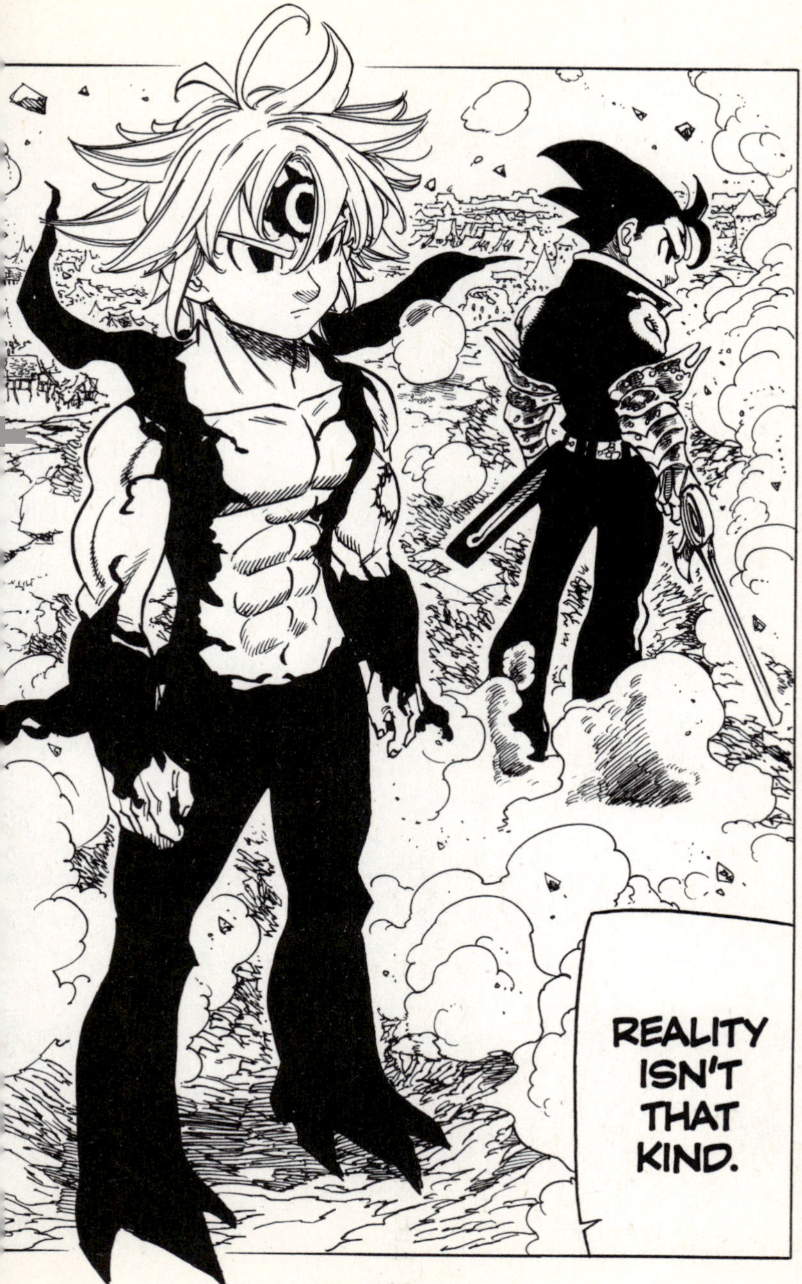
REALITY ISN'T THAT KIND.

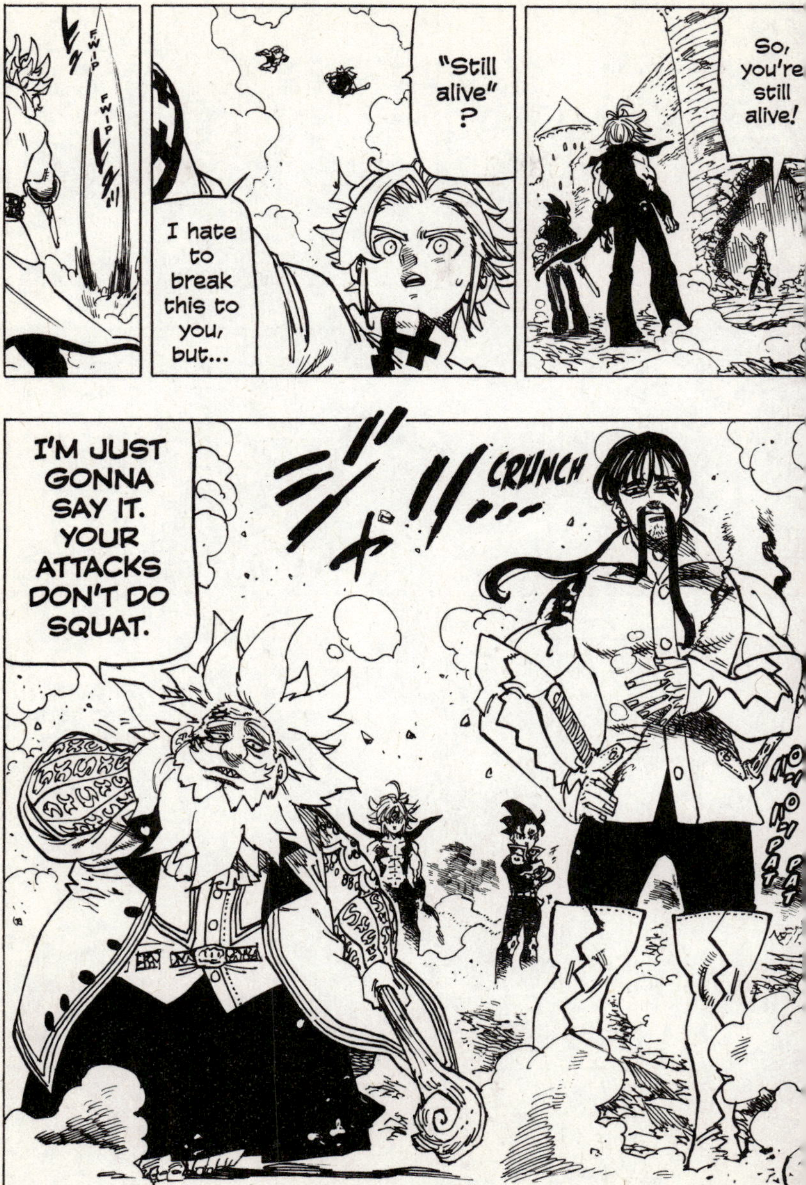
So, you're still alive!
"Still alive"?
I hate to break this to you, but...
FWIP FWIP
ジャリ…
CRUNCH
I'M JUST GONNA SAY IT. YOUR ATTACKS DON'T DO SQUAT.
PAT PAT

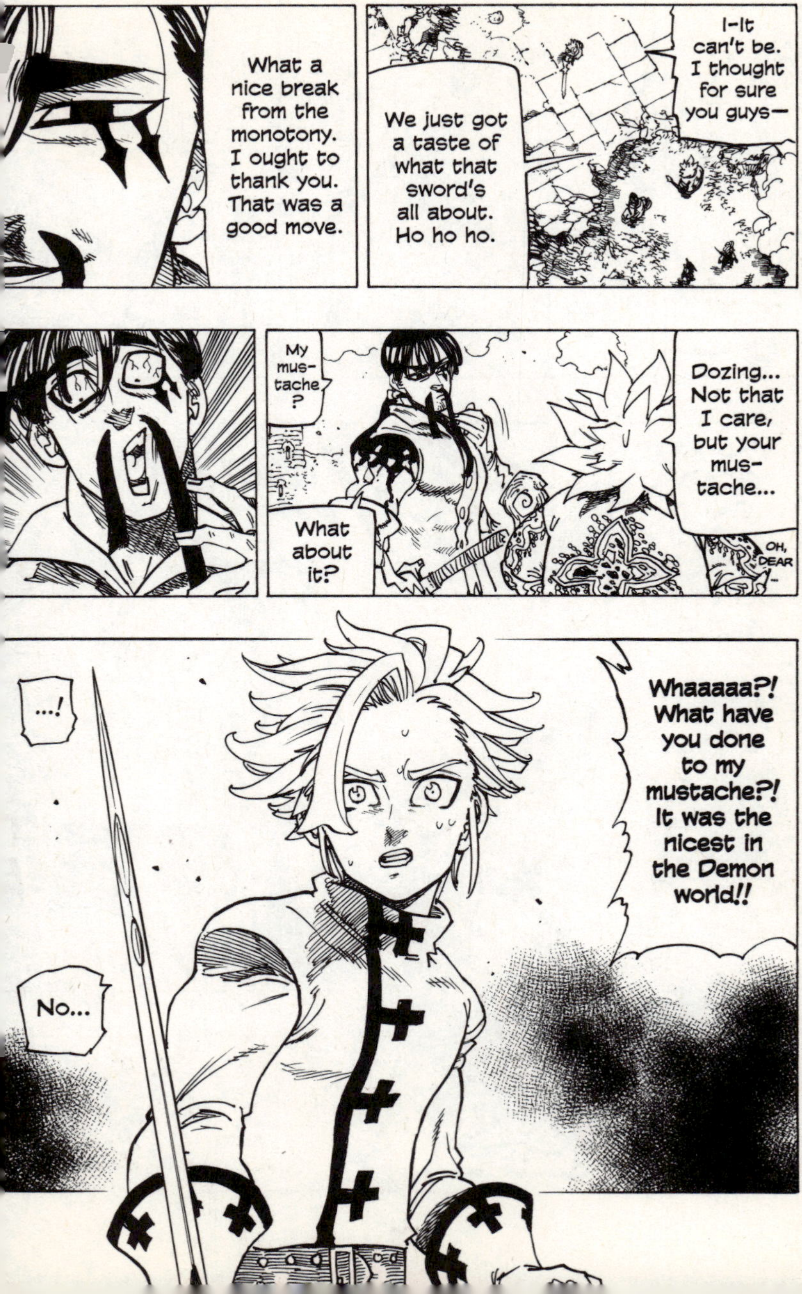
I-It can't be. I thought for sure you guys—
We just got a taste of what that sword's all about. Ho ho ho.
What a nice break from the monotony. I ought to thank you. That was a good move.
Dozing... Not that I care, but your mus-tache...
OH, DEAR...
My mus-tache?
What about it?
Whaaaaa?! What have you done to my mustache?! It was the nicest in the Demon world!!
...!
No...

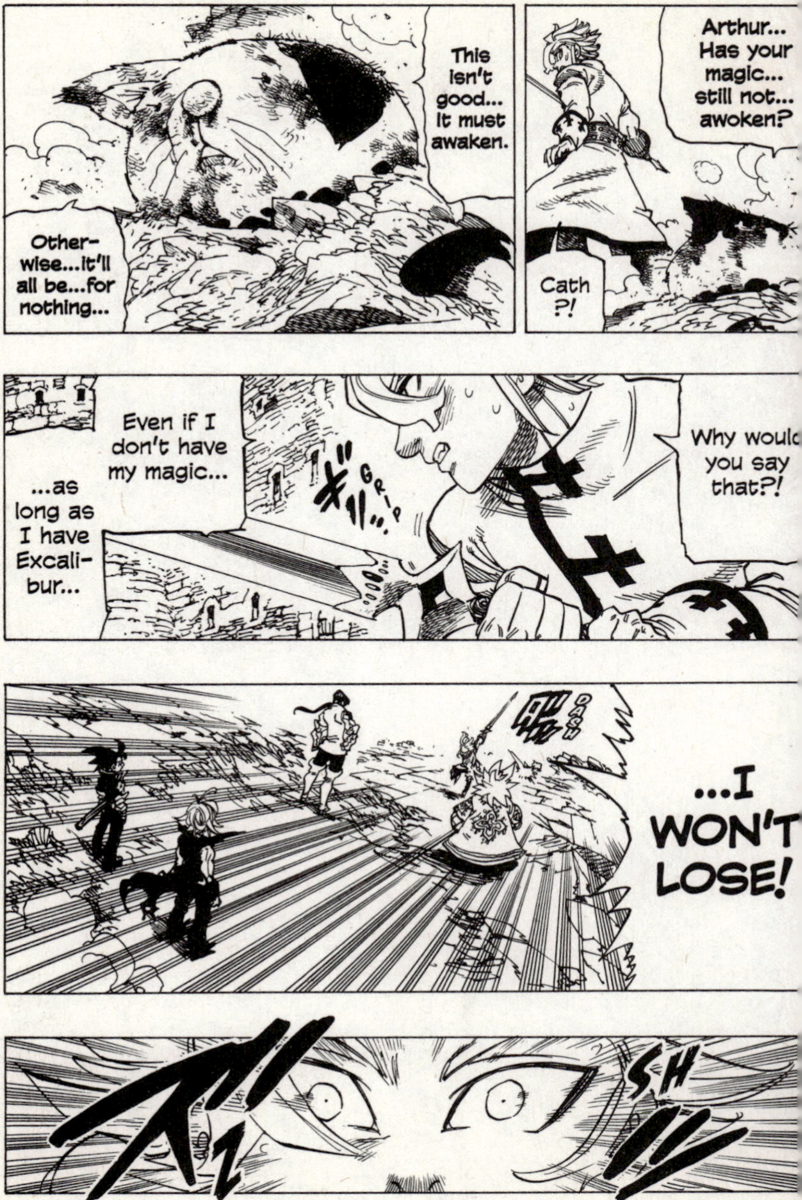
Arthur... Has your magic... still not... awoken?
Cath ?!
This isn't good... It must awaken.
Other-wise...it'll all be...for nothing...
Why woul
you say that?!
GRIP
Even if I don't have my magic...
...as long as I have Excali-bur...
...I WON'T LOSE!
DASH
SH

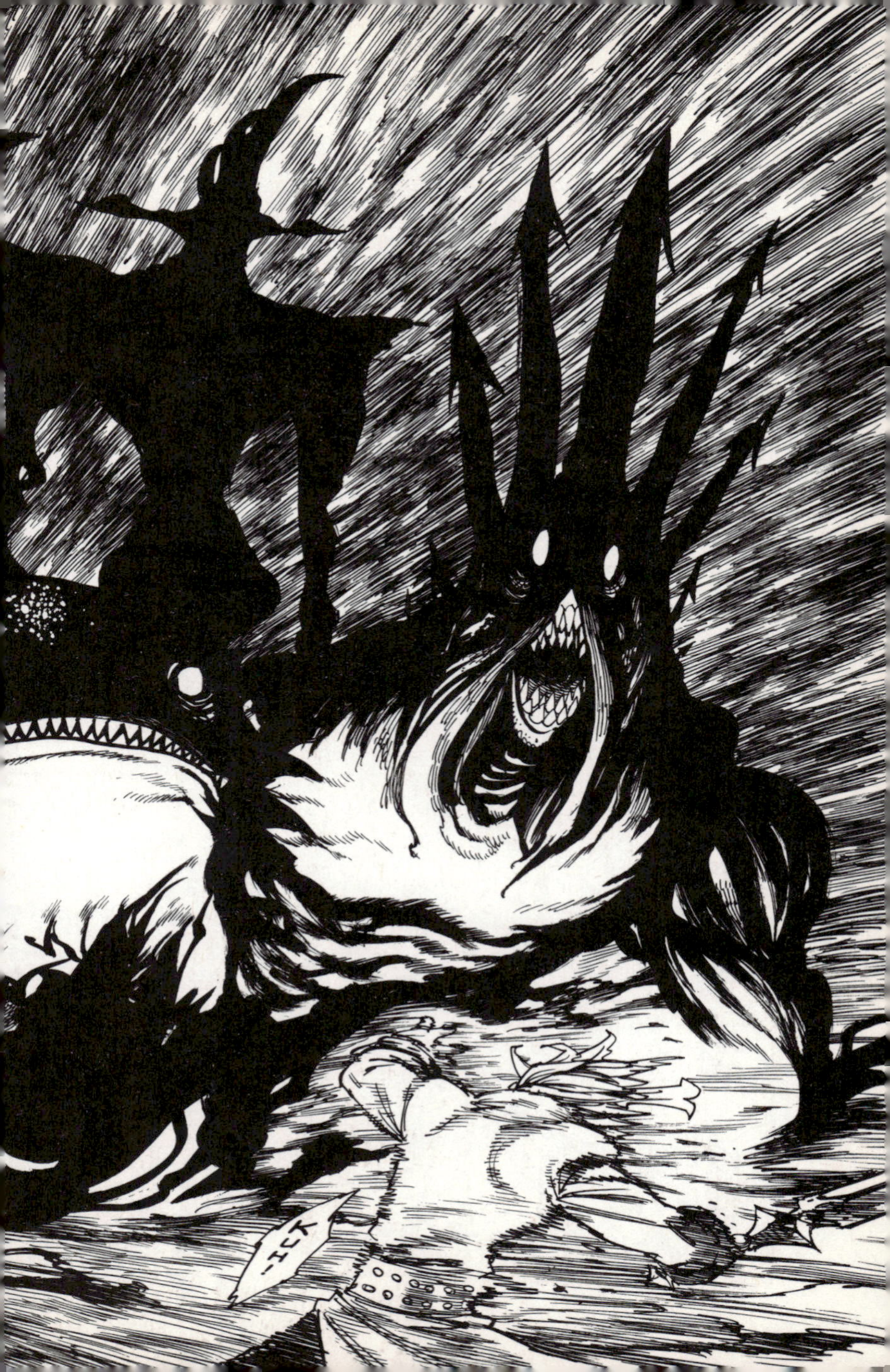
KUH!

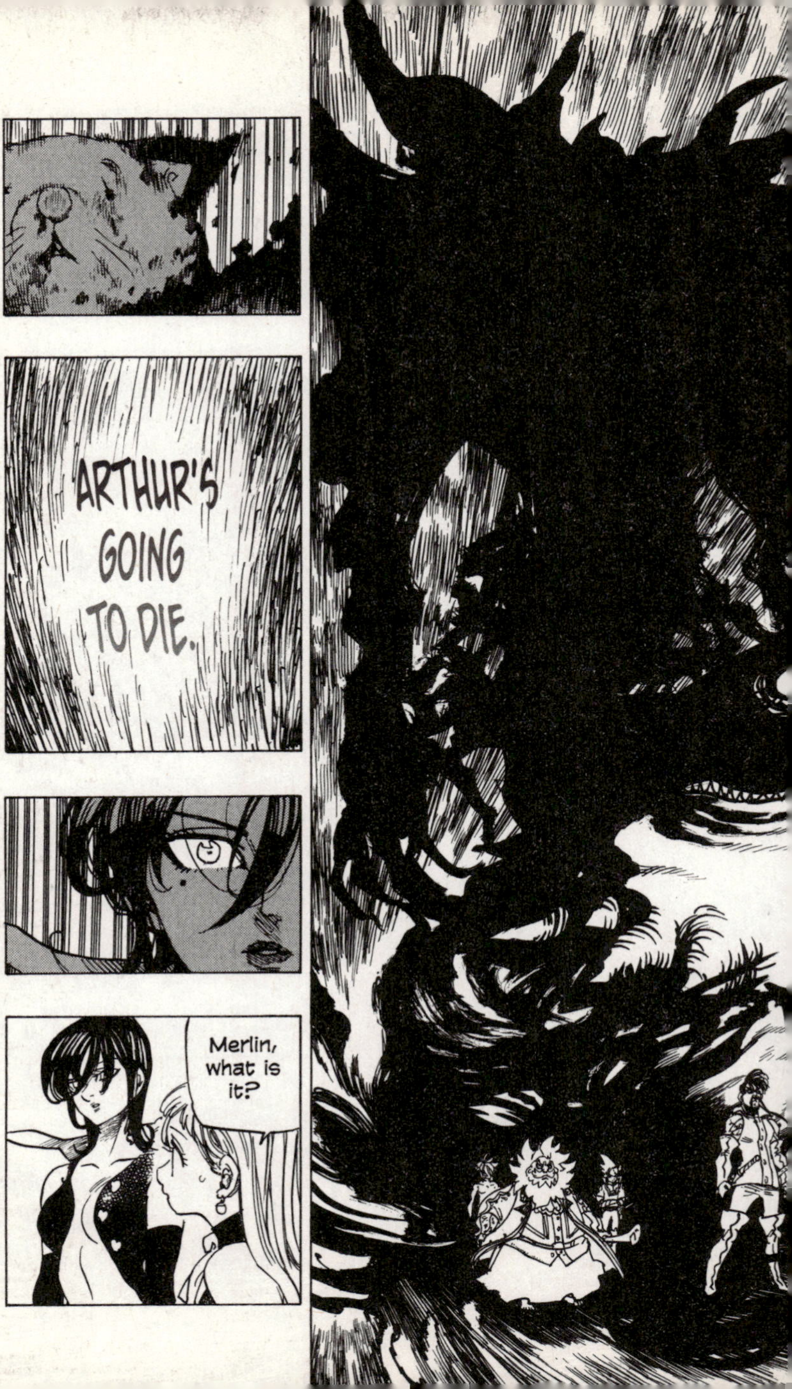
ARTHUR'S GOING TO DIE.
Merlin, what is it?

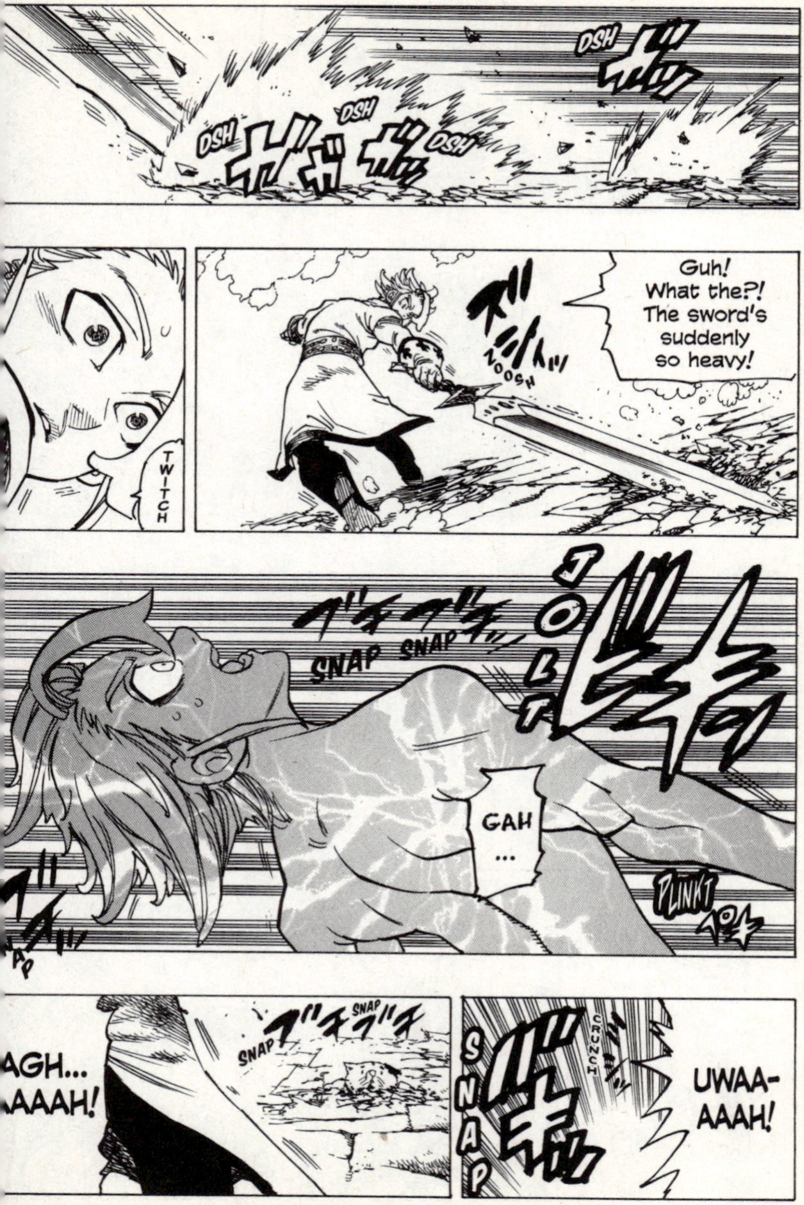
DSH
DSH
DSH
DSH
ZOOSH
Guh! What the?! The sword's suddenly so heavy!
TWITCH
JOLT
SNAP SNAP
GAH ...
PLINK!
AP
UWAA-AAAH!
CRUNCH
SNAP
SNAP
SNAP
AGH...
AAAH!

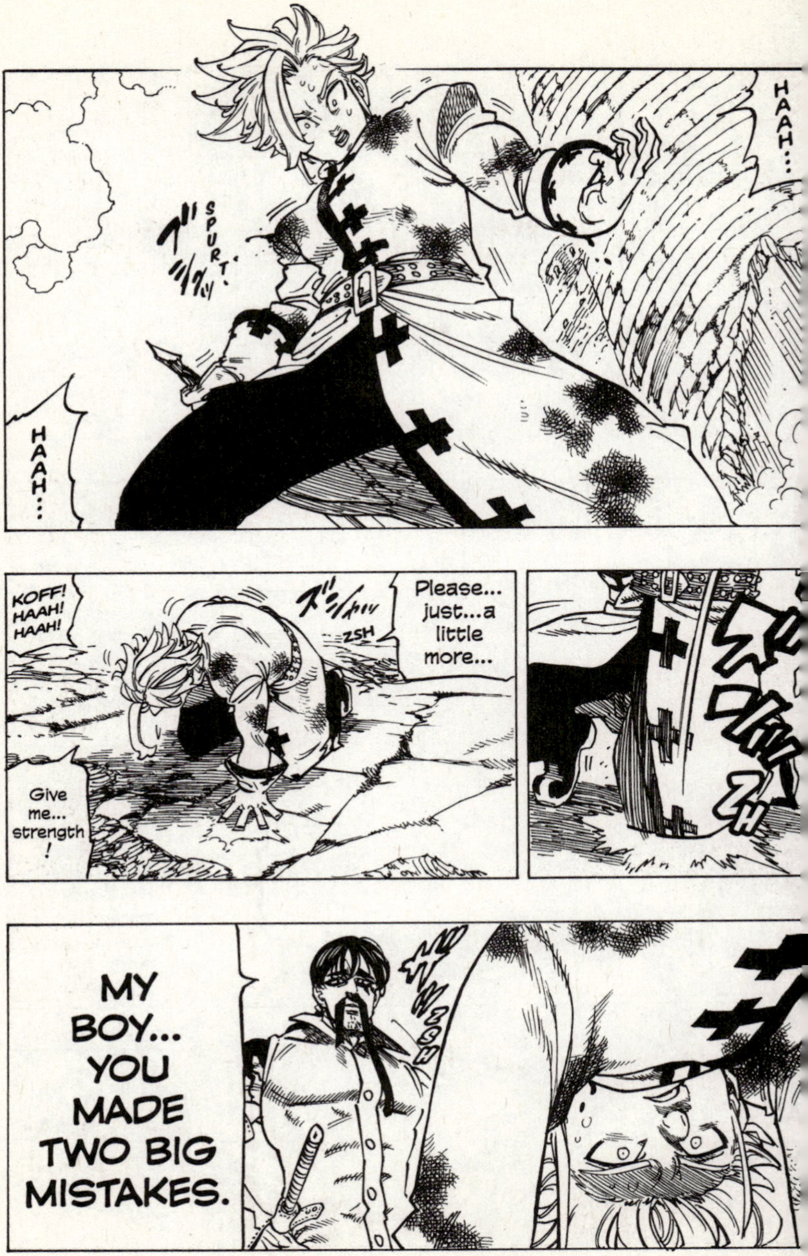
HAAAH...
SPURT
HAAH...
ZH
Please... just...a little more...
ZSH
KOFF! HAAH! HAAH!
Give me... strength!
MY BOY... YOU MADE TWO BIG MISTAKES.

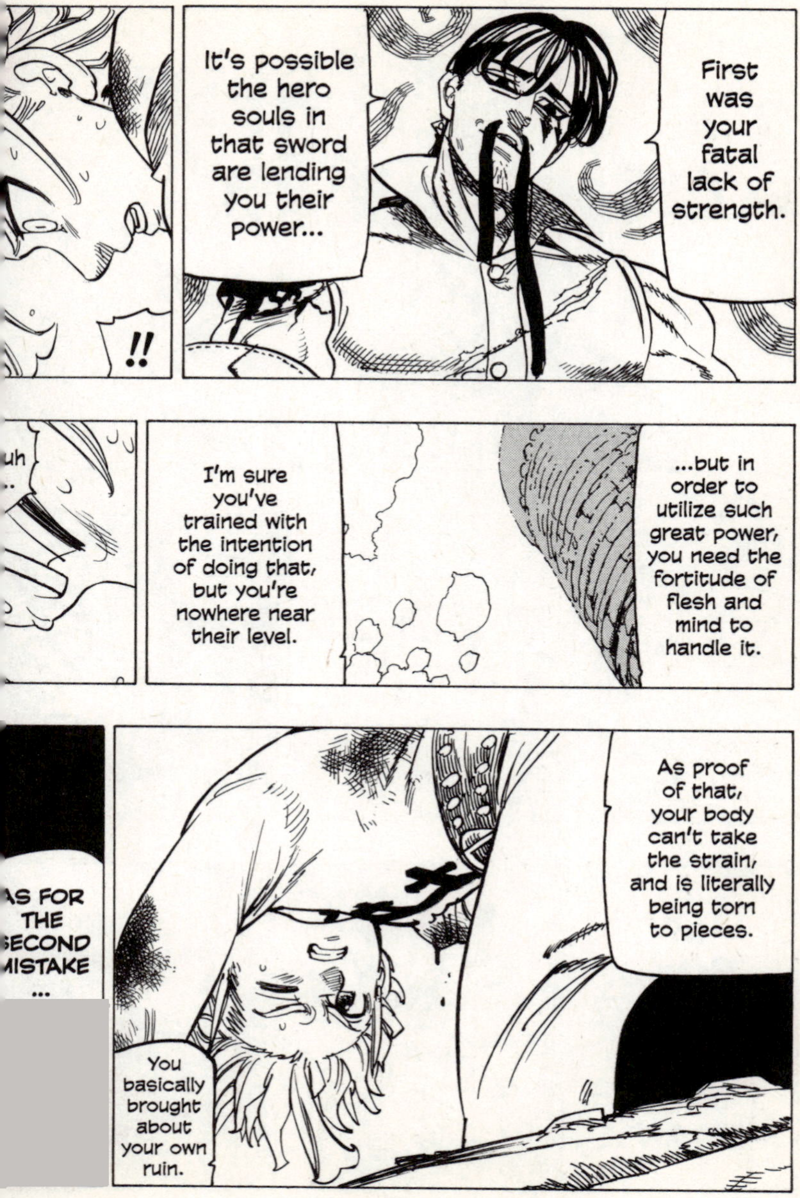
First was your fatal lack of strength.
It's possible the hero souls in that sword are lending you their power...
!!
...but in order to utilize such great power, you need the fortitude of flesh and mind to handle it.
I'm sure you've trained with the intention of doing that, but you're nowhere near their level.
uh ...
As proof of that, your body can't take the strain, and is literally being torn to pieces.
You basically brought about your own ruin.
AS FOR THE SECOND MISTAKE ...

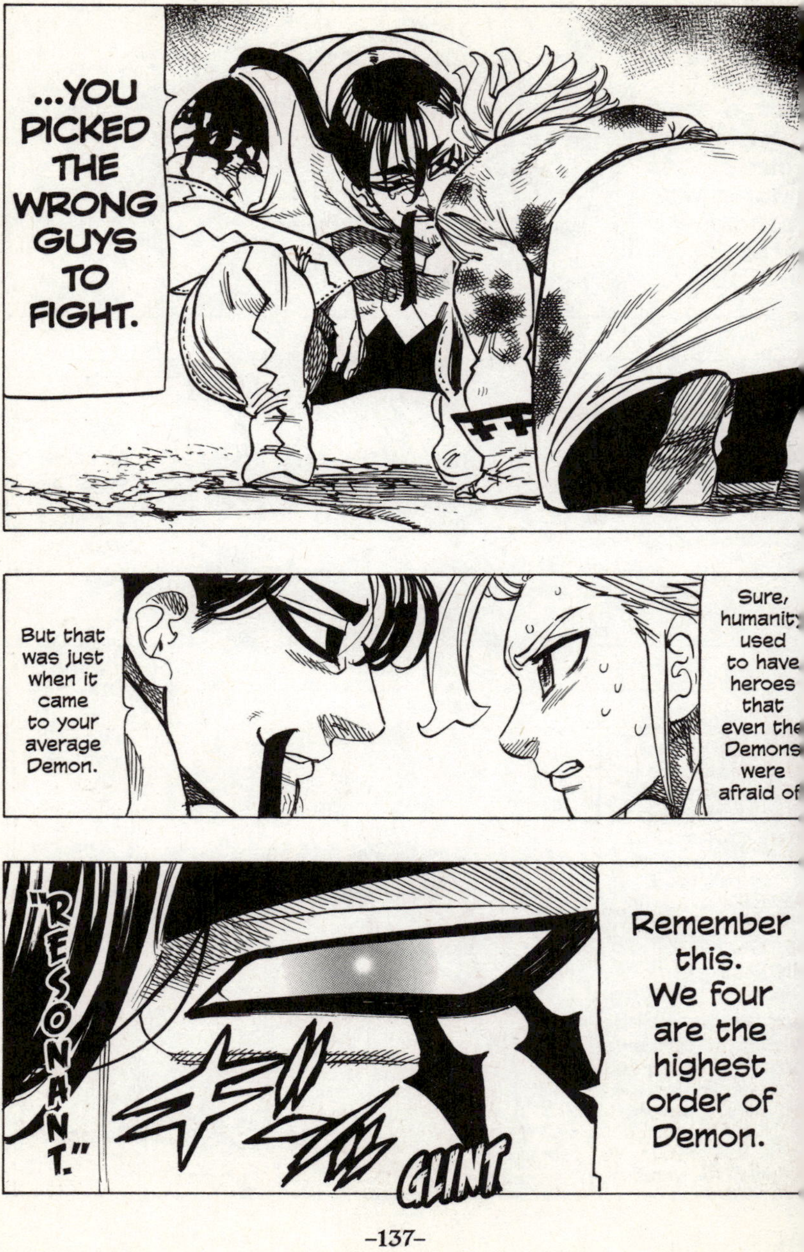
...YOU PICKED THE WRONG GUYS TO FIGHT.
Sure, humanity used to have heroes that even the Demons were afraid of
But that was just when it came to your average Demon.
Remember this. We four are the highest order of Demon.
"RESONANT."
GLINT

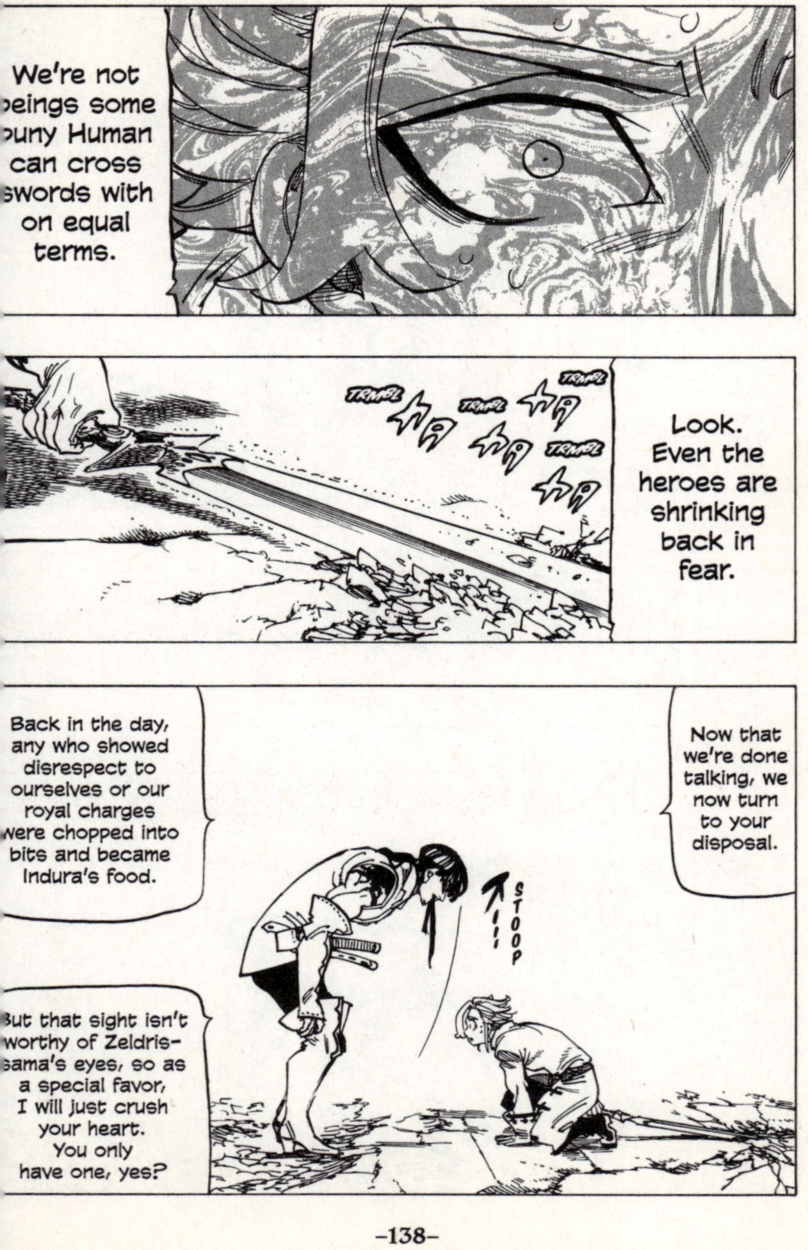

We're not eings some uny Human can cross swords with on equal terms.
TRMBL
TRMBL
TRMBL
TRMBL
Look. Even the heroes are shrinking back in fear.
Now that we're done talking, we now turn to your disposal.
Back in the day, any who showed disrespect to ourselves or our royal charges were chopped into bits and became Indura's food.
STOOP
ut that sight isn't worthy of Zeldris-sama's eyes, so as a special favor, I will just crush your heart. You only have one, yes?

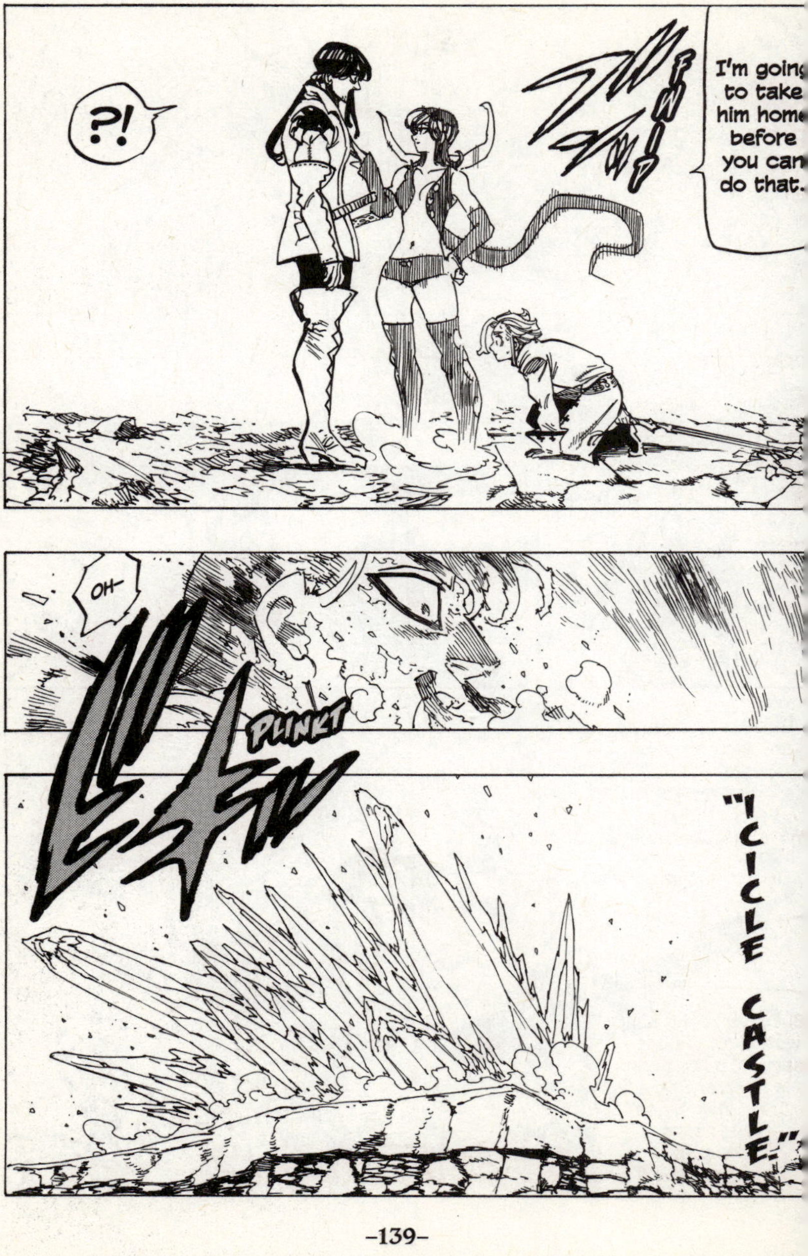
I'm going to take him home before you can do that.
FWIP
?!
OH-
PLINKT
"ICICLE CASTLE."

YOU!!

PLICK
PLACK *PLICK*

...!!

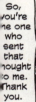

So, you're the one who sent that thought to me. Thank you.

BOUNCE

BOUNCE

You did well to stay alive, Arthur.

SHATTER

MERLIN!!

Hand over the Commandment of "Faith."

SHATTER

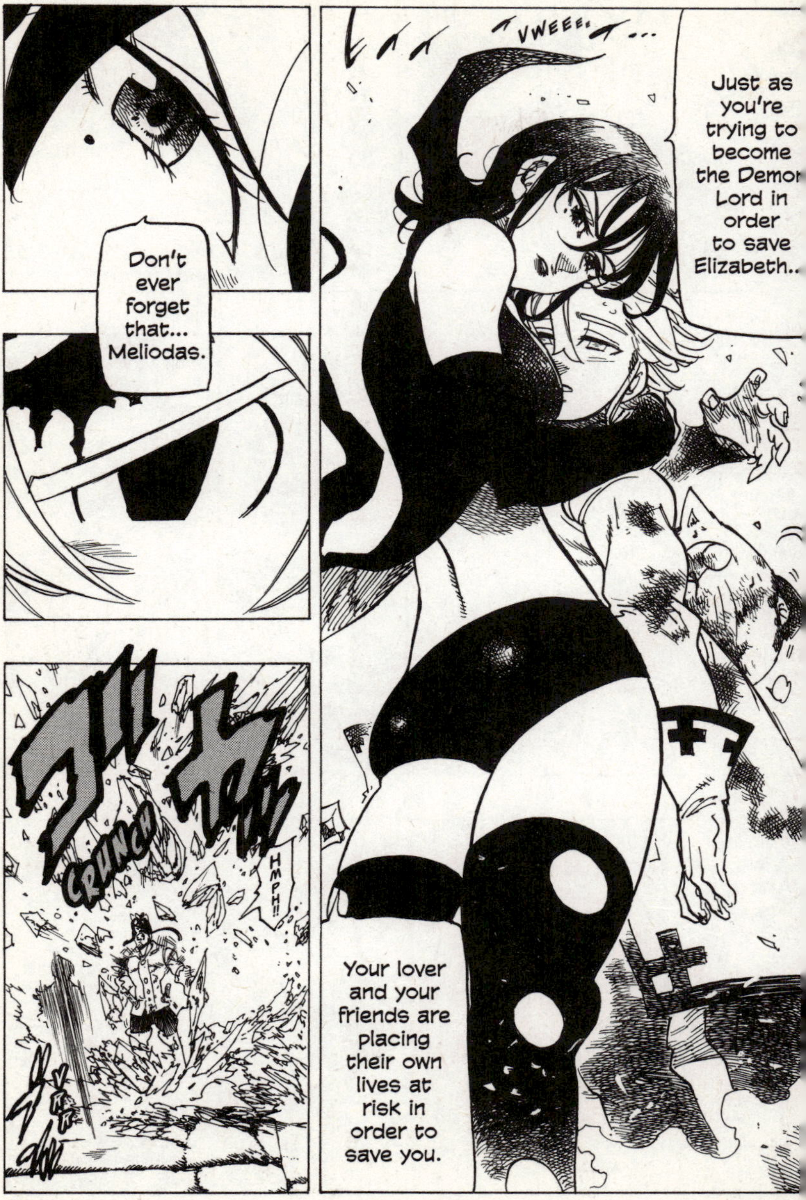
VWEEE...
Just as you're trying to become the Demon Lord in order to save Elizabeth...
Your lover and your friends are placing their own lives at risk in order to save you.
Don't ever forget that... Meliodas.
CRUNCH
HMPH!!

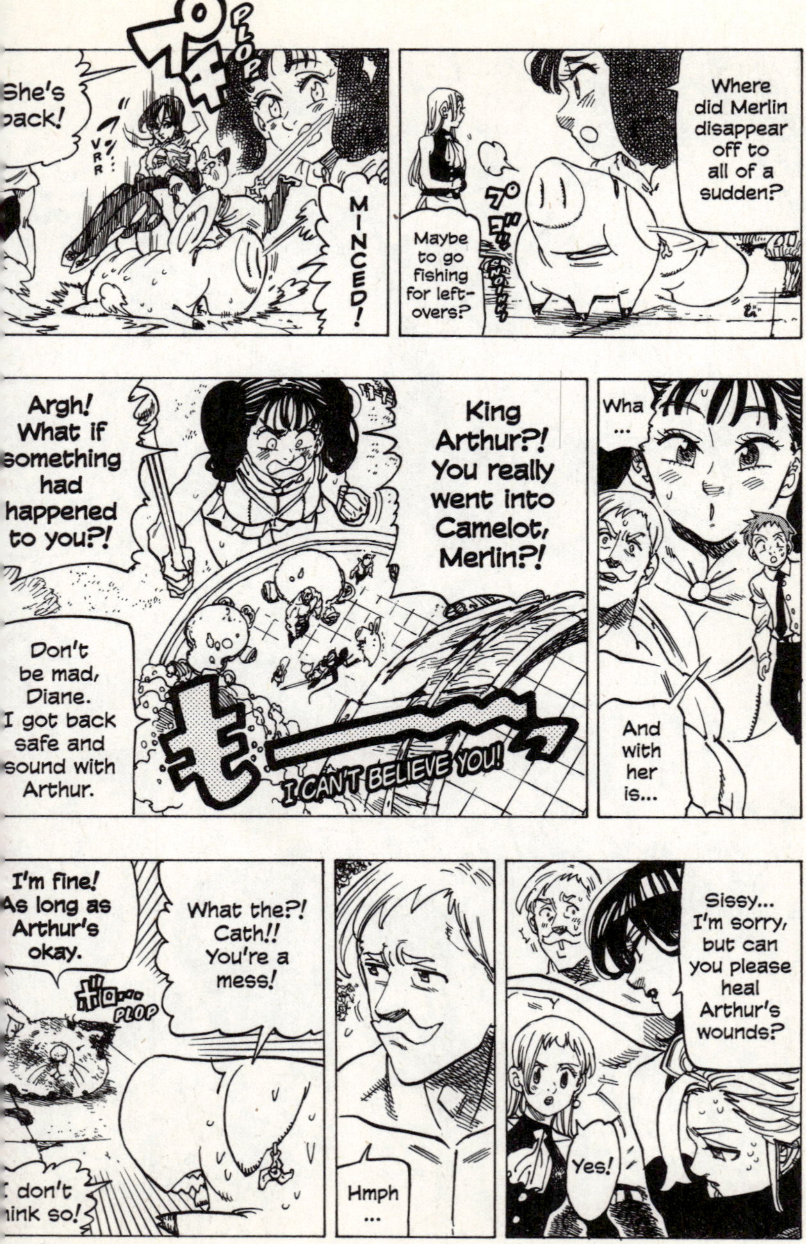
Where did Merlin disappear off to all of a sudden?
Maybe to go fishing for left-overs?
OINK
She's back!
VRR
PLOP
MINCED!
Wha...
And with her is...
King Arthur?! You really went into Camelot, Merlin?!
Argh! What if something had happened to you?!
Don't be mad, Diane. I got back safe and sound with Arthur.
I CAN'T BELIEVE YOU!
Sissy... I'm sorry, but can you please heal Arthur's wounds?
Yes!
Hmph...
What the?! Cath!! You're a mess!
I'm fine! As long as Arthur's okay.
PLOP
don't hink so!

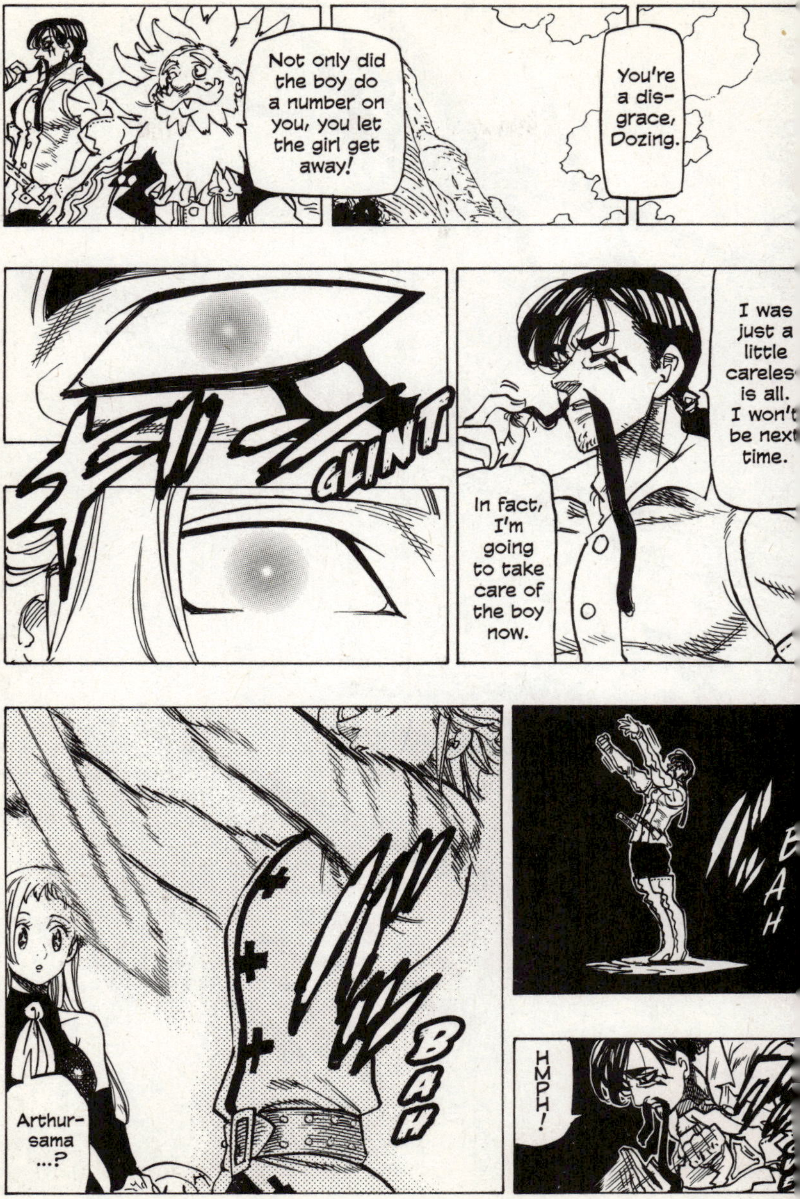
You're a disgrace, Dozing.
Not only did the boy do a number on you, you let the girl get away!
I was just a little careles is all. I won't be next time.
In fact, I'm going to take care of the boy now.
GLINT
BAH
HMPH!
BAH
Arthur-sama ...?

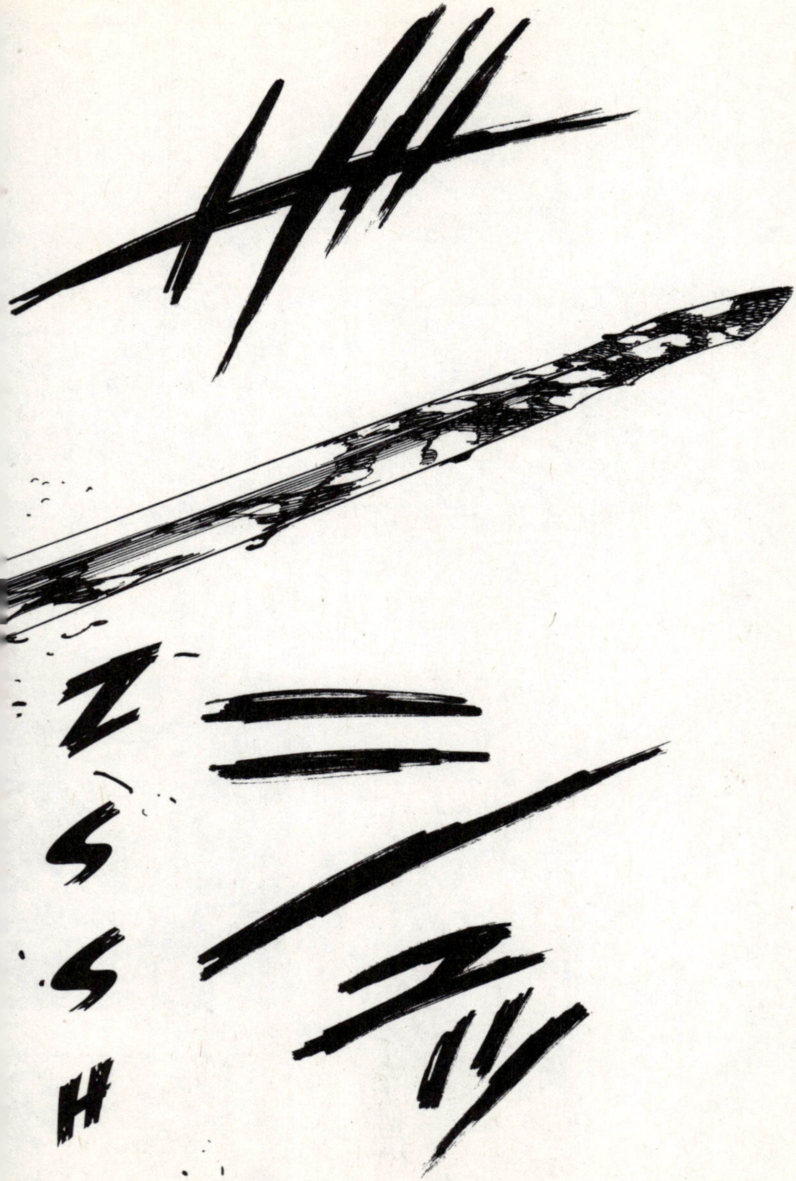
ZSSH

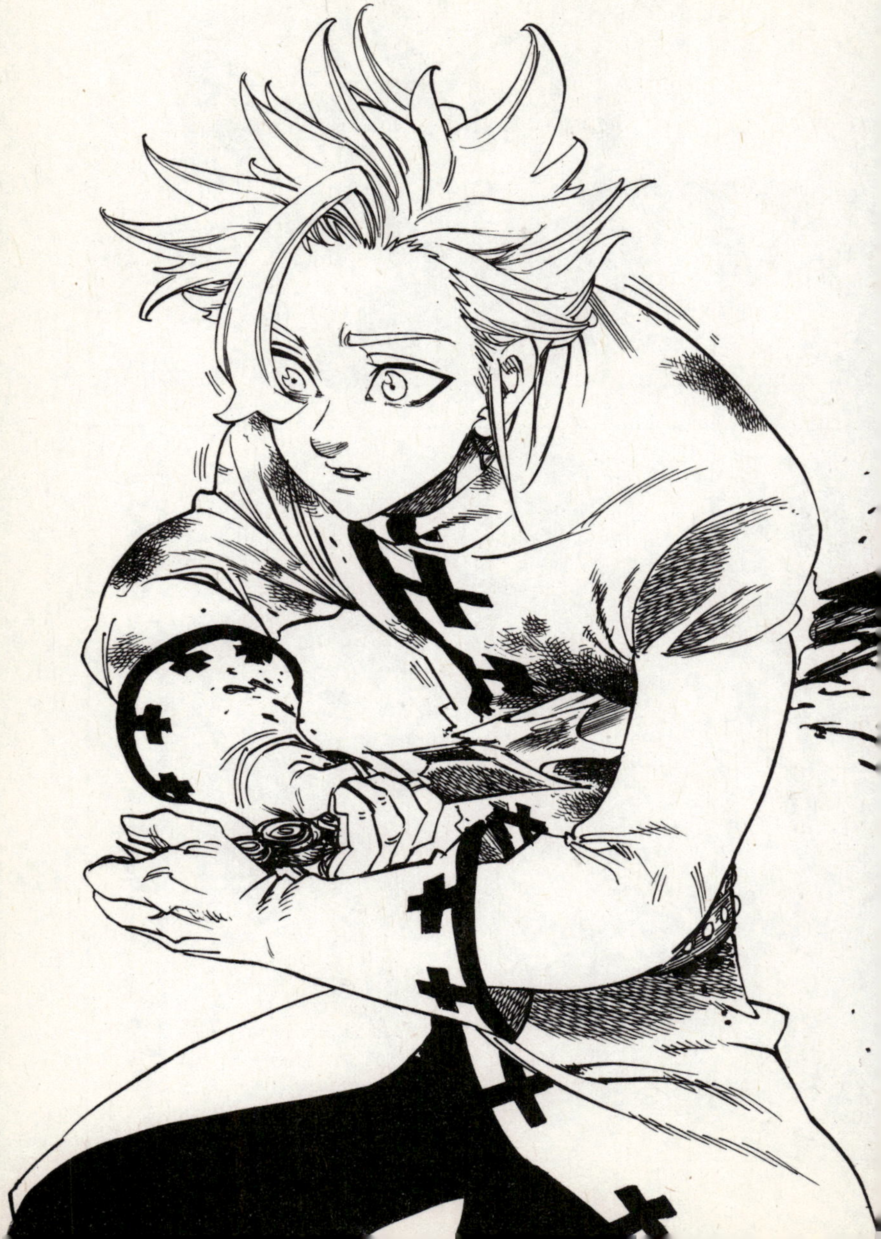

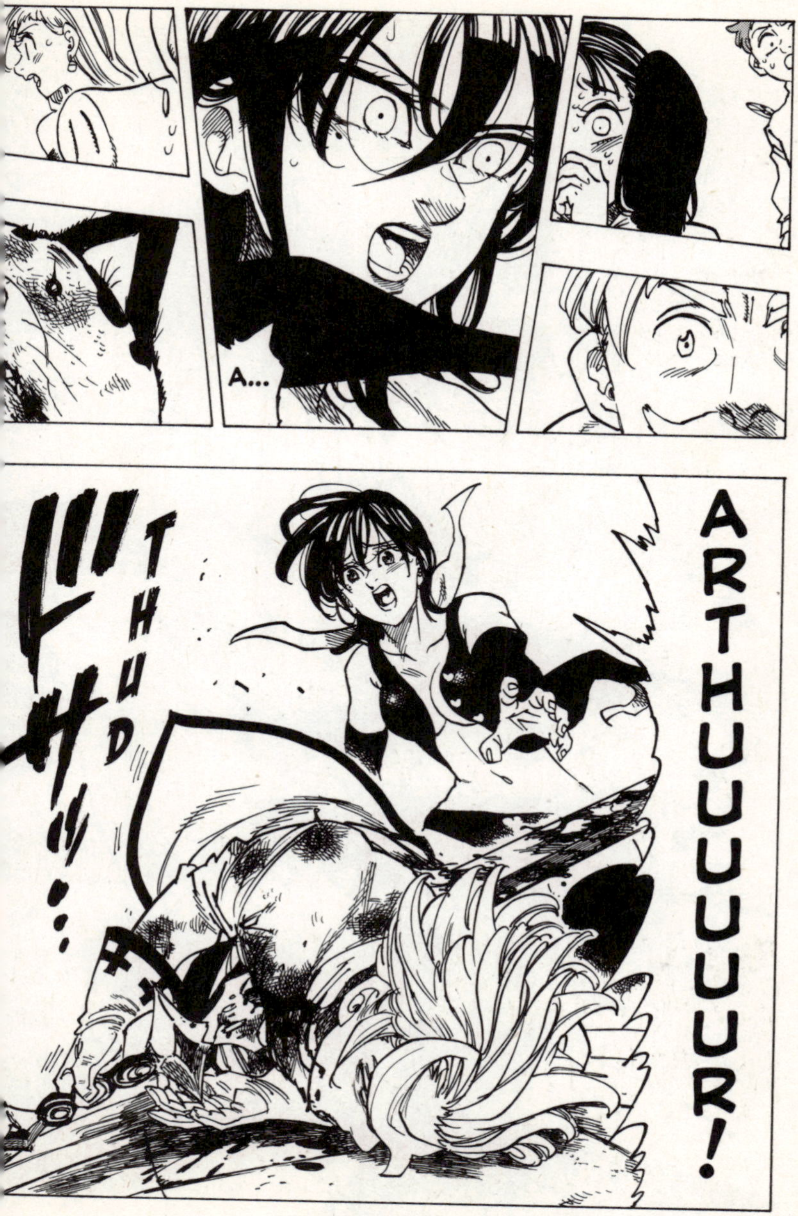
A...
ARTHUUUUUR!
THUD

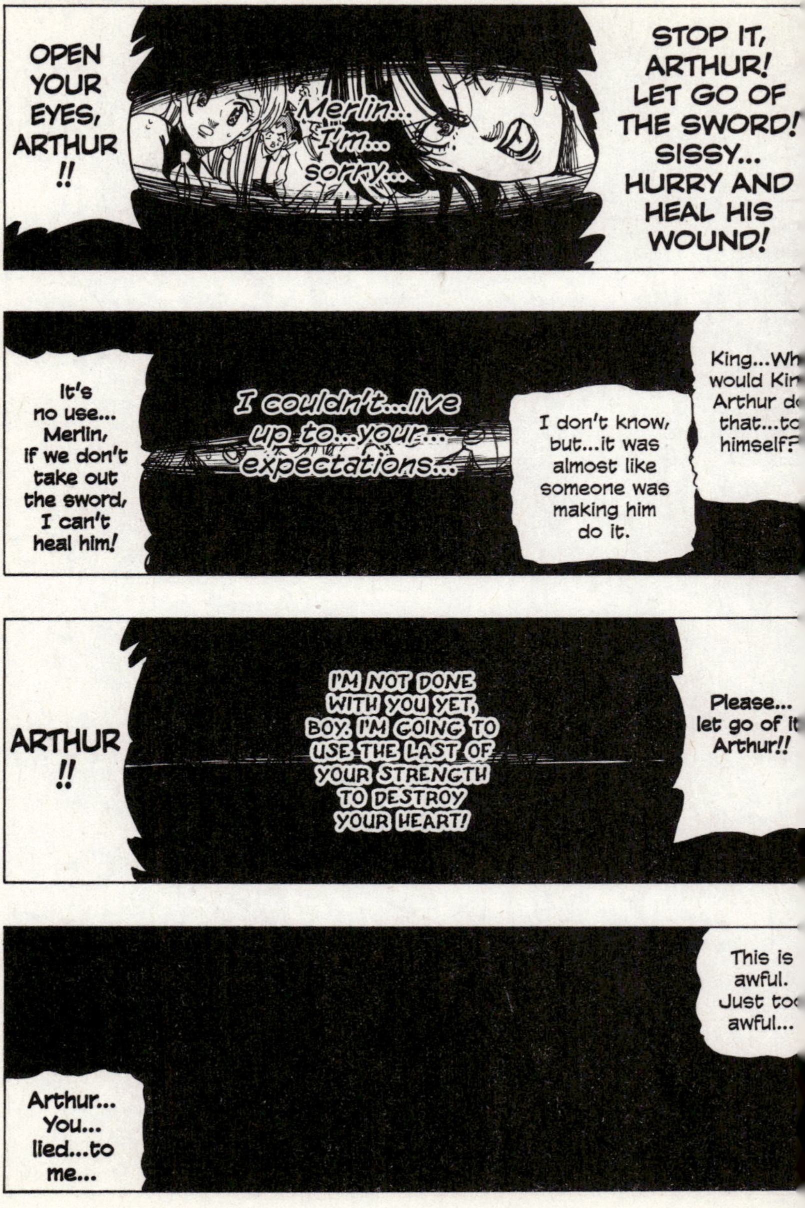
STOP IT, ARTHUR! LET GO OF THE SWORD! SISSY... HURRY AND HEAL HIS WOUND!
Merlin... I'm... sorry...
OPEN YOUR EYES, ARTHUR!!
King...Wh would Kin Arthur d that...to himself?
I don't know, but...it was almost like someone was making him do it.
I couldn't...live up to...your... expectations...
It's no use... Merlin, if we don't take out the sword, I can't heal him!
Please... let go of it Arthur!!
I'M NOT DONE WITH YOU YET, BOY. I'M GOING TO USE THE LAST OF YOUR STRENGTH TO DESTROY YOUR HEART!
ARTHUR!!
This is awful. Just too awful...
Arthur... You... lied...to me...

Chapter 257 - Sallying Forth

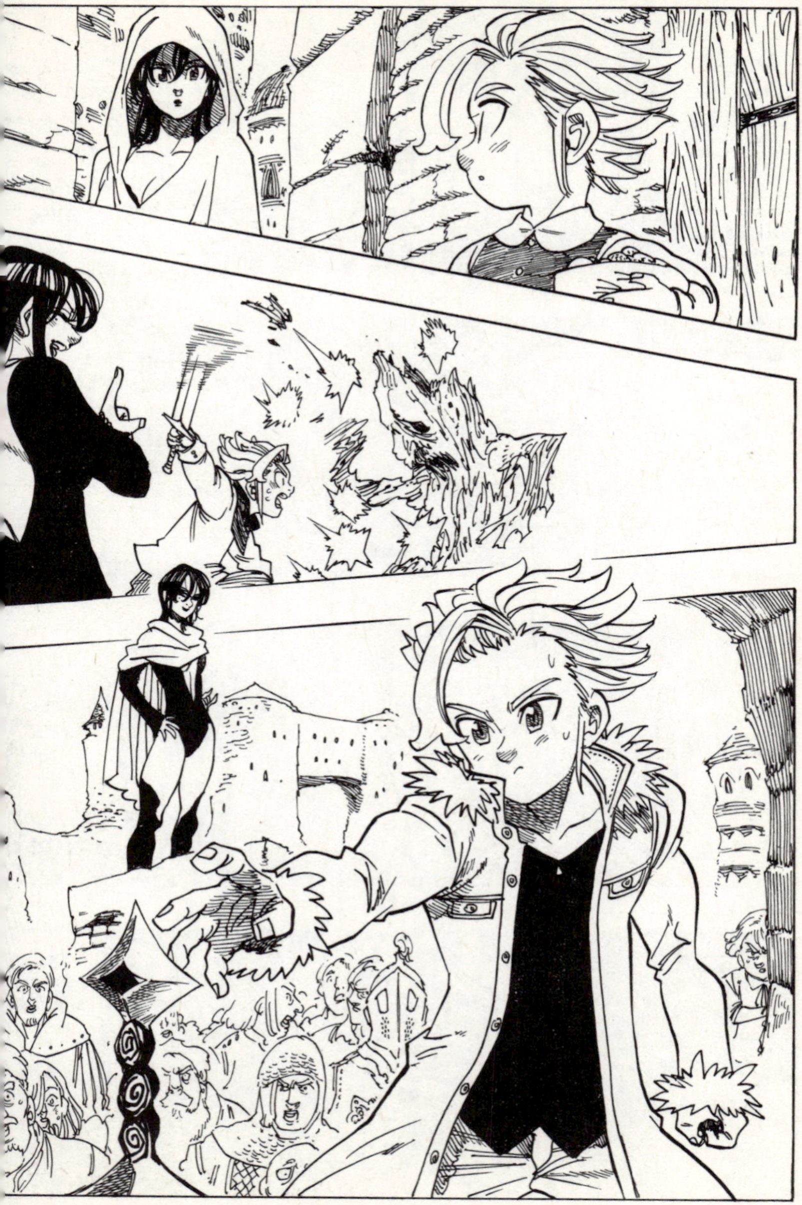

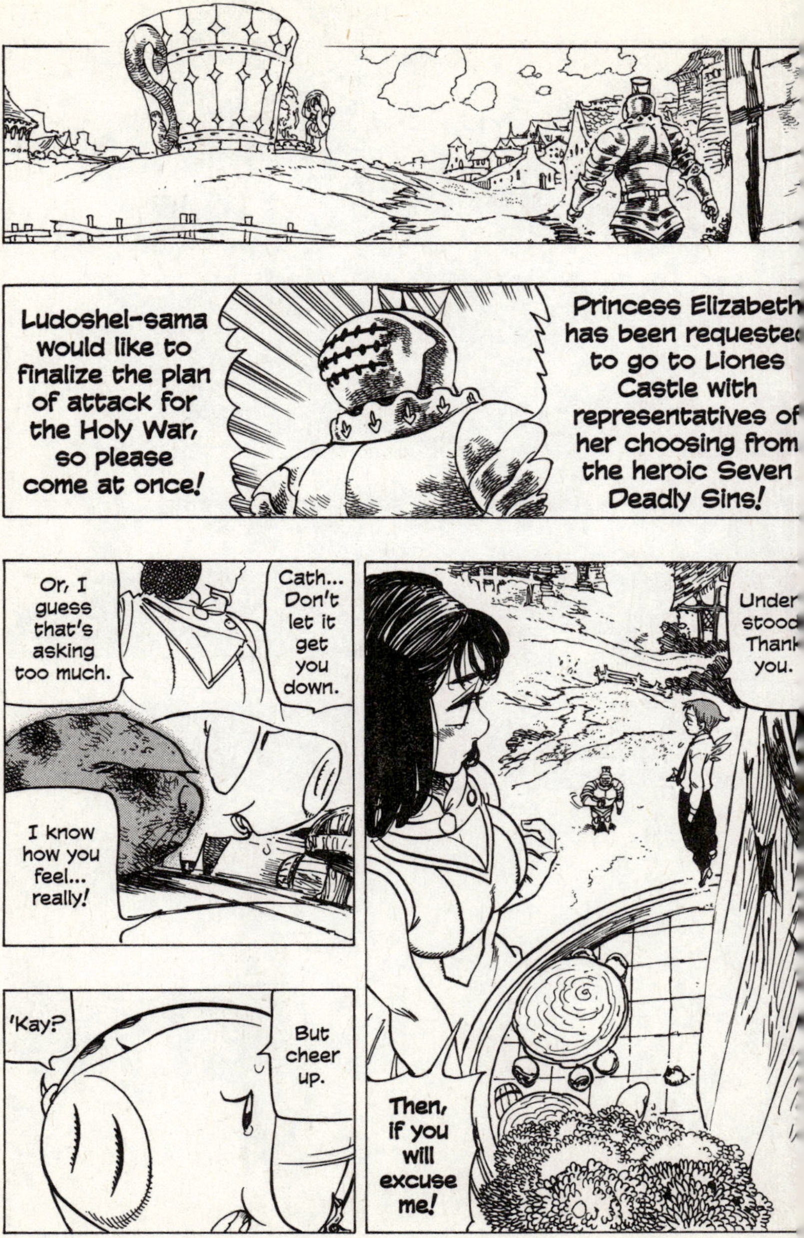
Princess Elizabeth has been requested to go to Liones Castle with representatives of her choosing from the heroic Seven Deadly Sins!
Ludoshel-sama would like to finalize the plan of attack for the Holy War, so please come at once!
Understood. Thank you.
Then, if you will excuse me!
Cath... Don't let it get you down.
Or, I guess that's asking too much.
I know how you feel... really!
But cheer up.
'Kay?

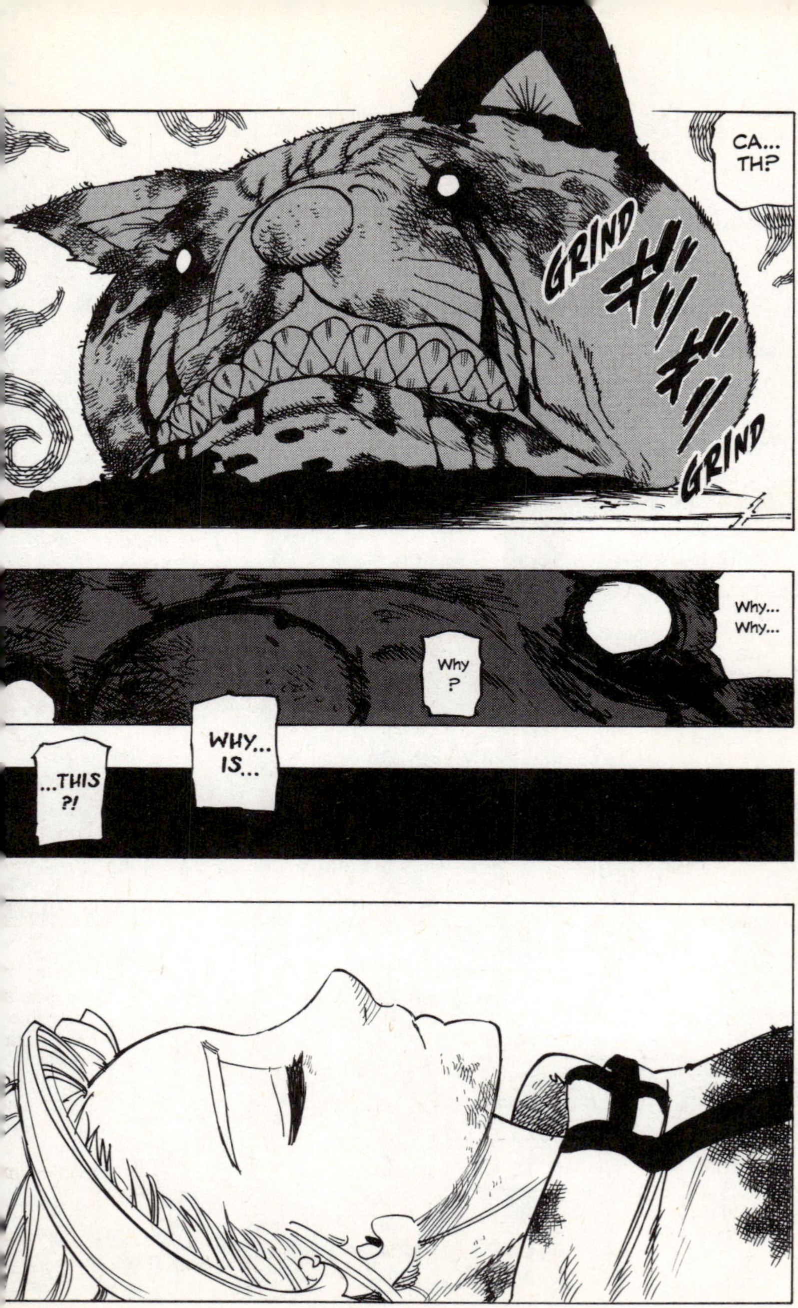
CA... TH?
GRIND
GRIND
Why... Why...
Why ?
WHY... IS...
...THIS ?!

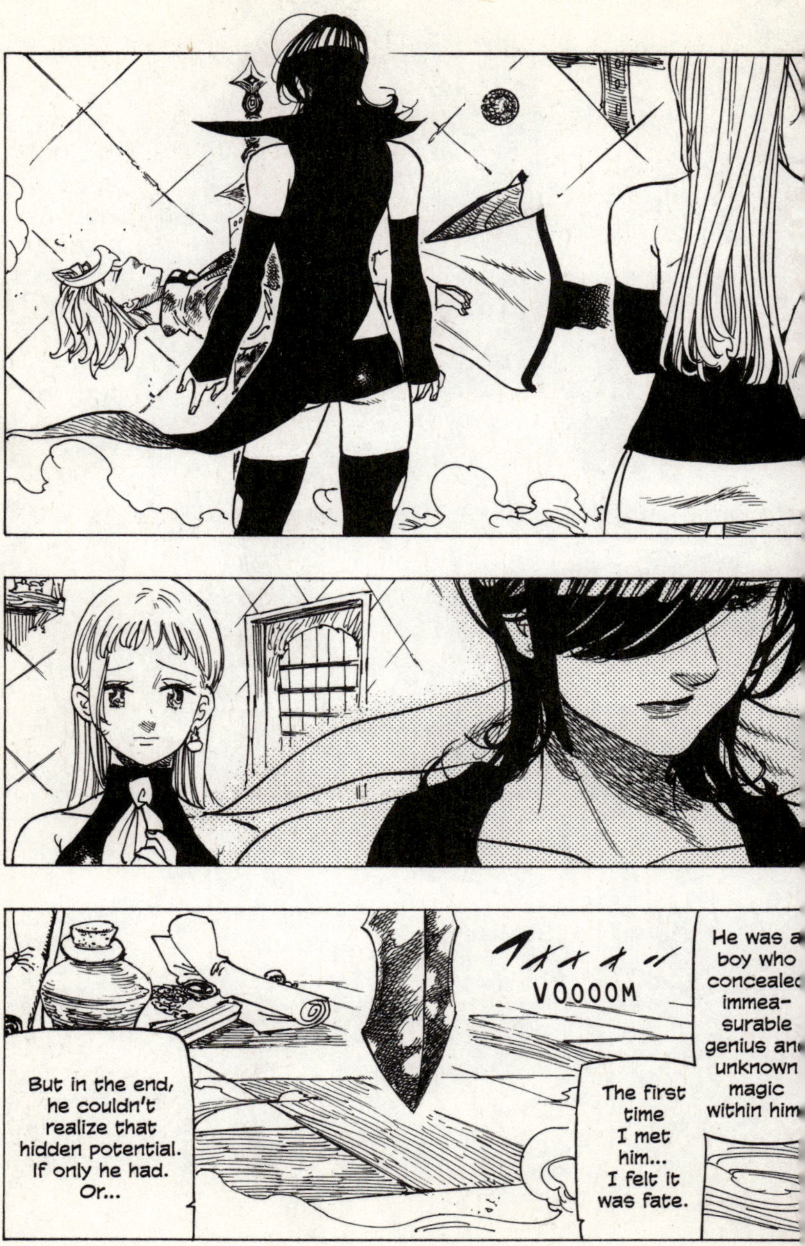
He was a boy who concealed immea-surable genius and unknown magic within him
VOOOOM
The first time I met him... I felt it was fate.
But in the end, he couldn't realize that hidden potential. If only he had. Or...

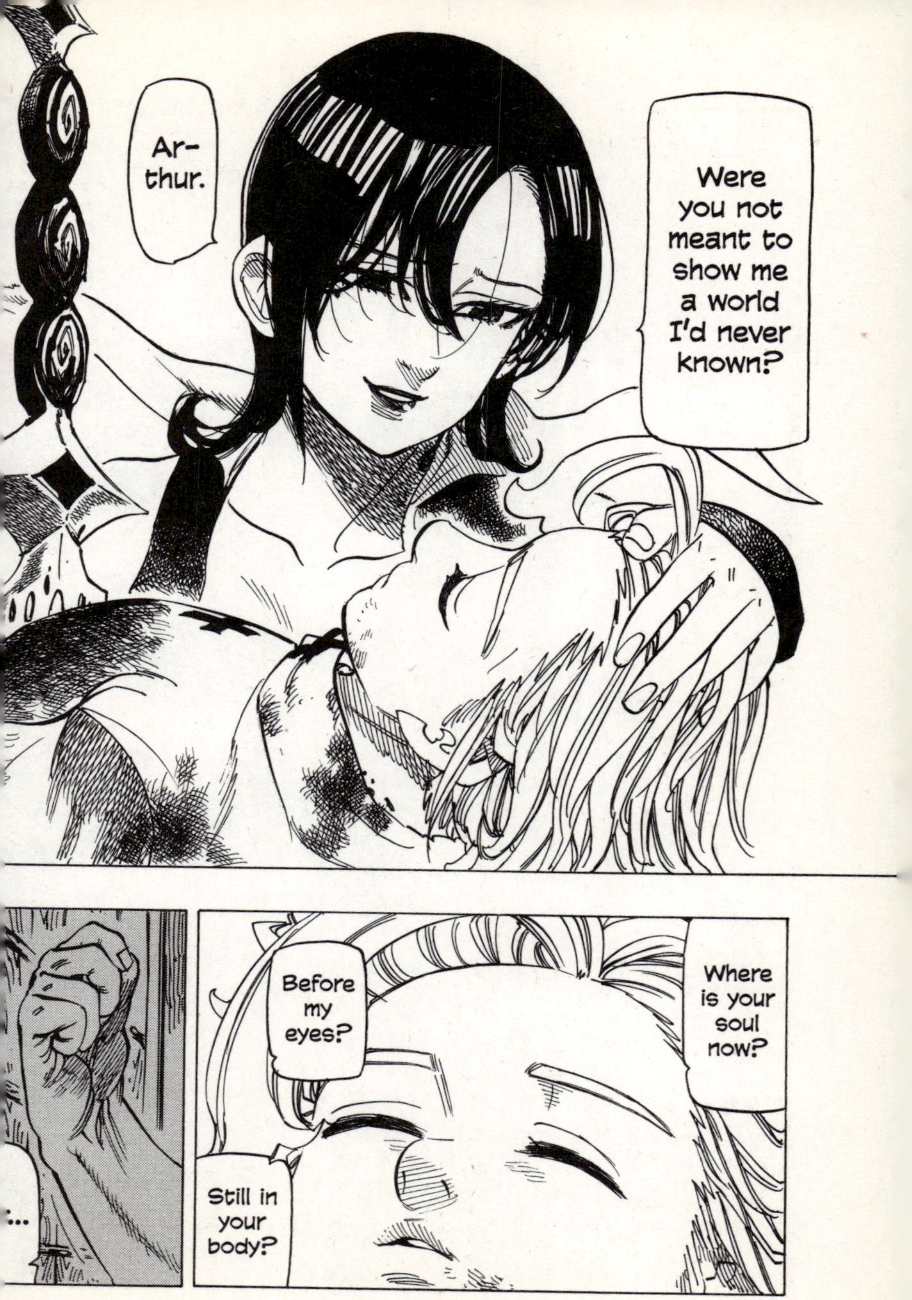

Were you not meant to show me a world I'd never known?
Ar-thur.
Where is your soul now?
Before my eyes?
Still in your body?
...

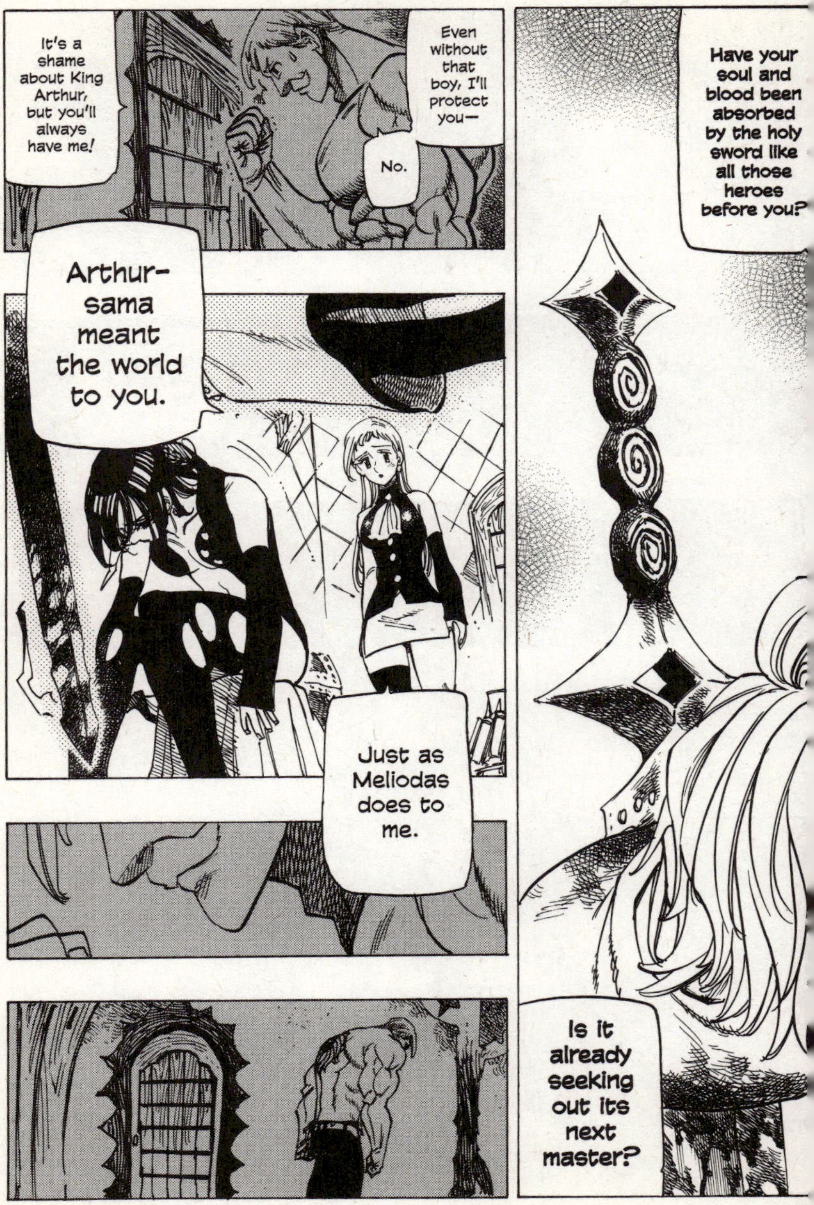
Have your soul and blood been absorbed by the holy sword like all those heroes before you?
Is it already seeking out its next master?
Even without that boy, I'll protect you—
It's a shame about King Arthur, but you'll always have me!
No.
Arthur-sama meant the world to you.
Just as Meliodas does to me.

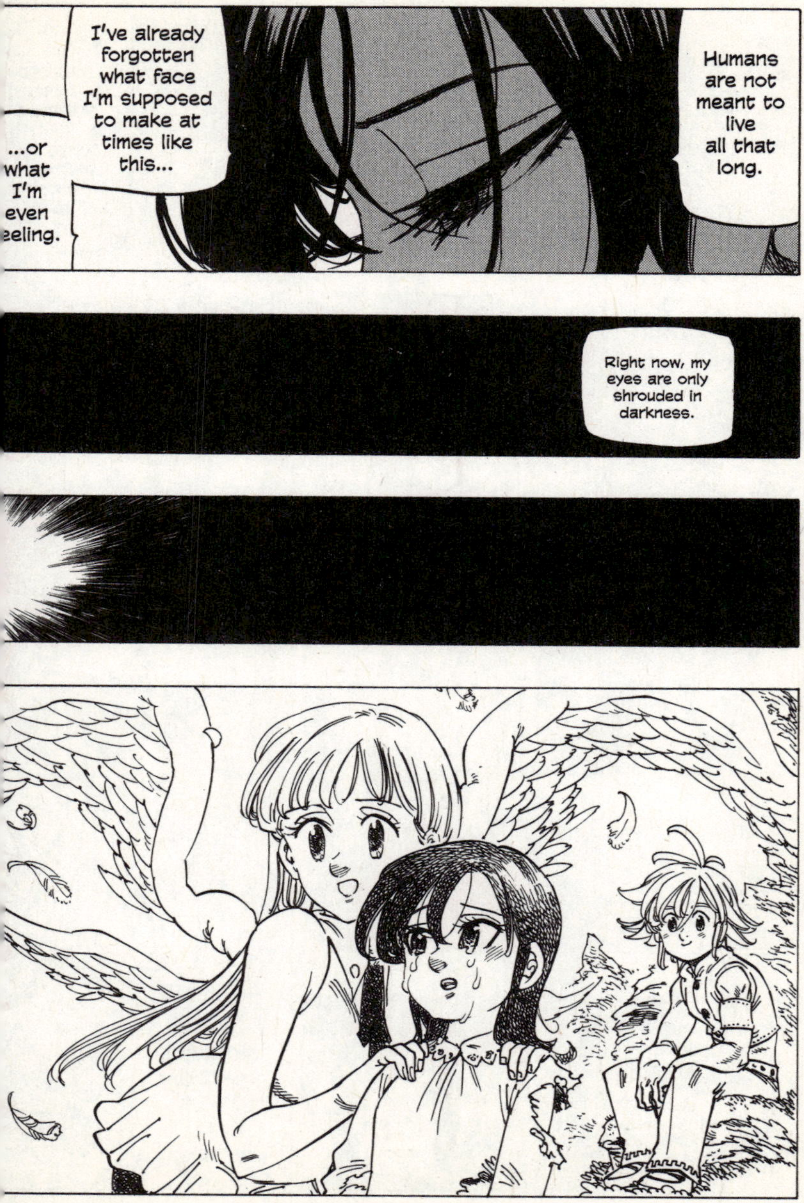
Humans are not meant to live all that long.
I've already forgotten what face I'm supposed to make at times like this...
...or what I'm even eeling.
Right now, my eyes are only shrouded in darkness.

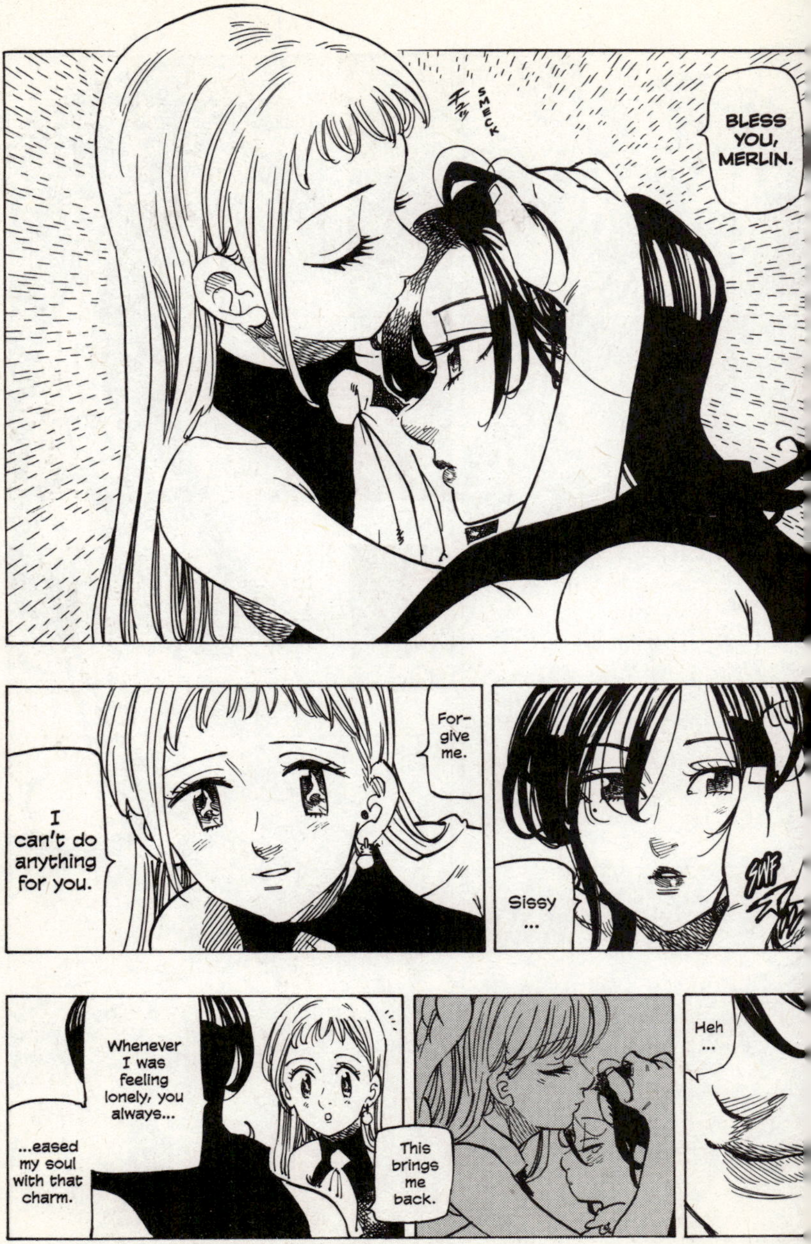
BLESS YOU, MERLIN.
SMECK
Sissy ...
SWF
For-give me.
I can't do anything for you.
Heh ...
This brings me back.
Whenever I was feeling lonely, you always...
...eased my soul with that charm.

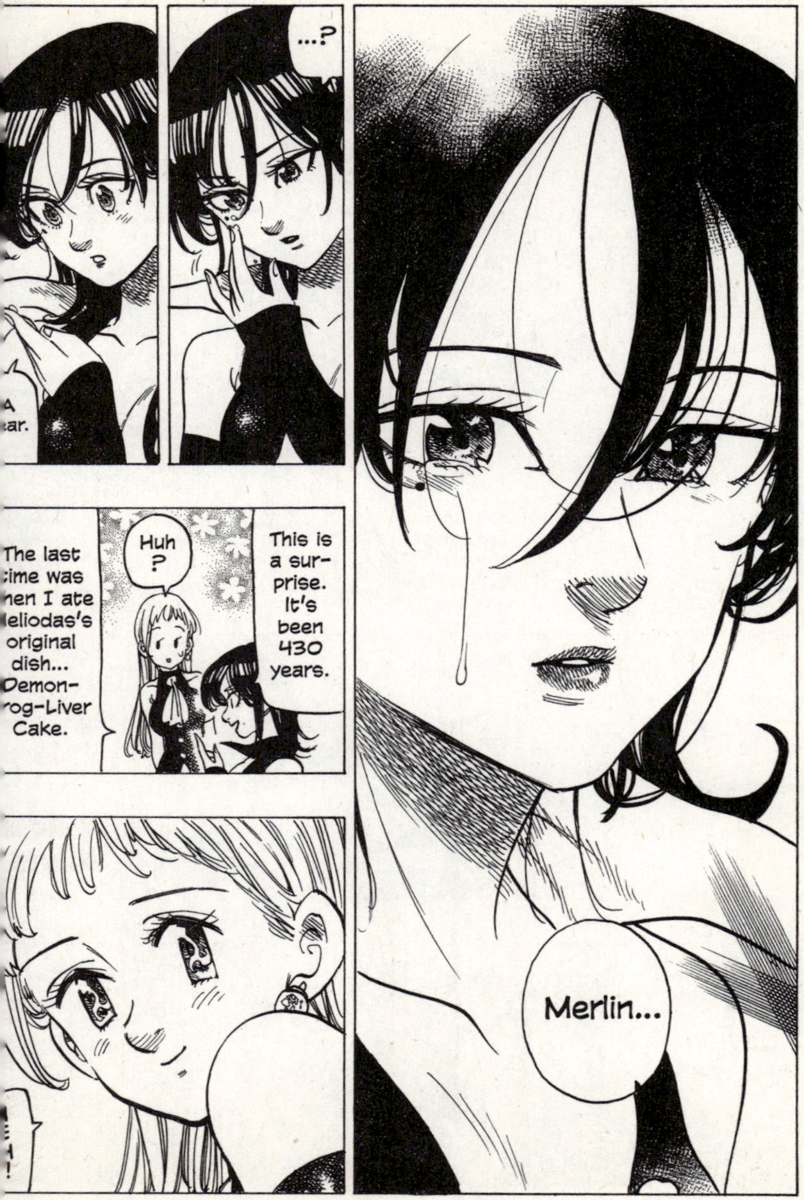

Merlin...
...?
A
ar.
This is a surprise. It's been 430 years.
Huh?
The last ime was hen I ate leliodas's original dish... Demon-rog-Liver Cake.

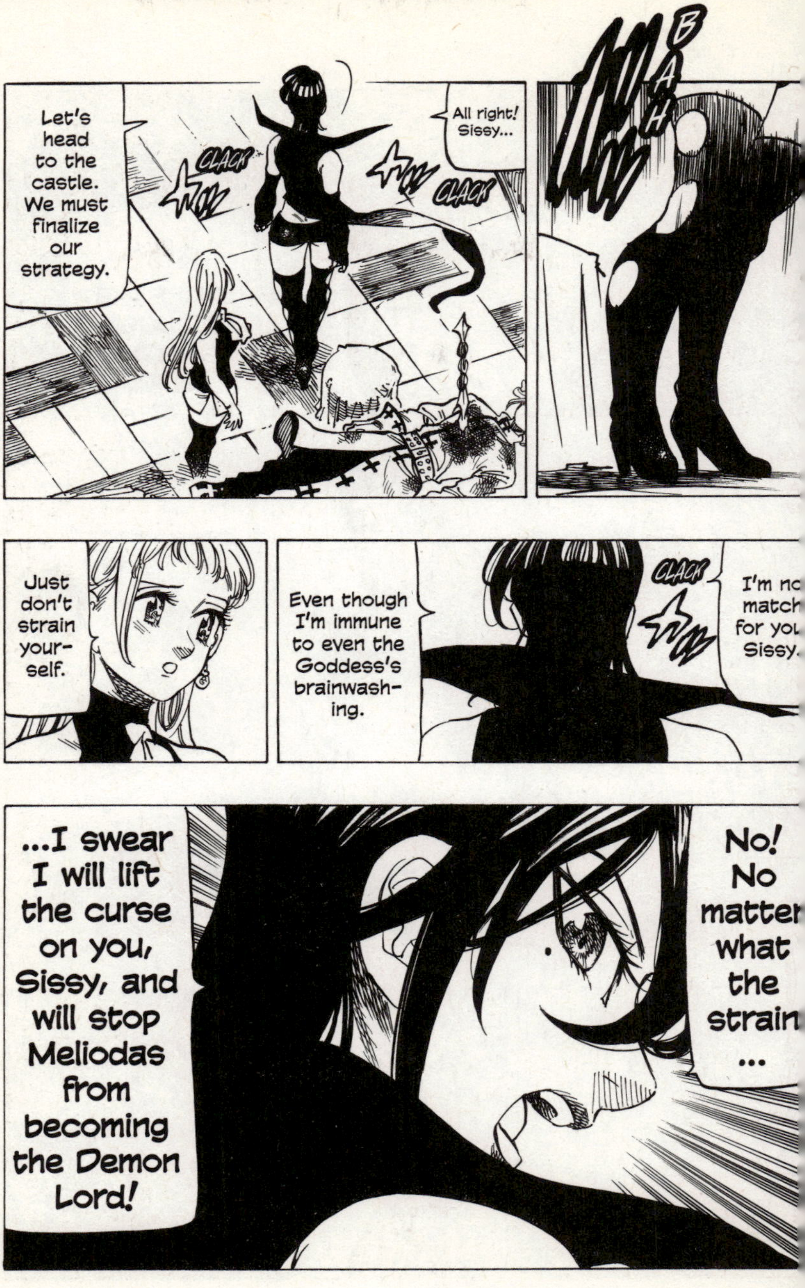
BAH
All right! Sissy...
CLACK
CLACK
Let's head to the castle. We must finalize our strategy.
I'm no match for you Sissy.
CLACK
Even though I'm immune to even the Goddess's brainwash-ing.
Just don't strain your-self.
No! No matter what the strain...
...I swear I will lift the curse on you, Sissy, and will stop Meliodas from becoming the Demon Lord!

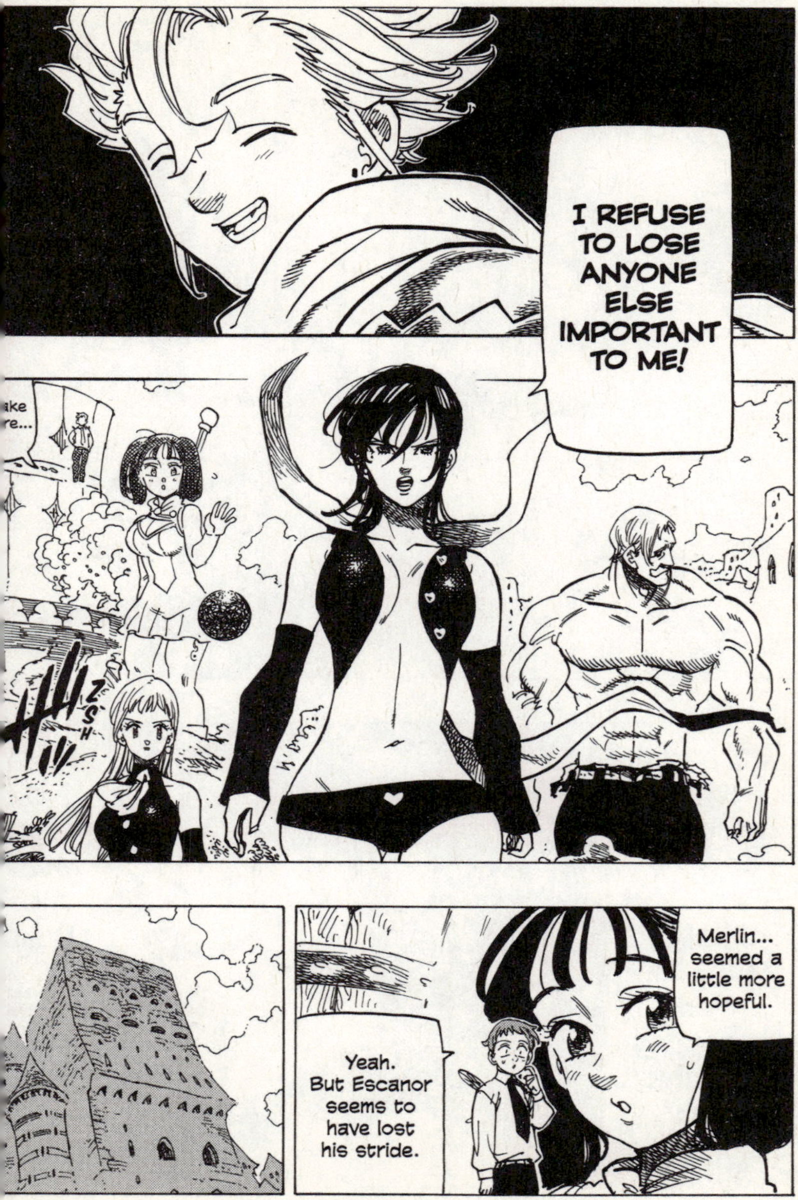
I REFUSE TO LOSE ANYONE ELSE IMPORTANT TO ME!
ZSH
Merlin... seemed a little more hopeful.
Yeah. But Escanor seems to have lost his stride.

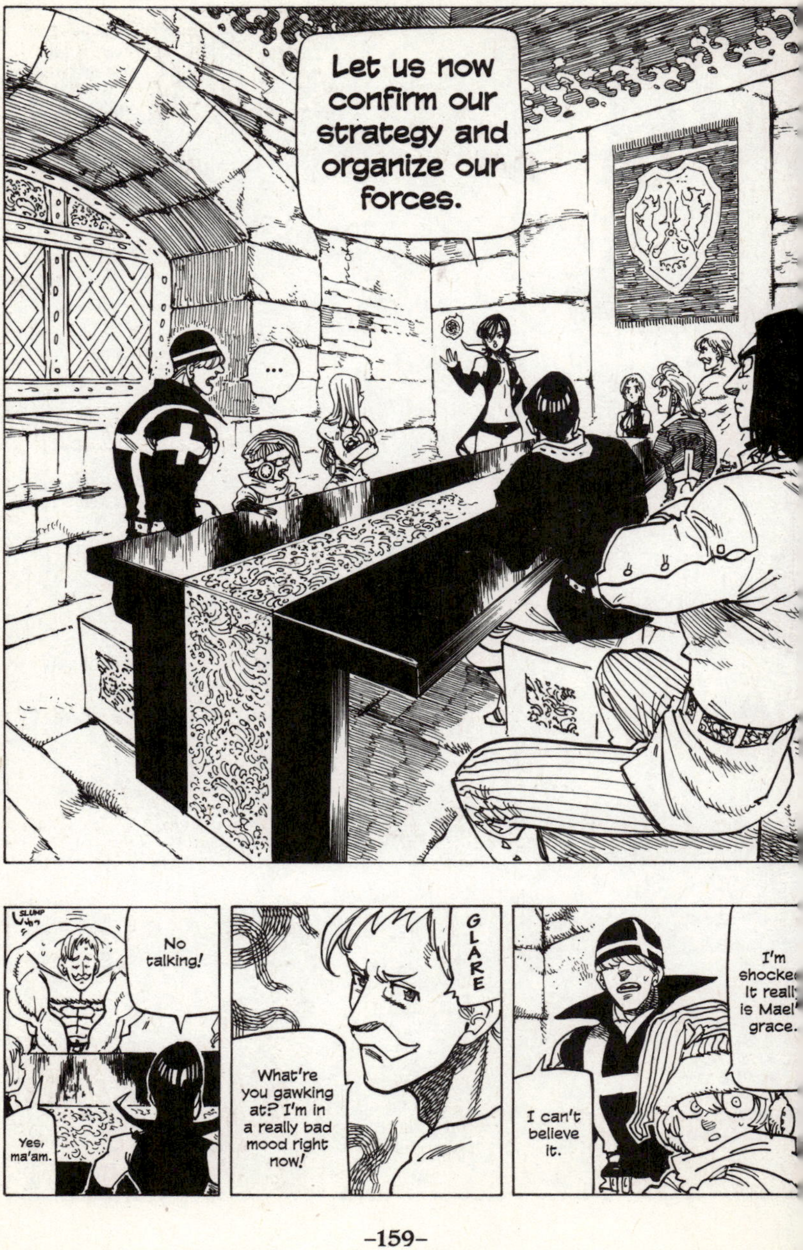
Let us now confirm our strategy and organize our forces.
...
I'm shocke
It reall
is Mael
grace.
I can't believe it.
GLARE
What're you gawking at? I'm in a really bad mood right now!
SLUMP
No talking!
Yes, ma'am.

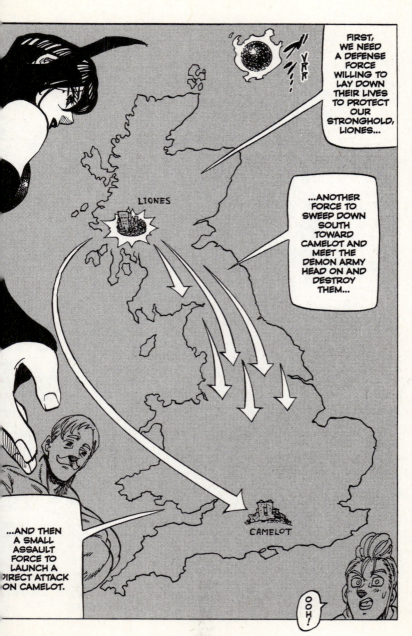

FIRST, WE NEED A DEFENSE FORCE WILLING TO LAY DOWN THEIR LIVES TO PROTECT OUR STRONGHOLD, LIONES...

...ANOTHER FORCE TO SWEEP DOWN SOUTH TOWARD CAMELOT AND MEET THE DEMON ARMY HEAD ON AND DESTROY THEM...

LIONES

...AND THEN A SMALL ASSAULT FORCE TO LAUNCH A DIRECT ATTACK ON CAMELOT.

CAMELOT

OOH!

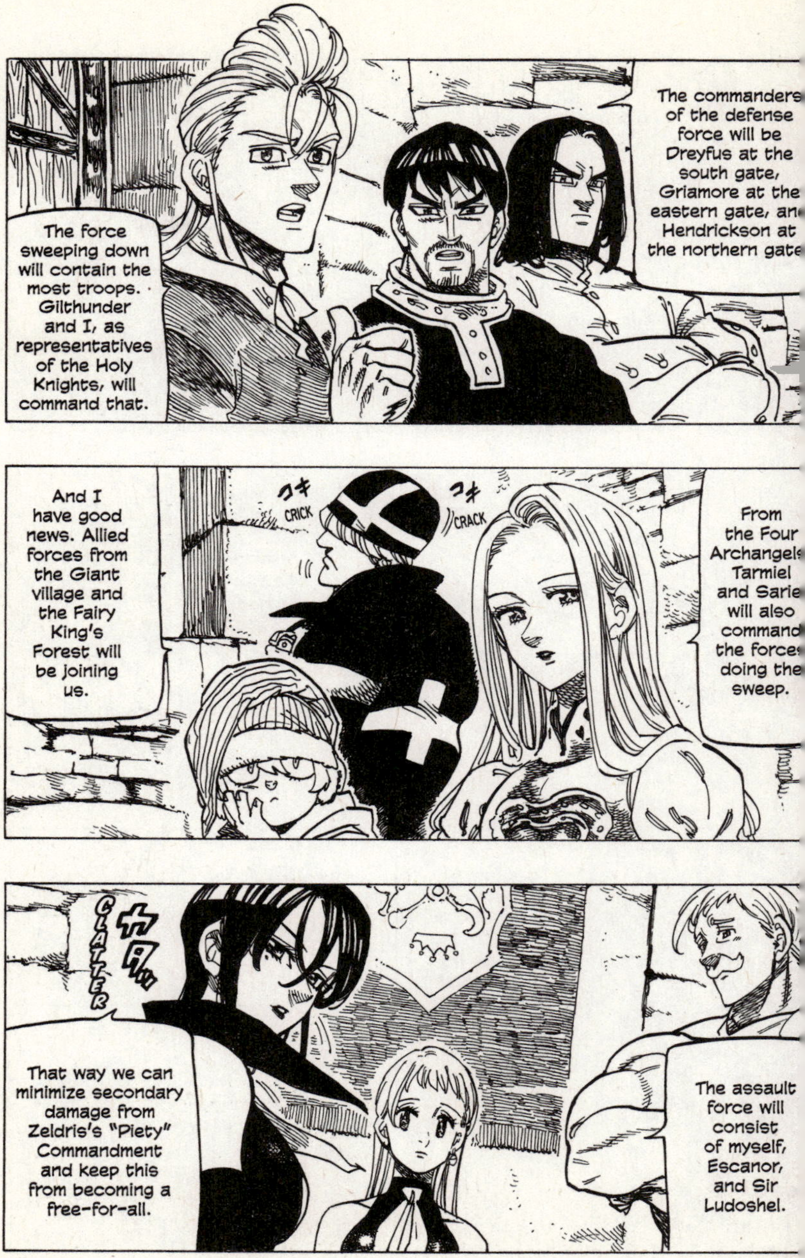
The commanders of the defense force will be Dreyfus at the south gate, Griamore at the eastern gate, an Hendrickson at the northern gate
The force sweeping down will contain the most troops. Gilthunder and I, as representatives of the Holy Knights, will command that.
コキ CRACK
コキ CRICK
From the Four Archangels Tarmiel and Sarie will also command the forces doing the sweep.
And I have good news. Allied forces from the Giant village and the Fairy King's Forest will be joining us.
The assault force will consist of myself, Escanor, and Sir Ludoshel.
カタ CLATTER
That way we can minimize secondary damage from Zeldris's "Piety" Commandment and keep this from becoming a free-for-all.

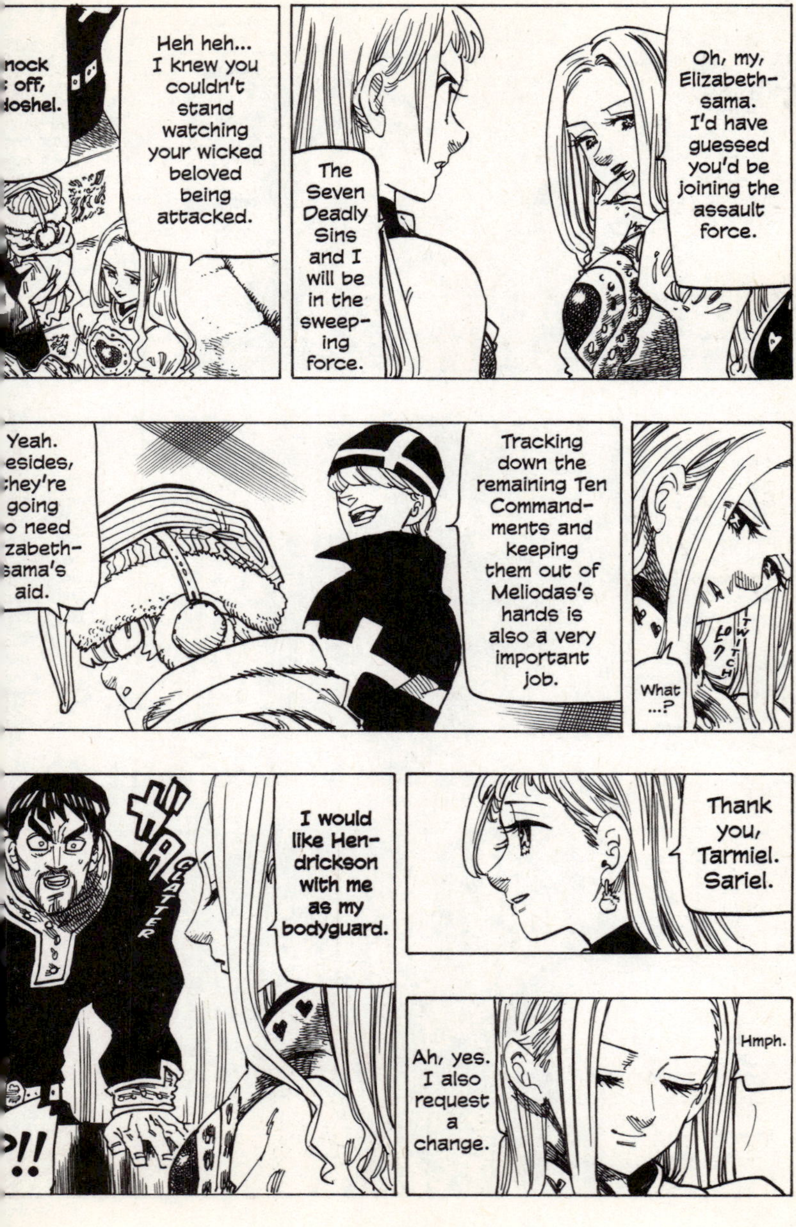
Oh, my, Elizabeth-sama. I'd have guessed you'd be joining the assault force.
The Seven Deadly Sins and I will be in the sweeping force.
Heh heh... I knew you couldn't stand watching your wicked beloved being attacked.
nock off, doshel.
What ...?
TWITCH
Tracking down the remaining Ten Commandments and keeping them out of Meliodas's hands is also a very important job.
Yeah. esides, hey're going o need zabeth-sama's aid.
Thank you, Tarmiel. Sariel.
Hmph.
Ah, yes. I also request a change.
I would like Hendrickson with me as my bodyguard.
CLATTER
?!!

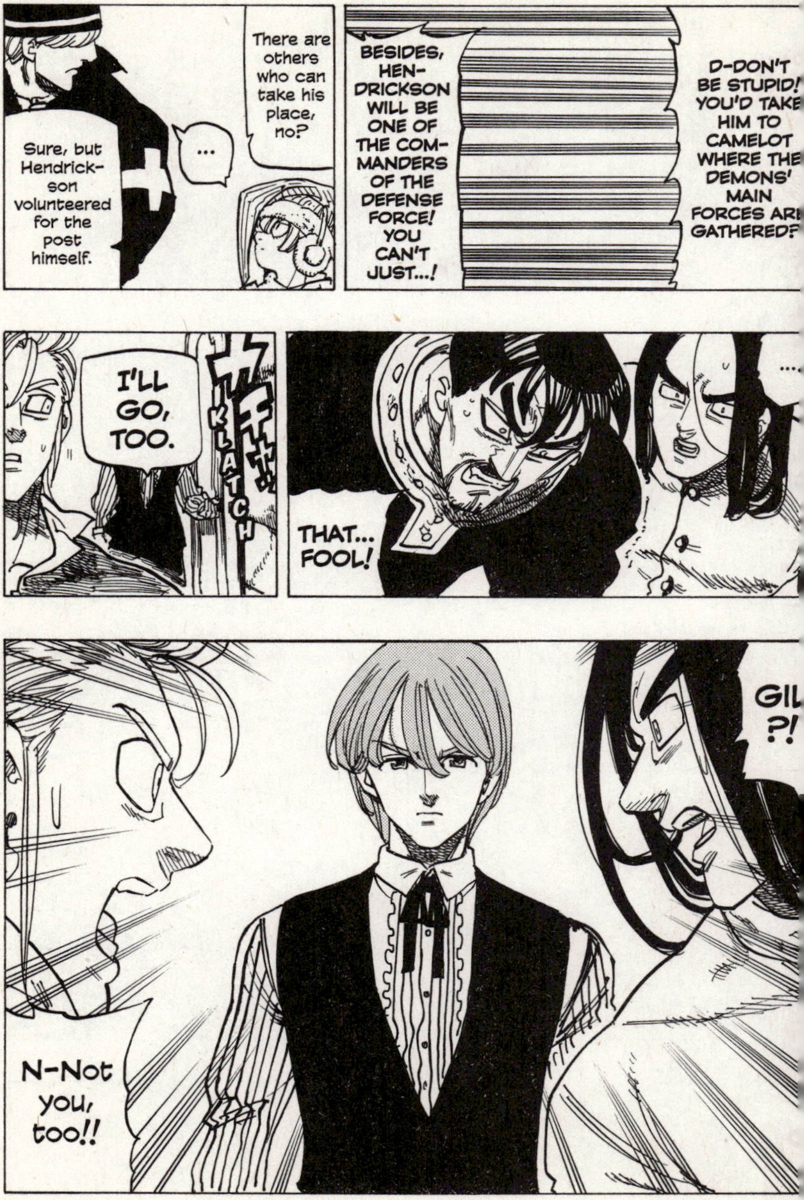

D-DON'T BE STUPID! YOU'D TAKE HIM TO CAMELOT WHERE THE DEMONS' MAIN FORCES ARE GATHERED?
BESIDES, HENDRICKSON WILL BE ONE OF THE COMMANDERS OF THE DEFENSE FORCE! YOU CAN'T JUST...!
There are others who can take his place, no?
...
Sure, but Hendrickson volunteered for the post himself.
....
THAT... FOOL!
KLATCH
I'LL GO, TOO.
GIL?!
N-Not you, too!!

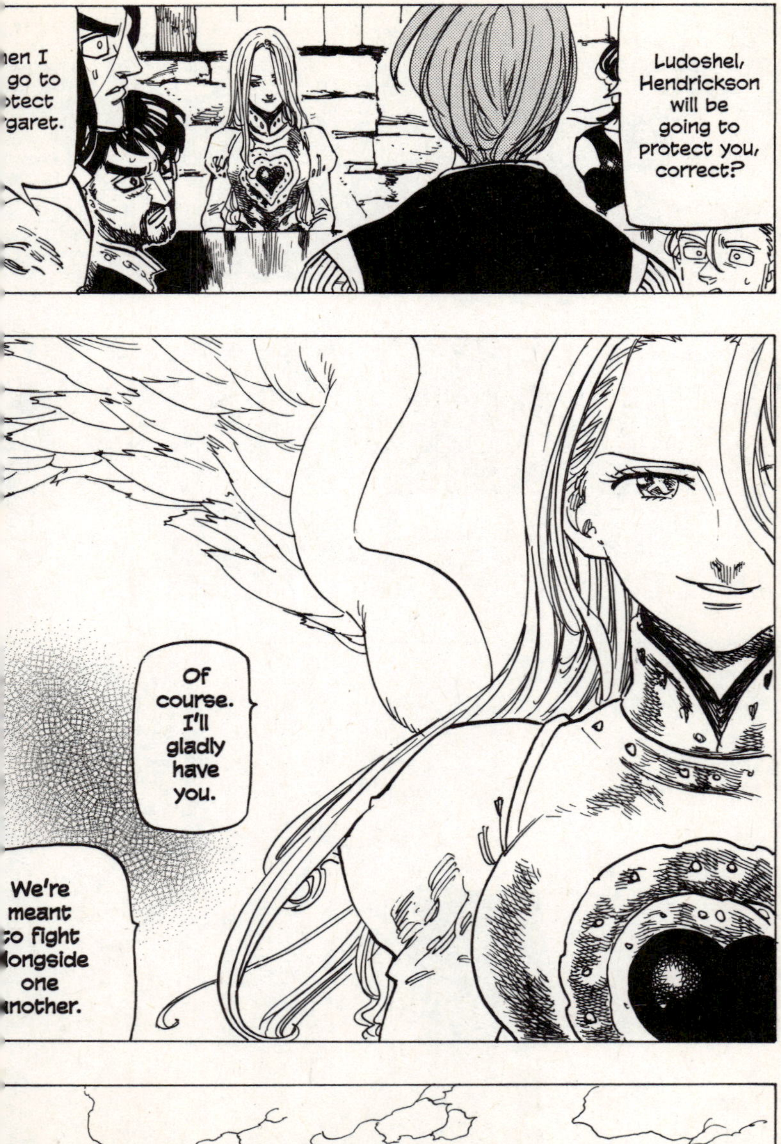
Ludoshel, Hendrickson will be going to protect you, correct?
en I go to otect rgaret.
Of course. I'll gladly have you.
We're meant o fight longside one nother.

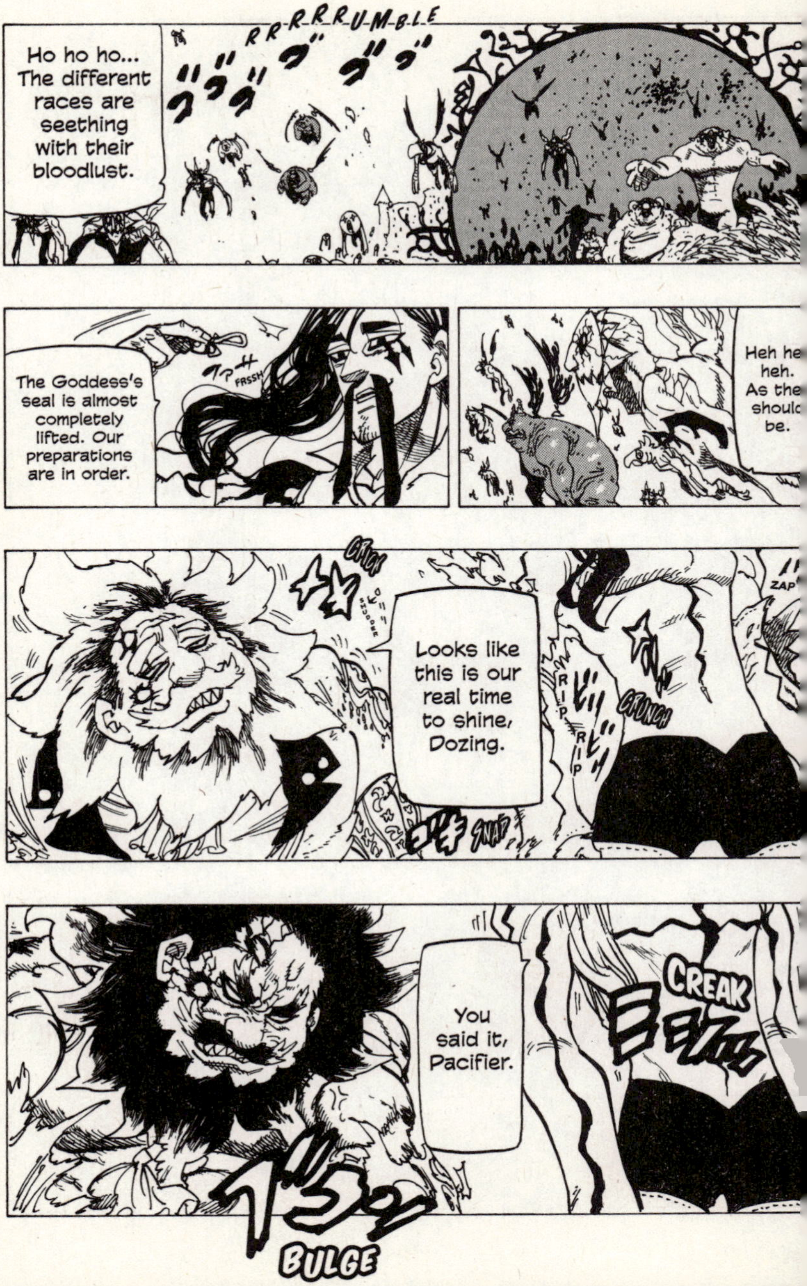
RR-R-R-R-U-M-B-L-E
Ho ho ho... The different races are seething with their bloodlust.
Heh he heh. As the should be.
FRSSH
The Goddess's seal is almost completely lifted. Our preparations are in order.
ZAP
RIP RIP
CRUNCH
Looks like this is our real time to shine, Dozing.
CRACK
SHUDDER
SNAP
CREAK
You said it, Pacifier.
BULGE

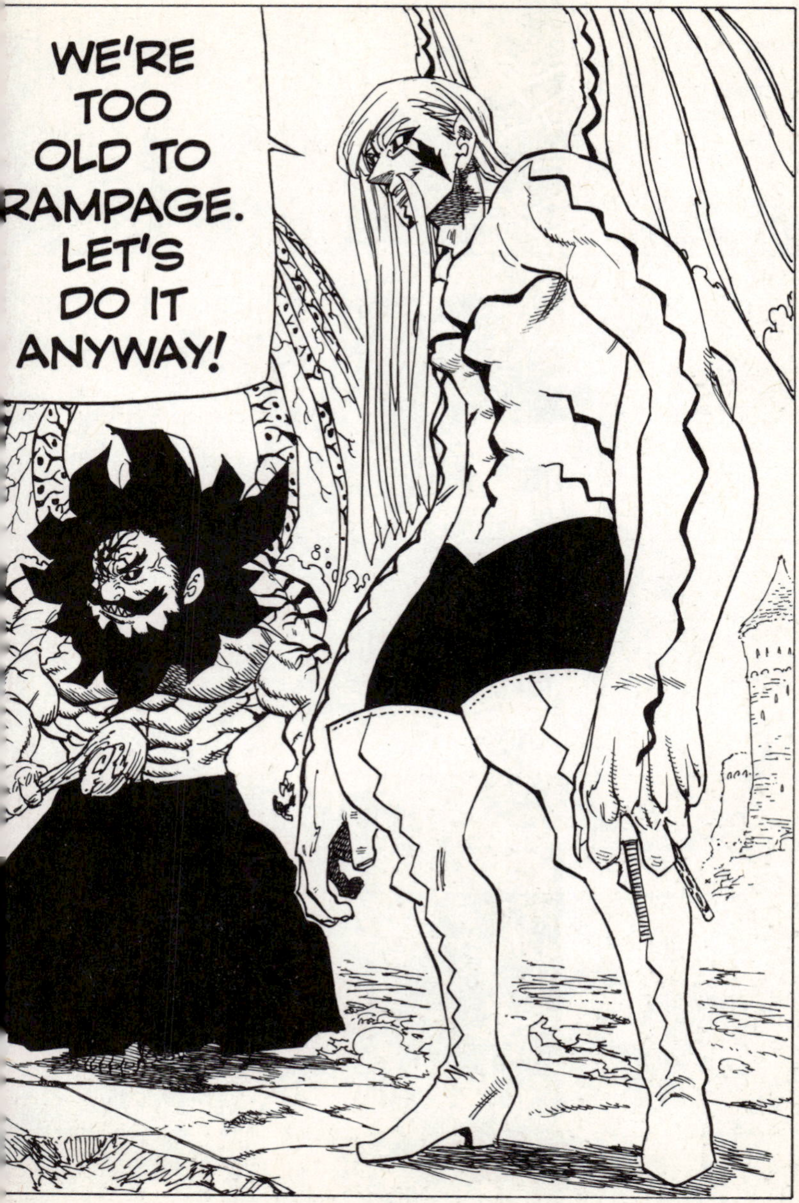
WE'RE TOO OLD TO RAMPAGE. LET'S DO IT ANYWAY!

THE SEVEN DEADLY SINS

Chapter 258 - Dawn of the Holy War

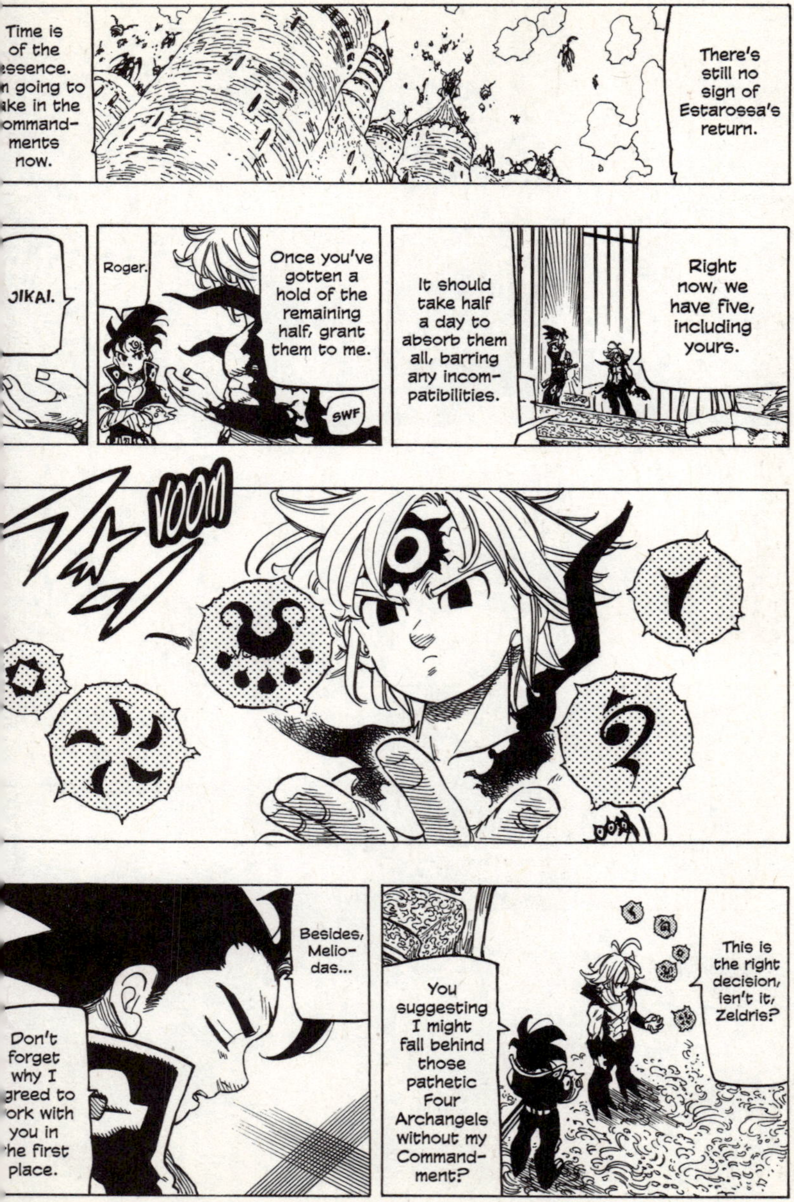
There's still no sign of Estarossa's return.
Time is of the essence. n going to ake in the ommand- ments now.
Right now, we have five, including yours.
It should take half a day to absorb them all, barring any incom- patibilities.
Once you've gotten a hold of the remaining half, grant them to me.
SWF
Roger.
JIKAI.
VOOM
This is the right decision, isn't it, Zeldris?
You suggesting I might fall behind those pathetic Four Archangels without my Command- ment?
Besides, Melio- das...
Don't forget why I greed to ork with you in he first place.

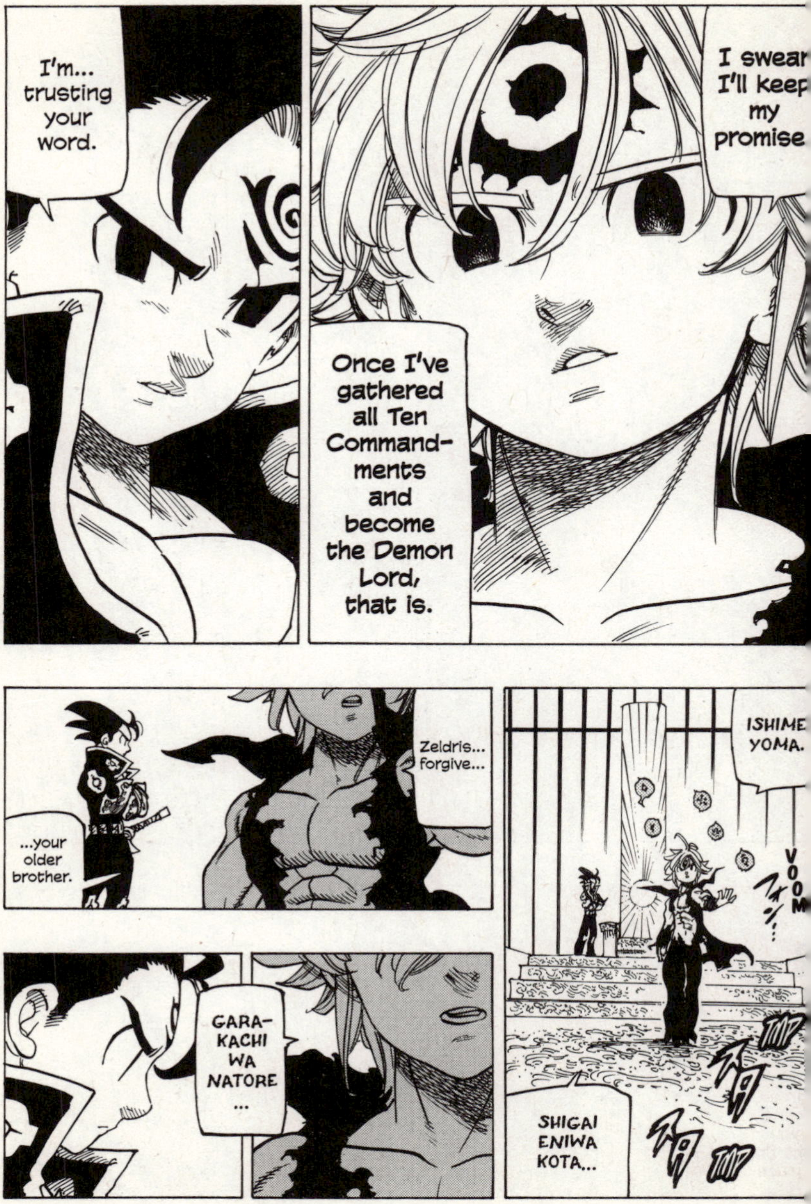
I swear I'll keep my promise
Once I've gathered all Ten Commandments and become the Demon Lord, that is.
I'm... trusting your word.
ISHIME YOMA.
VOOM
TMP
SHIGAI ENIWA KOTA...
TMP
Zeldris... forgive...
...your older brother.
GARA-KACHI WA NATORE ...

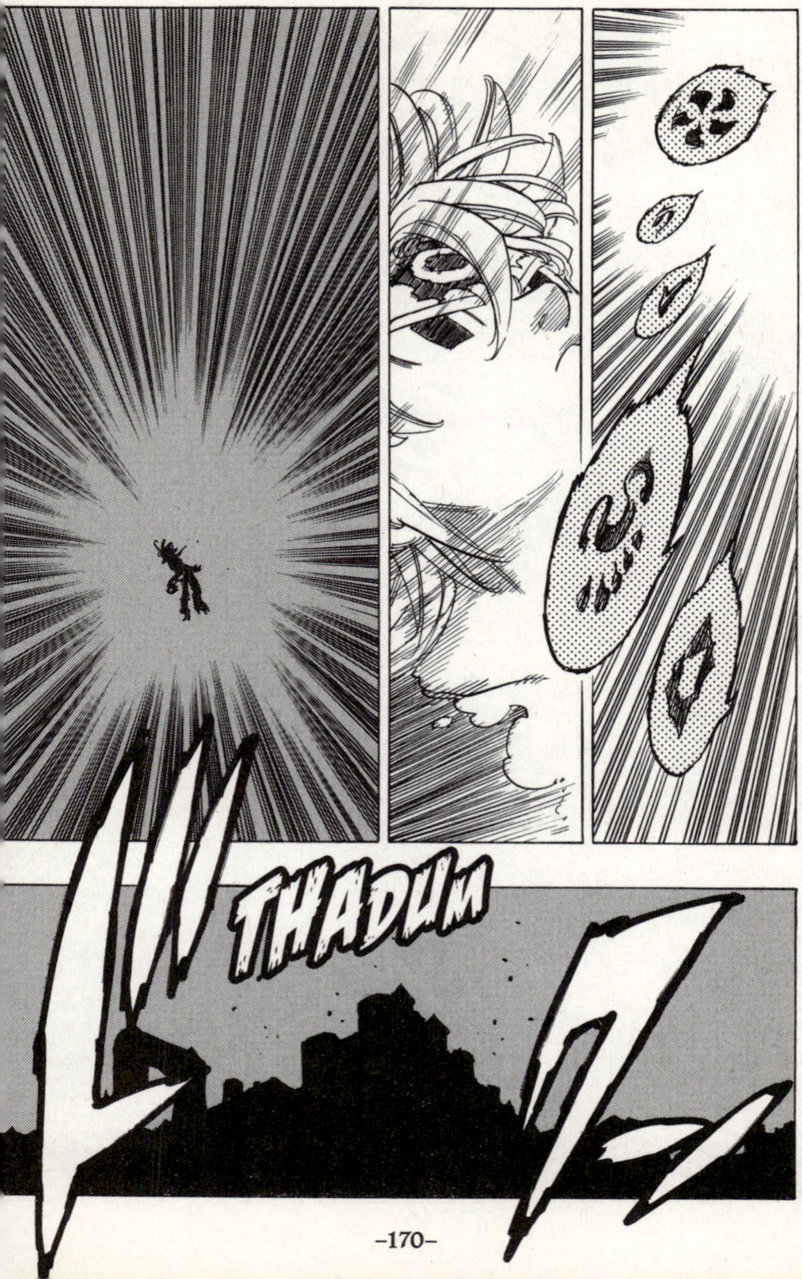
THADUM

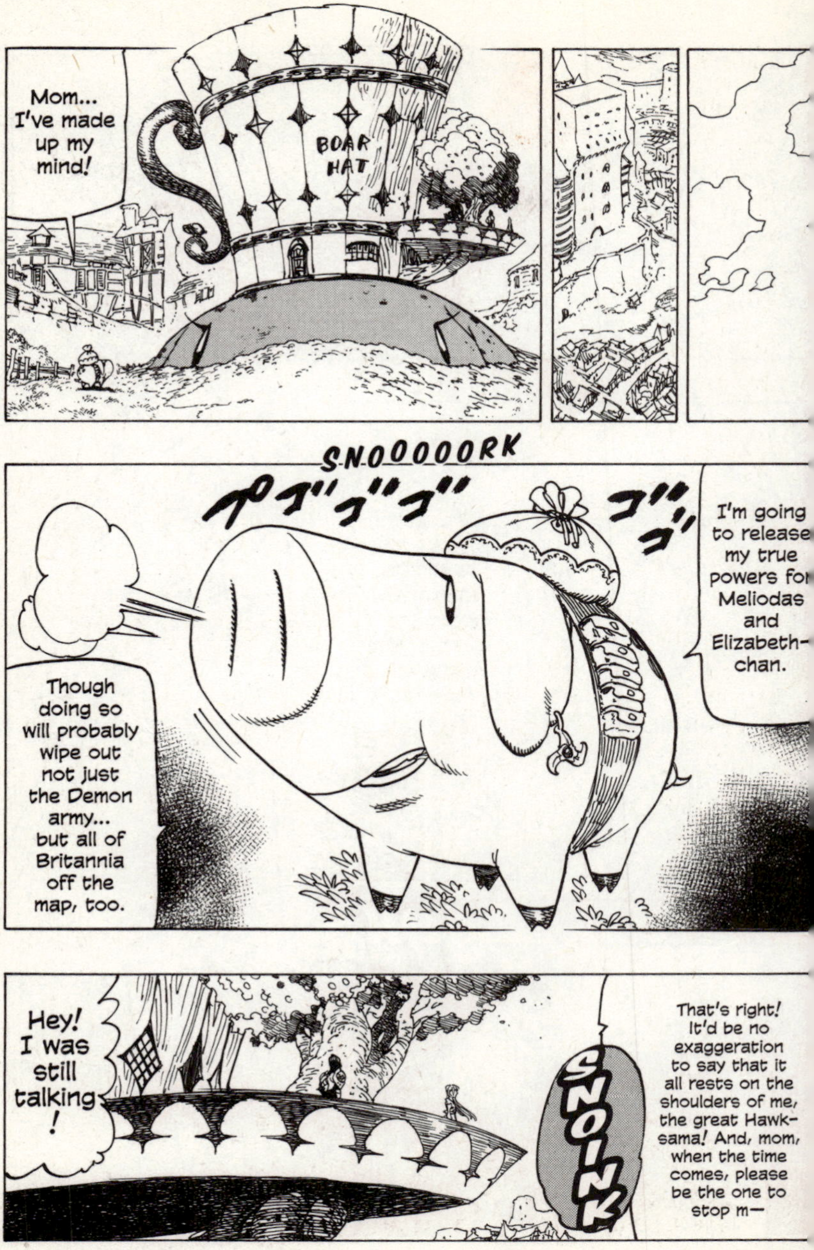

Mom... I've made up my mind!
I'm going to release my true powers for Meliodas and Elizabeth-chan.
SNOOOOORK
Though doing so will probably wipe out not just the Demon army... but all of Britannia off the map, too.
That's right! It'd be no exaggeration to say that it all rests on the shoulders of me, the great Hawk-sama! And, mom, when the time comes, please be the one to stop m—
SNOINK
Hey! I was still talking!

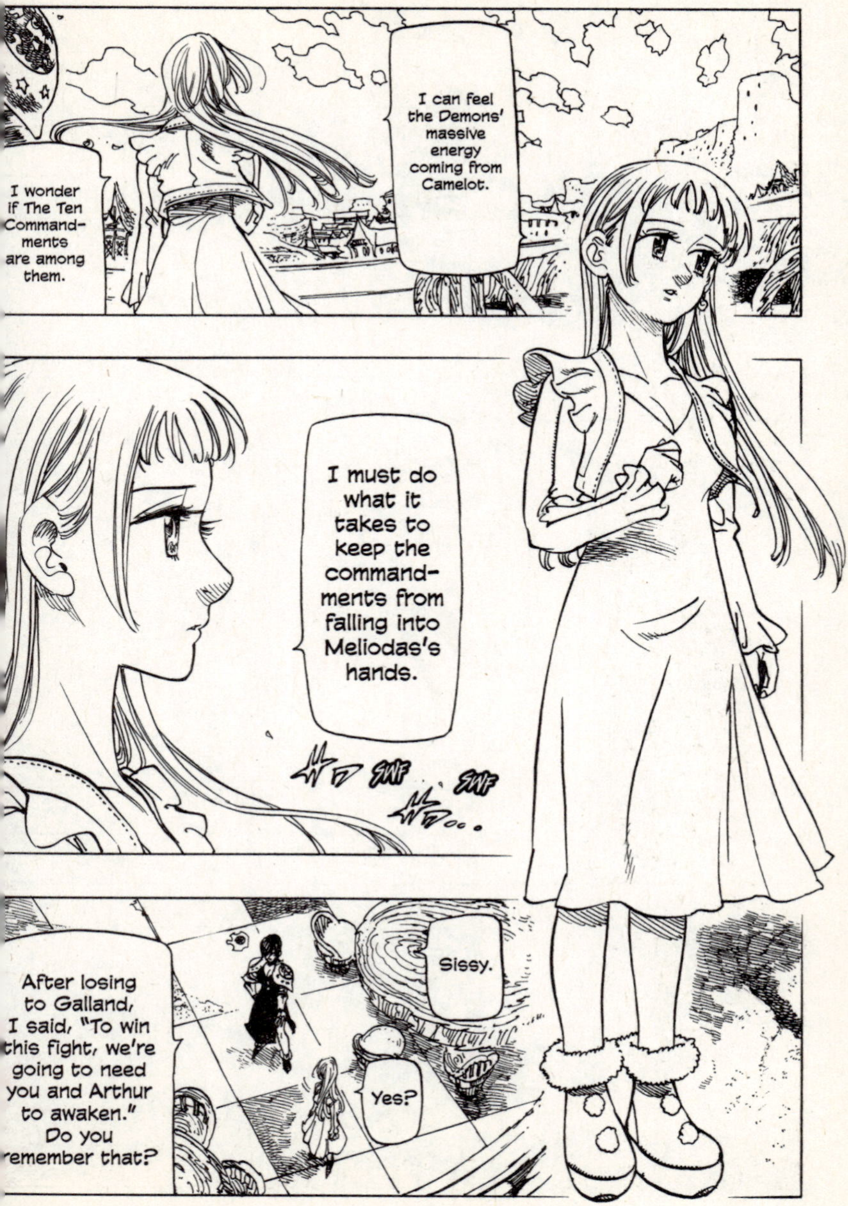
I can feel the Demons' massive energy coming from Camelot.
I wonder if The Ten Command-ments are among them.
I must do what it takes to keep the command-ments from falling into Meliodas's hands.
SWF
SWF
Sissy.
Yes?
After losing to Galland, I said, "To win this fight, we're going to need you and Arthur to awaken." Do you remember that?

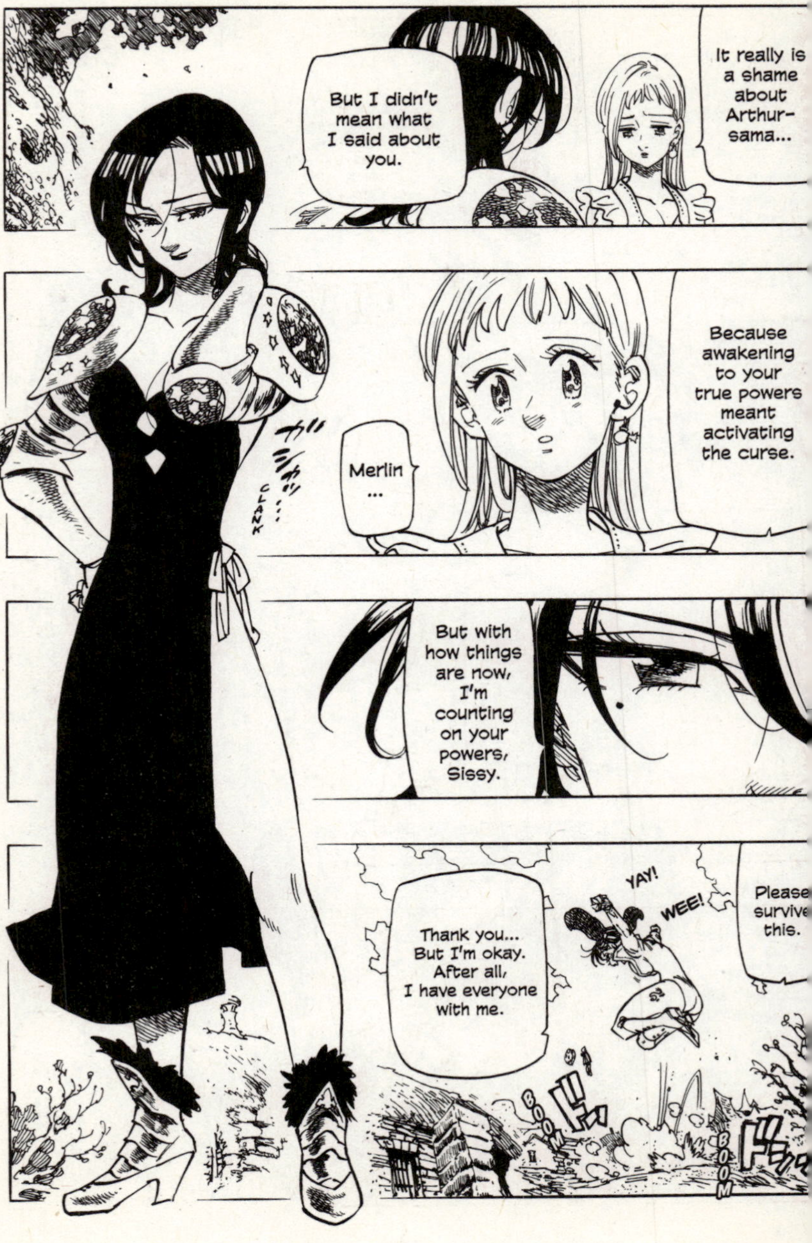
It really is a shame about Arthur-sama...
But I didn't mean what I said about you.
Because awakening to your true powers meant activating the curse.
Merlin ...
But with how things are now, I'm counting on your powers, Sissy.
Please survive this.
YAY!
WEE!
Thank you... But I'm okay. After all, I have everyone with me.
BOOM
BOOM
CLANK

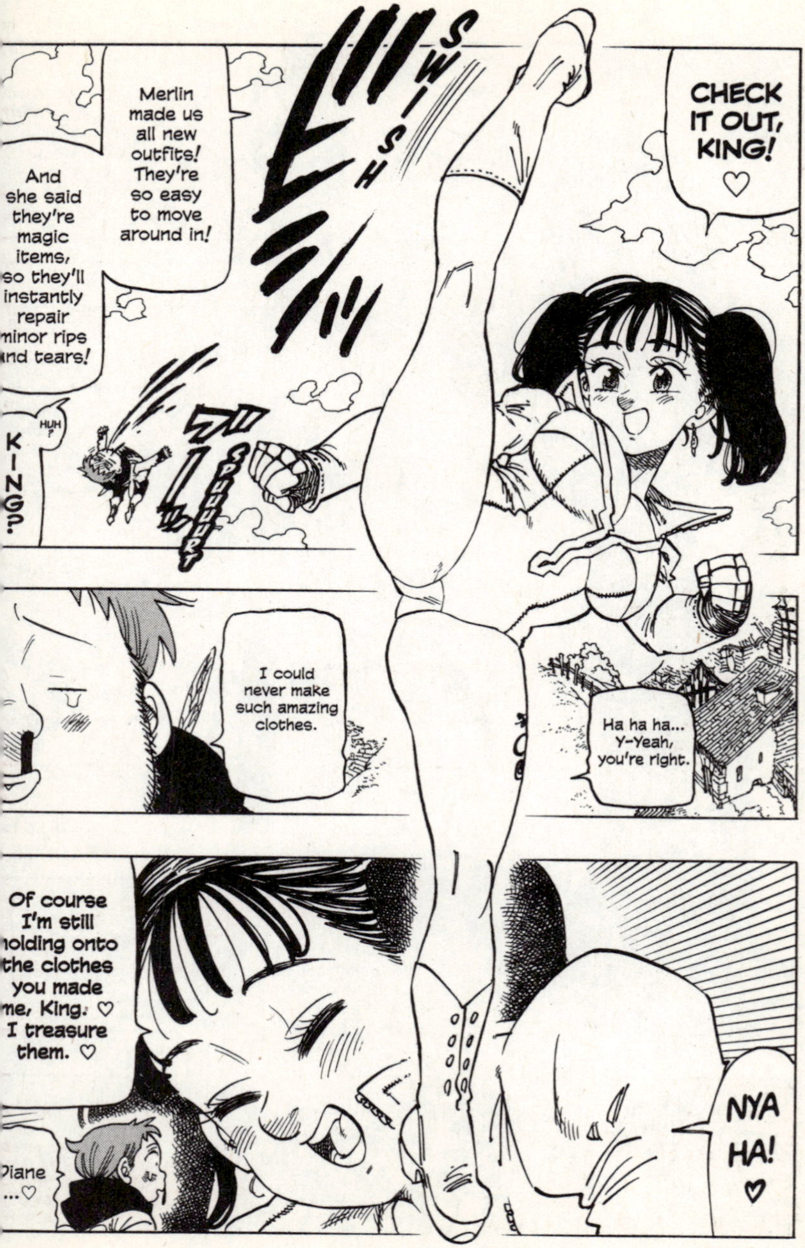
CHECK IT OUT, KING! ♡
SWISH
Merlin made us all new outfits! They're so easy to move around in!
And she said they're magic items, so they'll instantly repair ninor rips nd tears!
HUH?
SPLUUURT
KING?
Ha ha ha... Y-Yeah, you're right.
I could never make such amazing clothes.
NYA HA! ♡
Of course I'm still olding onto the clothes you made me, King. ♡ I treasure them. ♡
iane ...♡

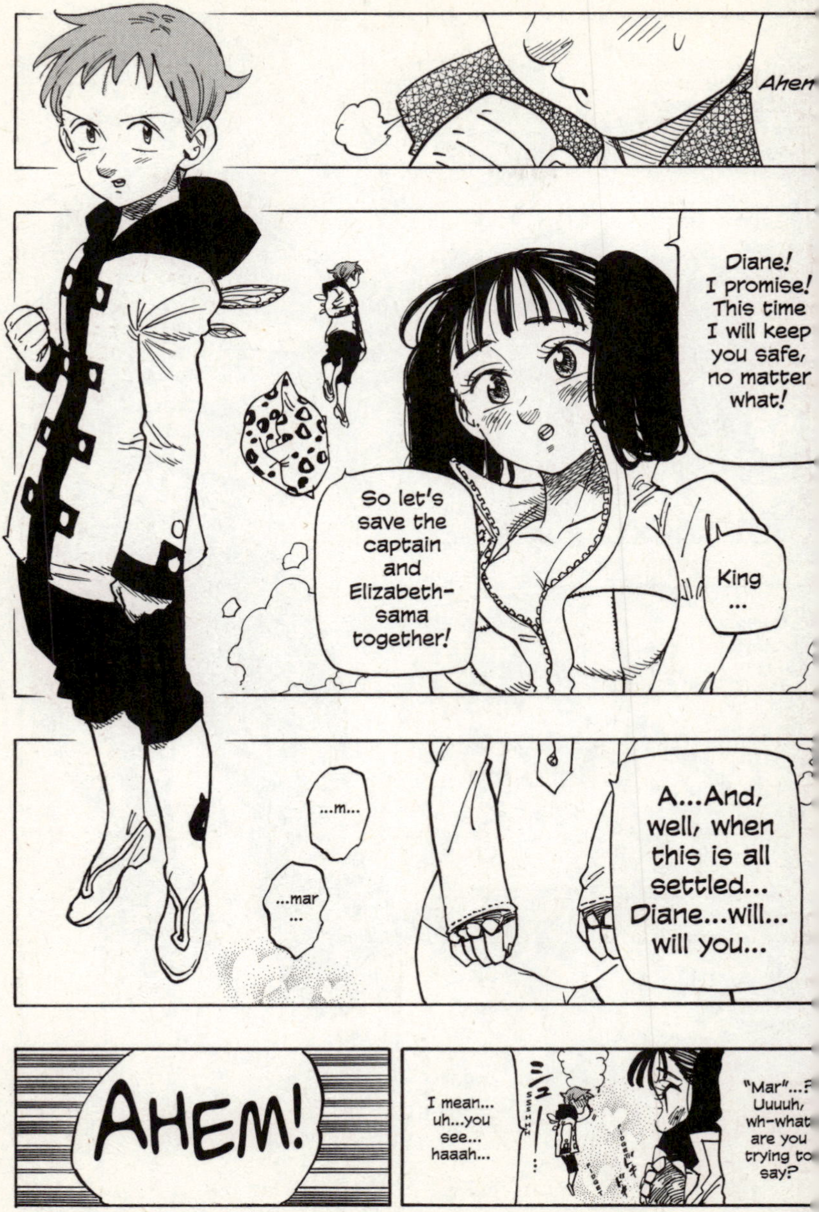
Ahem
Diane! I promise! This time I will keep you safe, no matter what!
King ...
So let's save the captain and Elizabeth-sama together!
A...And, well, when this is all settled... Diane...will... will you...
...m...
...mar ...
"Mar"...? Uuuh, wh-what are you trying to say?
I mean... uh...you see... haaah...
AHEM!

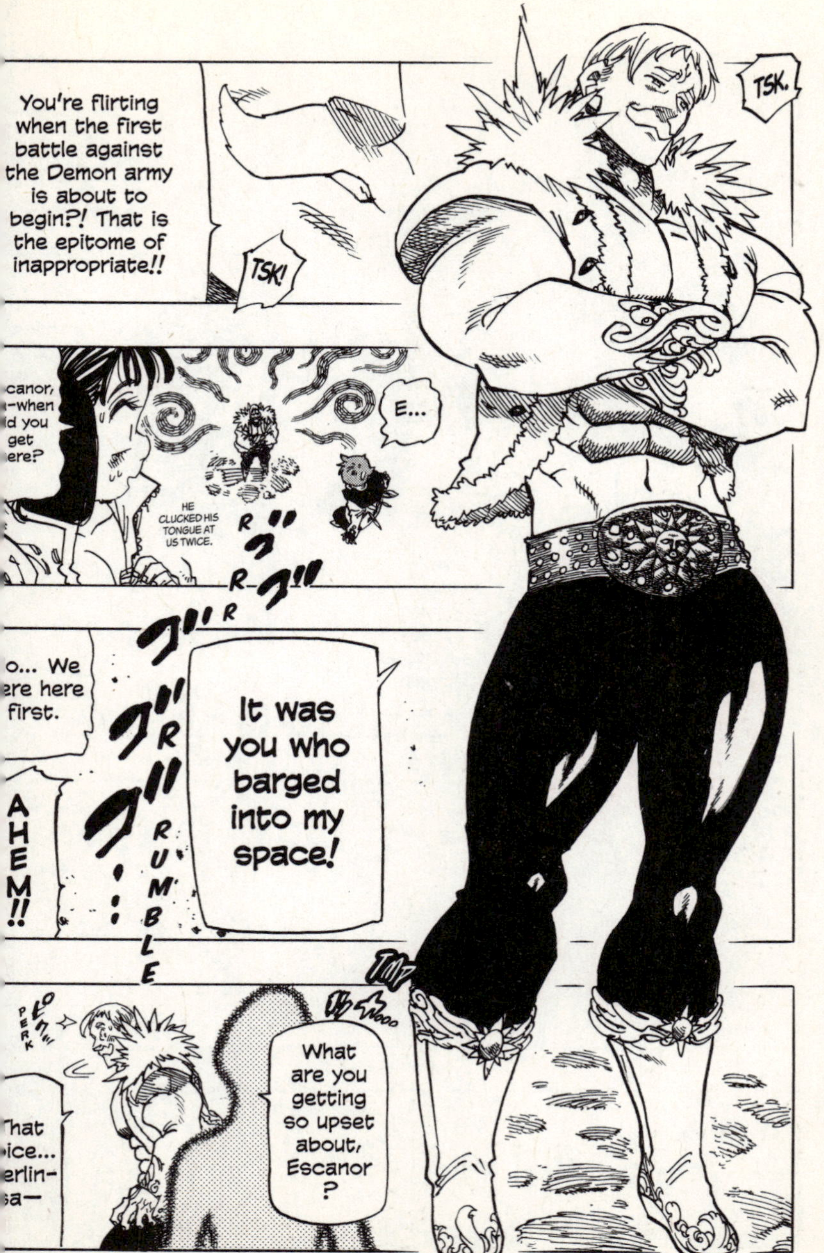
TSK.
You're flirting when the first battle against the Demon army is about to begin?! That is the epitome of inappropriate!!
TSK!
E...
HE CLUCKED HIS TONGUE AT US TWICE.
canor, -when id you get ere?
It was you who barged into my space!
o... We ere here first.
AHEM!!
RUMBLE
What are you getting so upset about, Escanor?
PERK
That ice... erlin-sa—

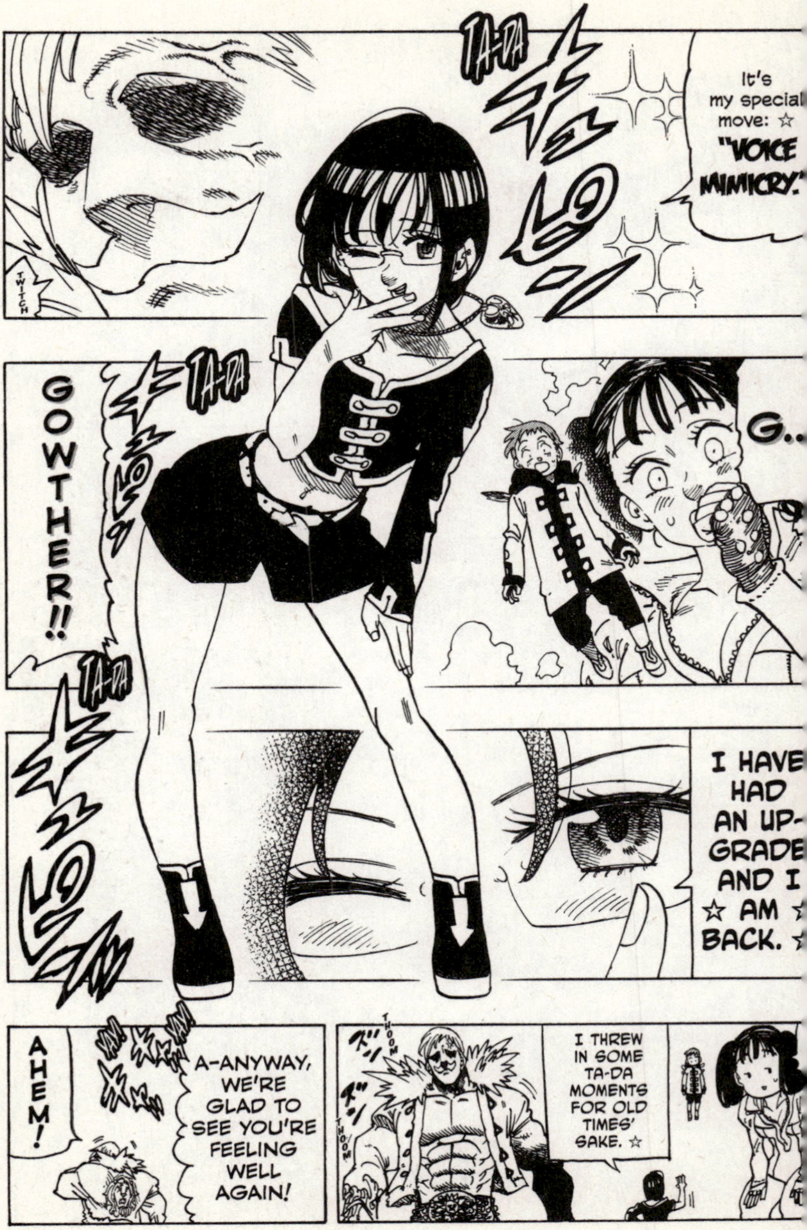
It's my special move: ☆ "VOICE MIMICRY."
TA-DA
TWITCH
G...
TA-DA
GOWTHER!!
I HAVE HAD AN UP-GRADE AND I ☆ AM BACK. ☆
TA-DA
I THREW IN SOME TA-DA MOMENTS FOR OLD TIMES' SAKE. ☆
THOOM
THOOM
A-ANYWAY, WE'RE GLAD TO SEE YOU'RE FEELING WELL AGAIN!
AHEM!

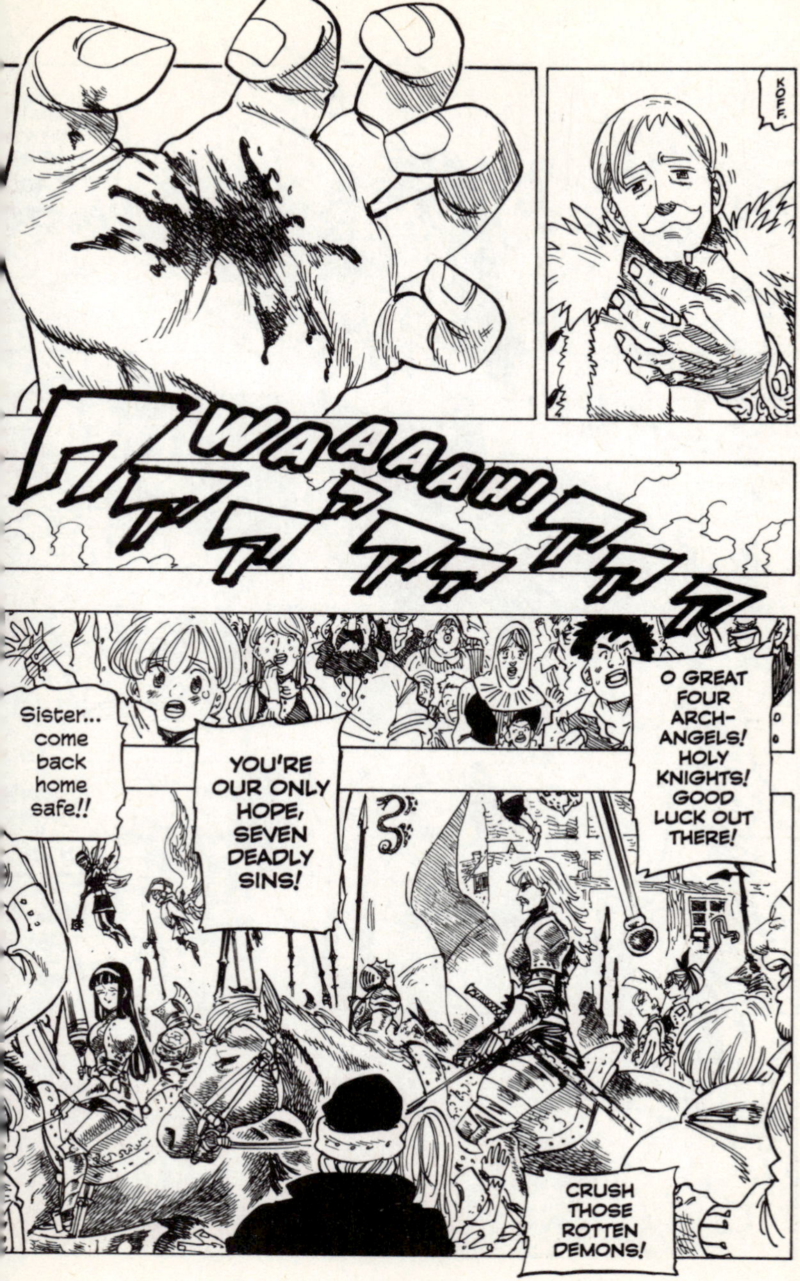
KOFF.
WAAAAAH!
O GREAT FOUR ARCH-ANGELS! HOLY KNIGHTS! GOOD LUCK OUT THERE!
YOU'RE OUR ONLY HOPE, SEVEN DEADLY SINS!
Sister... come back home safe!!
CRUSH THOSE ROTTEN DEMONS!

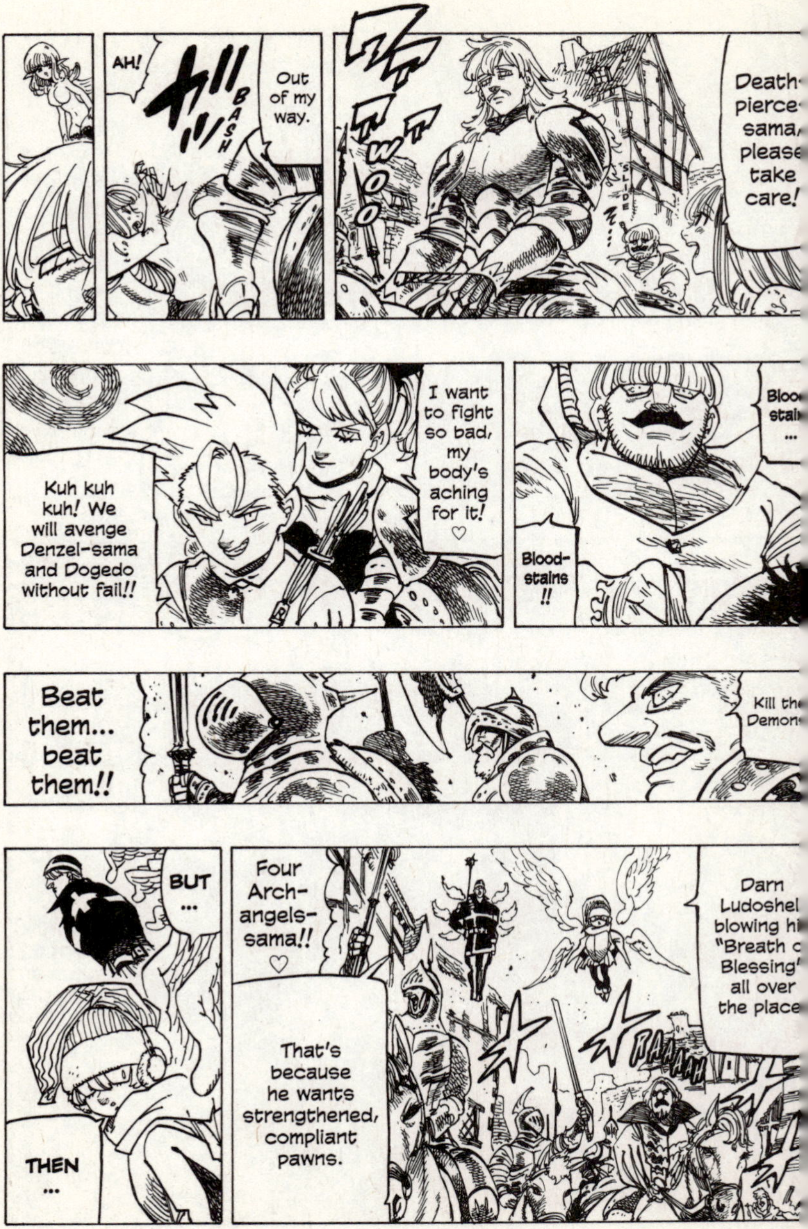

Death-pierce-sama, please take care!
SLIDE
WOOO
Out of my way.
BASH
AH!
Bloo stai ...
Blood-stains !!
I want to fight so bad, my body's aching for it! ♡
Kuh kuh kuh! We will avenge Denzel-sama and Dogedo without fail!!
Kill the Demon
Beat them... beat them!!
Darn Ludoshel blowing hi "Breath o Blessing" all over the place
RAAAAH
Four Arch-angels-sama!! ♡
That's because he wants strengthened, compliant pawns.
BUT ...
THEN ...

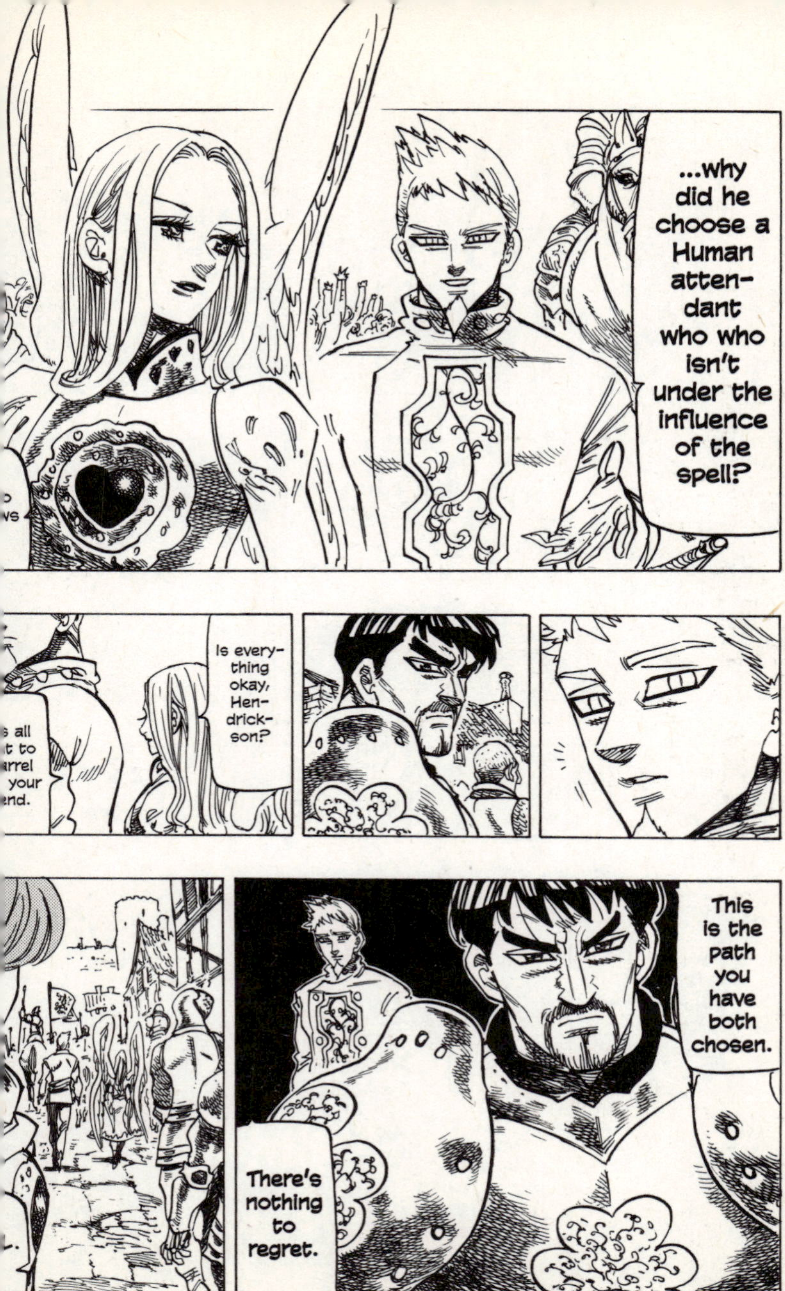
...why did he choose a Human attendant who who isn't under the influence of the spell?
Is everything okay, Hendrickson?
This is the path you have both chosen.
There's nothing to regret.

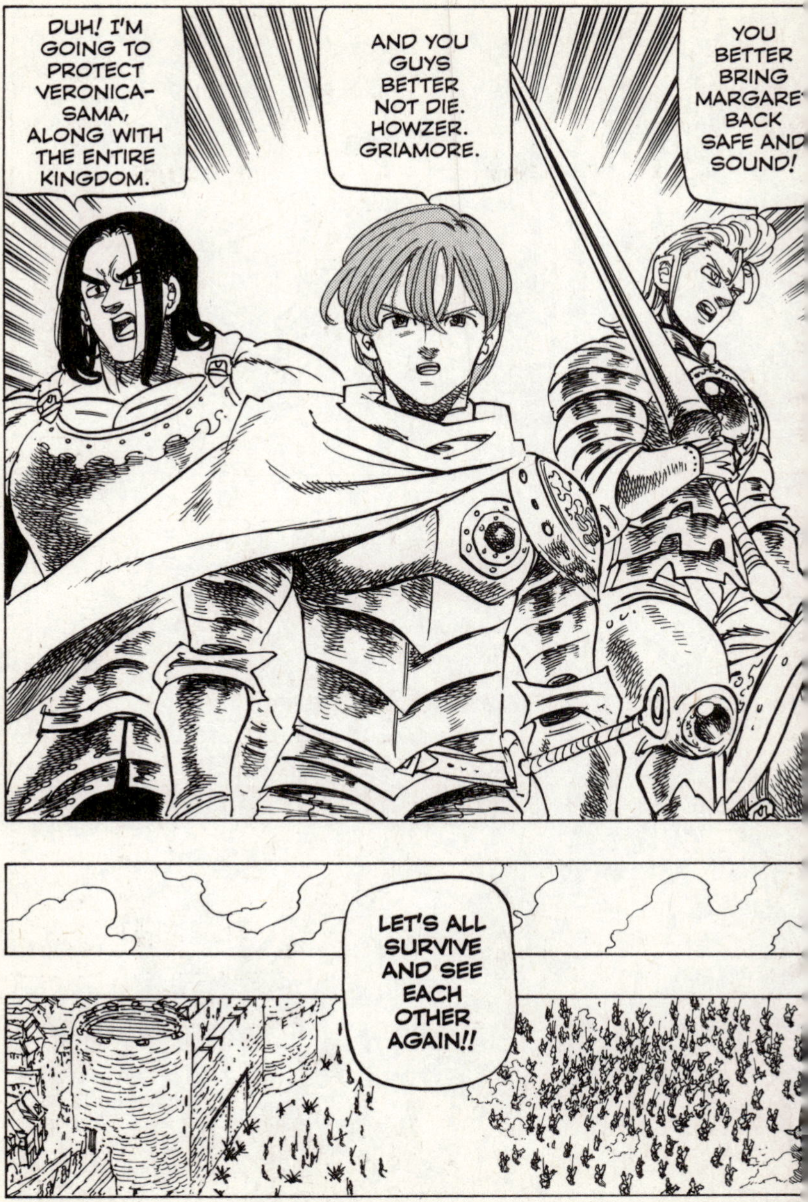
YOU BETTER BRING MARGARE BACK SAFE AND SOUND!
AND YOU GUYS BETTER NOT DIE. HOWZER. GRIAMORE.
DUH! I'M GOING TO PROTECT VERONICA-SAMA, ALONG WITH THE ENTIRE KINGDOM.
LET'S ALL SURVIVE AND SEE EACH OTHER AGAIN!!

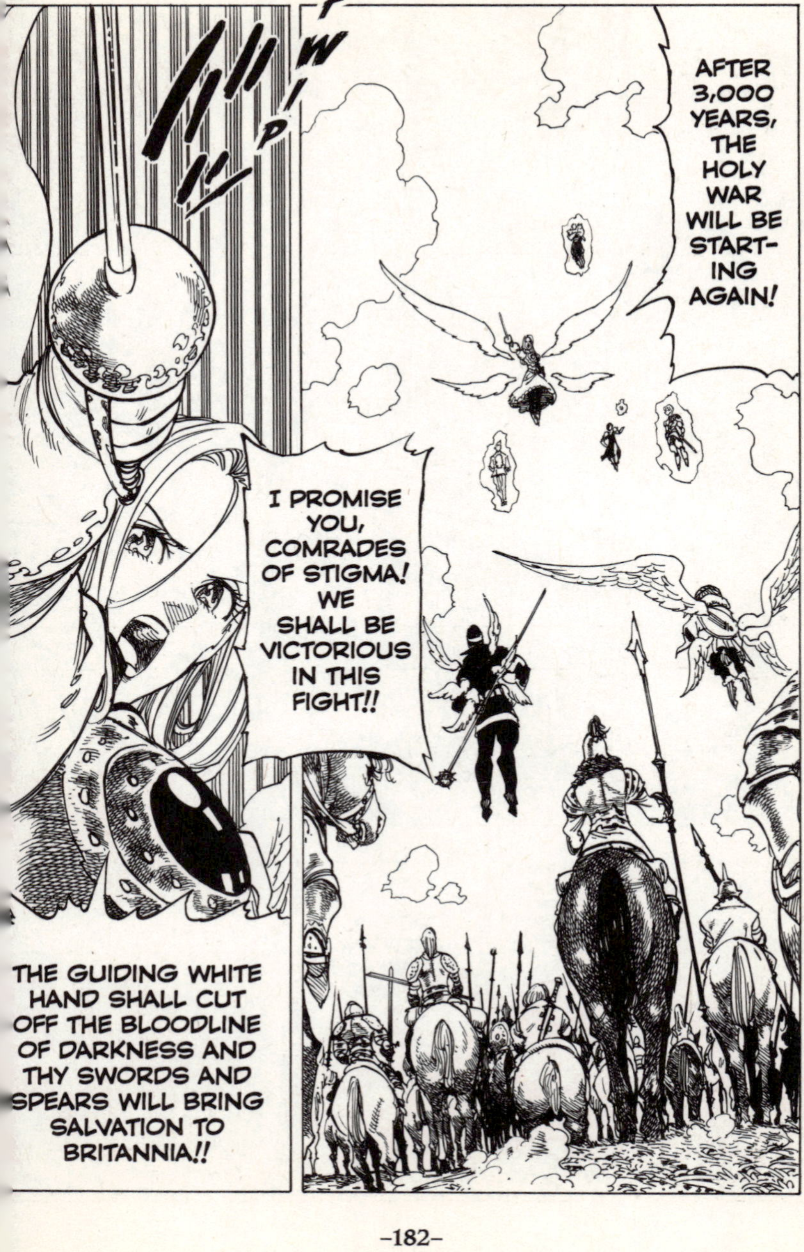
AFTER 3,000 YEARS, THE HOLY WAR WILL BE STARTING AGAIN!
I PROMISE YOU, COMRADES OF STIGMA! WE SHALL BE VICTORIOUS IN THIS FIGHT!!
FWIP
THE GUIDING WHITE HAND SHALL CUT OFF THE BLOODLINE OF DARKNESS AND THY SWORDS AND SPEARS WILL BRING SALVATION TO BRITANNIA!!

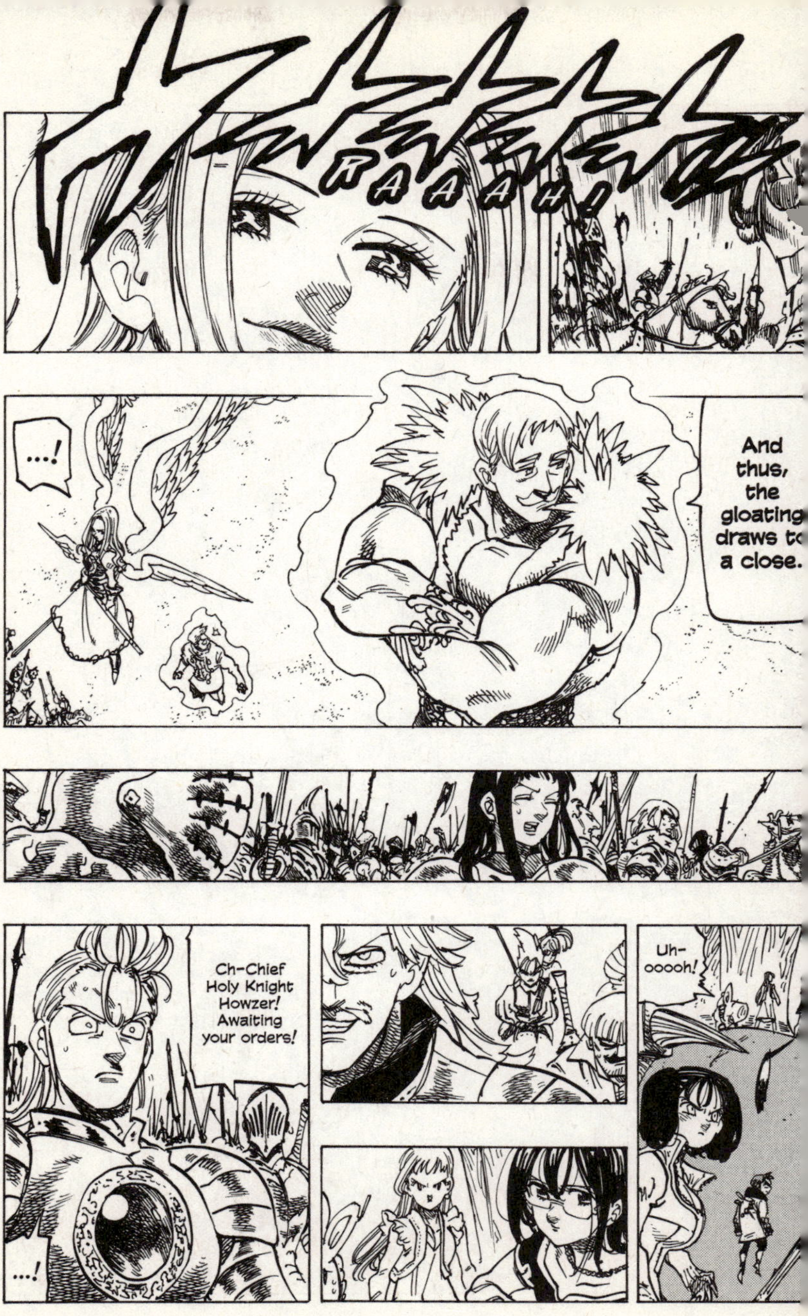
RAAAAH!
And thus, the gloating draws to a close.
...!
Uh-ooooh!
Ch-Chief Holy Knight Howzer! Awaiting your orders!
...!

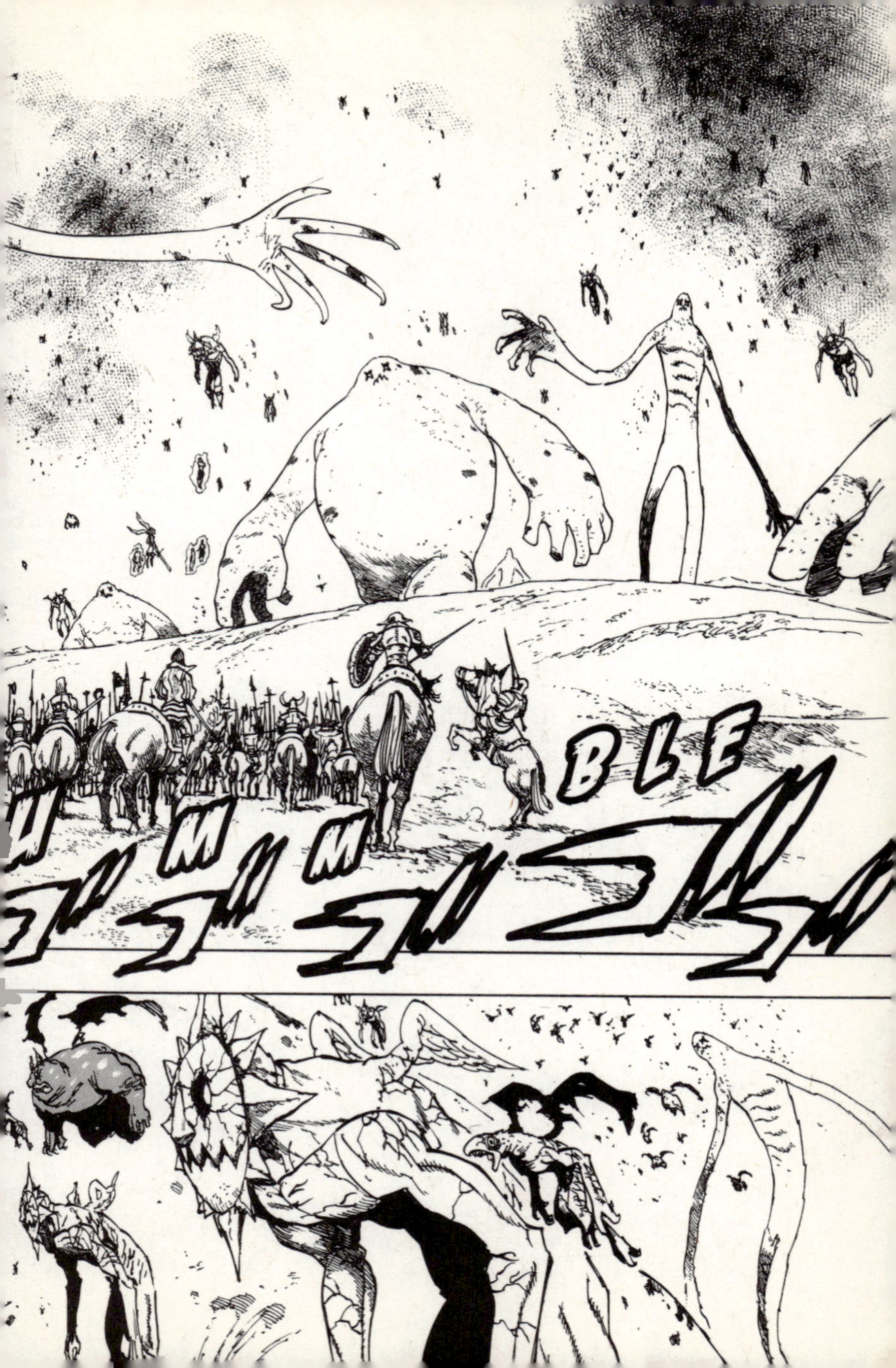
UMMBLE

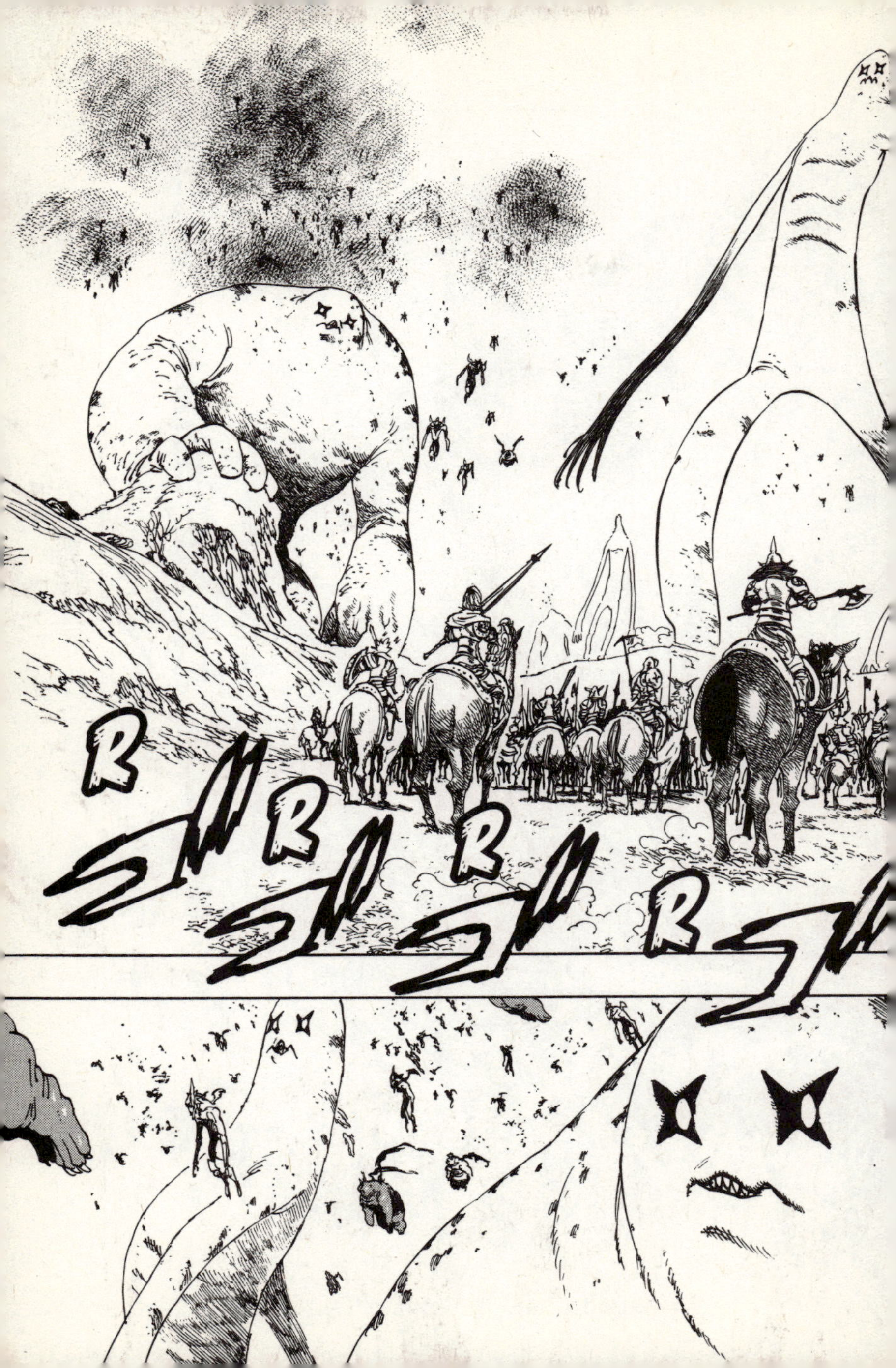

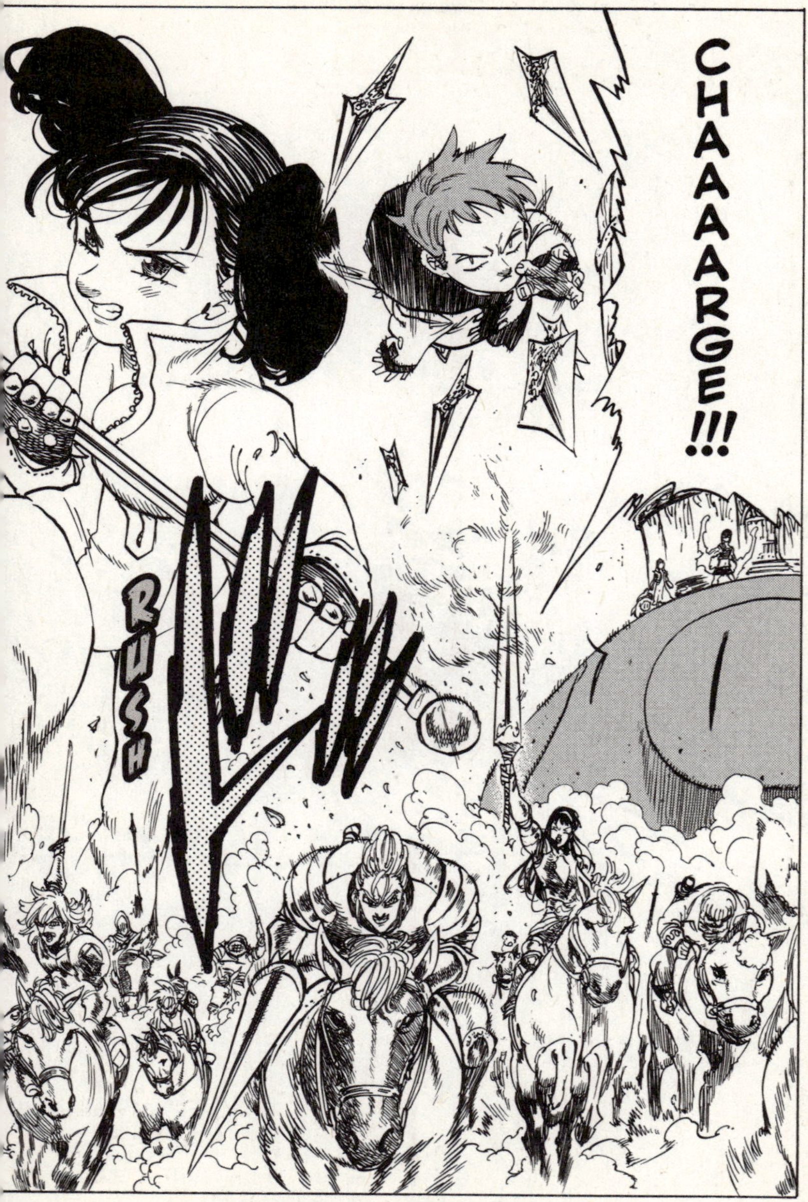
CHAAAARGE!!!
RUSH

To Be Continued in Volume 32...

"THE SEVEN DEADLY SINS" ILLUSTRATION CORNER

"THE DRAWING KNIGHTHOOD" SPACE

Be sure to include your name and address on your postcard!

M =
H =
E =
D =
B =
K =
G =
Mer =
Esc =
El =
J =

SPECIAL PRIZE

"Elaine..."

"Ban's doing everything he can for Meliodas right now, so I'm going to do everything I can for Ban!"

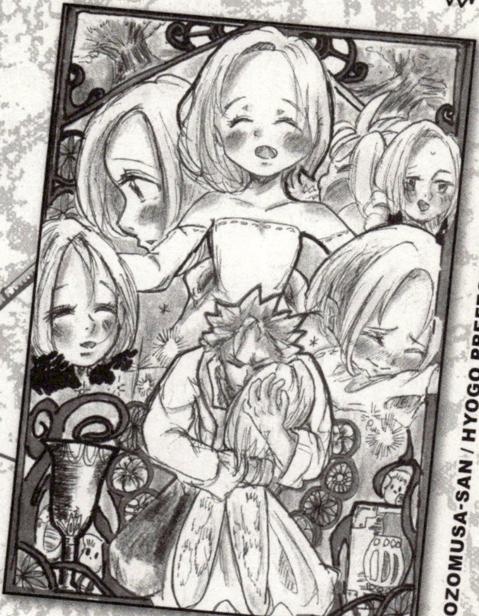

NOZOMUSA-SAN / HYOGO PREFECTURE

D "Pokey poke poooke. ♥"

K "Come on, Diane. Everybody's looking. ♥"

H "With icy stares..."

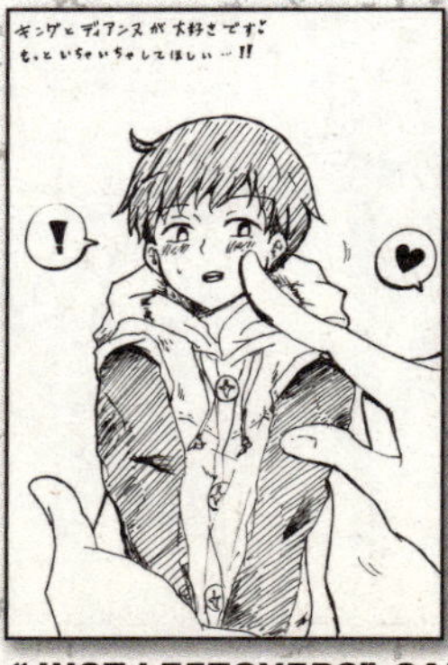

"JUST LEFTOVERS"-SAN / NAGANO PREFECTURE

ERINGI-SAN / NIIGATA PREFECTURE

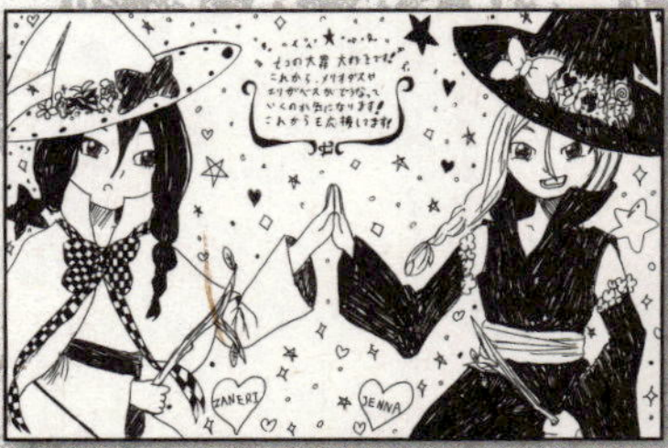

ZANERI
JENNA

Jenna "I can't believe Ludoshel-sama a his troops are back..."

Zaneri "I'm really worried...about Meliodas..."

D "Ah! Elizabeth with pigtails! ♥ I think I like that cute new look on her. ♥"

G "May I try it, too?"

K "Nah, maybe you'd better not."

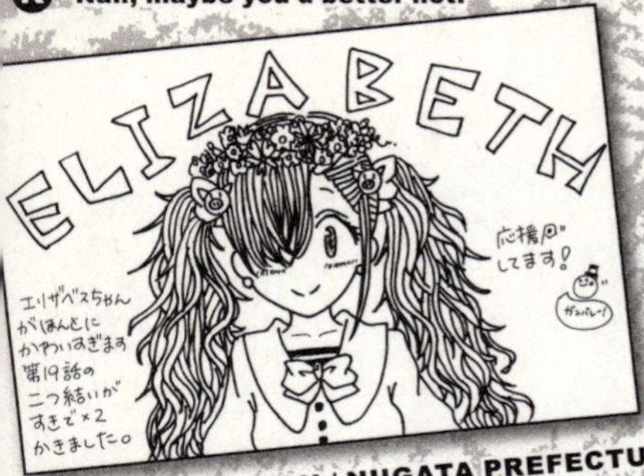
ELIZABETH
応援してます!
エリザベスちゃんがほんとにかわいすぎます
第19話の二つ結いがすきで×2かきました。

CHOCO-MOCHI-SAN / NIIGATA PREFECTURE

H "And just when I thought these two were finally free. Is it just me, or are the Goddesses actually the real Pig Jerks around here?!"

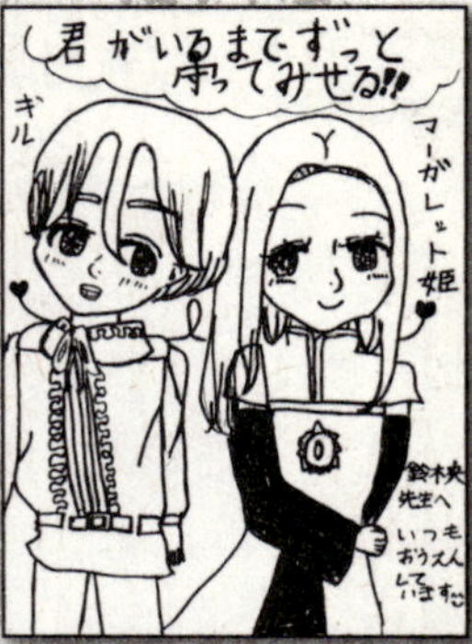
ギル
マーガレット姫
鈴木央先生へ
いつもおうえんしてます

MORE THAN PORK-SAN / NAGANO PREFECTURE

E "He'll be fine. I'm sure he'll be back and to his old self again!"

Esc "Captain... I hope you come back home safe and sound."

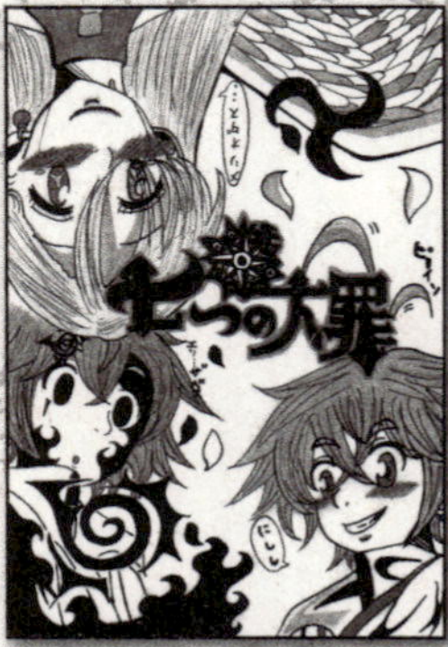
七つの大罪

KOKONO HIROSAWA-SAN / OSAKA

H "W...Wow, that's impressive!"

Mer "They say that one member of the Four Archangels possesses as much power as two members of The Ten Commandments combined."

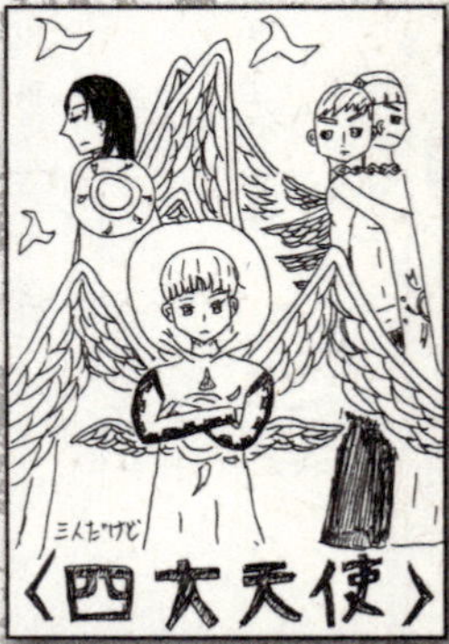
三人だけど
〈四大天使〉

HARUNA HASEGAWA-SAN / AICHI PREFECTURE

E "THROB!"

H "Elizabeth-chan's journey in manga... I bet she'd draw shojo manga of her and Meliodas getting all lovey dovey."

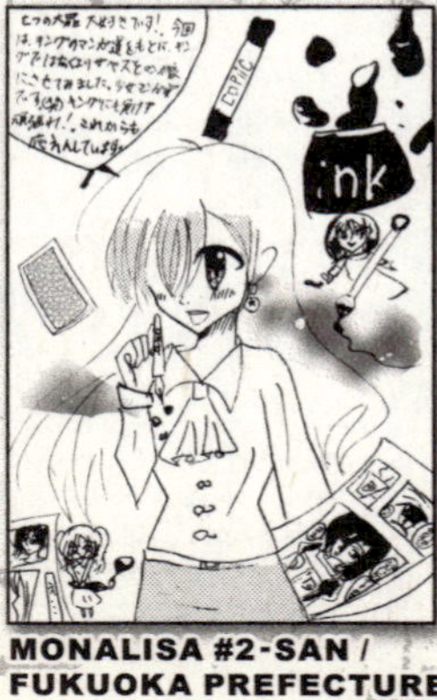
COPIC
ink

MONALISA #2-SAN / FUKUOKA PREFECTURE

Mer "I'd say he's about 30 times as strong... as Hawk."

H "S...So his Combat Class is 90,000?!"

Mer "..."

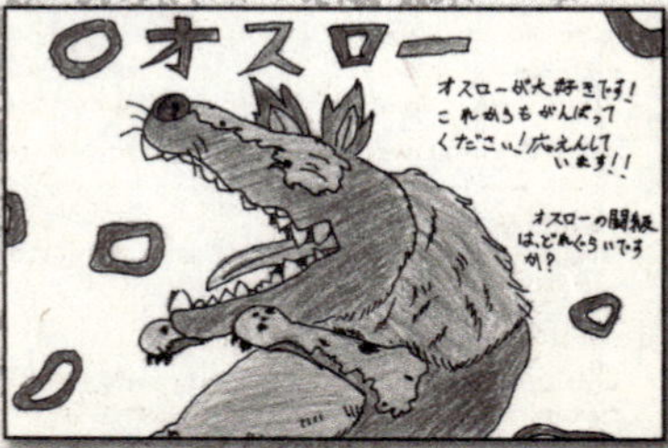
オスロー
オスローの闘級はどれぐらいですか?

AIKO YAGI-SAN / KYOTO

TAKAO KURUMIZAWA-SAN / NAGANO PREFECTURE

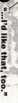

〈残飯処理騎士団〉
ホークちゃん 大好きです。
鈴木央先生
これからも応援してます!!

"Behold, the valiant figure of Hawk-sama! Dragon Rider!!"

"...More like, you're just the bait to catch a dragon with...?"

NAAGA-SAN / HOKKAIDO

E "I want to travel again with Meliodas and Hawk-chan someday."

H "...I'd like that, too."

MERLIN

MINORI CHIBA-SAN / SAITAMA PREFECTURE

Esc "Merlin-san... You sinful succubus! You're too gorgeouuuuus!!!"

Now Accepting Applicants for the Drawing Knighthood!

- Draw your picture on a postcard, or paper no larger than a postcard, and send it in!
- Don't forget to write your name and location on the back of your picture!
- You can include comments or not. And colored illustrations will still only be displayed in B&W!
- The Drawing Knights whose pictures are particularly noteworthy and run in the print edition will be gifted with a signed specially made pencil board!
- And the best overall will be granted the special prize of a signed shikishi!!

Send to:
The Seven Deadly Sins Drawing Knighthood
c/o Kodansha Comics
451 Park Ave. South, 7th floor,
New York, NY 10016

- Submitted letters and postcards will be given to the artist. Please be aware that your name, address, and other personal information included will be given as well.

new
ries
om the
eator
Soul
ter, the
egahit
anga and
ime seen
Toonami!

un and lively...
great start!"
-Adventures in
Poor Taste

FIRE FORCE

By Atsushi Ohkubo

e city of Tokyo is plagued by a deadly phenomenon: spontaneous
uman combustion! Luckily, a special team is there to quench the
ferno: The Fire Force! The fire soldiers at Special Fire Cathedral 8
e about to get a unique addition. Enter Shinra, a boy who possesses
e power to run at the speed of a rocket, leaving behind the famous
evil's footprints" (and destroying his shoes in the process).
an Shinra and his colleagues discover the source of this strange
idemic before the city burns to ashes?

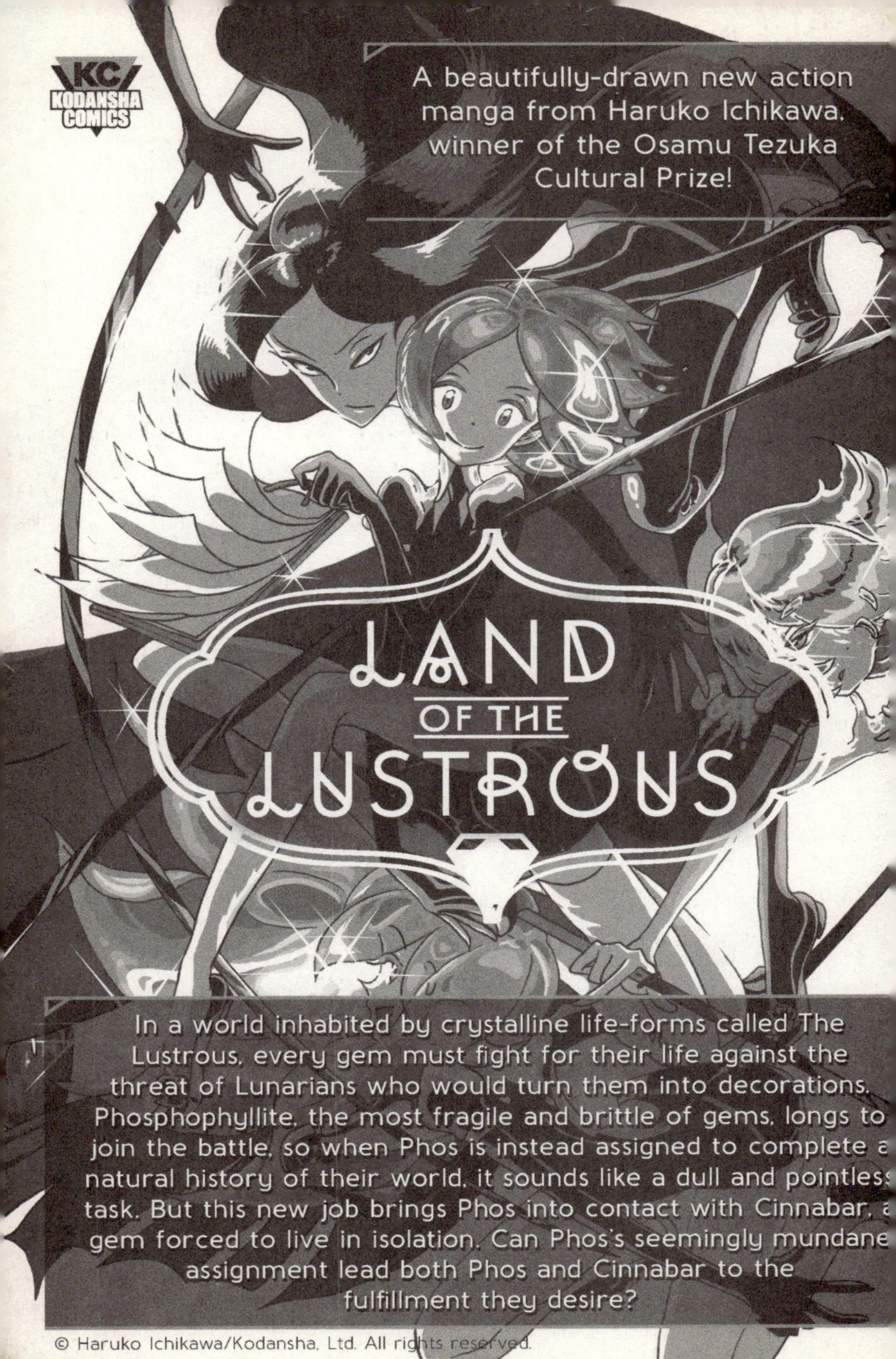
KC KODANSHA COMICS
A beautifully-drawn new action manga from Haruko Ichikawa, winner of the Osamu Tezuka Cultural Prize!
LAND OF THE LUSTROUS
In a world inhabited by crystalline life-forms called The Lustrous, every gem must fight for their life against the threat of Lunarians who would turn them into decorations. Phosphophyllite, the most fragile and brittle of gems, longs to join the battle, so when Phos is instead assigned to complete a natural history of their world, it sounds like a dull and pointless task. But this new job brings Phos into contact with Cinnabar, a gem forced to live in isolation. Can Phos's seemingly mundane assignment lead both Phos and Cinnabar to the fulfillment they desire?

The Seven Deadly Sins volume 31 is a work of fiction. Names, characters, places, and incidents are the products of the author's imagination or are used fictitiously. Any resemblance to actual events, locales, or persons, living or dead, is entirely coincidental.

A Kodansha Comics Trade Paperback Original.

Published in the United States by Kodansha Comics, an imprint of Kodansha USA Publishing, LLC, New York.

Publication rights for this English edition arranged through Kodansha Ltd., Tokyo.

First published in Japan in 2018 by Kodansha Ltd., Tokyo.

ISBN 978-1-63236-731-0

Printed in the United States of America.

www.kodanshacomics.com

9 8 7 6 5 4 3 2 1

Translation: Christine Dashiell
Lettering: James Dashiell
Editing: Lauren Scanlan
Kodansha Comics edition cover design: Phil Balsman